Transformational Leadership and Not for Profits and Social Enterprises

Recent decades have seen a significant transformation of the not-for-profit (NFP) sector. This includes a rise in the number of organisations and people employed, a shift from charities and philanthropic agencies to hybrid social enterprise business models, competing stakeholder interests and increasing expectations regarding accountability and transparency. The role of NFPs has also become more complex—they not only serve the disadvantaged and fulfil social needs but also actively advocate for and implement public policies and promote social and economic inclusion.

This growth and complexity has brought with it a need for innovative and entrepreneurial approaches to leadership that stems from an in-depth understanding of the changing nonprofit landscape. Addressing this need, *Transformational Leadership and Not for Profits and Social Enterprises* will help readers navigate extant challenges by drawing on conceptual literature, both theoretical and empirical and emphasising practical real world experience through case studies and vignettes

The key aim of this book is to help existing and future NFP leaders at all organisational levels to support their organisations and employees and in turn clients and communities, through theoretical insights and practical approaches by focusing on transformational leadership aspects for contemporary Not for Profits.

Transformational Leadership and Not for Profits and Social Enterprises is key reading for researchers, academics and policy makers in the areas of Non-profit Management, Leadership, Public Sector Management and Charity Management as well as related disciplines such as Philanthropy and Social Entrepreneurship.

Kenneth Wiltshire is the emeritus J. D. Story Professor of Public Administration at the University of Queensland Business School, Australia.

Aastha Malhotra is Vice-Chancellor's Research Fellow at University of Southern Queensland, Australia.

Micheal Axelsen is a Lecturer (Business Information Systems) at University of Queensland Business School, Australia.

Routledge Studies in the Management of Voluntary and Non-Profit Organizations

Series Editor: Stephen P. Osborne (University of Edinburgh, UK)

This series presents innovative work grounded in new realities, addressing issues crucial to an understanding of the contemporary world. This is the world of organised societies, where boundaries between formal and informal, public and private, local and global organizations have been displaced or have vanished, along with other nineteenth century dichotomies and oppositions. Management, apart from becoming a specialized profession for a growing number of people, is an everyday activity for most members of modern societies.

Similarly, at the level of enquiry, culture and technology, and literature and economics, can no longer be conceived as isolated intellectual fields; conventional canons and established mainstreams are contested. Management, Organization and Society addresses these contemporary dynamics of transformation in a manner that transcends disciplinary boundaries, with books that will appeal to researchers, student and practitioners alike.

Transformational Leadership and Not for Profits and Social Enterprises

Edited by Kenneth Wiltshire, Aastha Malhotra, and Micheal Axelsen

Routledge
Taylor & Francis Group

LONDON AND NEW YORK

First published 2018 by Routledge

2 Park Square, Milton Park, Abingdon, Oxfordshire OX14 4RN
52 Vanderbilt Avenue, New York, NY 10017

Routledge is an imprint of the Taylor & Francis Group, an informa business

First issued in paperback 2019

Library of Congress Cataloging-in-Publication Data
A catalog record for this book has been requested

ISBN: 978-1-138-20482-9 (hbk)
ISBN: 978-0-367-35549-4 (pbk)

Typeset in Sabon
by Apex CoVantage, LLC

Contents

Tables and Figures

Tables

Figures

Foreword

Since the establishment of Australia's first charity and first not for profit entity in 1813 in Sydney, The Benevolent Society, the not for profit sector has not only contributed to the economic, social and cultural aspects of our nation, it has shaped the very social fabric of our society.

From the smallest community-based association to the largest of our health, education and community service providers each has acted in the pursuit of enhancing the wellbeing of Australians and the common good of our society. This endeavour has reached beyond our national boundaries through international development and engagement.

Today the NFP sector has grown to involving over one million employees, over four million volunteers and generating an annual turnover of some $100 billion. It reaches into every city, town and community. It delivers vital services, advocates for just causes, galvanises local communities and action, embraces voluntary endeavour, builds bridges between diverse parts of our society and engages with the government and business sectors. It has the capacity to value add each dollar of donation and tax benefit given to it and to optimise each hour of work so generously volunteered.

Yet challenges remain. Some of those are long standing—for example, how do good concepts and projects move to a sustainable footing and be replicated in different areas and locations? This is a great challenge especially for Indigenous-based projects that are often viewed favourably but disappear too quickly or remain isolated and not replicated. Others are newer—for example the challenges associated with competing in highly competitive markets and emerging new social enterprise business models. And the changing nature, expectations and attitudes of government funders remain an ever-present source of sector anxiety.

The importance, constraints and challenges of the NFP sector were thoroughly identified in the Productivity Commission's Report on the Contribution of the Not for Profit Sector in 2010. Its analysis of the sector and emerging issues remains as relevant today as it did six years ago. In particular, it said:

> "*The NFP sector has different motivations and faces some different constraints to the government and the business sectors. These must*

be understood by government and business to improve their engage-
ment with NFPs, while NFPs need to understand the limitations they
impose.

- *NFPs are established for a community-purpose. Nevertheless, the*
  members' control over how the NFP goes about achieving this
  purpose can also be very important and even a reason for the
  existence of the NFP.
- *Many NFPs add value to the community through how their ac-*
  tivities are undertaken. The way in which NFPs are organised,
  engage people, make decisions, and go about delivering services
  is often itself of value. Yet, such participatory and inclusive pro-
  cesses can be time consuming and costly.
- *Many of the activities of the NFP sector would not be undertaken*
  by the for-profit or government sector. This could be because of
  lack of financial return, activities inherently being high risk, (po-
  litically as well as in terms of whether they will be effective), or
  because government or business lack the trust or client relation-
  ship to deliver the services effectively.
- *NFP activities may generate benefits that go beyond the recipi-*
  ents of services and the direct impacts of their outcomes. For
  example, involving families and the local community in the de-
  livery of disability services can generate broader community ben-
  efits (spill overs), such as greater understanding and acceptance
  of all people with disabilities thereby enhancing social inclusion.
  Smaller community-based bodies can play an especially impor-
  tant role in generating community connections and strengthening
  civil society."

Of course, even since that Report market based approaches to the funding
and financing of service delivery including consumer focussed reforms in the
areas of disability, housing, aged care and other human service areas have
made the environment an even more complex one for leaders in the NFP
sector. Competition with for profits has grown. Yet the overall growth of
the sector and the consequential spill over effects of NFP endeavour, whilst
insufficiently measured or understood, continue to remain very important to
the wellbeing of our national community.

Importantly the Commission recognised the pivotal role and need for
sound leadership of the sector. The sector and our society need leaders of
integrity, vision and commitment. They deserve leaders who understand the
value, significance and contribution of not-for- profit endeavour. They need
leaders who respect and value the past contributions of the sector yet are
able to respond to emerging challenges and opportunities. They need leaders who are able to comprehend the changing context and circumstances
of our times and adapt to their environment whilst being committed to the
mission, purpose and values of their organisations.

Above all leaders of NFP organisations need to understand it is the unique qualities, values and aspirations that drive NFP endeavour that is their greatest strength and even their competitive advantage in this ever changing and contested environment. Such qualities aid, not undermine, efficiency and effectiveness in such organisations and give organisational clarity and distinction in a contested environment. That is why the community supports generous NFP taxation benefits and public donations remain strong. Of course there are similarities to any business operator of a hospital, childcare centre or aged care facility. Yet there are differences and spill over benefits that should be understood and valued. NFP boards and leaders need to constantly acknowledge, value and promote those differences.

Whilst discussing service delivery the Productivity Commission alluded to this in the following:

> *"This recognises that the community is best served when service delivery systems play to the relative strengths of each participant and maximise the potential for complementarities. The potential contribution of the NFP sector to addressing disadvantage and promoting a more inclusive society can be substantially eroded by attempts to turn these organisations into pale imitations of either government or business."*

For the leaders of small, community based NFPs the challenges remain the empowerment of local communities to come together for a common purpose and to maintain the enthusiasm and commitment of their members and volunteers. From sporting clubs to local aid societies the maintenance of local participation remains a core goal and challenge. Participation is key to their existence. Some are challenged by the need to meet and adapt to increasing cultural and ethnic diversity in order to meet emerging local needs. Some are trying to find their place in a highly competitive world and an environment of increasing dominance by large players in service delivery across the nation. All are challenged by creating safe places for children and adults to carry out their activities.

For leaders of religions and faith based NFP organisations their challenges are to be relevant to the world in which they operate yet remain true to their foundational beliefs and values. As trust in all institutions, including religions, has waned, religious leaders need to understand, reflect and discern new ways and means to renew their mission and build the trust and confidence of their adherents and the community at large. For many leaders, the need for new governance and accountability regimes may cause conflict with past practices and powerful interests and will require competent and thoughtful leadership that can articulate well the necessity for and the benefits of a new way.

For the leaders of larger human service delivery agencies, the challenges are many and varied including responding to new funding and financing arrangements including consumer directed models, increased competitive based market models, changing relationships with government and business and evolving community needs. Many leaders are now confronted with issues such as mergers and acquisitions, lead agency arrangements, partnering with businesses to achieve social purpose outcomes. Developing social enterprise models, and responding to the changing aspirations of clients, workers and the community at large. New innovative financing and funding arrangements such as social bonds and social venture capital also pose new issues as well as creating new opportunities. And a thorough understanding of risk and its management has emerged as a much-needed skill in today's world. For some however the greatest risks are their own ambitions which can see a 'growth at all costs' strategy emerge aided by an overly compliant board.

Yet there are some fundamental principles that apply to effective leadership in the NFP sector irrespective of scale or structure of individual organisations.

No one leader is more important than the collective effort of his or her workforce and stakeholders and no one leader has more wisdom, understanding or insight than the collective intellect and wisdom of those involved in their organisation. NFP endeavour needs strong leaders who are prepared to listen, engage and motivate people to achieve the great and simple things that makes an organisation achieve its outcome. Leaders need to demonstrate through their actions that they are people of integrity, ethics and values that are in line with the values of their agency. Where such an alignment does not exist, the organisation will fracture and ultimately fail in its core objectives.

Leaders in the NFP sector need to fully embrace good governance and promote and demonstrate transparency and accountability. The days of the so called 'private' organisation has gone. NFPs are accountable to their members, their clients, their funders and the community. Today the Australian Charities and Not for Profits Commission has demonstrated that good governance, transparency and accountability ultimately aid NFP enterprises and enhance the good standing of the sector as a whole. Good governance is essential to the creation of an efficient, effective and outcomes focussed organisation.

Leaders in the NFP sector need to be willing to educate themselves and their key staff as to the changing context and societal circumstances and be adaptive to those changes. Too many leaders are so preoccupied with day to day management that they fail to read the changing signs and conditions. Leaders lead through being aware of what is happening, examining options and seizing opportunities. They also develop new skills when necessary. Responding to new market based environments will pose immense challenges and will be dangerous places for the ill-informed, unaware or unskilled leaders. It will be perilous for the arrogant or complacent leader alike.

In order to meet new conditions some leaders will consider mergers, acquisitions and new joint ventures. Such considerations will require skilful analysis not only of the commercial and market environments but a deep consideration of the issues of shared vision, values and the ethos of the various parties. The latter issues, unless carefully managed and fully anticipated, can ultimately undo the most attractive deals or arrangements and too often leaders become blinded by the financial or other issues and fail to fully take into account the fundamental underpinnings needed for such success in an NFP environment.

Above all leaders must be absolutely faithful to the mission of their NFP organisations. External challenges can place great pressures on organisations. This has been especially so as governments have played a much more directive role determining how, where, by whom and for how much services will be delivered. Notions of cooperation and collaboration have been weakened. And mission drift is rife within the sector. Good leaders understand the value of maintaining integrity in the mission of their organisation. More importantly the community values organisations that know what they stand for and live out that mission with consistency and courage. Dare I say, so will clients and consumers. That is not to say that some organisations should not evaluate the relevance of their mission as community needs change and a new or modified mission emerges. Certainly, new ways of delivering the mission will always need to be examined. But that is a conscious process, with a full consideration of the pros and cons of such change or adaptation. That is the opposite of mission drift where often that which is most precious is unintentionally lost.

Finally, in relation to engagement with government there is the need for better mutual understanding to improve new forms of engagement in the future. In relation to government and NFP engagement, it is important that governments have a good understanding of NFP agencies, their diversity, individual missions, service mixes, resource constraints, histories and degree of dependence on government funding. Similarly, it is important that NFP agencies have a good understanding of the government's objectives in relation to the services they are being funded to provide, the policies and programs of the relevant government agency and the public policy making process more generally. NFP leaders need to explore and foster new forms of engagement whilst advocating for the causes and values that they represent. Equally good leaders need to know when it is right to walk away, when the best interests of the organisation or more importantly those it serves will not be respected or benefitted.

Australia needs good leaders in its politics, businesses and civil society. The not for profit sector needs to embrace good leadership. Leadership is always contextual as to time, place and environment. It is contextual as to the nature and culture of an organisation. Yet it is always responsive, adaptive and creative.

Above all it is leadership that is also true to the core ethos of the organisation, its mission and its values. Success is built on this commitment.

Not for profit endeavour will continue to shape the very fabric of our society. Good leadership will ensure that Australia has a sector of which it can be justly proud, one that serves the common good.

Robert Fitzgerald AM
Inaugural Chair, Advisory Board (2012–2016)
Australian Charities and Not-for-Profits Commission

Preface

Throughout the world Not for Profit organisations have long played a vital role in the communities they serve, and their numbers have proliferated in response to constantly emerging social and economic issues. Their founders have typically been mission-driven leaders with a compassion for the people whom they seek to help, and these qualities have attracted a myriad of volunteers to the vision and mission.

However, the contribution of both these organisations and their leaders has tended to be passively accepted rather than celebrated and positively recognised. This is changing as governments have become motivated by desire or necessity to engage with them to deliver public policies in complex social arenas. As well, many private sector organisations have now realised the potential benefits which association with them can bring to the whole community, and to the morale of their own workforce.

Indeed, official inquiries in the UK, Europe, North America, and Australasia have in recent times revealed not just the social value of these bodies but also their contribution to GDP, employment and productivity of the nation.

There is an extensive literature in this field that is somewhat confusing as authors grapple with the array of nomenclature including Charities, Not for Profits, NGOs, Civil Society, Social Enterprises, and Social Entrepreneurs. Indeed there is a growing school of thought that would seek to change the familiar label of "Not for Profit" to "Not for Dividend." This would reflect more accurately the features of the sector, and affirm that there is no issue in making profits provided they are retained and directed to the fundamental mission of the organisation.

It is clear from both the literature and the vast array of practical experience in the sector that the common and key feature required for success is sound and inspiring leadership. Indeed, this book is based on the premise that what is required is Transformational Leadership.

In the modern era, challenges for Not-for Profits are becoming more intense, especially regarding sources of funding and other resources, and general support. Both those who have depended on traditional donors and those depending heavily on government funding have been forced to adopt different strategies to achieve their mission and maintain their identity.

Often this involves actually reinventing themselves whilst remaining true to their original purpose. New approaches include partnerships with governments, for profit organisations and other Not-for-Profits; new fund raising approaches, marketing initiatives and brand differentiation; and ways of keeping all stakeholders motivated including through the use of new technology. All of this at a time of greater scrutiny of the sector through regulation, taxation, transparency provisions, and demands for performance based outcomes.

In short, many traditional Not-for-Profits/Charities are looking to become Social Enterprises, and it is this journey which is the focus of this book, addressing the various leadership challenges which are encountered along the way.

Doing good works is now as much a profession as a calling.

We have become aware of these leadership challenges through extensive research as well as our conduct of leadership courses for the sector which have included a widely diverse range of Not-for-Profits. The contents of this book are based on this experience. In particular, it has become very apparent to us that there is a paucity of resource material for leadership courses of this kind offered by educators, for training by the organisations themselves and the sector as a whole, and those wanting to gain a greater understanding of the sector. We hope this book will go some way to filling this gap and be of material assistance to leaders whose organisations wish to embark on this journey or are already well advanced.

The book is based on the recent path-breaking research by Malhotra (the basis of Chapter 2) on the challenges that face leaders on the journey, as revealed in her longitudinal study of the literature and a number of cases studies. There are then a number of conceptual chapters on leadership itself and its many dimensions relevant to Not-for-Profit organisations. These are followed by chapters from experts that address the many specific challenges that have been identified. All of the authors have extensive experience in relevant research and engagement with the sector.

To enhance its usefulness for training and professional development courses, the book is structured in three parts: "The Leadership Journey," "Shaping the Journey," and "New Journeys, New Horizons." The first part is conceptual, the second is practical and relates to the current day challenges, and the final third part addresses the leadership challenges of the future. The book also features a number of vignettes ('Leadership in Practice') and case studies ('Stories from the Field') to showcase a sample of Not-for-Profit organisations who have successfully transformed, even re-invented themselves as social enterprises, to address the challenges which are emerging. These cases provide candid and valuable insights into the leadership challenges facing the Not-for-Profit sector today.

Many of these case studies include examples of leaders who are embracing new technologies and digital strategies to engage with current and future stakeholders and funders, motivate employees and volunteers, achieve brand recognition, and link those who have with those who need. The experience spans a wide range of fields including focuses that are faith based, indigenous health, animal welfare, humanitarian goals, the needs of the old and young, health, education, housing, emergencies and natural disasters. Many of the organisations featured are employing modalities and language that appeals to younger generations and their aspiration to be involved and contribute to society.

The book canvasses international experience as well as a particular focus on Australia. It is designed to be a practical resource rather than merely a theoretical one, and is squarely focussed on Transformational Leadership which we believe is the approach required to address the identified challenges that are facing Not-for-Profit leaders, and will continue to do so, in this ever-important sector of all societies.

Emeritus Professor Kenneth Wiltshire
(*University of Queensland*),
Dr Aastha Malhotra
(*University of Southern Queensland*)
Dr Micheal Axelsen
(*University of Queensland*)

Part I

The Leadership Journey

1 Leadership Concepts and Approaches

Kenneth Wiltshire

Introduction

Sound leadership is often the most crucial factor in the survival, success, and advancement of any organisation, community, or nation. This has been true from ancient times to the present day. However, the notion and type of leadership required are not a constant, and usually depend on the contemporary circumstances. The very nature of leadership itself has also been progressively subjected to wide ranging analysis thereby enhancing our understanding of the dynamics involved.

This chapter is not meant to be a comprehensive or definitive coverage of all leadership literature. It is merely intended as a snapshot of the changing nature of the concepts and theories of leadership and their evolution, attesting to the fact that there is no single definition of leadership, although there would be many who would say that they can recognise leadership when they see it.

The history of the evolution of leadership theories and concepts has been well documented.[1] The earliest focus was on personal traits of leaders; such factors as lineage, physical aspects such as height, strength, voice, presence, and appearance; and qualities such as courage, determination, resourcefulness, and even a messianic vocation and sense of destiny. The basic assumption was that there were such people as 'born leaders'. The image of the leader was the person out in front, clearly on a personal mission, controlling and accruing all power to themselves, taking all the decisions and issuing all the commands. Sometimes they have one or a few trusted advisers but they take all the responsibility for strategies and tactics, including alliances, leading to the final result.

Notions of what constitute leadership traits has been a moveable feast. To illustrate this a new light on traits was provided by Stogdill in a 1948 analysis of 124 studies of leadership traits which had been conducted between 1904 and 1947.[2] The majority of these studies showed that leaders tended to be intelligent, more dependable or responsible, and more active in social situations. The old supposed traits especially those related to physical characteristics had little relation to leadership. Stogdill's conclusion was that leaders had a strong capacity for organising and generating cooperative behaviour and this involved intelligence, alertness to the needs of others and insight into situations, reinforced by habits such as responsibility, initiative, persistence and self-confidence.

His work continued with a later 1974 analysis of 163 studies which suggested that leaders are characterised by: a strong drive for responsibility and task completion, considerable vigour and persistence in pursuit of goals, creativity and originality in problem solving, initiative in social situations, self-confidence and a strong sense of personal identity, willingness to accept consequences of their decisions and actions, a capacity for absorbing stress, willingness to tolerate frustration and delay, ability to influence the behaviours of others, and a capacity to organise groups to achieve the purpose at hand.[3]

In both studies he was quick to point out that the mere possession of these traits was not enough to ensure effective leadership—the actual behaviour and style of the crucial was crucial.

There then emerged a perspective that personal traits alone were not enough. The contingency in which leadership was required and displayed was also a key factor. The contingency might, for example, be war, crisis, rehabilitation, growth, competition, or sustainability. This gave rise to the modern expression, well known in the corporate and military worlds, that there are "certain leaders for certain times or situations". The approach became known as situational leadership.

Leaders and Followers

For a long period the leader himself or herself remained the focus of attention in leadership literature and studies. Then a paradigm shift occurred when it was realised that a key way to understand the concept of leadership was to study the leader-follower relationship. If it were possible to ascertain why people were prepared to follow a particular leader the notion of leadership would become clearer and easier to identify. In combination with previous concepts this school of thought spawned a range of other explanations of the nature of leadership.

The idea of transactional leadership arose in this context. This was the thought that leaders could enter some kind of bargaining or negotiating process to convince people to follow them. Some attempt was made to identify levers of power and influence by which this might be achieved. However, this was a short-lived leadership concept, as might be expected.

Charismatic theory was another, often-wobbly strand of thought which sought to give an explanation for followers' behaviour. 'Charisma', a word derived from Greek roots meaning spiritual or metaphysical power or energy, was an additional element added to the traits of leaders who attracted a large following. This thinking harked back to Weber's categorisations of authority—traditional authority (where some people possess authority because those in their position or community have always possessed it);

rational authority (where society calculates and determines that this person needs to have such authority); and charismatic authority (based on the mystical influence which some person has over others).[4] Of course, charismatic leadership can be exploited with evil as well as good intent, leading to dire consequences, as in the case of Hitler and many dictators past and present.

Role Models

Yet another popular approach to understanding the leader-follower relationship has been role modelling. Successful and well-respected leaders have been scrutinised to determine just what qualities they possessed. For example, a scan of hundreds of leadership texts has revealed that the people throughout history most often cited as inspirational leaders include:

- Joan of Arc
- Winston Churchill
- Mother Teresa
- Martin Luther King
- Mahatma Gandhi
- John F Kennedy
- Aung San Suu Kyi
- Nelson Mandela

In the particular fields of business, adventuring, and sport many role models have also been cited predominantly of leaders who triumphed through adversity, turning around the declining fortunes of companies or teams, or who achieved long running stellar results, for example CEO of General Electric Jack Welch, and Antarctic Explorer Ernest Shackleton.*

Interestingly it has also been observed that many, if not most, role models do often have a flaw, sometimes a fatal flaw, which is usually not known by their contemporaries, or if known is overlooked in the light of their achievements for the nation, community, or project. The most often cited cases refer to drinking, gambling, health disorders, or aspects of morality. Apparently, leaders do not necessarily have to be perfect in every aspect of their personal lives even though this is considered desirable.

At any event the full scope of leader-follower perspectives reveals a long distance from the notion underpinning trait theory—that people would follow a born leader in blind faith. Now key factors which figured in any explanation of the leader-follower dynamic included vision, trust, values, integrity, inspiration, sense of direction, clear communication, and a team approach.

---

* For an interesting and forensic analysis of Shackleton's leadership, see Margot Morrell and Stephanie Capparell's, *Shackleton's Way: Leadership Lessons from the Great Antarctic Explorer* (New York: Hachette, 2011).

Organisational Leadership

Much of the leadership literature previously mentioned has been based on general and random observations of leadership behaviour. However, there is now also a body of work which purports to be based on close empirical studies of the behaviour of successful leaders and which often leads to prescriptions or formulae which authors say can be replicated. Bookshops at airports and train stations abound in these tomes—the 10 key factors of leadership, the seven ways to success, the 12 thoughts of pathfinders etc. etc. A fair proportion of this is pulp fiction but there are some works which are based on well cited examples of actions and behaviour. Most of it is written in the context of organisational leadership and it pops up usually in the section of the shelving labelled 'Management'.

Indeed, this gives rise to one of the key debates in the literature, and one which is of considerable significance to Not-for-Profits and Social Enterprises viz. *"Is there a difference between leadership and management?"*

Leadership or Management

Basically there are three points of view to be found: (a) that the two concepts, leadership and management, are completely different; (b) that they are the same; and (c), as is so often the case in academic deliberations, a hybrid approach which says that aspects of leadership can be found in management and that leadership requires elements of good management.

In the real world, this dilemma is also often to be found. Visit a school and ask for the leader, (i.e. the school Principal), and you will be directed to a block labelled 'Administration'. Audiences sitting in an orchestral concert could be forgiven for thinking that the conductor is the leader of the orchestra given that conductors are always out in front waving their baton and taking bows, but the real leader of an orchestra is the first violin player. And just who is the leader of a sporting team? Some would say the captain is the leader but captains do not choose players for the team, nor rotate them during the match, nor decide their remuneration, nor determine the strategy for the match, nor take the full credit or blame for the result. Indeed, the coach and often the CEO of the club make these key decisions which in the corporate world would fall to the front person of the business i.e. the captain. Even on the field where captains do have a near monopoly on immediate tactics, the modern practice in many sports is for the captain to have a leadership team of three or four players who jointly decide such matters.

Those who say that leadership and management are different are often espousing the thoughts contained in the literal definition of each concept. The word 'leadership' is derived from a Greek word which, roughly translated, relates to the path of a ship at sea. Hence leadership has strong overtones of dynamic motion including long term vision, a goal or destination, a passage to that destination, and strategies and tactics to keep to that pathway or change course when required: in essence they have an overview of the progress of the mission and also of the team below on the decks.

'Management', on the other hand, derives from a Latin word which relates to 'the hand'. Thus, the word gives rise to images of control, command, direction, monitoring, oversight, performance measurement, all mainly oriented to short to medium considerations: in essence a 'hands-on', active rather than reflective posture.

One of the strongest advocates of a clear distinction between leadership and management, John Kotter, claims that leaders focus on change by setting direction and vision, aligning people to that vision, and motivating people to achieve the vision. In contrast managers plan and budget to produce results. They organise staff, and structure jobs and reporting relationships to implement plans; and they control, problem solve, and correct deviations from the plan. So, it is a leadership task to develop a shared plan, and a management task to coordinate its implementation.[5]

By contrast, one of the key proponents of the hybrid approach, Yukl, says that in influencing task objectives and strategies, commitment and compliance in task behaviour to achieve these objectives, group maintenance and identification, and in influencing the culture of the organisation the terms manager and leader can be used interchangeably.[6]

Interestingly whereas some people used to follow the Kotter line and argue that the Board should provide the leadership and the CEO the management, today leadership is considered a shared responsibility.

Whatever your view may be in this debate, we live in an era where many leaders of organisations are concerned that they are being swamped too much by demands that they focus on management issues thereby reducing their capacity and time to focus on their true leadership responsibilities. This can be seen best in organisations situated in a professional context such as Heads of Hospitals who regard themselves as medical leaders, or School Principals who used to be regarded as Curriculum leaders. However, their job descriptions and performance measures are often struck in purely management terms, including micro-management requirements. (Government employers are the worst in this respect.) Some of this burden, but not all, can be mitigated by delegating management to deputies or buying in expertise: after all it is far easier to buy in management than leadership. This issue is also plaguing Not-for-Profit Organisations where Board membership may not have a full range of skills, or may be focussed solely on short term factors. Government regulations may impose all manner of management responsibility on the leader. It is becoming clear that CEOs of most organisations are being considered predominantly as managers and not given enough space or encouragement to practice and enhance their leadership capacity.

By the same token, within the public sector itself, those who head government organisations are nowadays also required to have skills in the arena of public policy leadership. This has been described as the act of stimulating the formulation and implementation of public policy among multiple, diverse, stakeholders and constituencies. Not a great deal of attention has been given to the nature of this domain but it is clear that it includes—

- Raising the issue to the public and policy agendas
- Convening stakeholders to address the issue
- Forging agreement on policy options and alternatives
- Policy implementation: sustaining action and maintaining momentum.[7]

Leaders of Not-for-Profit organisations would do well to remember that the government bureaucrats sitting opposite them in any discussion on policy or funding are motivated by these factors as well as others.

Lessons from Organisation Theory

Despite the debates and different perspectives in the various theories of leadership, empirical analysis of leadership in organisations has produced a large amount of consensus on what are the key attributes of modern day leadership. Scanning some of the most cited studies, the aspects which appear most regularly include the following:

Common Characteristics of Successful Leaders

Qualities

- Demonstrating core values, high standards, honesty, and integrity.
- Completely sharing the values of the organisation and total alignment with its mission and dedicated to protecting its brand and reputation.
- Inspiring Trust (the notion of trust is becoming increasingly recognised as a key factor in all situations requiring leadership).
- Vision and long term goals and perspectives, pathfinding.
- Decisiveness, choice makers not choice takers.
- Self-confidence including no pretensions nor attempts to be someone other than themselves; in other words, "comfortable in their own skin" (People can quickly spot a fake).
- Being prepared to give power away rather than attempting to control all the levers of power and influence, and being prepared to hire someone smarter than yourself.

Competencies

- Keeping the wellbeing of the clients always foremost in every deliberation and decision.
- Protecting the brand though all aspects of governance, management, operations and communications.

- Possessing detailed knowledge of the industry and sector. There is a clear danger in hiring people who claim to be generic leaders and managers. It rarely works out as employees quickly lose respect for someone who does not appreciate the context and nature of their work, and stakeholders and partners quickly small a rat in their deliberations with such a person. A generic leader needs to devote much of their first year to learning about the origins and history of the enterprise and its milieu.
- Being aware of all the forces surrounding the organisation and sector. Without overdoing it too much, a leader needs to belong to all relevant industry bodies, read several newspapers and magazines, keep up to date with relevant trending social media issues, and remain aware of key research being conducted in the space of the organisation, and where appropriate and possible fund research which will advance the cause.
- Strategic thinking- from formulation to executing and evaluating of strategies. (Case studies reveal that the major shortcoming of all strategy is failure to implement.)
- Clear and persuasive communication: perhaps the most important leadership competency in the modern world, including communicating within and outside the organisation. Also, being seen to be sharing information honestly.
- Accompanying communication ability is the capacity to monitor the message being sent and anticipate its effect on the recipients including the way in which it will be interpreted.
- Rational decision making based clearly on evidence, or, where values are involved, making those values clear and the weight being given to them.
- Then there is sheer competency itself. 'Competent' leaders can fulfil all the tasks expected of them and it is useful if they can also handle, or at least understand the fundamentals of the tasks of all their leadership team members; even better if they spend time understanding the tasks of employees right down the line. (Many modern leaders spend at least a day a month serving on the counter or working in the production room.)
- Maintain a balance between the outward and inward elements of the role, particularly the wellbeing of the staff and the maintenance of key external stakeholders.
- Ensuring sustainability of the organisation particularly in relation to maintaining a diversity of funding sources.
- Attaining effective partnerships whilst ensuring that the brand is not submerged or even captured by any partner.

Personal Attributes

- Always being visible, approachable and accessible and an empathetic listener (harder in a large organisation, but successful leaders find ways to achieve this goal, as long as it has a personal dimension and does not rely on technology alone.)

- Exuding energy and enthusiasm (this of course also implies that a leader needs to be healthy and fit.)
- Showing sensitivity, consideration, and empathy for all employees.
- Being a team builder and remaining a team player.
- Celebrating team and individual successes and challenging team members to achieve even greater heights.
- Constantly endeavouring to be creative and innovative and allowing all team members the freedom to suggest changes to current thinking and practice.
- Promoting responsibility among followers.
- Acting as mentor, coach, role model and motivator to all team members, nurturing and instilling a sense of belonging among workers.
- Remaining resilient. Leadership can sometimes be a lonely affair, partly because of the occasional need to keep some distance from colleagues, and occasionally because there are some matters that can only be addressed alone. A leader may then be forced to fall back on his or her own values, judgement, and instincts. It is a good idea to belong to associations/circles of leaders of like organisations to share similar challenges and solutions.

Transformational Leadership

So, the literature on leadership, and especially that derived from the empirical experience of leaders, has effectively taken us full circle. Leadership is now usually considered as a process or a dynamic, rather than in terms of a position or hierarchy.

Leading from within is just as important as leading from the front. Delegating power is often a more important aspect of leadership than accumulating it. Personal qualities and approaches are more important than just structures and lines of reporting. "Servant Leadership" is an expression capturing the modern belief that dedication to serve is the wellspring from which all manner of leadership flows, especially in Not-for-Profit contexts.

Motivating team members and celebrating their successes and contribution to the organisation's performance is the key to what is now recognised as being transformational leadership. There are two broad usages of this term. One is a broad or macro approach which focuses on cultural change and innovation across societies. The other has a narrower focus particularly on the leader-follower paradigm within an organisation. Bass is a leading exponent of this approach and for him the transformational leader, rather than focusing on how the current needs of subordinates might be met, concentrates on arousing or altering their needs.[8] Bass claimed that transformational leaders achieve good results by employing one or more of four strategies: Idealised influence (transformational leaders are admired and respected by their followers and they act as role models or positive influences); inspirational motivation (transformational leaders communicate high expectations for subordinates and encourage them to aspire to high performance); intellectual stimulation (transformational leaders encourage their followers to be creative and innovative and to try new solutions to old problems); individual consideration (transformational leaders provide a supportive climate in which individuals are encouraged to grow and develop). So, whereas transactional leaders achieve expected outcomes, transformational leaders move the organisation beyond expectations.[9] Although Bass did not specify it, all of this transformation should be motivated by the broader public interest and by self-interest. There must be a moral dimension to transformational leadership.

So, we have indeed come full circle. Transformational Leadership is a concept where anyone adopting the right approach can demonstrate leadership wherever they may be located in the organisation. Such a leader is not a 'born leader', and does not need a specified list of traits, although the leadership talents which they do possess can be materially enhanced. Of course, not all leaders will be the same in terms of their personal style and approach as leadership is both an art and a science.

Indeed, there is now a comprehensive body of thought on transformational leadership which takes its place as a fully- fledged leadership concept. Moreover, it is a highly relevant concept for Not-for-Profit organisations experiencing a transition to becoming also a social enterprise, which is the topic of this book. Leaders are now regarded as agents of change.

The literature on transformational leadership is fairly vast but perhaps the best known is the work of Kouzes and Posner, whose formula has been successfully employed in numerous contexts:[10]

Practices and Commitments of Leadership

Challenging the process:

- Search out challenging opportunities to change, grow, innovate, and improve
- Experiment, take risks and learn from the accompanying mistakes

Inspiring a shared vision:

- Envision an uplifting and ennobling future
- Enlist others in a common vision by appealing to their values, interests, hopes and dreams

Enabling others to act:

- Foster collaboration by promoting cooperative goals and building trust
- Strengthen people by giving power away, providing choice, developing competence, assigning critical tasks and offering visible support

Modelling the way:

- Set the example by behaving in ways that are consistent with shared values
- Achieve small wins that promote consistent progress and build commitment

Encouraging the heart:

- Recognise individual contributions to the success of every project
- Celebrate team accomplishments regularly

Warning: It is vital to recognise that formulae such as this do not mean that leadership is just a box of tricks which can be switched on and off at will to become mere "Pretend Leadership." They must be real personal attitudes and genuine approaches or they will have no transformational power.

Leadership for the Not-for-Profit and Social Enterprise Sector

Much of the leadership literature which has been canvassed can be readily applied to the Not-for-Profit/Social Enterprise sector. Indeed, there are many similarities which are shared with both public and For Profit sectors. Most are related to management aspects and some characteristics of governance. Human and financial resource management throw up very similar challenges wherever they occur.

However, there are a substantial number of leadership challenges of particular pertinence for the Not-for-Profit sector. They include the importance given to the vision of the founders and the mission they carved out for the organisation. These values, which have usually long underpinned the organisation, often carry more lasting and permeated significance than can be found in any modern-day generic 'Mission Statement' of the kind which adorns the walls of government departments or large corporates.

The focus on the needs of the client, which is espoused for all organisations, assumes a much more intense and compelling imperative for Not-for-Profit organisations since this is their real *raison d'etre*.

Sustainability is far more of a challenge in this sector which is reliant so often on none too permanent government grants or the vagaries of philanthropy. This is often why a move into social enterprises and commercialisation is pursued to obtain a more reliable stream of resources. However, that in turn gives rise to the danger that these business activities may occupy the main focus of the Board and Management and cause the original vision and mission to be downplayed or even overlooked, which will alienate the clients and foundation stakeholders. All of this will be exacerbated if partnerships which are formed with the altruistic goal of improving sustainability result in the partners diluting or even swamping the brand and hence reputation of the Not-for-Profit. These are balancing acts which leaders in other sectors do not face in anything like the same dimension. Not-for-Profit leaders are constant jugglers.

Marketing and fund raising by Not-for-Profits faces these same hazards, and innovation and entrepreneurial behaviour are far riskier in the Not-for-Profit environment. There can be a lot to lose in terms of service to clients and their wellbeing if the organisation stumbles. Boards of Not-for-Profits, as custodians of the heritage and brand may need to refine their understanding of the notion of 'stewardship' in investing funds and endeavouring to lift returns in a world of ever changing financial markets.

The regulatory and governance requirements for Not-for-Profits are complex and very time consuming especially for smaller predominantly volunteer led Not-for-Profits. This arena becomes even more complicated if the organisation has an advocacy role and is then occasionally obliged to seek reform from the same governments who impose these governance arrangements and provide funding for the organisation. Leaders have to be very careful when they bite the hand that feeds them, and this situation has not been helped until very recently by the weak nature of the peak bodies in the Not-for-Profit sector who need to take on stronger advocacy roles as well.

Leaders in this sector are usually strongly oriented to identifying and encouraging emerging leaders in their midst but this is more difficult than in other sectors because staff numbers and hence vacancies are not all that large, salaries are typically lower, and there is less flexibility for the design of remuneration packages. Where there is a blend of paid and volunteer positions in the workforce, added complications arise which can cause challenges to the maintenance of harmony.

These and many other dimensions are addressed throughout this book in the chapters and case studies. The overall message is that Transformational Leadership is essential in modern day Not-for-Profits and Social Enterprises, and that requires these leaders to stay not just on top but ahead of the game.

Notes

1. Greg Latemore and Victor J. Callan. "Odysseus for Today: Ancient and Modern Lessons for Leaders." *Asia Pacific Journal of Human Resources* 36, no. 3 (1999): 76–86.
2. R. Stogdill. "Personal Factors Associated with Leadership." *Journal of Psychology*, 54 (1948): 259–269.
3. R. M. Stogdill. *Handbook of Leadership* (New York: Free Press, 1974); Martin Albrow. *Bureaucracy* (London: Palgrave Macmillan, 1970).
4. Martin.
5. John Kotter. "What Leaders Really Do." *Harvard Business Review* (May–June 2001): 103–111.

6. G. Yukl. *Leadership in Organisations*, 4th edn. (Englewood Cliffs, NJ: Prentice Hall, 1998).
7. Herrington J. Bryce. *Players in the Public Policy Process: Nonprofits as Social Capital and Agents* (Berlin: Springer, 2012).
8. B. M. Bass. *Leadership and Performance Beyond Expectations* (New York: Free Press, 1985).
9. B. M. Bass and B. J. Avolio (eds). *Improving Organizational Effectiveness Through Transformational Leadership* (Thousand Oaks, CA: Sage, 1994).
10. James M. Kouzes and Barry Z. Posner. *The Leadership Challenge*, 4th ed. (San Francisco, CA: Jossey-Bass/Wiley-Blackwell, 2007).

Bibliography

Albrow, Martin. *Bureaucracy*. London: Macmillan, 1970.

Bass, B. M. *Leadership and Performance Beyond Expectations*. New York: Free Press, 1985.

Bass, B. M. and B. J. Avolio, (eds). *Improving Organizational Effectiveness Through Transformational Leadership*. Thousand Oaks, CA: Sage Publications, 1994.

Bryce, Herrington J. *Players in the Public Policy Process, Nonprofits as Social Capital and Agents*. 2nd Edition. New York: Palgrave Macmillan, 2005.

Kotter, John. "What Leaders Really Do." *Harvard Business Review* (May–June 2001): 103.

Kouzes James M., and Z. Posner Barry. *The Leadership Challenge*. 4th Edition. San Francisco: Jossey-Bass/Wiley, 2007.

Latemore G., and V. Callan. "Odysseus for Today: Ancient and Modern Lessons for Leaders." *Asia Pacific Journal of Human Resources* (March 1999).

Morrell, Margot and Stephanie Capparell. *Shackleton's Way*. New York: Penguin, 2002.

Stogdill, R. M. *Handbook of Leadership*. New York: Free Press, 1974.

Stogdill, R. M. "Personal Factors Associated With Leadership: A Survey of the Literature." *The Journal of Psychology* 25, no. 1 (1948): 35–71.

Yukl, G. *Leadership in Organisations*. 4th Edition. Upper Saddle River, NJ: Prentice Hall, 1998.

2 Three Schools of Nonprofit Thought

Evolution of the Field and Implications For Leadership

Aastha Malhotra

Introduction

The nonprofit sector is a wide and diverse field constituted by organisations ranging from charities to social service agencies. Together these organisations serve the disadvantaged by fulfilling social needs, advocating and implementing public policies, promoting social inclusion and building economies by generating employment. In recent decades however, these organisations have been confronted by various social, economic and political changes. Challenges confronted by nonprofit managers and leaders include a tightening funding environment, growing competition for donors and grants, rising demand for services and increasing calls for accountability. Against this background, nonprofit leaders and managers are being forced to explore new ways of working. This includes adoption of highly formalised institutions, corporate tools and solutions, capacity building initiatives and experimenting with innovative social business models, thus transforming the very landscape of the nonprofit sector. Some however, argue that nonprofits cannot be managed in the same way as for-profits due to contextual differences. They stress the importance of community engagement and volunteerism. The transformation has thus lent itself to diverse and sometimes contradictory perspectives on nonprofit functioning and decision-making.

This introductory chapter builds on my doctoral research and a previous paper (Malhotra, Verreynne and Zammuto, 2012) that traced out the evolutionary development of not-for-profit management in the literature.[1] The chapter synthesises the competing perspectives into three distinct schools of thought where each school is based on unique values and motivations, and has different strengths and shortcomings. The emergent framework provides a clarification in language and facilitates movement of the 'either—or' debate that has dominated current discussions towards a more holistic approach that stems from an in-depth understanding of where each perspective is coming from, how it is evident and its implications for leadership.

The chapter is structured as follows. It begins with an explanation of the review process and then discusses the three schools of thought, covering their origins, the key drivers that prompted their emergence, the key characteristics and practices associated with each school as well as the reasons behind the transitions from one school to another. This is followed by the theoretical and practical implications of the framework for various stake-holder groups of nonprofit organisations and social enterprises, thus setting the scene for the remainder of the book.

Review and Analysis Process

The methodological approach draws on insights from the work of scholars who have traced the creation and evolution of fields such as new public management and organisational strategy. The primary motivation was to include a range of methodologically and intellectually diverse sources that have influenced the development of the nonprofit field and thus inclusion of editorial pieces, chronicles and government reports that provided important contextual information along with research articles, relevant stock-taking efforts and reviews conducted by other authors' commentaries and opinion pieces, research notes and reports pertaining to nonprofits was deemed critical to this review. In addition, noting that the nonprofit sector is a diverse group of organisations ranging from small religious groups to large universities and many of these nonprofits operate within unique institutional settings, thus making it improper to view them as a homogenous group, the review process concentrated on the conceptual development of nonprofit practice within the social service nonprofit organisations (SSNPO's).

Reading through the publications facilitated a development of a sense of the field and research findings, developments and observations put forward by other scholars and propagated views along with the respective time period. These were documented chronologically in a simple Microsoft Excel table. A close examination of the resulting list showed that even though the field was dotted with diverse and often competing ideas and research directions, as indicated by previous researchers, some views and insights were expressed repeatedly over time. Adopting the process of 'qualitative clustering', the data was synthesised further by looking for patterns and forming categories of similar and recurrent views and comparing and contrasting insights within each to identify commonalities and variations.[2] Using the emerging patterns as an organising lens and adopting a simple colour-coding scheme, the developments were re-organised according to the underlying perspective. For example, information related to the acceptance of management tools were assigned one colour while the ones related to new approaches combining management expertise with social aims were assigned another. It is, however, important to note that the aim of this organisation process was not to categorise the work of individual scholars, but rather to delineate the observed contradictions and bring some order to the present state of theorising in nonprofit functioning.

Drawing parallels with the work of scholars in other fields of management and leadership that have classified fields of studies into 'schools of thought' to effectively show how a field has evolved over time, the data was further distilled into "origins, characteristics as well as associated strengths and weaknesses," a classification typically visible in the literature.[3] Creation of sub-categories, identification of relevant content and the writing process was iterative and involved multiple drafts. Termed Traditional, Contemporary and Hybrid respectively, the three schools have appeared at different stages in the evolution of nonprofit practice and more importantly, each school continues to have a considerable influence on nonprofit organisations. The next three sections present each school in further depth.

The Traditional School: 1960s and Before

Dating back to the pre-twentieth century, the first of the three schools is the Traditional School. It reflects the earliest views towards nonprofit functioning and its origins are synonymous with those of the nonprofit sector—the practice of charity. Although charitable activities have religious underpinnings and trace back to ancient times, some of the most influential developments resulting in the creation of the modern-day nonprofit sector came about and gained prominence after the seventeenth century. Examples include the establishment of alm houses across Europe and United States of America and most significantly the passing of the English Poor Law of 1601 in England. The need for such services was cemented in the nineteenth century with the coming of the Industrial Revolution. Rapid urbanisation and mass migration into cities lead to problems such as poverty, overcrowding, poor housing, disease and substance abuse.[4] In an attempt to combat these problems, existing agencies, such as courts and hospitals, began to offer support services. As the presence of and demand for these services grew, so did attempts to organise and institutionalise them, which led to the formation of the very first social service agencies and nonprofit organisations.

Key Characteristics and Illustrative Practices

Deeply linked to these foundations, the Traditional School is underpinned by the values of compassion for those living in difficult circumstances, collaboration and community concern for public good. The foremost of these shows in the importance that some scholars place on a nonprofit organisation's mission. The Traditional School not only endorses these views, but also deems that focussing on anything other than the mission diminishes an organisation's ability to stay true to its purpose. For example, scholars observe that nonprofit organisations often prioritise service delivery over infrastructure, capacity and financial survival.[5]

The focus on client well-being and social goals is also visible in the second characteristic of the school, efforts at professionalising the field through government initiatives and establishment of formal social service departments, academic institutions and associations. Earliest examples include a Summer School in Philanthropic Work organised in New York City in 1898 (which became the New York School of Social Work in 1917) and the International Association of Schools of Social Work formed in France in 1928. Ensuing endeavours have focussed on unifying community and welfare services, improving skills and techniques for service delivery, developing high standards of work and maintaining ethical conduct.[6] Illustrative practices include supervision and formation of ethical codes that continue to govern practice and prescribe service ideals.

Another characteristic is the emphasis on collaboration and community engagement, a practice which has been a part of the nonprofit sector since the 1930s and allows organisations to maximise the participation of everyone concerned, combine contacts, information and resources in order to provide support to clients.[7] Advocates of the school recognise the importance of fostering inter-organisational collaborations and suggest that such practices not only allow nonprofits to address challenges that may be too complex for a single organisation alone to solve but also work with likeminded peers to collectively advocate for policy change and increased government funding.[8] A predisposition towards community engagement is also visible in volunteerism. Supporters of the Traditional School go beyond the operational perspective of viewing volunteers as a resource, and instead exalt the value of celebrating them and their spirit.[9] Notions such as "we must encourage, feed, and reward the altruistic 'habits of the heart' " sum up the Traditional School's approach towards the role of volunteers and broader community members.[10]

While the Traditional school of thought reflects the earliest views towards nonprofit management, its presence has been somewhat displaced in recent years. There are two main causes for this. First, the perception that the characteristics and practices of the Traditional School threaten nonprofit organisations' functioning and survival—thereby hampering their ability to continue delivering services as well as casting doubt over their credibility and accountability. It is important to note that while this discontent found impetus in the 1960's, it continues to be reflected in recent nonprofit work. For example, the emphasis on service delivery is linked to a reduced focus on building organisation's capacity, cutting back or hiring underqualified employees to reduce overhead costs, omitting to build financial reserves for unforeseen or future expenses and not investing in appropriate resources or infrastructure.[11] The absence of proper systems, performance measurement tools and standard measures of success further complicates assessing the social impact of nonprofit organisations; some even extend this lack of procedures to general functioning and question other organisational practices.[12] Disapprovals include the unrestricted discretion of social workers thus leading to concerns about the quality and consistency of service delivery and continued appointments of board members who, albeit passionate, lack relevant expertise and are ineffective at making decisions

The second cause can be linked to the broader changes, societal level shifts and policy reforms including the growing attractiveness of new public management and neoliberal views that became a part of the nonprofit land-scape in the 1970s and 1980s. Resulting challenges include funding cutbacks that led to a scarcity of resources, competition for government contracts and clients, entry of for-profit organisations into the nonprofit arena, ability to form cross-sector partnerships, decreasing voluntary support, intense media scrutiny and demonstrated accountability from donors among others.[13] These changes forced nonprofits to revisit traditional nonprofit practices of empowerment, volunteerism and community building and instead consider more businesslike practices for functioning, thus laying the foundation for the next school of thought.

The Contemporary School: Early 1970s to 1990s

While the Contemporary School emerged primarily in response to the changing operating environment, other factors such as research findings, practitioner efforts, government directives and funder demands also served as momentum drivers. Prominent examples include the first ever Private Philanthropy and Public Needs Survey in 1973 which revealed that nonprofit organisations were facing a range of management con-cerns and that the sector lacked academic programs to prepare nonprofit leaders.[14]

Subsequent government directives included budget cuts by the Reagan administration in the US in the 1980s and encouragement for nonprofits to develop management expertise and stringent control measures by the Thatcher government in Great Britain. These changes brought with them onerous regulations and reporting systems and compelled nonprofits to cut back less financially feasible activities, seek endorsements and establish ad-ditional revenue sources, all practices that demanded managerial skills.[15] Advocates of the Contemporary School not only encouraged this shift but also suggested that operating like a business would improve any non-profit organisation. Benefits promised include setting an organisation's direction, reduced financial uncertainty, increased competitive advantage and compli-ance with growing demands for accountability and transparency.

Key Characteristics and Illustrative Practices

The most prominent characteristic of this school is 'managerialism', a practice that acknowledges a proliferation of conventional business val-ues and skills within nonprofits. Illustrative practices include increased managerial training and education, appointment of people on the basis of their managerial competencies and even hiring management consul-tants.[16] Other examples include the adoption of tools such as cash-flow management, accumulation of surplus revenue, and cost-conscious bud-get regulations to strengthen organisations financially, subsidise loss-making services and offset uncertainty in funding. The literature suggests that nonprofits have placed special emphasis on practices such as strategic planning and strategic alliances and often linked them to enhanced organisational performance.[17]

Another characteristic of the Contemporary School is the 'marketisation' of the nonprofit sector.[18] This includes adoption of a market orientation, application of marketing tactics and establishment of commercial and revenue-generating arms.[19] The notion of *operating like a business* is further reflected in the third and fourth characteristics of the school—the acceptance of evaluation and performance measurement, and the need of nonprofit organisations to build capacity. One reason for the acceptance of performance evaluation and measurement is the pressure to appease funders and public perceptions as well as fulfil reporting conditions.[20] Capacity building, on the other hand, is often based in the aspiration of nonprofits to become self-reliant by developing their core organisation skills and resource management techniques.[21]

In spite of its popularity, the Contemporary School has been the subject of intense debate and criticism.[22] Numerous views contribute to this debate. Some scholars emphasise differences in mission, attitude, processes and structure between the for-profit and nonprofit sectors and, in turn, question the appropriateness and transferability of for-profit business practices. Points of contention include the challenge of measuring the fulfilment of a nonprofit's altruistic goals, personnel motivational factors such as mission and commitment to social cause rather than monetary gain and profitability motives. There is also the view that pursuit of efficiency-driven managerialist practices can result in mission displacement and mission deflection, a situation where organisations "move away from their founding principles" and engage in a reduction of services or client focus to promote efficiency.[23] Another view comes from researchers who express the concern that adopting for-profit business practices places undue pressure on smaller nonprofits. For example, Zimmerman and Stevens note that the paperwork and formalities required for procuring funding strain the already tight resources of smaller organisations.[24]

As a consequence, many nonprofit practitioners have resisted the rise of the Contemporary School. There is a growing awareness that 'superimposition' of for-profit practices does not always produce the greatest or desired results and nonprofit and activities and strategies specific to the nonprofit context are necessary.[25] Adding to this dispute are continuing changes in the nonprofit environment and the resulting concerns about the sustainability of organisations including steadily decreasing financial support that have become prominent since the late 1990s. In response, many nonprofits have turned to revenue-generating ventures and other practices that allow them to pursue efficient operations and financial sustainability while providing services, thus paving the way for the third and most recent school of thought.

The Hybrid School: 1990s to Present

The Hybrid School responds to the dual challenge of fulfilling a social mission while maintaining a financially sustainable approach and calls for 'blended' practices that combine social passion with business acumen to generate social and economic value and to increase access to resources.[26] While there has been a high level of interest in the Hybrid School in recent years, 'hybrid' practices that meet social and financial sustainability goals can be traced back to the early 1900's. One of the earliest and enduring examples is Goodwill that sells donated clothes and other unwanted items to raise funds for charitable activities since 1902.

Other prominent examples include the Grameen Bank, established in 1983 in Bangladesh to empower communities and eradicate poverty through micro-financing initiatives and the Ashoka Foundation, a nonprofit venture established in 1980, which encourages innovative practices by providing start-up funding to entrepreneurs with a social vision.[27] Recent developments that have cemented the presence of this school include publication of how-to manuals and practice-led initiatives (e.g., Yale School of Management's National Business Plan Competition for Nonprofit Organisations seeking to start or expand successful profit-making ventures in 2002), academic developments such as dedicated journals (e.g., Stanford Social Innovation Review, started in 2003), and education and research centres (e.g., the Skoll Centre for Social Entrepreneurship at the University of Oxford in 2003).

Advocates of the school argue that adopting Hybrid approaches can offset the weaknesses of the Traditional and Contemporary Schools by catalysing social transformation, allowing nonprofits to seize opportunities and achieve sustainable competitive advantage, which facilitates the long-term viability of an organisation.[28]

Key Characteristics and Illustrative Practices

The foremost characteristic of the Hybrid School is visible in 'dual-natured' practices that blur boundaries between nonprofit and for-profit work. The most widely-accepted of these are social entrepreneurship and social enterprises. Social entrepreneurship is broadly understood as entrepreneurial behaviour combined with a social mission or goal that emphasises and integrates economic and social value.[29] Examples include fee-for-service programs, social enterprises that aim to generate employment in disadvantaged communities, for-profit organisations set up for a social purpose that direct their profits to a social cause, socially responsible commercial businesses engaged in cross-sector partnerships as well as nonprofits applying business expertise and market-based skills for alternative resources.

Another characteristic of the Hybrid School relates to the role of innovation within the nonprofit domain, where scholars assert that nonprofits are inherently innovative in tackling social problems.[30] Although research on innovation within nonprofits is largely anecdotal with limited empirical research,[31] supporters of the Hybrid School actively promote innovation to use existing resources creatively and generate new products and services and gain competitive advantage.[32]

The third characteristic of the Hybrid School relates to relationships across sectors, which includes initiatives such as venture philanthropy that pertains to the adoption of venture capital principles in projects that aim to achieve social change.[33] Such investors provide both growth capital and strategic assistance; they also emphasise capacity building by investing in organisational infrastructure and governance practices within the nonprofits they fund. Other examples include tools that combine performance measurement with social value such as the Social Return on Investment (SROI) established by the Roberts Enterprise Development Fund (REDF), Social Impact Analysis, and Social Impact Assessment; tools which have revolutionised nonprofit performance measurement, as they incorporate financial data and the social impact of social policies and programs.[34]

Hybrid practices have received tremendous attention in recent years because they promise profits, poverty eradication and empowerment in one seamless package.[35] The feasibility and sustainability of this school is, however, still in question. The concern that the social focus of nonprofit commitments and the revenue-driven nature of commercial practices are fundamentally different means that divergent expectations can force organisations to deliver services that are commercially viable rather than those their communities need and focus on clients who are able to pay and refuse those who cannot.[36]

Similarly, organisations working across two distinct sectors may face contradictory pressures while trying to establish legitimacy within each; for example, a cafe that is a social business will compete with for-profit cafes.[37] The nascent stage of empirical evidence around the actual consequences of Hybrid practices adds to the ambiguity. For example, while numerous scholars have exalted the positive attributes of the Grameen Bank, the unintended consequence of increased violence against married women, owing to the empowerment of women and their resultant refusal to hand over the funds to their husbands in a male-dominated society, is less discussed.[38] To summarise, although the need to pursue practices that draw on the nonprofit sector's values and mission-based strengths with a sustainability outlook is being increasingly recognised, the Hybrid School's exact contribution to the sector remains uncertain.

Discussion and Setting the Context for the Book

At the outset of this chapter, the transformational nature of the nonprofit landscape and the contrasting and contradictory perspectives that exist towards nonprofit functioning and the resulting debates were highlighted.

The Three Schools of Nonprofit Thought provides an understanding of how the perspectives have evolved within the nonprofit context and brings the multiple perspectives together.

While the three perspectives have been recognised and discussed individually in previous research, scholars have applauded or criticised the diverse perspectives individually (Mulhare, 1999; Siciliano, 1997), drawn attention to their inherent contradictions (cf. Jackson 2009; Anheier, 2000), or highlighted the importance of understanding with equal rigour the positive and negative consequences and harnessing the benefits of each (cf. Conner and Epstein, 2007; Maier, Meyer and Steinbereithner 2014).[39]

The perspectives have not yet been positioned collectively in a single framework, showing that they continue to influence the functioning of the nonprofit organisations. I suggest that it is the co-existence of these perspectives or schools of thought that embodies the inherent tension and conflict that nonprofit leaders may experience in not only day-to-day operations but also their overall aims and objectives. A collective understanding of these perspectives as presented in the framework contributes in three ways.

Enhanced Understanding

First, the framework brings order and coherence to the academic and practitioner debates and uncovers the motivations behind the three schools and what has shaped them, practices that show how they may translate into practice as well as the outcomes associated with each, and their potential impact on the organisation. An enhanced understanding of own priorities and insight into others' priorities builds comprehensive insight into organisational functioning and can facilitate better leadership and decision-making in areas such as funding, investment and partnership decisions.

Platform to Embrace

Second, the integrative nature of the proposed framework captures the complex, turbulent yet realistic view of what it means to lead and manage a nonprofit. From a practical perspective, it highlights the interplay of the three schools which helps to explain the inherent tension and conflict that organisations may experience in not only day-to-day operations, but also their overall aims and objectives. An example of these implications can be seen in insights the framework holds for the emerging social enterprise literature. Insights related to the Hybrid school of thought within the framework not only contributes to the clarity of the discussions around what constitutes social entrepreneurship, but also places it within the context of the broader development of nonprofit functioning and some of the unintended consequences on vulnerable communities.

It also raises queries for authors who assert that hybrid organisations are the key to profits, poverty eradication and empowerment as well as those who attribute their emergence to 'heroic' individuals who want to fulfil a social aim using business acumen as noted in this chapter. Such claims downplay the value of the sector's charitable and philanthropic heritage and obscure the institutional and regulatory changes that have compelled nonprofit organisations to seek alternative sources of income—one of the significant activities of social enterprise activity. The framework brings such insights to the forefront of theorising thus paving the way for generation of insightful and penetrating research questions as well as a more nuanced understanding of how nonprofits should be led and managed.

Proactive Rather than Reactive Approach

Third, the Three Schools build on the work of past scholars who have identified the impact of these perspectives. For example, while Moore (2000) observes that processes such as strategic planning that are integral to the Contemporary school have been linked to changes in the mission which may have a negative impact on the reputation thus threatening its survival, Zimmerman and Stevens's (2006) research found that the formalities required for procuring funding strained the already tight resources of smaller organisations. The Three Schools can be used to pre-empt consequences and adopt a more proactive rather than reactive approach to functioning and help navigate the transformation that is characteristic of the current nonprofit environment.[40]

Valuable insights about strengths and criticisms associated with each school of thought, while not exhaustive, can serve as a starting point for nonprofit leaders to adopt a more informed approach to decision making, anticipation of outcomes and possibly employment of organisational processes to leverage the positive or mitigate the untoward or negative consequences and thereby reducing some of the ambiguity surrounding nonprofit practice.

Conclusion

The real challenge to understanding the nonprofit context is not to advocate one school over another or to combine the three schools which, given the diverse theoretical heritage and characteristics of each school, would lead to nothing more than an impasse. Nor is it to promote a one-size-fits-all approach—by avoiding a strong bias towards any one school of thought, nonprofit leaders can make sure they remain aware of the complexity surrounding nonprofit management practice (due to the presence of competing perspectives).

Instead, it is to examine and reflect on how the three schools manifest in practice across different functional areas (for example, governance, information systems) and the resulting implications, an exercise that is at the core of my research endeavours. The content presented in this book draws parallels with the evolutionary journey presented in this chapter. The leadership journeys demonstrate how people leading them have coped with changes, the theoretical chapters highlight the prevalent models and the case studies provide insight into the complex decision-making that occurs across functional areas.

The critical role played by nonprofit organisations in today's environment, and the nature of their responsibilities, makes it crucial to understand these complexities, eliminate the ensuing ambiguity and mitigate the associated risks. The three schools of thought presented in this chapter make an important first step in this direction.

Acknowledgement: I would like to express my gratitude to my PhD supervisors, Associate Professor Martie-Louis Verreynne and Professor Raymond Zammuto who provided support, offered comments, edited and encouraged me—without them the content presented in this chapter would have never seen the light of the day.

Notes

1. Aastha Malhotra, Raymond Zammuto and Martie-Louise Verreynne. "Three Schools of Not-for-Profit Management Thought—Exploring the Influence of Management Ideologies on Managerial Responses," in *Australian and New Zealand Academy of Management Conference* (Perth, Australia, 2012).
2. M. Miles and A. M. Huberman. *Qualitative Data Analysis: An Expanded Sourcebook* (Thousand Oaks, CA: Sage, 1994).
3. c.f. A. D. Meyer, A. Tsui and C. R. Hinings. "Configurational Approaches to Organizational Analysis," *Academy of Management Journal* 6 (1993); H. Mintzberg, B. Ahlstrand and J. Lampel. *Strategy Safari: A Guided Tour Through the Wilds of Strategic Management* (New York: Free Press, 1998); Daniel A. Wren. *The Evolution of Management Thought*, 4th edn. (Canada: John Wiley and Sons, 1994).
4. Nigel Horner (ed). *What Is Social Work? Context and Perspectives*, 3rd edn. (Exeter: Learning Matters, 2009).
5. A. S Blackwood and T. H. Pollak. *Washington-Area Nonprofit Operating Reserves* (Washington, DC: Urban Institute, Center on Nonprofits and Philanthropy, 2009); Thomas H. Jeavons. "When the Management Is the Message: Relating Values to Management Practice in Nonprofit Organizations," *Nonprofit Management and Leadership* 2, no. 4 (1992); Robert E. McDonald. "An Investigation of Innovation in Nonprofit Organizations: The Role of Organizational Mission," *Nonprofit and Voluntary Sector Quarterly* 36, no. 2 (2007); Daniel Stid and Jeffery Bradach. "How Visionary Nonprofits Leaders Are Learning to Enhance Management Capabilities," *Strategy and Leadership* 37, no. 1 (2009).
6. John Harris. "Professionalism Takes a Pounding [Online]," in *Moving Beyond Managerialism in Human Services*, eds. Michael Muetzelfeldt and Linda Briskman (Melbourne: RMIT Publishing, 2003); Mary Langan. "A Crisis in Care? Challenges to Social Work," in *A Crisis in Care? Challenges to Social Work*, ed. John Clarke (Milton Keynes: The Open University, 1993).

7. Joseph Galaskiewicz, Wolfgang Bielefeld and Myron Dowell. "Networks and Organizational Growth: A Study of Community Based Nonprofits," *Administrative Science Quarterly* 51, no. 3 (2006); Sharon Oster, *Strategic Management for Nonprofit Organizations—Theory and Cases* (Oxford: Oxford University Press, 1995); D. L. Rogers and C. L. Mulford. "The Historical Development," in *Interorganization Coordination: Theory, Research, and Implementation*, eds. D. A. Whetten D. L. Rogers and Associates (Ames, IA: Iowa State University Press, 1982); Melissa Stone, Barbara Bigelow and William Crittenden. "Research on Strategic Management in Nonprofit Organizations—Synthesis, Analysis and Future Directions," *Administration & Society* 31, no. 3 (1999).
8. Bin Chen and Elizabeth A. Graddy. "The Effectiveness of Nonprofit Lead-Organization Networks for Social Service Delivery," *Nonprofit Management and Leadership* 20, no. 4 (2010); Alfred Vernis and Angel Saz-Carranza. *Nonprofit Organizations Challenges and Collaboration* (New York: Palgrave Macmillan, 2006).
9. Jeffrey L. Brudney and Beth Gazley. "Moving Ahead or Falling Behind? Volunteer Promotion and Data Collection," *Nonprofit Management and Leadership* 16, no. 3 (2006); Richard Bush. "Survival of the Nonprofit Spirit in the a for-Profit World," *Nonprofit and Voluntary Sector Quarterly* 21, no. 4 (1992); Fred Setterberg and Kary Schulman. *Beyond Profit: The Complete Guide to Managing the Nonprofit Organization* (New York: HarperCollins, 1985).
10. Bush.
11. c.f. Blackwood and Pollak; K. A. Froelich, T. W. Knoepfle and T. H. Pollak. "Financial Measures in Nonprofit Organization Research: Comparing Irs 990 Return and Audited Financial Statement Data," *Nonprofit and Voluntary Sector Quarterly* 29, no. 2 (2000); Stid and Bradach.
12. Harris; Clyde Eirakur Hull and Brian H. Lio. "Innovation in Non-Profit and for-Profit Organizations: Visionary, Strategic, and Financial Considerations," *Journal of Change Management* 6, no. 1 (2006); Paul J. Jansen and Andrea R. Kilpatrick. "The Dynamic Nonprofit Board," *McKinsey Quarterly* 2 (2004).
13. Helmut Anheier. *Nonprofit Organizations Theory, Management and Practice* (New York: Routledge, 2005); Mark Lindenberg. "Are We at the Cutting Edge or the Blunt Edge? Improving Ngo Organizational Performance with Private and Public Sector Strategic Management Frameworks," *Nonprofit Management and Leadership* 11, no. 3 (2001); Hillel Schmid. "Merging Nonprofit Organizations: Analysis of a Case Study." ibid.5, no. 4 (1995).
14. Lesley Chenoweth and Donna McAuliffe. *The Road to Social Work and Human Service Practice*, 2nd edn. (China: Cengage Learning, 2008); Peter D. Hall, "A Historical Overview of the Private Nonprofit Sector," in *The Nonprofit Sector: A Research Handbook*, ed. Walter W. Powell (New Haven: Yale University Press, 1987).
15. A. Abrahamson and L. M. Salamon. *The Nonprofit Sector and the New Federal Budget* (Washington, DC: Urban Institute, 1986); L. David Brown and Mark H. Moore. "Accountability, Strategy, and International Nongovernmental Organizations," *Nonprofit and Voluntary Sector Quarterly* 30, no. 3 (2001); S. L. McMurtry, F. N. Netting and P. M. Kettner. "How Nonprofits Adapt to a Stringent Environment," *Nonprofit Management and Leadership* 1, no. 3 (1991); W. Bielefeld. "Funding Uncertainty and Nonprofit Strategies in the 1980s," ibid.41, no. 2 (1992).

16. Peter J. Haas and Maynard G. Robinson. "The Views of Nonprofit Executives on Educating Nonprofit Managers," ibid.8, no. 4 (1998); Eileen M. Mulhare. "Mindful of the Future: Strategic Planning Ideology and the Culture of Nonprofit Management," *Human Organization* 58, no. 3 (1999); J. I. Siciliano. "The Relationship Between Formal Planning and Peformance in Nonprofit Organizations," *Nonprofit Management and Leadership* 7, no. 4 (1997); Gerhard Speckbacher. "The Economics of Performance Management in Nonprofit Organizations," ibid.13, no. 3 (2003); Dennis R. Young. *Casebook of Management for Nonprofit Organisations: Entrepreneurship and Organizational Change in the Human Services* (New York: Hawthorne Press, 1985).

17. Stone, Bigelow and Crittenden; Schmid; Lois M. Takahashi and Gayla Smutny. "Collaborative Windows and Organizational Governance: Exploring the Formation and Demise of Social Service Partnerships," *Nonprofit and Voluntary Sector Quarterly* 31, no. 2 (2002).

18. A. M. Eikenberry and J. D. Kluver. "The Marketization of the Nonprofit Sector: Civil Society at Risk?" *Pubic Adminstration Review*, no. 64 (2004); L. M. Salamon and H. Anheier. *Defining the Nonprofit Sector: A Cross-National Analysis* (Manchester: Manchester University Press, 1997).

19. M. J. Arnold and S. R. Tapp. "Direct Marketing in Non-Profit Services: Investigating the Case of the Arts Industry," *Journal of Services Marketing* 17, no. 2 (2003); David Hammack. "Accountability and Nonprofit Organizations: A Historical Perspective," *Nonprofit Management and Leadership* 6, no. 2 (1995); L. Kristoffersen and S. Singh. "Successful Application of a Customer Relationship Management Program in a Nonprofit Organization," *Journal of Marketing Theory and Practice* (2004); Salamon and Anheier.

20. J. G Carman. "Evaluation Practice Among Community-Based Organizations Research into the Reality," *American Journal of Evaluation* 28, no. 1 (2007); A. Fowler. "Assessing Ngo Performance: Difficulties, Dilemmas and a Way Ahead," in *Performance and Accountability: Beyond the Magic Bullet*, eds. M. Edwards and D. Hulme (London: Earthscan, 1995); E. Morley, E. Vinson and H. P. Hatry. *Outcome Measurement in Nonprofit Organizations: Current Practices and Recommendations* (Washington, DC: Independent Sector, 2001).

21. Philip O'Donoghue, Myles McGregor-Lowndes and Mark Lyons. "Policy Lessons for Strengthening Nonprofits," *Australian Journal of Social Issues* 41, no. 4 (2006).

22. Tammy E. Beck, Cynthia A. Lengnick-Hall and Mark L. Lengnick-Hall. "Solutions Out of Context Examining the Transfer of Business Concepts to Nonprofit Organizations," *Nonprofit Management and Leadership* 19, no. 2 (2008); Bronwen Dalton and John Casey. "Money for Mission or Moral Minefield? The Opportunities and Risks of Not-for-Profit Business Venturing," in *Strategic Issues for the Not-for-Profit Sector*, ed. Jo Barraket (Sydney: University of New South Wales Press, 2008); John Lawler. "The Rise of Managerialism in Social Work," in *Management, Social Work and Change*, eds. Elizabeth Harlow and John Lawler (Vermont, USA: Ashgate Publishing Limited, 2000).

23. W. W. Powell and R. Steinberg. *The Nonprofit Sector: A Research Handbook* (New Heaven: Yale University Press, 2006), 604.

24. Jo Zimmerman and Bonnie W. Stevens. "The Use of Performance Measurement in South Carolina Nonprofits," *Nonprofit Management and Leadership* 16, no. 3 (2006).

25. Gordon Dabbs. "Nonprofit Businesses in the 1990s: Models for Success." *Business Horizons* 34, no. 5 (1991): 68–71; R. Rojas. "A Review of Models for Measuring Organizational Effectiveness Among for-Profit and Nonprofit Organizations," *Nonprofit Management & Leadership* 11, no. 1 (2000); Mark Moore. "Managing for Value: Organizational Strategy in for-Profit, Nonprofit, and Governmental Organizations," *Nonprofit and Voluntary Sector Quarterly* 29, no. 1 (2000); David O. Renz. "Changing the Face of Nonprofit Management," *Nonprofit Management and Leadership* 11, no. 3 (2001); Michael Worth. *Nonprofit Management Principles and Practice* (Thousand Oaks, CA: Sage, 2009).
26. Eikenberry and Kluver; J. Elkington and P. Hartigan, *The Power of Unreasonable People: How Social Entrepreneurs Create Markets That Change the World* (Cambridge, MA: Harvard Business School Press, 2008); Romayne Hutchison and Ben Cairns. "Community Anchor Organizations:Sustainablity and Independence," in *Hybrid Organisations and the Third Sector*, ed. Billis David (London: Palgrave Macmillan, 2010); S. Johnson. "Social Enterprise Literature Review," (Edmonton, Alberta: Canadian Centre for Social Entrepreneurship, 2001); Burton A. Weisbrod, "Guest Editor's Introduction: The Nonprofit Mission and Its Financing," *Journal of Policy Analysis and Management* 17, no. 2 (1998).
27. Muhammad Yunus and Bertrand Moingeon. "Building Social Business Models: Lessons from the Grameen Experience," *Long Range Planning* 43 (2010); Johanna Mair and Ignasi Marti. "Social Entrepreneurship Research: A Source of Explanation, Prediction, and Delight," *Journal of World Business* 41 (2006).
28. S. H. Alvord, L. D. Brown and C. W. Letts. "Social Entrepreneurship and Societal Transformation: An Exploratory Study," *The Journal of Applied Behavioral Science* 40, no. 3 (2004); C. Debra Minkoff. "The Emergence of Hybrid Organizational Forms: Combining Identity-Based Service Provision and Political Action," *Nonprofit and Voluntary Sector Quarterly* 31, no. 3 (2002); J. Weerawardena and G. Sullivan Mort. "Learning, Innovation and Competitive Advantage in Not-for-Profit Aged Care Marketing: A Conceptual Model and Research Propositions," *Journal of Nonprofit & Public Sector Marketing* 9, no. 3 (2001); Shaker Zahra et al. "Globalization of Social Entrepreneurship Opportunities," *Strategic Entrepreneurship Journal* 2 (2008).
29. Mair and Marti.
30. Graham Dower and Thomas B. Lawrence. "The Role of Power in Nonprofit Innovation," *Nonprofit and Voluntary Sector Quarterly* 41, no. 6 (2012).
31. For an exception, see Robert E. McDonald. "An Investigation of Innovation in Nonprofit Organizations: The Role of Organizational Mission," ibid.36, no. 2 (2007).
32. Junseob Shin and George E. McClomb. "Top Executive Leadership and Organizational Innovation," *Administration in Social Work* 22, no. 3 (1998); John Thompson, Geoff Alvy and Ann Lees. "Social Entrepreneurship—A New Look at the People and the Potential," *Management Decision* 38, no. 5 (2000); McDonald; G. Sullivan Mort, J. Weerawardena and K. Carnegie. "Social Entrepreneurship: Towards Conceptualisation," *International Journal of Nonprofit and Voluntary Sector Marketing* 8, no. 1 (2003).
33. M. Morino and B. Shore. "High-Engagement Philanthropy: A Bridge to a More Effective Social Sector," (Venture Philanthropy Partners, 2004); D. M. Van Slyke and H. K. Newman. "Venture Philanthropy and Social

Entrepreneurship in Community Redevelopment," *Nonprofit Management and Leadership* 16, no. 3 (2006).

34. Worth.
35. C. K Prahalad. *The Fortune at the Bottom of the Pyramid: Eradicating Poverty Through Profits* (Upper Saddle, NJ: Wharton School Publishing, 2006).
36. Jennifer Alexander. "Adaptive Strategies of Nonprofit Human Service Organizations in an Era of Devolution and New Public Management," *Nonprofit Management and Leadership* 10, no. 3 (2000); S. L. McMurtry, F. N. Netting and P. M. Kettner. "How Nonprofits Adapt to a Stringent Environment," ibid.1 (1991); Mark Rosenman, Kristin Scotchmer and Elizabeth Van Benschoten. *Morphing into the Market: The Danger of Missing Mission* (Washington, DC: Aspen Institute, 1999).
37. Minkoff.
38. Schuler, Sidney Ruth, Syed M. Hashemi and Shamsul Huda Badal. "Men's Violence Against Women in Rural Bangladesh: Undermined or Exacerbated by Microcredit Programmes?" *Development in Practice* 8, no. 2 (1998): 148–157.
39. Mulhare; Siciliano; Terence Jackson. "A Critical Cross-Cultural Perspective for Developing Nonprofit International Management Capacity." *Nonprofit Management and Leadership* 19, no. 4 (2009): 443–466; Helmut Anheier. *Managing Non-Profit Organisations: Towards a New Approach* (London: Centre for Civil Society, LSE, 2000); A. Conner and K. Epstein. "Harnessing Purity and Pragmatism," *Stanford Social Innovation Review* (2007); Florentine Maier, Michael Meyer and Martin Steinbereithner. "Nonprofit Organizations Becoming Business-Like: A Systematic Review." *Nonprofit and Voluntary Sector Quarterly* 45, no. 1 (2016): 64–86.
40. Moore; Zimmerman and Stevens.

Bibliography

Abrahamson, A., and L. M. Salamon. *The Nonprofit Sector and the New Federal Budget*. Washington, DC: Urban Institute, 1986.

Alexander, Jennifer. "Adaptive Strategies of Nonprofit Human Service Organizations in an Era of Devolution and New Public Management." *Nonprofit Management and Leadership* 10, no. 3 (2000).

Alvord, S. H., L. D. Brown, and C. W. Letts. "Social Entrepreneurship and Societal Transformation: An Exploratory Study." *The Journal of Applied Behavioral Science* 40, no. 3 (2004): 260–82.

Anheier, Helmut. *Managing Non-Profit Organisations: Towards a New Approach*. London: Centre for Civil Society, LSE, 2000.

——— *Nonprofit Organizations Theory, Management and Practice*. New York: Routledge, 2005.

Arnold, M. J., and S. R. Tapp. "Direct Marketing in Non-Profit Services: Investigating the Case of the Arts Industry." *Journal of Services Marketing* 17, no. 2 (2003): 141–60.

Beck, Tammy E., Cynthia A. Lengnick-Hall, and Mark L. Lengnick-Hall. "Solutions Out of Context Examining the Transfer of Business Concepts to Nonprofit Organizations." *Nonprofit Management and Leadership* 19, no. 2 (2008): 153–71.

Bielefeld, W. "Funding Uncertainty and Nonprofit Strategies in the 1980s." *Nonprofit Management and Leadership* 41, no. 2 (1992): 381–401.

Blackwood, A. S., and T. H. Pollak. *Washington-Area Nonprofit Operating Reserves.* Washington, DC: Urban Institute, Center on Nonprofits and Philanthropy, 2009.

Brown, L. David, and Mark H. Moore. "Accountability, Strategy, and International Nongovernmental Organizations." *Nonprofit and Voluntary Sector Quarterly* 30, no. 3 (September 1, 2001): 569–87.

Brudney, Jeffrey L., and Beth Gazley. "Moving Ahead or Falling Behind? Volunteer Promotion and Data Collection." *Nonprofit Management and Leadership* 16, no. 3 (2006): 259–76.

Bush, Richard. "Survival of the Nonprofit Spirit in the a for-Profit World." *Nonprofit and Voluntary Sector Quarterly* 21, no. 4 (1992): 391–410.

Carman, J. G. "Evaluation Practice Among Community-Based Organizations Research Into the Reality." *American Journal of Evaluation* 28, no. 1 (2007): 60–75.

Chen, Bin, and Elizabeth A. Graddy. "The Effectiveness of Nonprofit Lead-Organization Networks for Social Service Delivery." *Nonprofit Management and Leadership* 20, no. 4 (2010).

Chenoweth, Lesley, and Donna McAuliffe. *The Road to Social Work and Human Service Practice.* 2nd Edition. China: Cengage Learning, 2008.

Conner, A., and K. Epstein. "Harnessing Purity and Pragmatism." *Stanford Social Innovation Review* (2007): 61–65.

Dabbs, Gordon. "Nonprofit Businesses in the 1990s: Models for Success." *Business Horizons* 34, no. 5 (1991): 68–71.

Dalton, Bronwen, and John Casey. "Money for Mission or Moral Minefield? The Opportunities and Risks of Not-for-Profit Business Venturing." In *Strategic Issues for the Not-for-Profit Sector*, edited by Jo Barraket. Sydney: University of New South Wales Press, 2008.

Dower, Graham, and Thomas B. Lawrence. "The Role of Power in Nonprofit Innovation." *Nonprofit and Voluntary Sector Quarterly* 41, no. 6 (2012): 991–1013.

Eikenberry, A. M., and J. D. Kluver. "The Marketization of the Nonprofit Sector: Civil Society at Risk?" *Pubic Adminstration Review* no. 64 (2004): 132–40.

Elkington, J., and P. Hartigan. *The Power of Unreasonable People: How Social Entrepreneurs Create Markets That Change the World.* United States of America: Harvard Business School Press, 2008.

Fowler, A. "Assessing Ngo Performance: Difficulties, Dilemmas and a Way Ahead." In *Performance and Accountability: Beyond the Magic Bullet*, edited by M. Edwards and D. Hulme. London: Earthscan, 1995.

Froelich, K. A., T. W. Knoepfle, and T. H. Pollak. "Financial Measures in Nonprofit Organization Research: Comparing Irs 990 Return and Audited Financial Statement Data." *Nonprofit and Voluntary Sector Quarterly* 29, no. 2 (2000): 232–54.

Galaskiewicz, Joseph, Wolfgang Bielefeld, and Myron Dowell. "Networks and Organizational Growth: A Study of Community Based Nonprofits." *Administrative Science Quarterly* 51, no. 3 (2006): 337–80.

Haas, Peter J., and Maynard G. Robinson. "The Views of Nonprofit Executives on Educating Nonprofit Managers." *Nonprofit Management and Leadership* 8, no. 4 (1998): 349–62.

Hall, Peter D. "A Historical Overview of the Private Nonprofit Sector." In *The Nonprofit Sector: A Research Handbook*, edited by Walter W. Powell. New Haven: Yale University Press, 1987.

Hammack, David. "Accountability and Nonprofit Organizations: A Historical Perspective." *Nonprofit Management and Leadership* 6, no. 2 (1995): 127–39.

Harris, John. "Professionalism Takes a Pounding [Online]." In *Moving Beyond Managerialism in Human Services*, edited by Michael Muetzelfeldt and Linda Briskman, 5–22. Melbourne: RMIT Publishing, 2003.

Horner, Nigel, ed. *What Is Social Work?: Context and Perspectives*. Edited by Jonathan Parker and Greta Bradley. 3rd Edition. Exeter: Learning Matters, 2009.

Hull, Clyde Eirakur, and Brian H. Lio. "Innovation in Non-Profit and for-Profit Organizations: Visionary, Strategic, and Financial Considerations." *Journal of Change Management* 6, no. 1 (2006): 53–65.

Hutchison, Romayne, and Ben Cairns. "Community Anchor Organizations: Sustainablity and Independence." In *Hybrid Organisations and the Third Sector*, edited by Billis David. London, United Kingdom: Palgrave Macmillan, 2010.

Jackson, Terence. "A Critical Cross-Cultural Perspective for Developing Nonprofit International Management Capacity." *Nonprofit Management and Leadership* 19, no. 4 (2009): 443–66.

Jansen, Paul J., and Andrea R. Kilpatrick. "The Dynamic Nonprofit Board." *McKinsey Quarterly* 2 (2004): 72–81.

Jeavons, Thomas H. "When the Management Is the Message: Relating Values to Management Practice in Nonprofit Organizations." *Nonprofit Management and Leadership* 2, no. 4 (1992).

Johnson, S. *Social Enterprise Literature Review*. Edmonton, Alberta: Canadian Centre for Social Entrepreneurship, 2001.

Kristoffersen, L., and S. Singh. "Successful Application of a Customer Relationship Management Program in a Nonprofit Organization." *Journal of Marketing Theory and Practice* (2004): 28–42.

Langan, Mary. "A Crisis in Care? Challenges to Social Work." In *A Crisis in Care? Challenges to Social Work*, edited by John Clarke, 47–67. Milton Keynes: The Open University, 1993.

Lawler, John. "The Rise of Managerialism in Social Work." In *Management, Social Work and Change*, edited by Elizabeth Harlow and John Lawler. Vermont, USA: Ashgate Publishing Limited, 2000.

Lindenberg, Mark. "Are We at the Cutting Edge or the Blunt Edge? Improving Ngo Organizational Performance With Private and Public Sector Strategic Management Frameworks." *Nonprofit Management and Leadership* 11, no. 3 (2001): 247–70.

Maier, Florentine, Michael Meyer, and Martin Steinbereithner. "Nonprofit Organizations Becoming Business-Like: A Systematic Review." *Nonprofit and Voluntary Sector Quarterly* 45, no. 1 (2016): 64–86.

Mair, Johanna, and Ignasi Marti. "Social Entrepreneurship Research: A Source of Explanation, Prediction, and Delight." *Journal of World Business* 41 (2006): 36–44.

Malhotra, Aastha, Raymond Zammuto, and Martie-Louise Verreynne. "Three Schools of Not-for-Profit Management Thought—Exploring the Influence of Management Ideologies on Managerial Responses." In *Australian and New Zealand Academy of Management Conference*. Perth, Australia, 2012.

McDonald, Robert E. "An Investigation of Innovation in Nonprofit Organizations: The Role of Organizational Mission." *Nonprofit and Voluntary Sector Quarterly* 36, no. 2 (2007): 256–81.

McMurtry, S. L., F. N. Netting, and P. M. Kettner. "How Nonprofits Adapt to a Stringent Environment." *Nonprofit Management and Leadership* 1, no. 3 (1991): 235–52.

Meyer, A. D., A. Tsui, and C. R. Hinings. "Configurational Approaches to Organizational Analysis." *Academy of Management Journal* 6 (1993): 1175–95.

Miles, M., and A. M. Huberman. *Qualitative Data Analysis: An Expanded Sourcebook.* Thousand Oaks, CA: Sage Publications, 1994.

Minkoff, C. Debra. "The Emergence of Hybrid Organizational Forms: Combining Identity-Based Service Provision and Political Action." *Nonprofit and Voluntary Sector Quarterly* 31, no. 3 (2002).

Mintzberg, H., B. Ahlstrand, and J. Lampel. *Strategy Safari: A Guided Tour Through the Wilds of Strategic Management.* New York: Free Press, 1998.

Moore, Mark. "Managing for Value: Organizational Strategy in for-Profit, Nonprofit, and Governmental Organizations." *Nonprofit and Voluntary Sector Quarterly* 29, no. 1 (2000): 183–204.

Morino, M., and B. Shore. *High-Engagement Philanthropy: A Bridge to a More Effective Social Sector.* Venture Philanthropy Partners, 2004.

Morley, E., E. Vinson, and H. P Hatry. *Outcome Measurement in Nonprofit Organizations: Current Practices and Recommendations.* Washington, DC: Independent Sector, 2001.

Mulhare, Eileen M. "Mindful of the Future: Strategic Planning Ideology and the Culture of Nonprofit Management." *Human Organization* 58, no. 3 (1999): 323–30.

O'Donoghue, Philip, Myles McGregor-Lowndes, and Mark Lyons. "Policy Lessons for Strengthening Nonprofits." *Australian Journal of Social Issues* 41, no. 4 (2006): 511–24.

Oster, Sharon. *Strategic Management for Nonprofit Organizations—Theory and Cases.* United States of America: Oxford University Press, 1995.

Powell, W. W., and R. Steinberg. *The Nonprofit Sector: A Research Handbook.* Yale University Press, 2006.

Prahalad, C. K. *The Fortune at the Bottom of the Pyramid: Eradicating Poverty Through Profits.* Upper Saddle, NJ: Wharton School Publishing, 2006.

Renz, David O. "Changing the Face of Nonprofit Management." *Nonprofit Management and Leadership* 11, no. 3 (2001).

Rogers, D. L., and C. L. Mulford. "The Historical Development." In *Interorganization Coordination: Theory, Research, and Implementation,* edited by D. A. Whetten, D. L. Rogers, and Associates, 32–53. Ames, IA: Iowa State University Press, 1982.

Rojas, R. "A Review of Models for Measuring Organizational Effectiveness Among for-Profit and Nonprofit Organizations." *Nonprofit Management & Leadership* 11, no. 1 (2000).

Rosenman, Mark, Kristin Scotchmer, and Elizabeth Van Benschoten. *Morphing Into the Market: The Danger of Missing Mission.* Washington, DC: Aspen Institute, 1999.

Salamon, L. M., and H. Anheier. *Defining the Nonprofit Sector: A Cross-National Analysis.* Manchester: Manchester University Press, 1997.

Schmid, Hillel. "Merging Nonprofit Organizations: Analysis of a Case Study." *Nonprofit Management and Leadership* 5, no. 4 (1995).

Schuler, Sidney Ruth, Syed M. Hashemi, and Shamsul Huda Badal. "Men's Violence Against Women in Rural Bangladesh: Undermined or Exacerbated by Microcredit Programmes?" *Development in Practice* 8, no. 2 (1998): 148–57.

Setterberg, Fred, and Kary Schulman. *Beyond Profit:The Complete Guide to Managing the Nonprofit Organization.* New York: HarperCollins, 1985.

Shin, Junseob, and George E. McClomb. "Top Executive Leadership and Organizational Innovation." *Administration in Social Work* 22, no. 3 (1998): 1–21.

Siciliano, J. I. "The Relationship Between Formal Planning and Peformance in Nonprofit Organizations." *Nonprofit Management and Leadership* 7, no. 4 (1997): 387–403.

Speckbacher, Gerhard. "The Economics of Performance Management in Nonprofit Organizations." *Nonprofit Management and Leadership* 13, no. 3 (2003): 267–81.

Stid, Daniel, and Jeffery Bradach. "How Visionary Nonprofits Leaders Are Learning to Enhance Management Capabilities." *Strategy and Leadership* 37, no. 1 (2009): 35–40.

Stone, Melissa, Barbara Bigelow, and William Crittenden. "Research on Strategic Management in Nonprofit Organizations—Synthesis, Analysis and Future Directions." *Administration & Society* 31, no. 3 (1999): 378–423.

Sullivan Mort, G., J. Weerawardena, and K. Carnegie. "Social Entrepreneurship: Towards Conceptualisation." *International Journal of Nonprofit and Voluntary Sector Marketing* 8, no. 1 (2003): 76–88.

Takahashi, Lois M., and Gayla Smutny. "Collaborative Windows and Organizational Governance: Exploring the Formation and Demise of Social Service Partnerships." *Nonprofit and Voluntary Sector Quarterly* 31, no. 2 (2002).

Thompson, John, Geoff Alvy, and Ann Lees. "Social Entrepreneurship—a New Look at the People and the Potential." *Management Decision* 38, no. 5 (2000): 328.

Van Slyke, D. M., and H. K. Newman. "Venture Philanthropy and Social Entrepreneurship in Community Redevelopment." *Nonprofit Management and Leadership* 16, no. 3 (2006): 345–68.

Vernis, Alfred, Maria Iglesias, Beatriz Sanz, and Angel Saz-Carranza. *Nonprofit Organizations Challenges and Collaboration.* New York: Palgrave Macmillan, 2006.

Weerawardena, J., and G. Sullivan Mort. "Learning, Innovation and Competitive Advantage in Not-for-Profit Aged Care Marketing: A Conceptual Model and Research Propositions." *Journal of Nonprofit & Public Sector Marketing* 9, no. 3 (2001): 53–73.

Weisbrod, Burton A. "Guest Editor's Introduction: The Nonprofit Mission and Its Financing." *Journal of Policy Analysis and Management* 17, no. 2 (1998): 165–74.

Worth, Michael. *Nonprofit Management Principles and Practice.* United States of America: Sage Publications, 2009.

Wren, Daniel A. *The Evolution of Management Thought.* 4th Edition. Canada: John Wiley and Sons, 1994.

Young, Dennis R. *Casebook of Management for Nonprofit Organisations: Entrepreneurship and Organizational Change in the Human Services.* New York: Hawthorne Press, 1985.

Yunus, Muhammad, and Bertrand Moingeon. "Building Social Business Models: Lessons from the Grameen Experience." *Long Range Planning* 43 (2010): 308–25.

Zahra, Shaker, Hans Rawhouser, Nachiket Bhawe, Donald Neubaum, and James Hayton. "Globalization of Social Entrepreneurship Opportunities." *Strategic Entrepreneurship Journal* 2 (2008): 117–31.

Zimmerman, Jo, and Bonnie W. Stevens. "The Use of Performance Measurement in South Carolina Nonprofits." *Nonprofit Management and Leadership* 16, no. 3 (2006): 315–27.

3   The Journey of A Social Leader

Leading and Transforming Organisations for Social Impact

Anna Krzeminska, Andreas Heinecke,
and Christian Koch

Introduction

Thousands and thousands of books are published on leadership training, and American companies alone spend 14 billion annually to develop leadership skills among their managers. Critical voices state clearly that this is a waste of time and money. Studies have found that adult learners in a lecture setting forget nearly 50% of what they learn within two weeks. And the most highly trained leaders—CEOs of multinational companies—are often unable to translate their knowledge into practice, and fail within their first 18 months on the job.[1] Another public saying boldly states that leaders are born and not made.[2] That's tough.

Leaders in the social sector,* no matter whether they are working for a social enterprise, running a social business or doing classical community work, certainly face additional adversities. Although many of them haven't studied management or finance and could benefit from business training, they usually don't have the financial resources to sit in a lecture hall for hours and listen to skilled teachers.** They don't have the time and the patience to follow theoretical models or be entertained in boot camps. Social leaders are usually not promoted, and even if they would have the opportunity to join

---

* Social sector is a collective term for a range of organisations that trade for a social purpose. They adopt one of a variety of different legal formats but have in common the principles of pursuing business-led solutions to achieve social aims, and the reinvestment of surplus for community benefit. Their objectives focus on socially desired, nonfinancial measures of the implied demand for and supply of services Organisations within the social sector may occur in any legal form, such as agencies, clubs, foundations—any innovative nonprofit enterprise, or profit organisations addressing a social problem, or hybrid organisations with charitable status with elements of both types, or be imbedded in other organisations as corporate social entrepreneurship (through CSR).

** According to Katherine Milligan, Managing Director of the Schwab Foundation of Social Entrepreneurs, only 50% of the recently elected fellows came from a MBA background/ previous business career. The others have various backgrounds and worked in different industries and foremost in the non-for-profit sector.

leadership classes for non-profits, the offerings are quite limited compared to the thick catalogue of leadership trainings for for-profits.***

Furthermore, there are the blurred boundaries between for profit and not-for profit, the financial constraints across all phases of organisational development, the scarcity of human resources due to low wages, the problematic measurement of social impact, the broad spectrum of organisational forms, the cross-sector approach, the threat of a mission drift, the unclear future of the organisation due to a lack of defined and approved exit strategies.

Finally, the sector is currently transforming towards market-based mechanisms leading to the increased rise of new social ventures (social enterprises) and the transformation of established non-profits in the market. In Australia, this transformation manifests, for example, through new regulations such as the introduction of the National Disability Insurance Scheme (NDIS). This transformation is affecting a significant number of organisations. An Australian Government study conducted in 2010[†] identified approx. 59,000 economically significant NFPs employing approx. 900,000 people (2006/07 data), which amounts to 8% of the overall workforce.[3]

Despite those difficulties, social leaders often succeed to cope with the permanent Titan's task of balancing a social mission with financial sustainability, based on their broad spectrum of professional and life experiences before they decide to contribute to the common good. They weren't born leaders. But they were people, who became leaders without necessarily having the ambition to take a leadership role. They are collateral leaders, and embarked on a journey within an unclear framework and a very vague destination.

What does that mean for our topic of how to successfully lead and transform organisations in the social sector? To better understand the specific challenges social leaders face two of the authors of this chapter conducted a global survey among social leaders in collaboration with the Schwab Foundation for Social Entrepreneurship,[‡] one of the world's largest non-profit organisations that support social enterprise. Published as a pioneering leadership manual entitled 'Leadership in Social Enterprise: How to Manage Yourself and the Team' in 2014 the study aims to support the founders and chief executive officers of social enterprises by providing advice that is tailored to the realities of mission-driven organisations at various stages of their development. The practitioner-oriented manual was derived from an extensive literature review, as well as interviews and a

---

*** A simple Google research shows the significant differences. 14 million hits are shown by social leadership programs while 438 million hits pop up when it comes to business leadership programs in general.

  † The rough estimate for the overall number of NFPs in the study is 600,000, yet this does include a majority of 440,000 of small, often informal and incorporated organisations such as neighbourhood tennis or babysitting clubs that do not operate in a market.

  ‡ The detailed report is available at www.schwabfound.org/sites/default/files/file_uploads/leadership_in_social_enterprise_2014.pdf

global survey among key Schwab staff and almost 100 of the then approx. 250 fellows of the Schwab Foundation. The results of the global survey are relevant for both new social ventures and NFPs given that 26.1% of Schwab Fellows are Leveraged Non-Profit, 53.3% are Hybrid Non-Profit, while only 20.7% are Social Business. What the results of the study suggest is that, while social leaders are often inspirational, highly ethical and visionary, important leadership behaviours seem to be underdeveloped in many social leaders. These behaviours are associated with the more managerial side of running the organisation and as a result social leaders mainly face the following four 'managerial type' leadership challenges:

- Building a management team
- Delegation and succession
- Balancing and integrating
- Personal and professional development

In this chapter, we will explore the implications of the general challenges and recent transformation in the social sector for its leadership. We do so by conceptually linking leadership challenges to different stages in the lifecycle of social organisations, distinguishing between social start-ups and established NFPs. For each stage we link leadership challenges to the empirical results of the global survey of social leaders and develop recommendations for transforming organisations for social impact.

The Journey of a Social Leader

In the following, we will relate leadership tasks to the process of organisational development as it is described in two popular models: The first is indicated in the Open Book of Social Innovation and differentiates between six steps from the initial idea to systemic change.[$] Obviously, the tasks and challenges of a social start-up are quite different from an established organisation, which is able to improve the situation of their beneficiaries in a systemic and sustainable way. The second model is based on the research of Friedrich Glasl and Bernard Lievegoed, who differentiate between four stages of the organisational lifecycle, i.e., the phases of pioneering, differentiation, integration, and association.[4]

Pioneering Phase

Before the pioneering phase actually starts one person has to take the lead to formulate a social cause and be convinced about the solution approach.

[$]   We apply a social systems perspective of organizations, as e.g. described in Kühl, Stefan 2013, Organizations. A systems approach, Routledge. In this view, organizational culture is an aspect of the informal side of an organization which comprises all those expectations and rules that are not (or cannot) be formalized as terms of membership.

Especially in newly established initiatives, the founder is the main driver and plays the key role as fund-raiser, human recruiter, strategist, communicator, hands-on practitioner, trouble-shooter etc. It's a 24/7 job, and the founder is quickly perceived as an asset (with all key contacts, personal reputation, vision), and a threat (as no one can be equally capable in all domains, and the competence to delegate is hardly developed). Usually the first followers are coming from close social networks ("friends, fools & family"). The social enterprise at this stage is not necessarily an 'organisation', and can be more seen as a loose net. Improvisation dominates, as processes are not well planned. The whole venture is mainly opportunity driven, stays flexible and reacts spontaneously.

The results of the Schwab Foundation leadership survey confirm the popular notion that Social Entrepreneurs are visionary, charismatic, inspiring, as well as highly ethical and values-driven. Furthermore, social entrepreneurs empower those around them and therefore, facilitate strong commitment of their team members to their cause and organisations. Thus, they are perfectly suited to act as pioneers in the early phase of their fledgling organisations.

However, dangers of this first phase for social start-ups are failures due to lack of experiences, too many concurrent activities, personality cult, power struggles, chaos, obscurities, employees who are emotionally dependent, but without professional performance. And from an organisational development perspective, this early stage in the lifecycle has wide-ranging implications, as it lays the foundations not only regarding structures and processes, i.e. the "formal side" of the organisation, but as well for what is to become the "organisational culture" later on.[#] A lot of the leadership challenges cited above have their roots here, in the way the founder and the "first followers" interact, communicate, solve (or create) problems. Because gradually, over time, these patterns become rules, rituals, habits, and newcomers start adopting them, they become socialised into the 'organisational culture' that is taking shape. This culture is still quite fluid in the beginning, but it quickly stabilises and then becomes increasingly difficult to change.

Recommendation—Early Interaction and Communication Patterns Matter

Understandably, the 'organisational culture' is seldom the first concern of the founder in the pioneering phase as so many things happen in parallel and pressure is high. Nevertheless, interaction and communication patterns that emerge in the early pioneering phase cause a lot of the problems, inefficiencies and energy loss later on. Therefore, it is an important leadership task to create sufficient time for reflection and exchange in the team to avoid that small quarrels turn into major conflict lines. Often, it is enough to consciously address this

---

\# Referring to the famous quote by Ross Ashby: "Only variety absorbs variety" in Ashby, Ross 1956, An Introduction to Cybernetics.

topic periodically in small workshop formats. External facilitation can help as it makes it easier for the team to address critical leadership behaviour, too.

Differentiation Phase

For social start-ups, the second phase usually begins with the first successes. The approach is tested, the concept proven, and financial sources identified. The organisation is growing, and becomes more process oriented and a sort of rational apparatus. Due to third sources funding, governance structures need to be implemented, and cause additional work load to serve all needs in terms of accountability, transparency, business planning, financial management, codes of conducts for the organisation, etc. Growth is often a very painful process, and lots of social enterprises fail especially in times of success. They cannot organise the growing demand and market pressure, and the founder is often perceived as a bad manager, who isn't able to organise the growth process.

Dangers in the second phase are inability to transform the "club into a company," the demotivation of the founder due to administrative work and the loss of flexibility, and primarily personal (intuitive) decisions. Employees may see a mission drift and loss of culture, and leave the organisations or stay with low motivation.

This is very much in line with the leadership challenges reported in the global survey related to transforming the "club into a company" during the differentiation phase, which centre on recruiting a management team and balancing the increasing demands from running their enterprise. Nevertheless, responding to these challenges remains highly relevant for established NFPs, too. When recruiting managers to their growing organisations social leaders face the challenge of attracting followers who share similarities with the founder in terms of the social mission and culture but complement the founder in terms of his/her strengths and weaknesses. While anecdotal evidence suggests that hiring for-profit managers may negatively impact the social enterprise and dilute its mission, the results from the Schwab study suggest the contrary. Almost 60% of the respondents said they have successfully recruited and retained managers with a for-profit-background, and only 20% reported they have had conflicts with newly recruited managers from a for-profit-background. Also, while relying heavily on volunteers during this stage may provide the organisation with cost-effective support of followers with a strong social mission and cultural fit, it bears its own risks. The survey shows there is more emotional conflict and tension among members and between staff from different backgrounds in organisations with more volunteers. Also, organisations with more volunteers report significantly more conflicts with recruited managers from for-profit companies.

The challenge of balancing increasingly complex and sometime conflicting demands during the differentiation phase depends on successful recruiting. Survey results show that focusing on the work that the entrepreneur enjoys most and that best suits their strengths is easier once a professional and cohesive management team is in place. Highlighting the importance of complementarity in team composition, Schwab Social Entrepreneurs who employ a higher proportion of staff with a completely different background than theirs report fewer struggles with balancing. Diversity in recruitment and team building, however, seems to differ based on the entrepreneurs' own work background: Schwab Social Entrepreneurs with a strong business background employ significantly fewer people with different backgrounds, while those with strong volunteer work experience employ significantly more people with a different background. Thus, the latter will likely be better able to balance their responsibilities and focus on leveraging theirs strengths to the benefit of the organisation.

Recommendation—Diversity is Key in the Management Team

The Schwab survey results provide a very clear orientation regarding recruiting for NFPs: a variety of backgrounds in the management team is beneficial to cope with the multiple challenges and tasks involved in following a social cause and building the organisation to do so in the differentiation phase.[5] Managers with a for-profit-background can bring in valuable perspectives, but for NFPs that already have a strong business minded team, the search direction has to be opposite, bringing in people with complementary competencies.

Integration Phase

While the differentiation phase is very challenging, as the leader cannot cover all needs, the integration phase combines the enthusiasm of the pioneering phase with the rationality of the differentiation phase, and the organisation grows to an organism. The boundaries blur between ordinary for-profit companies and mission driven 'more than profit' organisations, which can lead to significant conflicts within the organisation. That's quite bitter, as by then the approach seems to be proven and the social impact increases, but the organisation needs to integrate efficiency and impact to fully harness its potential. Thus, smaller manageable units of work are often formed, to make the organisation flexible again. The smaller units also incorporate holistic tasks and can largely plan themselves, organise and exercise self-control. A central office controls and offers support and consulting services, but does not regulate.

The danger at this stage is, inter alia, that the organisation is too focused on their own world and their functioning, so that the external stakeholders such as clients and partners disappear from the view. Elements of almost all four leadership challenges from the global survey are associated with the characteristics of the integration phase. After successful recruitment during differentiation, the founder needs to retain talent to ensure the sustainable success of the organisation during the integration phase. However, this can be challenging as especially talented and ambitious staff want to broaden their experience and take over responsibility and are often lost if they are not offered interesting career and development prospects within the organisation. While many social enterprises are growing fast, new leadership positions cannot always be translated into promotion opportunities. This situation can worsen if the leader struggles with delegating responsibility, which seems to affect approx. half of the Schwab sample of social entrepreneurs.

According to the global survey one of the main challenges of the integration phase is to successfully combine social and commercial goals, which are often conceptualised as conflicting. However, asked about conflicts within their organisations, Schwab Social Entrepreneurs did not perceive them to be a big problem. Still, a deeper analysis of the survey results showed some interesting factors. The social entrepreneurs perceived balancing responsibilities and stakeholder interests as more challenging when conflicts in the organisation were stronger, probably because it makes the act of balancing external demands more difficult when internal stakeholders are in conflict as well. There was also a connection of conflict to the kind of people working with the organisation. Emotional and personality conflicts between members of the organisation were reported as higher in organisations with more employees with a social work background. Conflicts related to different goals, mindsets or professional backgrounds were reported as higher in organisations with more employees with a business background.

Recommendation—Self-Management, Wholeness and Purpose Orientation

Looking at the leadership challenges outlined above for NFPs in the integration phase, a lot of them have to do with finding adequate organisational models that help balancing between structures and openness, mission and economic orientation and keeping staff motivated and conflicts at bay. Consultants and financiers often propose NFPs adopt rather classical organisational designs that originated in the business sector. But these usually involve hierarchical structures with typical line functions such as marketing/communications, sales, production, R&D etc. which don't fit the culture and style of working of NFPs. They are often introduced anyway because they are deemed 'professional' and create trust with external stakeholders. Yet, NFPs should be careful not to embrace these models too quickly. *Reinventing organisations*, a book by former McKinsey partner Frederic Laloux[6] dealing with organisational design, is probably the most discussed release in this field in the last years. It promotes (and empirically backs) the advent of a new type of organisations that rely on self-management (structures/processes), strive for wholeness (general practice/HR processes) and purpose orientation (strategy development). Instead of introducing more structures, processes and back-office functions, Laloux proposes a radical form of self-management and simplification of internal bureaucracies. This might be very interesting for NFPs because it is close to values shared in the sector, reduces frustrations for mission-driven staff members and provides them an attractive work environment with a lot of freedom and responsibility. The organisations surveyed in *Reinventing Organisations* all delegated hiring of new team members, negotiating about roles and responsibilities, even payment issues into the sub-teams, with positive effects on team spirit and culture. Hence, it could be an interesting approach to manage internal conflicts, too, but it requires a very cooperative leadership style to implement these models.

Association Phase

The integration phase is followed by the association phase, which this is scientifically least explored. In the Open Book of Social innovation this phase would be the achievement of a systemic change. In this phase the idea can become bigger than the founder, and s/he and the organisation may become obsolete. The danger in this stage is a leader who doesn't want to let it go. Missing succession plans and clear exit scenarios may block this process, and the final success of the social venture may be hindered due to personal agendas.

In the survey, Schwab Social Entrepreneurs rated the improvement of their own managerial skills and leadership style as the least problematic of all leadership challenges. Less than one third of respondents perceived developing their own management skills and leadership style to suit their organisation's needs as challenging. This lack of self-reflection can become problematic for those who underestimate the importance and time, which usually amounts to years, to build a succession plan. Of course, many social leaders are worried about the risk of mission drift once they leave the organisation. However, there are various governance mechanisms such as asset locks and legal forms that can be implemented to counter potential mission drift. The qualitative interviews conducted with selected social entrepreneurs prior to the global survey, however, clearly showed the perceived importance of continuous personal development. Concerning their development as effective leaders, social entrepreneurs heavily emphasised the need to reduce the role of the ego in decisions and conflicts, and the value of religious values or spiritual practices such as meditation to achieve this goal. Mastering the key challenge of personal development seems to be the basis for mastering all other leadership challenges.

Recommendation—Change Starts with the Leader

Leaders have a role model and enabling function, especially when it comes to learning and the inevitable change processes in the lifecycle of the organisation. They need to demonstrate the readiness to admit themselves to uncertainty—and also have experience in re-stabilising in challenging situations.[7] Rather than striving single-handedly for bold objectives, it is often more important to create the space for group learning and exchange in the team. This attitude of *post-heroic management* is very much in line with the Schwab survey results that suggest that social leaders stressed the need to reduce the role of the ego in decisions and conflicts, and the value of religious values or spiritual practices to achieve this goal. As well, it is a precondition for planning and implementing succession solutions—for long-term social impact, probably the most important change processes in the career of a social leader.

Conclusion

The journey of a social leader has lots of trade-offs. It's a roller coaster, and not everybody is robust enough to stay motivated over decades. The unbreakable belief in the mission is key to keep the energy high to make the impossible possible.

Notes

1. Pierre Gurdijian, Thomas Halbeisen and Kevin Lane. "Why Leadership Development Programs Fail," *McKinsey Quartely*, 2014.
2. Shinnosuke Nakayama, Leaders Are Born, Not Made, Fish Study Finds, Scientific America August 2013, www.scientificamerican.com/article/leaders-are-born-not-made-fish-study-finds/
3. Productivity Commission 2010, Contribution of the Not-for-Profit Sector, Research Report, Canberra.
4. Robert Murray, Julie Caulier-Grice, Geoff Mulgan. "The Open Book of Social Innovation," 2010, www.nesta.org.uk/sites/default/files/the_open_book_of_social_innovation.pdf
5. Friedrich Glasl and Bernhard Lievegoed, 2010, www.ngo.de/images/stories/organisationsentwicklung/oe-prozesse/glasl-phasen.pdf
6. Laloux, Frederic 2014, Reinventing Organisations, Nelson Parker.
7. Varga von Kibéd, Matthias; Schneider, Karin 2016, Führungskräfte und Veränderungen—die Haltung macht den Unterschied. Zeitschrift SyStemischer, 08/2016.

Bibliography

Ashby, Ross. *An Introduction to Cybernetics*. London: Methuen, 1956.
Glasl, Friedrich, and Bernhard Lievegoed. Die Phasen einer Organisation nach Friedrich Glasl. 2010. Retrieved from www.ngo.de/images/stories/organisationsentwicklung/oe-prozesse/glasl-phasen.pdf
Gurdijian, Pierre, Halbeisen, Thomas, and Lane, Kevin. "Why Leadership Development Programs Fail." *McKinsey Quarterly* (2014).
Heinecke, Andreas, Magdalena Kloibhofer, and Anna Krzeminsa. Leadership in Social Enterprise: How to Manage Yourself and the Team. Schwab Foundation for Social Entrepreneurship, 2014. Retrieved from www.schwabfound.org/sites/default/files/file_uploads/leadership_in_social_enterprise_2014.pdf
Kühl, Stefan. *Organizations. A Systems Approach*. London: Routledge, 2013.

Laloux, Frederic. *Reinventing Organisations*. Nelson Parker, 2014.

Murray, Robert, Julie Caulier-Grice, and Geoff Mulgan. The Open Book of Social Innovation. 2010. Retrieved from www.nesta.org.uk/sites/default/files/the_open_book_of_social_innovation.pdf

Nakayama, Shinnosuke. "Leaders Are Born, Not Made, Fish Study Finds." *Scientific American* August 2013. Retrieved from www.scientificamerican.com/article/leaders-are-born-not-made-fish-study-finds/

Productivity Commission. *Contribution of the Not-for-Profit Sector, Research Report*. Canberra. 2010.

Varga von Kibéd, Matthias, and Karin Schneider. Führungskräfte und Veränderungen—die Haltung macht den Unterschied. Zeitschift SyStemischer. 2016.

Stories From The Field: The Red Cross and Red Crescent Movement

Introduction

The Red Cross and Red Crescent Movement is by its very nature a unique organisation which has evolved continually since its formation in 1864 when the First Geneva Convention was signed by 12 nations in Geneva Switzerland and the International Committee of the Red Cross (ICRC) was formed. At that time, the organisation was focussed solely on human conflict. The visionary founder of the organisation was a young Swiss businessman Henri Dunant who observed at first hand the Battle of Solferino in Italy. He was appalled that the wounded Austrian soldiers were not assisted by the local population in the same way the wounded French soldiers were. He wrote a book urging that a respected independent and neutral international organisation be founded to assist the wounded and prisoners of war and that they operate under a well-recognised and protective emblem, the red cross on a white background (which was the reverse image of the Swiss flag).

The Geneva Conventions and their Additional Protocols form the core of international humanitarian law, which regulates the conduct of armed conflict and seeks to limit its effects. They are also designed to protect those not taking part in hostilities (adjacent civilians, medics and aid workers) and those who can no longer fight (wounded, sick, shipwrecked troops and prisoners of war).

The original 1864, 1906 and 1929 Conventions were consolidated and updated in the Geneva Conventions of 1949 which have been ratified by most States around the world.

The original Conventions have had three Protocols added with two in 1977 and one in 2005, which approved a third protective emblem, the Red Crystal.

The Movement Structure

Since 1864, Red Cross (and since 1929 Red Crescent) Societies are able to be found in countries which have ratified the Geneva Conventions and its protocols.

The Red Cross and Red Crescent Societies are not strictly non-Government organisations as they can only be formed in any country with the approval of the Government of that country and they are said in the Geneva Conventions to be 'auxiliaries to Government' in the humanitarian field.

So today the Red Cross and Red Crescent Movement (the Movement) has National Societies in 190 countries and organisations in several other countries are making applications to join the Movement.

The Movement has two central bodies, the ICRC (which as mentioned earlier was formed in 1864) and it continues today to be guardian of the Geneva Conventions and it monitors conflicts in over 80 global conflict zones at present. It is a fiercely independent body whose central committee is composed of Swiss citizens and it has over 30,000 skilled employees.

The International Federation of the Red Cross and Red Crescent Society (the International Federation) was not formed until 1919 (at the same time the League of Nations was formed) at the urging of the then United States President Woodrow Wilson. The Federation secretariat is also located in Geneva but it also has significant regional offices in other parts of the globe. The International Federation has approximately 400 employees and it provides services to assist National Red Cross and Red Crescent Societies to grow to be more efficient in the countries in which they operate. It facilitates the exchange of best practice, innovations and ideas between the different National Societies.

The 190 National Societies vary in size and strength and collectively have over 20 million active volunteers who work principally in the humanitarian areas of disaster preparedness, response and recovery as well as in a wide range of health and community services.

The Standing Commission of Red Cross and Red Crescent (on which I serve and had the privilege of chairing from 2011 to 2015) is an overarching body of nine senior Movement representatives including the two senior executives of the ICRC and International Federation. Its task is to work to achieve Movement harmony and to address whole of Movement matters and to organise the regular international meetings of the Movement including the International Conference held every four years with Governments as well as National Societies with one vote each. This body approves changes to the Geneva Conventions.

It works hard to ensure the 190 National Societies, who are ruggedly independent, work harmoniously with the ICRC and International Federation on combined Movement humanitarian responses to major conflicts and disasters. All components of the Movement work under the Seven Fundamental Principles in all they do and these Principles are Humanity, Independence, Impartiality, Neutrality, Unity, Universality and Voluntary Service.

The overall mission of the Red Cross and Red Crescent Movement is to use the power of humanity (utilising volunteers wherever possible) to help the most vulnerable people in the world and in any given country.

Movement Leadership

The Red Cross and Red Crescent Movement does not have one leader who is the equivalent of the Secretary General of the United Nations and a team of Under Secretaries General and middle managers reporting to him.

The ICRC has an Executive President and a Director General as its leaders with the former having a more external focus while the Director General tends to be responsible more for the internal management of the organisation.

The International Federation has a volunteer President (usually also the President of a National Society) and a Secretary General (or full time CEO).

Each National Society has a President, some of whom are full time executive presidents while the remainder are volunteers with other jobs and a full time Secretary General (or CEO). The Australian Red Cross Society has an unpaid volunteer as its national President.

There is no obligation on these global leaders to work together and the role of the Standing Commission first formed in 1929 has been partly to provide a mechanism for any concerns about differences of opinion or approach in major humanitarian matters or global operations.

The International Conference of the Red Cross and Red Crescent in Seville in 1997 ratified an agreement (known today as 'the Seville Agreement') which provides considerable guidance on which organisation takes the lead in major field operations where the ICRC, the International Federation and National Societies are all involved.

Beyond this formal mechanism, there are regular meetings between the global leaders to discuss particular matters of concern at any given time. Since 2011 the ICRC and International Federation with the strong support of the Standing Commission and many National Societies have been working on an overall RCRC Movement Co-ordination and Co-operation project to provide more guidance especially in matters not covered by the Seville Agreement such as global fundraising, use of the social media and leadership training.

The Movement leaders are chosen by their Annual General Meetings (or equivalent named bodies) except for the ICRC President who is chosen by the international committee itself. The ICRC, the International Federation and the larger National Societies like the Australian Red Cross Society endeavour to follow sound governance principles with strategic plans discussed widely within their organisations with staff and members. External grievance experts are often engaged to assist in improving the internal grievance procedures and to review performance of key officers and board members and the effectiveness of the current strategic plans the different components have adopted.

Other Leadership Challenges for the Movement

The challenges faced by the Movement with its complex structure of 192 independent entities are immense as the world considers the Red Cross and Red Crescent Movement (or the Red Pillar as it is often termed) to be a single organisation. Hence there is a need for effective co-ordination and co-operation mechanisms internally to ensure in a major conflict zone like Syria, Afghanistan or Iraq or in a national disaster response, there is a common approach and no duplication of effort or waste of our precious resources.

The Standing Commission works hard on its 'Movement Harmony' remit to ensure that the two Geneva based institutions are working together effectively and that as far as possible the National Societies are also working with the two big institutions in a co-ordinated and co-operative way.

As mentioned previously, protocols and procedures have been established to determine which major institution or National Society is the 'lead institution' in any major humanitarian response involving multiple actors. Increasingly we are finding that it is best if the host National Society is the 'lead institution' as is the case in Syria during the present time of conflict where the Syrian Arabic Red Crescent Society is the lead institution for the Movement response and the ICRC, the International Federation and all participating National Society follow the SARC volunteers (as often do the UN organisations and NGOs) into conflict areas to do their humanitarian work.

An operational challenge for the organisation is the fact that it has more than one international symbol, the Red Cross and the Red Crescent. There are 29 Red Crescent Societies (mainly in Islamic countries) who work seamlessly with Red Cross Societies in joint humanitarian responses. This can be confusing to the general public especially in a given country which does not recognise the second emblem.

Another challenge for the Red Cross and Red Crescent Movement is language as it has four official languages which can be spoken at its international meetings and these are English, French, Spanish and Arabic. More recently, Russian has been added as an unofficial fifth language of the Movement.

Much time is spent in the Movement on translation and interpreting the language used at meetings and in documents. It is also difficult to achieve our goal of standard procedures and practices. All National Societies have been urged for instance to have a young person on their national board. However in some cultures young people are not considered to be sufficiently wise or experienced to be included on a national board and hence this recommendation is not followed there.

A further challenge for the organisation and especially the International Federation is the need to be perceived as even handed in establishing international committees and working groups. These cannot be sourced from one continent, gender or age group. Hence all committees, boards and working groups need to have broad geographic, gender, age and skill based representatives so that their findings or recommendations gain global acceptance.

Another issue for the Movement is the independence of each component and the lack of any means to compel a national society to act in a particular way. As in any federation, the international leaders and boards can only hope that good sense prevails and that good ideas and practices will be taken on board. It can take considerable time and patience to get universal or even wide acceptance of common practices and solutions to humanitarian problems. Members need great patience and resolve.

Given the mission of the organisation is to mobilise the power of humanity to help vulnerable people (who are not being helped effectively by others) it is not easy to compromise the main mission except sometimes because of lack of resources or because of the perceived antipathy of Government or opposition forces, some National Societies may choose not to put their limited resources into areas in which it will be difficult to make any real difference.

Australian Red Cross Society

The Australian Red Cross Society was formed in 1914 as a branch of British Red Cross and it was initially focussed on providing support for Australian Servicemen in World War I and sending parcels and communications to prisoners of war.

After World War I the Australian Red Cross expanded its range of services into health and community services and it for instance established blood banks around the country.

After World War II the Australian Red Cross expanded its activities even further as it considered how best to implement its mission to help the most vulnerable people in country and abroad. Today it provides over 70 humanitarian services grouped under eight headings:

- The Australian Red Cross Blood Service
- Disaster Response (domestic and international)
- Disseminating International Humanitarian Law (IHL)
- Aboriginal and Torres Strait Islander services
- Migrants, refugees and asylum seekers
- International aid and assistance
- Locational disadvantage
- Social inclusion

The Australian Red Cross Royal Charter of Rules were changed by the National Council at their annual meetings in 2005 and 2007 from a federal body to a united national body with a single national strategy, one decision making board, a single management and budget. This was a major undertaking and it was driven by the need to have in place effective risk management and to avoid duplication of services and administration with resultant cost savings.

The change process required a national governance committee with some experienced governance professionals on it and some external assistance from governance experts to develop a model for a functioning unitary structure taking into account the long history of the organisation and the views and feelings of its members, many of whom had been members for well over 3 decades.

Once a coherent set of reforms were developed and approved (after much vigorous debate) by the national executive (now the national Board), an explanatory paper and a Power Point presentation were developed to better explain it. The senior leadership conducted workshops in all States and Territories over a three-week period, in two-hour separate interactive meetings with States Boards, their senior staff and other key members and stakeholders. Good suggestions and new ideas were taken on board to improve the overall proposal. The main driver for change was risk management. It was strongly argued that the organisation needed one overall body to have oversight and responsibility for all activities of the Society in every part of the country to help meet its workplace health and safety and other legislative requirements. The first raft of changes were unanimously adopted by the National Council at its annual meeting in November 2004 and approved by the Governor General in 2005 and the changes were gradually implemented over a 12-month period.

Brand and Marketing

Australian Red Cross is challenged by the breadth of its activities. Only the blood service operates as a national monopoly. In other areas the Australian Red Cross operates side by side with Government owned enterprises and other non-profit organisations in its service offerings.

Different operational and marketing strategies are required depending on the area and location of the services being provided. Increasingly we have developed procedures to operate co-operatively with other humanitarian actors recognising that our donors and supporting governments expect there to be joint action by all humanitarian actors in a crisis situation to the maximum extent possible to minimise any waste of resources.

In West Africa during the Ebola crisis, the Secretary General of the International Federation of Red Cross and Red Crescent and his staff worked to develop applicable procedures in the three main affected countries in establishing the key operational roles and responsibilities. Thus MSF took primary responsibility for the medical treatment while the RCRC Movement took primary responsibility for keeping an updated register of victims and their families and it also attended to the respectful burial of the Ebola dead.

There are specific guidelines on the promotion and use of the Red Cross symbol (or brand as our symbol is often known). As mentioned earlier it is a protective emblem under the Geneva Convention and International Humanitarian Law demands that use of the emblem not be trivialised or in any way impugned or brought into disrepute.

These guidelines do not permit the Australian Red Cross to allow its name or more importantly its emblem to be used by others without its express approval. This approval is never given to companies or organisations involved in weapon manufacturing, tobacco, alcohol or illicit drugs or any form of human trafficking.

The Australian Red Cross marketing team receives regular training by Australian Red Cross International Humanitarian Law officers on emblem abuse. This often leads to a conservative approach in decision making as marketing officers try hard to avoid any suggestion that the Red Cross emblem is being misused or compromised. Of course the Red Cross is one of the most visible and high profile global emblems, so there is no shortage of external businesses eager to be involved as a partner in Red Cross services and activities, such is its brand strength.

Engagement with Donors

The Australian Red Cross has over the past 15 years received massive support from ordinary Australians in times of crises. In the Victorian Bushfire response for instance there were over 600,000 donors, at least two thirds of whom made their donations online.

Since the Bali bombing appeal in 2002 the Australian Red Cross has put in place a system of regular reporting to donors on its activities to show how donor funds are being employed. The internet has been a great boon in allowing electronic messaging to donors to save on posting and printing costs.

Donors are free to opt out of reports on disaster or appeal responses but unless they do that, regular reports are provided on the use of donated funds in any given project. In the case of larger donations and business partners, more complete reports on the use of funds are provided.

Partnerships

Despite the Red Cross fundamental principle of independence, the Movement at the higher level has recognised that the organisation could not and should not act alone in a major conflict or disaster response. The expectation of Government and other stakeholders is that there will be a co-ordinated humanitarian response from all actors

This comes quite naturally to the Red Cross and Red Crescent Movement as it has co-operated and co-ordinated mechanisms in place for its 192 separate Movement components.

It is relatively simple then to adopt or extend these co-ordinating and co-operating measures to encompass other humanitarian agencies working in the same space at the same time.

Formal partnerships can occur at times with other humanitarian agencies (especially UN agencies) and more recently with businesses. As in the area of marketing there are international and national guidelines. Bodies involved in arms manufacture, alcohol, tobacco, etc. are not able to partner with Australian Red Cross or even to make donations in many cases.

Human Resource Management and Volunteers

As an organisation which has always relied heavily on volunteers being part of its humanitarian response, Australian Red Cross has considerable experience in training and managing volunteers. It has volunteer codes of conduct. It provides insurance for them while performing their allocated duties. The national human resources team of the organisation has a specific responsibility to manage paid staff and volunteers, to monitor the conditions under which they work, and to evaluate their performance on a regular basis.

Volunteers are required to commit to the seven Fundamental Principles of the organisation and failure to do so (and indeed any inappropriate actions or omissions) will lead to a volunteer's services being terminated immediately.

A challenge for the organisation arises in major disaster responses when the number of trained staff and volunteers are inadequate to deal with the response. In such cases volunteers from other agencies are utilised and at times there will be spontaneous volunteers from the affected community who need to be quickly vetted before they are allowed to assist. Initially they will be required to work with a trained volunteer who can assist them and monitor their performance.

Naturally, any volunteer working with children is required to have a 'blue card' (in Queensland) or its equivalent in other States if they are in a situation where they will be working with children.

Interface with Stakeholders including Governments

As mentioned earlier, the Australian Red Cross is cognisant of the need to regularly inform others (especially donors) of the way in which its donated funds are being acquitted.

It naturally follows that the same principles apply to stakeholders other than donors. Regular electronic updates are provided to them on the work and activities of Australian Red Cross on any given project or disaster response in which the stakeholders are involved. For Government and business partners more complex reporting including audited financial statements are provided where that is appropriate. It is appreciated that stakeholders do need to be told what good works are being undertaken or, in the rare instance where mistakes occur, what is being done to remedy these inevitable human errors we all make from time to time.

On the flipside to this, an important stakeholder in any humanitarian response is the beneficiary, and Australian Red Cross has modified its protocols and procedures in the past 15 years to ensure there is adequate briefing and discussions with beneficiaries on the services with which they are being provided.

During the Asia Tsunami response in Aceh ARC emergency response representatives sat on the ground with local villagers in remote areas so the Red

Cross recovery team could listen to the views of beneficiaries on the type of new housing to be provided to replace the homes lost in the tsunami. Various options were provided as it was recognised that one size does certainly not fit all!

Use of Innovation

The Australian Red Cross in common with all other national societies and other humanitarian agencies is open to modifying its standard procedures and service delivery to take on board innovations and new opportunities to help reduce administrative costs and to provide more effective assistance for those in need. This and our significant local volunteer base helps that vital donated dollar go further.

Australian Red Cross staff are encouraged to attend seminars in new technologies and those are gradually trialled and if successful introduced into the organisation's formal procedures going forward.

As mentioned earlier, the Victorian Bushfire saw over 600,000 donations made on line which helped reduce the cost of accounting for the over $300 million contributed by so many donors. Regular reports by email were given to all donors providing email addresses as opposed to the need to post out materials to those providing only a postal address.

Staff who pioneer new and innovative ideas are celebrated in the organisation. Two years ago a Red Cross staff member and a volunteer were awarded the Greg Vickery Scholarship to help them develop a live platform and e-learning bay on the dissemination of International Humanitarian Law to young people. This was an excellent example of the organisation encouraging innovation in a unique service area of the organisation.

Greg Vickery AO
*Member of the Standing Commission of Red Cross and
Red Crescent, and the immediate Past President of
the Australian Red Cross Society*

Part II

Shaping the Journey

4 Stakeholder Partnerships and the Delivery of Services

Stephen Jones

Introduction

Non-profit institutions (NFPs) in Australia are a wide-ranging group of organisations established to provide charitable goods and services for the public benefit.[1] Key to the success of NFPs is their ability to form strategic alliances and partnerships with a variety of stakeholders: policy makers, other service delivers, sponsors, and coaches/mentors. Forming and maintaining these relationships has become a key challenge for NFPs as the wellbeing of their clients, and their own survival in a dynamic regulatory period from 2010 depends upon these relationships. This chapter examines the case of the Australian NFP sector and explores how the charities have needed to operate through partnership arrangements to enhance their ability to contribute to the wellbeing of their clients and their own sustainability as they pursue their service obligations.

The discussion presented here looks primarily at issues surrounding partnership arrangements between the NFP sector and the Australian Government as the primary funder of organisations that have been contracted to provide services classed as 'public goods'. The rationale is that core social services such as childcare, healthcare, disability services, and employment services are difficult to fund privately for the people who need the services the most.[2] With the government as the primary source of NFP funding, Australia is similar to the UK, New Zealand and Canada and dissimilar to the USA, where the majority of NFP funding comes from philanthropic foundations and private donors. The provision of help and support to those in need is increasingly viewed as a three-sector solution based on contributions from government, private business and NFP organisations. There is an increasing role for private sector individuals and organisations such as banks, superannuation funds and private corporations contributing to social enterprises as a component of their Corporate Social Responsibility (CSR) programmes.[3] However, despite the emergence of these philanthropic contributions they still represent a small proportion of the pool of financial support for the majority of NFPs. In 2015 the 50,908 charities in NFP sector in Australia received a total revenue of $134.5b; $11.1b (8.3%) in donations, with $55.6b (41.4%) of direct government support.[4] Long-standing partnership arrangements have existed between the NFP sector and governments in

Australia, including local, state and federal levels. Of particular importance in this chapter are the arrangements between federal government agencies with social welfare responsibilities that undertake specific arrangements with relevant NFP organisations.

This chapter will first place the emergence of partnership arrangements in the broader theoretical context of neoliberal ideas that have reformed relationships between governments and the private sector, including NFP organisations, since the 1990s. Second, the chapter will examine the nature of the partnership arrangements, including the areas of engagement, and the approaches taken by government agencies and NFP organisations. Third, the areas of concern regarding partnership arrangements raised by both sectors in recent surveys will be outlined. Finally, the chapter will consider possible ways in which partnership arrangements can be improved to maximise the delivery of services to the most vulnerable sectors of the community.

The NFP Sector in Australia

The NFP sector in Australia makes a considerable social and economic contribution. Table 4.1 provides a snapshot of the situation as recorded by the Australian Bureau of Statistics in 2015. The Australian NFP sector is comprised of approximately 600,000 diverse organisations the majority of which are small, non-employing organisations, and 10% of which are registered charities. In 2012–13 there were approximately 57,000 NFPs with an active tax role. In 2014 there were approximately 60,000 charities registered with the Australian Charities and Not for Profits Commission (ACNC). The top 1,000 NFPs are involved in the following sectors: health, education & research, social services, culture & recreation; environment; development & housing; law & advocacy; international philanthropy; religion; and business and professional associations including unions.[5]

In 2015 charities in Australia reported sources of income that were largely from 'other income and revenue income primarily from donations and bequests'. Table 4.2 highlights the main sources of income for the NFP sector.

Table 4.1 NFP Key Results (Source: Australian Bureau of Statistics, 2015)[6]

Not for Profit Institutions in Australia 2012–2013	
Number of organisations	56,894
Value added to national accounts	$54.8b
Income	$107.5b
Assets	$176b
Employment	1,081,900 persons
Volunteers	3,882,300 persons
Volunteering hours	520.5 million hours

Table 4.2 Key Indicators of Income Sources, 2015[7]

Income Source	Charities which received any income (%)	Mean per charity ($)
Government Grants	35.1	1,093,425
Donations & bequests	62.8	219,399
Other income & revenue	91.2	1,329.641
Total	98.1	2,642,302

The process for awarding contracts for human services provision is competitive and used on major programs. Government funding comprises a large portion of the budgets for the NFPs, but does not fully fund services except in 25% of cases where the government would have fully funded services they have elected to outsource.[8] According to contemporary government attitudes, accountability and transparency for delivery of services is best be achieved by clear regulatory standards that standardise contracts, finance and performance reporting.[9]

A Preference for Partnership Arrangements

Contemporary NFP activity has developed within a neoliberal political and economic ethos. Essentially, this ethos privileges the idea that competition in the market maximises utility and brings benefits to the priorities of the state.[10] The increasing application of a neoliberal, market-based framework starting from the late 20th century has changed the relationship of NFPs with the state and ultimately other NFP stakeholders.[11] The Keynesian, community-based model of NFP organisation has been supplanted by the state setting policy for public sector goods & services by a disaggregated, decentralised group of providers.[12] The rationale is that instead of relying on a single provider (e.g., the government) to provide public sector goods & services, multiple providers across a range of for profit and NFP organisations will better meet the demand more efficiently and according to consumer choice. "Neoliberals cast the non-profit sector as an independent third force closely cooperating with government to sustain social provision."[13]

Neoliberal approaches to governance arrangements have also been written about extensively under the term 'New Public Management' (NPM). The ideas under this approach incorporate the above points but also meet the goals of minimising government bureaucracies, establishing contractual arrangements with stakeholders in delivering services and increasing results and privatising services.[14] The movement towards NPM has successfully introduced new approaches into many developed economic contexts, including Australia. However, the movement has also had the paradoxical effect of prioritising economic efficiency over embodying traditional values of care. There is focus on establishing more choice at a lower cost and in some cases a better value aligned with a need for decentralised organisations to report on their activities, through contractual arrangements. Partnership agreements established on these ideas has helped to create competing demands on both NFP staff and volunteers to keep a delicate balance between serving their clients within the mission of their organisations, and remain accountable to the state for their income, expenses, activities and retention of NFP status, useful for tax purposes.

NPM has traditionally been rolled out with regulatory reforms as the mechanism for changing the culture of public service departments and ministries as they downsize and devolve service-delivery responsibilities to external providers.[15] The application of NPM principles has had consequences for government agencies and is closely linked with wide-ranging dissatisfaction with and lowered confidence in government as the best provider of public services. The key characteristics of NPM are synthesised from a wide range of sources by Carroll and Steane (2002) and Keating (2001) as:[16]

- Multiple providers of public services including: government, NFP and business actors
- Results-driven service as measured in terms of efficiency, quality and cost as determiners of which actors provide service
- Government primarily in governance role over public services
- Reliance on market mechanisms and contracts rather than rules to co-ordinate supply and demand for public services
- Accountability linked to results and separation of politics from management of public services

In surveys of Government Department employees, 88% view arrangements with NFPs as a partnership.[17] Some of the reasons why partnership arrangements with the NFP sector continue to be an attractive option for the delivery of government services, and the degree of importance placed on some of the characteristics by the government agencies surveyed, are outlined in Figure 4.1. Other, more nuanced, reasons include:

- Partnership arrangements permitted joint decision making and shared responsibility
- They facilitated the joint delivery of services
- NFP partners could co- contribute to the sharing of costs
- Partners could maintain a frequent communication on issues relating to service delivery
- NFP partner shared common goals with government agencies in terms of the groups receiving the services.[18]

Many agencies argued that the NFPs they work with are more efficient at delivering services than governments. NFPs are seen as best placed to

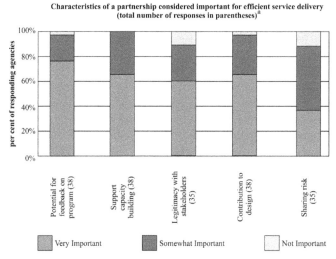

Characteristics of a partnership considered important for efficient service delivery
(total number of responses in parentheses)[a]

Very Important   Somewhat Important   Not Important

[a]Agencies were invited to select more than one response.

Figure 4.1 Characteristics of a partnership considered important for efficient service delivery[20]

address community needs as a result of being closer to the target group for which the service is aimed. In this Australian context this has been particularly true for agencies that fund services to Indigenous groups. NFPs in such instances can be closer to the Indigenous communities and have a better understanding of the needs and expectations of remote communities.[19]

Advantages of Partnership Arrangements

Partnership arrangements with the NFP sector are advantageous to governments in a number of ways. In countries like Australia with increasingly diverse heterogeneous societies the demands for government services are increasingly complex and challenging for individual organisations to provide. Where governments do well in providing services from tax dollars is where there is majority demand such as for roads, health care and schools which are classed as truly 'public' and can be met, on the whole, in a homogenous way.

There are at least three different ways to view the partnership arrangements, between governments and non-profits in providing services to a heterogeneous population with diverse needs, two of which are government failure theory and interdependence theory. Increasingly there are views that argue there is an inability of government to provide services across a range of interest groups with complex demands. One example from the Australian context is the challenges refugees bring to government services including the need to focus on issues relating to language, health, education and employment problems associated with individuals in this situation. Governments are seen to be failing to deliver services in circumstances where the needs are much more specific to groups and individuals with needs that may not configure with the overall general needs of the population. Faced with these more specific needs and niche groups, secondary markets open up such that alternate service providers begin to have relevance. Non-profit providers and third party, for-profit firms vie for market share in terms of quality and cost of services provided.[21] Some scholars refer to this view as remedialist meaning that non-profits step in when governments fail to deliver services.[22] Another set of ideas relating to the partnership arrangement looks at relative benefits and missional purpose of government and non-government organisations. Instead of regarding non profits as 'gap-fillers' for areas where the government is not poised to respond to needs of niche groups, 'interdependence' approaches propose that governments and non-profits work collaboratively in the areas of their respective strength. In this way, governments are investors in service providers who are missionally oriented towards addressing particular needs. Figure 4.2 provides an indication of the range of areas where NFPs provide services. A second way to refer to this view is essentialist, where values of altruism and cooperation are preferred to market mechanisms.[23] Governments are not the only investors, however. According to interdependence theory, philanthropists may also have an active role as stakeholders. They can be encouraged to work with government to augment the availability of public services for niche groups.[24]

The third set of ideas supporting the partnership arrangement describe government relationships with non-profits is adversarial where both parties

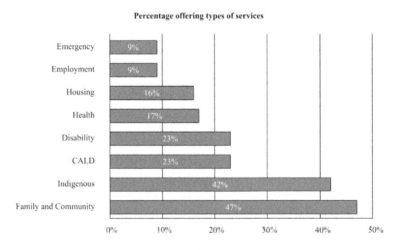

Figure 4.2 Australian NFP Service Types[25]

are suspicious of one another and are constantly holding each other to account.[26] This role is not necessarily separated from non-profit as either gap-filler or preferred provider. As direct service providers, non-profits are viewed as both more trustworthy and efficient than large government bureaucracies especially when it comes to accurately representing their needs.[27] In theory, they have the flexibility to respond more quickly to the needs of their clientele. In each of these partnership arrangements there are consequences for NFP organisations establishing closer relationships with government agencies. Areas where non-profits are vulnerable include: (1) becoming more bureaucratic in response to government reporting requirements; (2) spending more time pursuing philanthropic donations than on services; (3) paying more attention to the mission and staff of the non-profit than the clientele; and (4) not delivering services effectively or at all.[28]

Scholarship around partnerships between government and non-profits seems to be in agreement that they are ever more the norm than the exception in developed countries (McLoughlin 2011, p. 241). Governments see the benefits of partnership arrangements as they have a variety of reasons to pursue them including wanting to make sure that particular services are delivered in a high-quality way without interruption. Although the literature on these partnerships reflect inherent tensions between governments and non-profits including the management for partnership as well as how best to deliver and regulate services, the overall consensus at the macro level is that these partnerships are desirable for governments and the non-profit sector.[29]

Earlier iterations of government-NFP partnerships, starting in the 1990s, could largely be characterised by government setting the agenda and terms of engagement, including gag clauses preventing the NFPs from commenting on government policy affecting their clientele. More recently, NFPs have pushed back for the right to advocate and openly challenge government policy and in so doing have begun to shape the terms of the partnerships.[30] The literature cautions against viewing the government as a unitary body, however, where different departments of the government have more sector-specific views about their relationship with NFPs. The formal contracts between government departments and NFPs are not sufficient, by themselves, to fully encourage the development of partnerships between government and NFP agencies. In fact, actor-oriented leadership in the dialogical, inter-organisational interface can make a profound difference to the success of the partnership and the outcomes for clientele.[31] The relational element where trust, goodwill and collaboration are built lead to the most well-rounded solutions for service provision.

Some private sector organisations in Australia also provide funding to organisations via corporate sponsorships. Sponsorship is particularly common in the arts. However, it is also used to support social purpose organisations to finance (what is likely to be) a high-profile event or campaign. Box 1 provides a case study of one organisation in Melbourne that works together with the NFP organisation on goals of mutual interest. In such contexts, corporates will typically seek to promote their brand to existing or new customers through the initiative. The sectors receiving significant philanthropy were environment, development and housing, law, advocacy, philanthropic, international ($3,194m—37%); religion ($1,805m—20%); social services ($1,240m—14%); and culture and recreation ($1,082m—12.5%).[32] The observations of the NFP sector of corporate participation suggests there are some crucial elements to the relationship that need to be present for corporates to consider partnership arrangements. These elements include:

1. Prioritising issues: corporates supporting organisations that address social problems and needs that align with their own interests (e.g. education, health, the arts, etc.). For many corporates, these issues are aligned with their commercial priorities and focus
2. Matching geographies: corporates supporting organisations that operate in the same communities and locations as they do
3. 3. Picking growth stages: corporates supporting organisations at a particular stage (or cycle) of growth (e.g. start-ups, new initiatives or organisations looking to scale)
4. Supporting staff: corporates supporting organisations that their own staff already support, often resulting in matched giving programs, to maintain and deepen the relationship
5. Engaging partners: corporates seeking opportunities to work alongside organisations to deliver programs and activities, including through volunteer opportunities.[33]

Within Australia, property group The GPT Group (GPT) is an example of a corporate whose giving program demonstrates a number of the above trends. In particular, GPT's giving program focuses on sector priorities (including environmental sustainability, healthy living, social inclusion and learning and employment); supports partners in set geographies; and provides opportunities for employee engagement. GPT's approach also looks to support partners that deliver on business objectives, such as brand and reputation.

Box 1: Partnership to Support for the homeless in Melbourne[34]

STREAT's partnership with The GPT Group (GPT) began in 2010 with the opening of a STREAT coffee cart in Melbourne Central. Over the last year, STREAT's pilot site with a monthly casual lease has evolved into a five year commercial agreement, becoming Melbourne Central's first social enterprise tenant.

Since opening its doors at Melbourne Central, STREAT has served more than 319,000 coffees and trained more than 175 young people who were homeless or at risk of homelessness. Beyond the direct benefits for the young trainees, the cart and subsequent kiosk has played a key role in boosting

STREAT's volunteer ranks and developing a loyal customer base. GPT also provides ongoing support to STREAT, helping to organise and promote other fundraising activities at the centre such as 'Sleepless in September'—a sleep-out at Melbourne Central which raised $48,000 towards STREAT's youth programs last year.

The co-founder and CEO of STREAT, likens the start of the relationship to dating where both parties tested the waters to see whether there was alignment between their priorities. After seeing how each operated and the early results, both organisations committed to the relationship and are now looking at opportunities to scale.

(*Source: Pro Bono Australia, 2014*)

Government Role to Regulate

Given the importance of the benefits to both current and future generations of Australians, it is vitally important that the NFP sector is well regulated so that it remains accountable to the communities it serves.[35] In Australia, regulation is seen as a vitally important mechanism towards ensuring that organisations, which exist for the express purpose of serving the public good, actually fulfil their mandate to do so. In regards to the NFP sector, the Australian Government has taken different positions over the past decade. It is the dual role of government as regulator and government as partner that has been a critical source of friction between federal agencies and NFP organisations. Submissions made to various parliamentary inquiries argue that the NFP regulatory environment has been overly complex and that action should be taken to reduce the regulatory burden on the sector. Without reductions in the burden NFPs argue they will be unable to achieve the efficiencies and more effective operations that makes them suitable as implementation partners. In 2012, the Australian Government established the Australian Charities and Non-profit Commission (ACNC) as a vehicle with the intended purpose of improving the quality of management of NFP organisations. In order to put some stability into the sector, and championed by the Association of Chartered Accountants, the ACNC was commissioned with the goal of putting some structure into a sector with variable public oversight across localities while at the same time reducing regulatory and reporting burden on NFPs. The establishment of the ACNC as an independent regulatory agency was a major development in the maturation of the NFP sector and formalising aspects of the sector's relationship with the broad range of government departments and agencies. The focus of the ACNC was to be on two specific areas: that they provide the public goods and services claimed in an efficient and transparent way; and, that their volunteer boards operate the charities in a transparent manner. Embedded in the establishment of the ACNC was legal clarity on the different forms of charities and NFPs and tailored reporting that allowed the public and funders to understand the financial health of these organisations.[36]

Principles underpinning the ACNC regulatory approach include:[37]

- *Fairness:* presumption that lack of compliance is more to do with lack of understanding or error than intentional fraud. ACNC is committed to responding proportionally and consistently in its role to uphold policies and procedures.
- *Accountability:* ACNC strives for transparency and mutual understanding with all stakeholders to charitable organisations.
- *Integrity:* "The ACNC is committed to acting with integrity, adhering to Australian laws and the Australian Public Service's Code of Conduct and Values, as well as our organisational values."
- *Independence:* "ACNC is an independent statutory office holder with its own budget. ACNC reports annually to Parliament."
- *Respect:* ACNC is committed to engaging with charities and their stakeholders in order to make informed decisions while respecting the autonomy of the charities.

Australia's NFP sector is similar in some respects to the USA, the UK, New Zealand and Canada but has distinctive characteristics. In many ways the Australian NFPs are younger than the NFP sectors in these other countries as evidenced by the relatively late, and highly-contested, appointment of the ACNC as a NFP regulator.[38] Despite various objections to the existence of the ACNC in the political discourse there has been a high level of support within the NFP community. Surveys of NFP organisations since 2013 reveal a strong preference for a quasi-independent body to manage regulation over the traditional monitoring and control by the Australian Tax Office. Over 80% of NFP organisations surveyed support the establishment of the ACNC. There is a strong preference for the regulatory approaches of the ACNC (44%) in comparison to the tax office (6%). The NFP sector continues to argue that reducing unnecessary regulations and compliance costs should be a high priority for the ACNC. The ACNC continues to survive political challenges to its existence by the newly elected federal government with a renewed effort to minimise the bureaucratic reporting requirements imposed on charities as a result of regulation.[39]

The decision to retain the ACNC in a highly-contested policy space remains in many ways 'dysfunctional' with the burden of compliance and managing partnership relationships with various government departments still falling to NFP agency staff. There is no agreement in the literature preceding the formation of the ACNC as to the desirability or appropriateness of partnerships between government and NFPs. One concern for leaders of not for profits has been that the government and NFPs cannot truly be collaborative partners because the government has both the top-down power and the financial leverage.[40] A second concern is the reliance on customers to be able to make the optimal decisions when choosing who they want to provide their social services.[41] Partnerships are not ipso facto good or bad, but in order for NFP partnerships with government and, secondarily, private sector companies, it is important to keep the original purpose of the NFP in frame.

If governments expect NFPs to show value per dollar spent as the primary measure of the partnership's success, then the strategic organisational form needed within NFPs is challenged. In this scenario, NFPs must meet the requirements of the funding body and the needs of the client base with limited material and human resources.[42] While in many ways government agencies state they prefer partnership arrangements there are ongoing issues that reflect the fundamental conflict of the principal/agent relationship. The next section will outline many of the key concerns raised by both government agencies and NFPs on the nature of the partnership arrangements.

Partnership Challenges

In the past some government agencies have expressed concern about the capacity within the NFP sector to undertake the management and administration of government programmes. The field of NFPs with the capacity to undertake much of the work available has been limited and it has been difficult to attract new entrants to make submissions through tender processes. Perhaps the first and most significant challenge is the overall view taken by a government agency and its staff to the concept of a partnership. As the 'principal' in the partnership relationship, government agencies wield tremendous power in terms of the contractual arrangements that determine the role of the relevant parties. Survey data suggests there are varying views

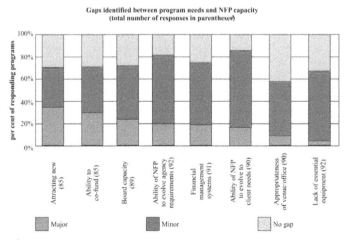

Figure 4.3 Gaps in NFP capacity.[44]

across agencies as to exactly what they mean by a partnership. Some prefer to maintain a top down approach that closely monitors and controls programme delivery, programme quality and safety. Other agencies seem to adopt an almost casual relationship with their partners where the arrangement is 'by intention and not in a legal sense'.[43] Other agencies adopt a more equal arrangement that reflects the nature of a true partnership agreement. In these partnerships there are strong consultation arrangements throughout the policy development and implementation stages.

The approach taken by the partners will largely determine the operation of the partnership, and in many respects the outcomes it achieves. When asked if they experience any difficulties in establishing an effective and efficient partnership, many agencies and their staff blame the NFP organisation for the problems. Figure 4.3 highlights some of the gaps that many government agencies existed in the capacities of NFP organisations. Agencies focus on what they see as weaknesses in the NFP organisation including poorly qualified staff and high staff turnover. They further criticise the NFPs for having objectives and priorities that are different from the government or that the requirements of the government are too high and onerous. Those agencies that take a more consultative approach to the partnership arrangements argue there may be issues on both sides. They take a more consultative and innovative approach that investigates and trails new approaches to areas such as monitoring and evaluation, contract arrangements, governance and accountability and risk management.[45]

For their part leaders of NFPs have been raising issues they find challenging in partnership arrangements with the federal government. A 2015 Senate Inquiry into the community service tendering process by the federal government revealed a range of issues that impact on the capacity of NFPs to undertake their contractual obligations when partnering with the government. At the fundamental level NFPs point to the contract terms and conditions as a key factor undermining their efforts to support and improve community outcomes.[46] The restrictions placed on funding allocated to programmes, and the inconsistency of this funding for any longer than three years, have both been restrictions and reduced NFPs flexibility in identifying needs in the communities they have been contracted to serve. This is particularly serious as it places many NFPs in highly precarious situations. On the one hand if they meet the contractual demands they will satisfy one aspect of the partnership arrangement. However, in meeting these contractual demands they risk failing to meet the requirements of the community they have missional obligations to serve. This is a self-defeating approach as the NFPs are selected as partners by the government on the basis of their capacity to meet the social demands of their clients. For these reasons NFPs have been claiming the contractual arrangements have challenged and 'in some cases destroyed, relationships and collaborative partnerships'.[47] Regarding social safety net services, such as social housing, veterans' affairs and unemployment assistance, there are intractable problems requiring ongoing and long-term commitment by government in order to continually meet variable needed in these two areas among others. In these instances, clear policy objectives need to be articulated, paired with funding transparency, and appropriate regulation.[48] In other instances, contractual terms have bound organisations together, irrespective of different operating methods, distinct missions and organisational governance methods. Such approaches again fail to maximise the opportunities of the distinctive nature of many NFPs that make them attractive as partners in the first place.

Gag clauses have been a long-standing cause for concern that prevent NFPs from advocating on behalf of their clients that have added extra pressure to the NFP sector and the collaborative nature of partnerships with government in Australia. Government agencies have demanded that NFPs not criticise the governments that provide more than 50% of their funding. While the gag clause was removed at the Federal level in 2013 (*Freedom to Advocate Bill 2013*) it is only partially removed by state governments. The impulse to restrict democratic freedoms to advocate on behalf of the vulnerable remains active among some ministers at the state and federal levels. The larger problem with periodically tying government funding to non-criticism clauses is that principles of participatory process and collaborative governance are put at risk in so far as NFP organisations accurately represent the citizens claimed.[49] The Australian Council of Social Services (ACOSS) argues that confidentiality requirements make it impossible for organisations to identify the level of resources and how to best use them within certain communities or population groups.[50] From a public policy perspective this weakness prevents NFPs from fulfilling a critical partnership role of providing policy learning that could contribute to the improvement in the delivery of service to vulnerable communities. Other areas of concern expressed by the NFP sector include:

- Micro management
- Proliferation of service agreement and contracts—cocktail funding & reporting
- Short term funding arrangements for long term problems
- Sub-contracting through lead agencies
- Variability across government agencies

Data gathered on NFP perspectives reflect that this partnership relationship is not satisfactory, in palpably dissatisfactory ways, regarding these same reporting requirements, which are viewed as micro-managing service delivery with short-term government contracts.[51] From the information outlined above it seems there is a disconnect between the government's view and the NFPs' perspectives on program improvement. Government program respondents tend to be more optimistic about the effectiveness of current arrangements, and the future of those arrangements, than NFPs.[52] The relationships between NFPs and government agencies remain subject to political interference and electoral cycles that create new agendas for change. The need for reform remains an ongoing issue where NFPs remain in a weak negotiating position with government agencies that hold the financial and political power. The next section will attempt some insights on the future directions these partnership arrangements may take.

Future Directions

Despite the benefits acknowledged by the agencies some scholars have argued that the application of neoliberal principles to the NFP sector has actually caused a cultural and institutional shift away from relationship-based service provision and a consequent diminution in the quality of services provided.[53] There are, of course, some advantages to both government and the NFP sector in ensuring that partnership arrangements work effectively in the delivery of services to those who need them the most.

Government agencies continue to prefer market based approaches, such as competitive tendering, not only for logic related to NPM ways of thinking, but because of concern to reduce risk around fraud and lack of appropriate governance.[54] One of the challenges is towards achieving a balance between the government's need for stringent reporting requirements against the NFP sector's limited capacity. Recent recommendations are that reduced red tape for NFPs can be achieved by streamlining and standardising these requirements across federal, state and territory agencies reducing the financial reporting burden to NFPs.[55] Moreover, it would reduce the compliance burden for NFPs. In 2016 the ACNC commissioned a report on options to reduce reporting requirements for ACNC registered charities. The report is a follow-up to 2013 research by the ACNC on reporting burdens on the charity sector produced by regulatory requirements. The 2016 report found that the greatest administrative, cost and reporting burden is related to fundraising due to differences between jurisdictions at the state, territory, Commonwealth and even international levels.[56] There are areas that charities have identified where reporting requirements (e.g., regulatory burden) can be reduced. These include streamlining and updating requirements to stay current with legislation and the pace of the charitable sector. By far the most attractive suggestion was that the ACNC would be a centralised entity for reporting on fundraising, taxation and incorporation across multiple jurisdictions.

In 2010 the Productivity Commission identified a willingness within the federal government agencies to improve relationships with NFPs. Agency staff recognised the difficulties in administering programmes and forming effective partnerships.[57] The submissions to the 2015 Senate Inquiry into social services reveals that many of the ideas raised by the Productivity Commission remain relevant. Some of these ideas include:

- Increasing flexibility in relationships; for example, creating consultation groups and discussion panels and establishing client centred arrangements (outcomes based).

- Increasing the capacity of NFPs; for example, working with peak bodies to build sector capacity, providing targeted infrastructure investments such as developing frameworks for best governance and business practices, training for staff and developing new standards.
- Better coordination and consistency in program requirements; for example, developing shared responsibility agreements, increased use of multi year agreements.[58]

There seems to be little doubt that there will continue to be an increase in demand for NFPs to deliver government services. This appears to be driven not only by the success of past and current engagement experiences but also by a public recognition and preference for the NFP sector to deliver these services. Public surveys have long revealed a preference for the NFP sector by people who said they had used a community service:

- 85% of people agreed that non-profit organisations should operate community services
- 47% agreed that for-profit organisations should operate community services.
- 57% said they preferred services run by non-profit organisations.[59]

In 2014 the ACOSS submission to the Australian Government inquiry into the not-for-profit sector listed 10 recommendations. These include: using ACNC's eight principles of good charity regulation as a NFP sectoral benchmark, protecting the independence of the NFP sector, reducing red-tape, and effectively using the meaningful data already gathered to guide policy decisions.[60] It remains to be seen whether the ambitions of public sector agencies and the desires of the NFP sector will be realised through recognition of the changes needed by political decision makers. The political will to change the dynamics of the government/NFP partnership arrangements will ultimately serve the interest of stakeholders involved in service delivery and most importantly the most vulnerable members of our society.

Notes

1. N. Cortis, A. Young, A. Powell, R. Reeve, R. Simnett, K. Ho and I. Ramia. *Australian Charities Report 2015* (Australia: Centre for Social Impact and Social Policy Research Centre, UNSW, 2016).
2. T. Boyd-Caine. "The Contribution of Not for Profits to Democratic Process," in *The Three Sector Solution: Delivering Public Policy in Collaboration with Not-for-Profits and Business*, eds. J. Butcher and D. Gilchrist (Australia: ANU Press, Acton, 2016), 87.
3. L. Black. "Policy Impediments to Social Investments by Australian Businesses," in *The Three Sector Solution: Delivering Public Policy in Collaboration with Not-for-Profits and Business*, eds. J. Butcher and D. Gilchrist (Australia: ANU Press, Acton, 2016), 116–117.
4. Cortis, Young, Powell, Reeve, Simnett, Ho and Ramia.

5. Productivity Commission. *Contribution of the Not-for-Profit Sector.* Research Report, Canberra, 2010.
6. Australian Bureau of Statistics (ABS), "Australian National Accounts: Non-Profit Institutions Satellite Account, 2012–2013," 2015, www.abs.gov.au/ausstats/abs@.nsf/mf/5256.0
7. Cortis, Young, Powell, Reeve, Simnett, Ho and Ramia.
8. Productivity Commission, XLIX.
9. Ibid., XXXIII.
10. M. N. Barnett and M. Finnemore, M. "The Politics, Power, and Pathologies of International Organizations," *International Organization* 53, no. 4 (1999): 699–732.
11. B. Evans, T. Richmond and J. Shields. "Structuring Neoliberal Governance: The Non-Profit Sector, Emerging New Modes of Control and the Marketisation of Service Delivery," *Policy and Society* 24, no. 1 (2005): 76.
12. Ibid., 77.
13. Ibid., 78.
14. Y. Hasenfeld and E. E. Garrow. "Non-Profit Human-Service Organizations, Social Rights, and Advocacy in a Neoliberal Welfare State," *Social Service Review* 86, no. 2 (2012): 302.
15. M. Keating. "Public Management Reform and Economic and Social Development." *OECD Journal on Budgeting* (2001): 158–159.
16. Keating, 145–146; P. Carroll and P. Steane. "Australia, the New Public Management, and the New Millennium," in *New Public Management: Current Trends and Future Prospects* eds. K. McLaughlin, S. Osborne and E. Ferlie (London: Routledge, 2002), 195–196.
17. Productivity Commission, D2.
18. Ibid.
19. Productivity Commission.
20. Ibid.
21. J. D. Lecy and D. M. Van Slyke. "Non-Profit Sector Growth and Density: Testing Theories of Government Support," *Journal of Public Administration Research and Theory* (2012): 3. doi:10.1093/jopart/mus010.
22. M. Considine. "Governance and Competition: The Role of Non-profit Organisations in the Delivery of Public Services," *Australian Journal of Political Science*, 38, no. 1 (2003): 65.
23. Ibid., 65.
24. J. D. Lecy and D. M. Van Slyke. "Non-Profit Sector Growth and Density: Testing Theories of Government Support," *Journal of Public Administration Research and Theory* (2012): 4. doi:10.1093/jopart/mus010.
25. Productivity Commission.
26. J. M. Brinkerhoff and D. W. Brinkerhoff. "Government—Nonprofit Relations in Comparative Perspective: Evolution, Themes and New Directions," *Public Administration and Development* 22, no. 1 (2002): 7.
27. J. E. Mosley and C. M. Grogan. "Representation in Nonelected Participatory Processes: How Residents Understand the Role of Non-Profit Community-Based Organizations," *Journal of Public Administration Research and Theory* 23, no. 4 (2013): 6.
28. J. M. Brinkerhoff and D. W. Brinkerhoff. "Government—Nonprofit Relations in Comparative Perspective: Evolution, Themes and New Directions," *Public*

Administration and Development 22, no. 1 (2002): 6; M. Considine. "Governance and Competition: The Role of Non-profit Organisations in the Delivery of Public Services," *Australian Journal of Political Science* 38, no. 1 (2003): 65.

29. C. McLoughlin. "Factors Affecting State—Non-Governmental Organisation Relations In Service Provision: Key Themes From The Literature." *Public Administration and Development*, 31, no. 4 (2011): 242.

30. Ibid., 243.

31. Ibid., 246.

32. M. McGregor-Lowndes, T. Flack, W. Scaife, P. Wiepking and M. Crittall. *Giving and Volunteering in Australia 2014: Environmental Scan/Literature Review* (Brisbane, Queensland: The Australian Centre for Philanthropy and Nonprofit Studies, Queensland University of Technology, 2014).

33. S.V.A. Quarterly. "How Corporate Partnerships Work," 2014, www.socialventures. com.au/sva-quarterly/how-corporate-partnerships-work/

34. Pro Bono Australia. "How Corporate Partnerships Work," 2014, https:// probonoaustralia.com.au/news/2014/09/how-corporate-partnerships-work/

35. The Treasury. "Final Report: Scoping Study for a National Not-for-Profit Regulator," Australian Government, 2011, http://archive.treasury.gov.au/ documents/2054/PDF/20110706%20-%20Final%20Report%20-%20Scop ing%20Study.pdf

36. AICD (Australian Institute of Company Directors). "Submission to the ACNC Implementation Task Force,": 2012: 8–9, www.companydirectors.com.au/~/ media/resources/director-resource-centre/policy-on-director-issues/2012/ aicd-submission_acnc-implementation-design-discussion-paper_27-feb-12. ashx?la=en

37. Australian Charities and Not-for-Profits Commission (ACNC). "Regulatory Approach Statement," 2014, www.acnc.gov.au/ACNC/About_ACNC/ Regulatory_app/RegApp_St2013/ACNC/Publications/Reg_App/RegAppr_ Powers.aspx?hkey=e8deb00c-f626-4813-8f50-1cf1ef8f0a6b

38. Australian Charities and Not-for-Profits Commission (ACNC); C. Porter and K. O'Dwyer. "Retention of the Australian Charities and Not-for-Profits Commission," Media Release, 4 March, Parliament House, Canberra, 2016.

39. S. Jeffery. "Federal Government Moves to Assure Charity Sector About ACNC's Future," 2017, www.theage.com.au/national/public-service/federal-government- moves-to-assure-charity-sector-about-acncs-future-20170607-gwm29m

40. R. Melville. "Token participation' to 'engaged partnerships': Lessons learnt and challenges ahead for Australian not-for-profits" in *Strategic Issues in the Not-for-Profit Sector* ed. Barraket, J. Sydney, UNSW Press, 2008.

41. R. S. Kaplan and D. P. Norton. "Balance without Profit." *Harvard Business Review* (January 2001): 23–26.

42. J. Barraket (ed). *Strategic Issues in the Not-for-Profit Sector* (Sydney: UNSW Press, 2008).

43. Productivity Commission, D19.

44. Productivity Commission.

45. Ibid., D3.

46. Australian Council of Social Service (ACOSS). "Submission to the Productivity Commission: Study into the Contribution of the Not-for Profit Sector," 2009, www.acoss.org.au/images/uploads/ACOSS_submission_-_PC_Study_into_the_ Contribution_of_the_Not_for_Profit_Sector.pdf

47. Ibid., 5.
48. Productivity Commission, 279.
49. J. E. Mosley and C. M. Grogan. "Representation in Nonelected Participatory Processes: How Residents Understand the Role of Non-Profit Community-Based Organizations," *Journal of Public Administration Research and Theory*, 23, no. 4 (2013): 2–3.
50. Australian Council of Social Service (ACOSS).
51. Productivity Commission.
52. Ibid.
53. R. Connell, B. Fawcett and G. Meagher. "Neoliberalism, New Public Management and the Human Service Professions: Introduction to the Special Issue," *Journal of Sociology*, 45, no. 4 (2009): 333.
54. BDO. "Not-for Profit: Fraud Survey 2014," 2014, 19–20, www.bdo.com.au/en-au/insights/surveys/not-for-profit/bdo-not-for-profit-fraud-survey-2014
55. Deloitte Access Economics. "Australian Charities and Not-for-Profits Commission: Cutting Red Tape: Options to align state, territory and Commonwealth charity regulation," Final Report. 2016: 44.
56. Ibid.
57. Productivity Commission.
58. Productivity Commission; Senate (Community Affairs References Committee). "Impact on Service Quality, Efficiency and Sustainability of Recent Commonwealth Community Service Tendering Processes by the Department of Social Services," Commonwealth of Australia. 2015, www.aph.gov.au/Parliamentary_Business/Committees/Senate/Community_Affairs/Grants/Final_Report
59. Australian Council of Social Service (ACOSS)
60. ACOSS3–4, 10.

Bibliography

ACOSS. *Briefing: DSS Discretion Grants Funding Round, February 2015.* 2015. Retrieved from www.acoss.org.au/images/uploads/External_Briefing_DSS_funding_2015.pdf
ACOSS. *Submission to the Inquiry Into the Australian Charities and Not for Profit Commission (Repeal) (No 1) Bill 2014.* Strawberry Hills, NSW. 2014.
ACOSS. *Improving the Adequacy and Outcomes of Community Sector Contracts: A Guide for Community Organisations.* 2015. Retrieved from www.acoss.org.au/wpcontent/uploads/2015/06/ACOSS_Contracting_Guide_for_the_Community_Sector-Final.pdf
AICD (Australian Institute of Company Directors). *Submission to the ACNC Implementation Task Force.* 2012. Retrieved from www.companydirectors.com.au/~/media/resources/director-resource-centre/policy-on-director-issues/2012/aicd-submission_acnc-implementation-design-discussion-paper_27-feb-12.ashx?la=en
Australian Charities and Not-for-Profits Commission (ACNC). *Regulatory Approach Statement.* 2014. Retrieved from www.acnc.gov.au/ACNC/About_ACNC/Regulatory_app/RegApp_St2013/ACNC/Publications/Reg_App/RegAppr_Powers.aspx?hkey=e8deb00c-f626-4813-8f50-1cf1ef8f0a6b
Australian Council of Social Service (ACOSS). *Submission to the Productivity Commission: Study Into the Contribution of the Not-for Profit Sector.* 2009. Retrieved

from www.acoss.org.au/images/uploads/ACOSS_submission_-_PC_Study_into_ the_Contribution_of_the_Not_for_Profit_Sector.pdf

Australian Bureau of Statistics (ABS), *Australian National Accounts: Non-Profit Institutions Satellite Account, 2012–2013*. 2015. Retrieved from www.abs.gov. au/ausstats/abs@.nsf/mf/5256.0

Barnett, M. N., and M. Finnemore. "The Politics, Power, and Pathologies of International Organizations." *International Organization* 53, no. 04 (1999): 699–732.

Barraket, J. (ed). *Strategic Issues in the Not-for-Profit Sector*. Sydney: UNSW Press, 2008.

BDO. *Not-for Profit: Fraud Survey 2014*. 2014. Retrieved from www.bdo.com.au/ en-au/insights/surveys/not-for-profit/bdo-not-for-profit-fraud-survey-2014

Black, L. "Policy Impediments to Social Investments by Australian Businesses." In *The Three Sector Solution: Delivering Public Policy in Collaboration With Not-for-Profits and Business*, ed. Butcher, J. and D. Gilchrist. Australia: ANU Press, Acton, 2016.

Boyd-Caine, T. "The Contribution of Not for Profits to Democratic Process." In *The Three Sector Solution: Delivering Public Policy in Collaboration With Not-for-Profits and Business*, ed. Butcher, J. and D. Gilchrist. Australia: ANU Press, Acton, 2016.

Brinkerhoff, J. M., and D. W. Brinkerhoff. "Government—Nonprofit Relations in Comparative Perspective: Evolution, Themes and New Directions." *Public Administration and Development* 22, no. 1 (2002): 3–18.

Carroll, P., and P.Steane. "Australia, the New Public Management, and the New Millennium." n *New Public Management: Current Trends and Future Prospects*, edited by McLaughlin, K., S. Osborne and E. Ferlie. London: Routledge, 2002 p195–209.

Connell, R., B. Fawcett, and G. Meagher. "Neoliberalism, New Public Management and the Human Service Professions: Introduction to the Special Issue." *Journal of Sociology* 45, no. 4 (2009): 331–8.

Considine, M. "Governance and Competition: The Role of Non-Profit Organisations in the Delivery of Public Services." *Australian Journal of Political Science* 38, no. 1 (2003): 63–77.

Cortis, N., A. Young, A. Powell. R. Reeve, R. Simnett, K. Ho, and I. Ramia. *Australian Charities Report 2015*. Australia, Centre for Social Impact and Social Policy Research Centre, UNSW, 2016.

Deloitte Access Economics. *Australian Charities and Not-for-Profits Commission: Cutting Red Tape: Options to Align State, Territory and Commonwealth Charity Regulation. Final Report*. 2016.

Evans, B., T. Richmond, and J. Shields. "Structuring Neoliberal Governance: The Non-Profit Sector, Emerging New Modes of Control and the Marketisation of Service Delivery." *Policy and Society* 24, no. 1 (2005): 73–97.

Hasenfeld, Y., and E. E. Garrow. "Non-Profit Human-Service Organizations, Social Rights, and Advocacy in a Neoliberal Welfare State." *Social Service Review* 86, no. 2 (2012): 295–322.

Jeffery, S. *Federal Government Moves to Assure Charity Sector About ACNC's Future*. 2017. Retrieved from www.theage.com.au/national/public-service/federal-government-moves-to-assure-charity-sector-about-acncs-future-20170607-gwm29m

Kaplan, R. S., and D. P. Norton. "Balance Without Profit." *Harvard Business Review* (January 2001): 23–26.

Keating, M. "Public Management Reform and Economic and Social Development." *OECD Journal on Budgeting*, (2001): 141–208.

Lecy, J. D., and D. M. Van Slyke. "Non-Profit Sector Growth and Density: Testing Theories of Government Support." *Journal of Public Administration Research and Theory* (2012). doi:10.1093/jopart/mus010.

McGregor-Lowndes, M., T. Flack, W. Scaife, P. Wiepking, and M. Crittall. *Giving and Volunteering in Australia 2014: Environmental Scan/Literature Review*. Brisbane, Queensland: The Australian Centre for Philanthropy and Nonprofit Studies, Queensland University of Technology, 2014.

McLoughlin, C. "Factors Affecting State—Non-Governmental Organisation Relations in Service Provision: Key Themes From the Literature." *Public Administration and Development* 31, no. 4 (2011): 240–51.

Melville, R. "Token Participation' to 'Engaged Partnerships': Lessons Learnt and Challenges Ahead for Australian Not-for-Profits." In *Strategic Issues in the Not-for-Profit Sector*, ed. J. Barraket Sydney. UNSW Press, 2008.

Mosley, J. E. and C. M. Grogan. "Representation in Nonelected Participatory Processes: How Residents Understand the Role of Non-Profit Community-Based Organizations." *Journal of Public Administration Research and Theory* 23, no. 4 (2013): 839–63.

Porter, C. and K. O'Dwyer. *Retention of the Australian Charities and Not-for-profits Commission*. Media Release, 4 March, Parliament House, Canberra, 2016.

Pro Bono Australia. *How Corporate Partnerships Work*. 2014. Retrieved from https://probonoaustralia.com.au/news/2014/09/how-corporate-partnerships-work/

Productivity Commission. *Contribution of the Not-for-Profit Sector*. Research Report, Canberra, 2010.

Senate (Community Affairs References Committee). *Impact on Service Quality, Efficiency and Sustainability of Recent Commonwealth Community Service Tendering Processes by the Department of Social Services*. Commonwealth of Australia. 2015. Retrieved from www.aph.gov.au/Parliamentary_Business/Committees/Senate/Community_Affairs/Grants/Final_Report

SVA Quarterly. *How Corporate Partnerships Work*. 2014. Retrieved from www.socialventures.com.au/sva-quarterly/how-corporate-partnerships-work/

The Treasury. *Final Report: Scoping Study for a National Not-for-Profit Regulator*. Australian Government, 2011. Retrieved from http://archive.treasury.gov.au/documents/2054/PDF/20110706%20-%20Final%20Report%20-%20Scoping%20Study.pdf

5   Corporate Social Responsibility, Government, and the Balancing Act

Kenneth Wiltshire

Introduction

Leaders are jugglers.

This is more so in the Not-for-Profit sector than any other, where one of the biggest juggling acts is balancing relationships with government on the one hand, and with the private sector on the other. While these partnerships can play a vital role in helping Not-for-Profits deliver their vision and mission to the benefit of their clients, it is crucial that leaders of Not-for-Profits understand the motivation and the drivers of these suitors, as well as some of the risks involved (Figure 5.1).

Figure 5.1 The Juggling Act

The Government Equation

The government interface has long been a factor for the sector, involving funding, taxation, regulation, and the need to lobby governments on behalf of clients to fulfil the mission of the organisation and maintain its sustainability. This in itself is a delicate operation since no sensible leader would want to bite the hand that feeds the organisation; at least not too often. That in itself can become more problematical since there have been several instances where governments have punished organisations who have dared to speak out against government action or policy. There have even been shameful examples of governments who have written clauses into funding arrangements forbidding public comment by the recipients of grants. This, together with the tendency of some governments to suddenly modify, reduce or even terminate program funding, has led many experts to advise Not-for-Profit organisations not to become too dependent on government grants as part of their revenue mix. A notional cap of 30% is often advocated.

Unfortunately, there is a tendency for program staff of Not-for-Profits to become hypnotised by government funding and support in the belief that it conveys some kind of imprimatur or legitimacy for the programs involved. This often leads to their developing a symbiotic relationship with the government bureaucrats administering their program funding. Imagine their surprise when the grant is often threatened as a result of government cutbacks or the ubiquitous 'reviews' which have become so commonplace, not to mention the vagaries of elections. Indeed, the shortness of the election cycle, (usually three or four years maximum), does not sit well with the 5–7 year cycle required to demonstrate the effectiveness of, say, a welfare, health, education, or housing program. It is crucial that the CEO and Board members of the Not-for-Profit do not become entrapped by this phenomenon.

This is not to say that Not-for-Profit Leaders should not take advantage of opportunities provided by various contemporary public sector reform platforms. These trends include—

- Privatisation
- Funder/Purchaser/ Provider Splits
- Contracting Out/Outsourcing
- Contestability and Competitive Tendering
- Public Private Partnerships
- Joint Ventures
- Franchising
- Community Ownership Programs with Government Empowerment
- Consumer Directed Care (despite mixed results with consumer choice and voucher schemes)

Indeed, many of these initiatives have allowed Not-for-Profits to obtain actual ownership of public assets and the care of the associated clients. Others have enabled beneficial partnerships with the public sector particularly in service delivery where Not-for-Profits are invariably superior given their intimate knowledge of their clients and their needs, and have a strong record of compassionate care.

The challenge for the Leader of the Not-for-Profit is to analyse carefully what is on offer from governments and only enter into these initiatives if there is symmetry with the mission and potentially significant benefits for the clients. There is no harm in letting a government sale or a grant offer sail by the window if they do not meet these tests. The same will be true if the government, through such mechanisms, tries to encourage amalgamation between Not-For-Profits, something which is becoming a more common, if subtle, motivation for governments who see possible reduced overheads in such moves, leading to their being able to reduce government funding of the relevant programs.

The Leader also needs to be courageous in standing up to coercion from governments who are trying to push them into these sometimes ideologically based programs. This is best done initially in a direct and confined manner, using evidence based arguments, but, if public action including resort to the media becomes necessary, it is best handled by the sector as a whole, or affected groups of organisations in the sector acting together. These are situations where an effective peak body for the Not-for-Profit sector becomes essential, especially one with a research/evidence based advocacy team.

Corporate Social Responsibility CSR

Not-for-Profit organisations have long enjoyed support from many private sector companies and entities, including sponsorship and donations in cash and in kind. Frequently, personal and institutional linkages have developed and personal connections have often played a large part, especially with founders. In recent times these relationships have become more widespread and formalised through the upsurge of what is now known as Corporate Social Responsibility (CSR). There are few definitions of CSR because it comes in many shapes and sizes. One comes from the World Business Council for Sustainable Development:[1]

> *"Corporate Responsibility is the continuing commitment by business to behave ethically and to contribute to economic development while improving the quality of life of the workforce, their families, and the local community and society at large. More than goodwill, corporate community involvement, or strategic corporate philanthropy, corporate responsibility is a genuine attempt by a company to build meaningful relationships between the corporate sector and the rest of society."*

Rather than being actually defined, CSR tends to be conceptualised, and this conceptualisation includes the following strands:

- *Business Ethics:* Some see CSR as simply a component of business ethics which embraces concern for something more than just profits, including community welfare.
- *Corporate Citizenship:* Being a 'good corporate citizen' has become something of a mantra these days and there are, once again, several perspectives of the concept. The three most common ones are:

- The limited view where CSR is seen as simply corporate philanthropy.
- An equivalent view where CSR equals corporate citizenship.
- An extended view where CSR extends to the political role of a corporation in society.
- A *globalisation conceptualisation:* CSR is intimately related to universal concern for the environment, absence of exploitation, and elimination of bribery and corruption. There are of course international and cultural differences in approach.
- *Beyond the Triple Bottom Line:* The boundary for corporate behaviour is pushed even beyond the triumvirate of concern for profits, people, and the environment, to include the values mentioned in the other conceptualisations including particularly ethics, role modelling as corporate citizens, wellbeing of communities and nations etc.

In relation to potential partnerships with Not-for-Profits we consider Corporate Social Responsibility to be a deep commitment which must involve more than just sponsorship, joint advertising, philanthropy, or donation schemes. It must involve physical engagement between the staff of the two partners and joint activity in the work of the Not-for-Profit. Good examples from Australian experience include the way the two major airlines Qantas and Virgin have participated in the actual work of charities and where senior executives of the corporates have devoted a number of days each year in mentoring and training staff of the charity; or the Broncos football team which has actively worked with staff of IUIH, an indigenous health organisation, through the innovative Deadly Choices program to encourage health checks and subsequent follow up.

Once again, Not-for-Profit leaders need to understand the drivers and motivation for CSR before they enter this arena.

The Drivers of CSR

The CSR phenomenon of the past two decades has been driven by both positive and negative forces. Scandals have often revealed unethical and antisocial behaviour which has caused companies to reform their practices and revisit their values base. If these scandals have caused crises including corruption, exploitation, and even destruction and death, such remedial action will follow more swiftly, either voluntarily or at the behest of the law and revision of regulation. The spread of ethical consumerism has had a salutary effect on the behaviour of companies worldwide and, along with social awareness and education, has prompted many to consider the formal adoption of CSR policies and strategies, which lead as well to ethics training. Of course, companies have been forced to address their corporate responsibilities by sheer laws and regulations introduced by governments across many areas of business activity, often in response to scandals or catastrophes.

All of these factors enter the equation in a stark manner when a competitor adopts CSR as a policy. So too when Generation Ys and Millennials, who are often attuned to global ethics and are being interviewed for a job, ask the company's interviewers whether the company has a CSR policy and practices. This is becoming an experience of growing frequency.

The Motivation for CSR

The business case for CSR was well expressed by one of the pioneers of the approach, Anita Roddick, founder of 'The Body Shop', when she stated that "Being good is good business." The argument is that it will result in more satisfied customers, attract committed employees, create brand differentiation, and achieve competitive advantage.

It will also serve as an aid to risk management and achieve long-term benefits from trading in a safer, better educated, more equitable, stable environment. Moreover, if businesses take voluntary action of the CSR kind, this will forestall regulation and will increase independence from government.

The Sceptics

Of course, there are sceptics regarding these arguments. Some say CSR is merely a cloak for self interest and profit maximisation, and the motives are questionable.

There is also a broader line of attack on the whole CSR concept by the likes of Milton Friedman, and 'The Economist' magazine (until recently), who simply say that CSR is contrary to the value and purpose of business; in fact it is not the role of business at all, and can also be anti—free trade.

Despite the persuasive language and argument surrounding the business case for CSR it is almost impossible to measure any causal relationship between CSR and the profitability of an enterprise, even though a significant improvement of morale within the organisation may be observed. It is also not clear whether CSR has contributed to financial success, or whether financial success has enabled the firm to 'indulge' in CSR.

This conundrum is well summed up in the statement, "*It is not so much a matter of whether profit subsequently arises from social actions, but whether profit or altruism was the main reason for the action in the first place.*"

The Moral Arguments for CSR

Given the ambiguity surrounding the real motivation to adopt CSR, its advocates often stress moral arguments. They include:

- Corporations can cause social problems (such as pollution) and hence have a responsibility to solve those problems they have caused and to prevent further problems arising.
- As powerful social actors, with recourse to substantial resources, corporations should use their power and resources responsibly in society.

- All corporate activities have social impacts of one sort or another, whether through provision of products and services, the employment of workers, or some other corporate activity. Hence corporations cannot escape responsibility for those impacts, whether they are positive, negative, or neutral.
- Corporations rely on the contribution of a much wider set of constituencies, or stakeholders in society, (such as consumers, suppliers, local communities), rather than just shareholders, and hence have a duty to take into account the interests and goals of these stakeholders as well as those of shareholders.

One way of conceptualising the nature of Corporate Social Responsibility is contained in the summation of the responsibilities of companies set out in Table 5.1.

Table 5.1 Corporate Social Responsibility and the social context

Corporate Social Responsibility	Social Context
Philanthropic responsibilities	Desired by society
Ethical responsibilities	Expected by society
Legal responsibilities	Required by society
Economic responsibilities	Required by society

Strategies and Stances

It has also been observed that companies have adopted several clearly identifiable strategies regarding these responsibilities. They have been categorised as:

- *Reaction*: The corporation denies any responsibility for social issues e.g. by claiming they are the responsibility of government, or by arguing that the corporation is not to blame.
- *Defence*: The corporation admits responsibility but fights it, doing the very least that seems to be required, or adopting a superficial public relations approach.
- *Accommodation*: The corporation accepts responsibility and does what is demanded of it by relevant groups
- *Proaction*: The corporation seeks to go beyond industry norms and anticipates future expectations by doing more than is expected.

This conceptualisation is taken further by experts in business strategies who have identified Corporate Social Responsibility stances which have been taken by firms and the role of leadership in each of the stances. This approach is also useful for leaders of Not-for-Profits and social enterprises in considering potential partners. For example, Angwin et. al identify four basic approaches taken by firms:[2]

- *Laissez-faire*: role is just to make a profit, observe legal compliance, pay taxes and provide jobs, defensive to outside pressures.
- *Enlightened Self Interest*: CSR makes sound business sense, reactive to outside pressures.
- *Forum for stakeholder interaction*: Good for sustainability or triple bottom line, proactive in social issues.
- *Shaper of Society*: engaged in social and market change, taking a defining role in society.

The outcome of these Corporate Social Responsibility strategies and stances may include the development of social policies, social programs, and social impacts. These might include country-based projects, community development projects, changes to employment and HRM policies and practices, refinement of purchasing and financing policies, health programs, education and training. Most importantly it will often lead to *partnerships with Not-for-Profits and NGOs*.

Incentives

There are powerful incentives nowadays for companies to adopt these strategies. Stock markets often have indices such as the FTSE 4 Good Index, which is an evaluation of the CSR performance of companies. Superannuation funds usually have a 'responsible investment' category. Social accounting standards have been developed such as various ISO categories, triple bottom line measures, sustainable development reporting such as the Global Reporting Initiative and Green Globe. The UN Global Compact reports on progress towards ten universal principles, and the UN Experts on International Accounting standards provide voluntary technical guidance on corporate social responsibility reporting.

A very pungent measure has been the UK Business in the Community/St. James Ethics Centre 'Corporate Social Responsibility Index' whose weighting of corporate behaviour is set out in Table 5.2.

Of course, there are many other incentives for companies to adopt Corporate Social Responsibility programs, especially where these involve intimate partnerships with effective Not-for-Profit organisations. This includes the sheer inner and outer glow which can surround the whole organisation in both tangible and intangible forms. It means a lot to the corporate community of employees and shareholders to be recognised as a good corporate citizen with a sincere desire to make a difference in the world by encouraging

Table 5.2 Weighting of Corporate Behaviour as part of Corporate Social Responsibility Index

Corporate Behaviour	Weighting
Corporate Social Responsibility Strategy	10%
Integration across the business	22%
Management of corporate responsibility within business across sections of community, environment, market, workplace	26%
Performance and impact in a range of social and environmental areas	36%
Level of assurance provided by participants	6%

recognising and supporting those who serve at the front line of bringing hope into the lives of the worthy and needy.

The Leadership Challenge and the Balancing Act

Thus emerges the balancing act confronting the leader of a Not-for-Profit: "How to maximise the benefits and avoid the pitfalls of partnerships with both government and corporate sectors?" For it can be a delicate act indeed. Essentially it involves catching and surfing the potential waves of support while avoiding being dumped or wiped out.

In relation to engaging with both potential partners, the dumpers can involve coming to see 'citizens' as merely 'clients' and thereby transforming a former personal client relationship into a purely contractual one. Another danger is becoming contract-driven so that goal displacement occurs and the aim becomes securing contracts rather than providing a service. It is also possible to become too dependent on donors, and even tailoring bids to donor's wishes. The brand can be weakened by too close a relationship with these partners, especially if they seek to take all the credit for the results being achieved. The credibility of the Not-for-Profit can also be tarnished by partners. Binding partnerships may also jeopardise capacity to lobby both governments and corporates on social and community issues of importance to the Not-for-Profit. It can also occur that the Not-for-Profit starts to mimic aspects of the partner's behaviour including becoming top heavy in staffing at the expense of front line resourcing and attention.

Taken to extremes these trends can cause a wipe out for an unprepared Not-for-Profit especially if the leader and staff start to look, sound, and speak like bureaucrats or capitalists, lose credibility and ruin the brand. There is also a real danger that close identification with one or other partner will narrow the traditional support base of the Not-for-Profit as its members become disenchanted or feel there is no longer any need for their support or funding. 'We' becomes 'they'. In short, the potential exists for the Not-for-Profit to be exploited and be seen as just an arm of government or business. In other words, it can lose its *raison d'etre*.

By the same token there are real potential benefits for an astute leader of a Not-for-Profit who can see emerging trends in both public and private sectors, identify niches and opportunities associated with these trends, and develop innovative ways and programs to help these potential partners achieve their goals without compromising those of the Not-for-Profit. The foundation must be a good fit between the vision and mission of the Not-for-Profit and those of its potential partner.

Benefits may include:

- Direct tangible benefits to clients
- Increased funding particularly for priorities in difficult arenas
- Support from a wider than traditional support base
- Enhanced sustainability
- Skills enhancement for the organisation
- Boost to staff morale
- More impetus to be able to mobilise the community to address the mission
- Enhance the image of the organisation
- Influence Public and Business policy
- Raise the status of the whole NFP sector.

In this scenario, the Not-for-Profit leader who is carefully surfing for partnerships will be catching the breakers for a rewarding ride to the shore for all concerned, especially the current and future clients of the organisation.

Notes

1. World Business Council for Sustainable Development. "Corporate Social Responsibility: Meeting Changing Expectations," World Business Council for Sustainable Development: Geneva, 1999, 3.
2. Angwin, Duncan Neil, Gerry Johnson, Richard Whittington, Patrick Regner and Kevan Scholes. "Exploring Strategy," (2017).

Bibliography

Angwin, Duncan Neil, Gerry Johnson, Richard Whittington, Patrick Regner, and Kevan Scholes. Exploring Strategy. 2017.
World Business Council for Sustainable Development. Corporate Social Responsibility: Meeting Changing Expectations. World Business Council for Sustainable Development: Geneva, 1999.

Leadership in Practice: Institute For Urban Indigenous Health

Introduction

Amongst all the issues facing indigenous Australians, health has long been the most important concern. With no discernible improvement in indigenous health over the decades a sense of doom and gloom has pervaded discussions of the matter despite successive rollouts of often well meaning, but usually misguided, government initiatives involving both incentives and penalties. The key focus for health, welfare, education, and employment, has come to be captured in the phrase 'Closing the Gap' between the indigenous and non-indigenous population, but little has been achieved nationwide to date.

Into this scenario stepped the creation of the Institute for Urban Indigenous Health, when four separate indigenous health associations based in different parts of South-East Queensland decided in 2009 to form IUIH as a regional, community controlled confederation whose key focus would be the improvement and advancement of the health of indigenous peoples of the region. IUIH is a company limited by guarantee under Corporations Law. Its vision is to reduce the disparity in health and well-being experienced by Aboriginal and Torres Strait Islander peoples in South East Queensland through access to comprehensive high quality and timely primary health care services, integrated with the broader health and human services system. The values of IUIH are laden with concepts such as community, cultural respect, holistic approaches, excellence, stewardship and collaboration.

The four members of IUIH who founded and now own IUIH are:

- the Aboriginal & Torres Strait Islander Community Health Service (ATSICHS) Brisbane Ltd;
- the Kalwun Health Service;
- The Kambu Medical Service; and
- The Yulu-Burri-Ba Health Service

Each of these organisations is located in separate parts of the South East Queensland region.

Some idea of the scale of health service requirements can be seen when it is realised that the indigenous population of the South-East Queensland, is more than the total indigenous population of each of Victoria or South Australia, more than two thirds of the indigenous population of the Northern Territory, and more than half of the total indigenous population of Western Australia. The indigenous population of South East Queensland is projected to be over 100,000 by 2031.

The Results

Past data has shown that the life expectancy of indigenous people in the region has been 12 years less than that for all Queenslanders, the gap being identified as due to cardio vascular (29%), diabetes (16%), chronic respiratory (11%), cancer (10%) and mental (9%).[1]

Given the magnitude of this health challenge the results achieved to date have been nothing short of outstanding. Since the founding of IUIH in 2009 there has been:

- An increase in health adjusted life expectancy by 0.6 years for all patients and 0.8 years for diabetics, achieved in just 15 months
- A more than tripling of indigenous patient access
- A 250% increase in visits to GPs
- A 2,500 % increase in 'Health Checks'
- A 500% increase in GP Chronic Disease Management Plans

The number of Primary Health Care Clinics in the region has increased from the original five to 18, also facilitating placements for 307 students across 16 disciplines. The active patient population is approaching two-thirds of the indigenous population of the region. Outside of government, the IUIH network is the largest employer of indigenous people in the region.[2]

Leadership Challenges

The leadership challenges of maintaining such an organisation are formidable. A key one has been the past reluctance of indigenous Aboriginal and Torres strait islanders to engage with the mainstream health system itself, including hospitals and General Practitioner clinics. It is often felt that they lack an understanding of indigenous issues and cultural factors. Moreover sheer practical matters such as inadequate transport and accessibility have proven to be barriers. So the fact that IUIH is community controlled has been crucial to its success as it generates a feeling of trust and empathy with the indigenous communities. It also is a key factor in designing services and support for indigenous patients which are tailored to their situation. Community Control is seen as the local community having control of issues that directly affect their community as well as being a practical expression of self-determination. So a Community Controlled Health Service is an incorporated Aboriginal and/or Torres Strait Islander organisation, is initiated by a local indigenous community and based in that community, is governed by an indigenous body which is elected by the local indigenous community, and is delivering holistic and culturally appropriate health services to the community which controls it.

However this has also meant a need to counter views of some extreme white groups (and occasionally politicians), who have attempted to depict community control as an aspect of segregation and even special treatment. There has also often been the risk that because governments have usually focussed their indigenous health initiatives on remote indigenous communities, there would be a strong temptation for them to attempt to mainstream indigenous health services in urban areas. Since the health results achieved by IUIH speak for themselves such views have been easily countered. Also the IUIH clinics are open to all and have many non-indigenous clients.

Potential for Innovation

The creation of IUIH was also based on the potential for development of 'new' models of delivery, and new business models to decrease dependency on grant funding from government by moving to a social enterprise model and becoming more community controlled. It would also facilitate the need for the sector to demonstrate leadership within indigenous specific and mainstream health system reforms. Coordination and integration would also open up considerable possibilities to achieve scale, consistency, and sharing of funding which could be redirected to emerging health challenges across various parts of the region.

Family

As might be expected the successful operation of the governance arrangements for the Institute poses considerable challenges. The unique design features a Board made up of four Directors each of whom is appointed by the four constituent indigenous health authorities and the Board Chair is selected from their number. They in turn appoint another four Directors who are skills based, and have mainly been non indigenous.

Integral to maintaining the harmony and synergy of the four indigenous bodies who make up the IUIH, has been the concept of 'family' which is deeply embedded in indigenous culture. However it has also strongly depended on the appointment of a talented CEO, trusted by all members of the family, who can provide the leadership required to maintain such harmony and maintain the focus on the main objective—improving indigenous health. The current CEO Adrian Carson, a well respected youthful indigenous leader, has proved adept at meeting this challenge even when some inevitable differences of view have arisen between some of the membership organisations. (In all fields of human activity managing any federation or confederation is always a hazardous occupation.)

Leading in a Hazardous Environment

Leadership in the very uncertain environment of indigenous health also requires considerable negotiating skills since managing the interface with governments and other stakeholders is crucial to the survival of the organisation. Given the complexity of the context in which IUIH operates this is arguably more of a challenge than that faced by leaders of large corporates. This is especially so in relation to the government interface since under Australia's cumbersome federal system responsibility for health policy and funding is split between national and state/territory governments. With often no love lost between the two levels of government, maintaining productive relationships with both requires dextrous skills on the part of the CEO, not to mention endless plane trips, and an acute antennae and other monitoring devices to measure the political temperature and wind direction. This is especially important since all governments keep shifting organisational responsibility for indigenous health between mainstream health departments, specially created agencies for indigenous health, and even Prime Ministers' or Premiers Departments.

Funding and Sustainability Challenges

IUIH is a Not-for-Profit organisation whose funding comes predominantly from governments through the healthcare funding systems. However this arena is fraught with uncertainty and instability for IUIH given the constant changes in government policies on health funding, especially that of the Medicare and health grants programmes which have been subject to constant tinkering and occasionally more radical overhauls including sudden withdrawal. The situation is not helped by the fact that both the Commonwealth and Queensland governments have operated under maximum, three-year terms, and elections are often held at even shorter intervals. This adds up to a very uncertain and unstable environment in which to provide leadership for survival and sustainability. Indeed, IUIH has occasionally been caught in such an electoral cycle when promised grants have not materialised or time frames for particular public health programs have been drastically shortened. In these situations Adrian Carson has convinced the Board that the objective of improving indigenous health is essential and the organisation should boldly step out, in faith, dipping into reserves in the hope that previous promised grants for programs such as the opening of new clinics in needy areas will be revived. This exercise of faith has generally paid off. Nonetheless it is all an abject lesson for Not-for-Profits who become very dependent on government funding.

IUIH funding sources are split between 65.8% in Grant Funding and 34.2 % in Non-Grant Funding, and the latest year saw a 9% growth in Non-Grant funding.

Rising to the challenge to diversify the funding base Adrian Carson has led the organisation into an array of partnerships, sponsorships, and entrepreneurial activities. The best known of these initiatives is the 'Deadly Choices' program whereby indigenous people are given access to sporting and cultural events and other programs and benefits, but only provided they have a health check and follow up on the results of that check. It has been an outstanding success causing a dramatic escalation in the number of health checks and ensuing health treatments. This program has also attracted the sponsorship and partnership with the Brisbane Broncos, a successful Rugby League team whose involvement includes publicity, support and advocacy for indigenous health and indigenous welfare more generally. Other sporting and business organisations, as well as Foundations, have followed the example and many partnerships have been forged.

The IUIH entrepreneurial approaches have also included commercialising the 'Deadly Choices' program as well as franchising the IUIH 'model of care' which includes skilful use of basic funding to address multiple aspects of personal health particularly dental health, establishing physical exercise programs including provision of gyms such as the 'Work it Out' program, 'Mums and Bubs' programs, and cultural programs including intergenerational forums with indigenous elders to improve mental as well as physical health. Indeed the focus on the health of elders and their continuous engagement is a prominent aspect of IUIH programs.

IUIH is fast becoming a social enterprise as well as a Not-for-Profit.

Leadership through Example and Sound Management

CEO Adrian Carson has a clear leadership and management style which has been key to the organisations' success. It includes as a foundation his philosophy:

- Leaders **build** consensus—they don't seek it. . .
- Leaders are positive about the **present** and the **future** of their communities— they can't influence the past but can determine the future. . .
- Leaders are **authentic**—they use their individual strengths and experiences. . .
- Leaders are **humble**—they understand the privilege and responsibility of serving their community. . .
- Leaders are **readers**—they are dedicated to continuous learning.[3]

Carson has introduced a database which would be the envy of every large corporate. Figures are readily to hand on health issues throughout the region, the take-up rate in engagement and health checks, the number of clients and their illnesses, the deployment of funds and staff, the comparative performance of all clinics, etc. This allows for evidence-based policy-making and strategy formulation. It has also proven crucial in approaches to governments for funding in an era when results based funding is the norm. The database is invaluable for management decisions, the best example being the location of transport needs for clients of the clinics. Transport for medical attention has been one of the greatest obstacles to provision of health services to indigenous people in the past and now IUIH has a series of transport arrangements operating across the region—a key factor in the success of the organisation.

The Board and staff of IUIH are significantly involved in devising the strategy for the organisation aided by sound work in use of the database and continuous environmental scans.

Fostering Leaders

The CEO is well respected and trusted by his staff, both medical and administrative. He has instituted an effective professional staff development program and paid special attention to identifying and training emerging leaders in the organisation. Carson constantly admonishes his team never to 'play the race card' i.e. dwell on past injustices to indigenous Australians. Indeed he seldom engages publicly in the many of Australia's often rancorous debates about indigenous rights, treaties, constitutional recognition, and perceived racism. His focus is steady on improving indigenous health although keeping aware of the perceptions of non-indigenous Australians whilst designing new initiatives.

The CEO has proven to be very successful in his liaison role with all stakeholder including governments, partners, sponsors, and the media. He is an effective communicator and advocate for his cause and IUIH effectively uses all the modern social media modalities. However getting traditional media interested in good news stories (which are abundant in IUIH) has proven very difficult. Carson possesses a good political nose and effectively establishes networks which keep him abreast of changes which are afoot in both public and private sectors. He is always innovative seeking new opportunities especially for the opening of clinics, seeking new funding sources, and exploring new modalities of service delivery. Many other regions of Australia are seeking to replicate the IUIH programs, and the organisation has received accolades and awards for its model of care and its sound approach to governance.

The CEO's outward facing qualities are supplemented by his inward management capabilities. He is open and accountable to the Board of IUIH and operates with particular respect for his indigenous colleagues. When a difficult situation has arisen in one of the four constituent bodies he has taken the positive step of sending in a 'Spearhead' to assist them in addressing the situation be it financial or management or human. This spearhead concept of using an experienced and trained person to assist parts of the organisation on a short-term basis is one that could well be copied by all organisations, including Not-for-Profits.

Future Leadership Challenges

As with so many organisations IUIH will have to be careful not to become a victim of its own success. This applies especially to the rapid rate of growth which it is experiencing in its client base and its staffing. Welding an organisation of its future size will be challenging, including ensuring that the organisation does not become too top heavy, making sure that amicable relations continue between head office and field clinics.

A key challenge is to guarantee that any risks associated with continuing and future funding avenues are well accounted for in the risk framework and monitoring of the organisation, because IUIH operates in a very uncertain environment. The past success in diversifying the funding base needs to continue to mitigate these uncertainties.

Carson himself has enumerated the major challenges for the South East Queensland Community Controlled Health Services as:[4]

- Operating and maintaining a strategic focus in an increasingly uncertain policy and funding environment
- Building the evidence base for Urban Indigenous Health and South East Queensland Community Controlled Health Services—including contribution to 'social determinants' of health
- Continuing to build leadership/capacity within the South East Queensland Community Controlled Health Services.

And what of the CEO himself? For all his many achievements and talents, he appears to be overloaded in terms of juggling his outward and inward facing leadership responsibilities. For the sake of the health of indigenous Australians, he will hopefully keep out of the way of buses, but it might be time to explore appropriate and innovative approaches to delegation and load sharing.

Message from the Chairperson

Whatever the future may bring in terms of leadership challenges the organisation has a sound base from which to face them. As the IUIH Chairperson Aunty Lyn Shipway says:[5]

> *"I am proud to state that the range of services now available to our people is at least equivalent to, if not greater, than that available to within the broader health system. Through our integrated approach to planning, development, and delivery of comprehensive primary health care to our communities, we have achieved a system of care that the various government reforms of the past decade have promised but failed to deliver. Our approach places the people-our families-at the centre of*

the system, with care and business models developed to ensure that our services are of the highest quality and sustainable." (5)

Kenneth Wiltshire
Non-Executive Director IUIH.

Notes

1. Stephen Begg, Theo Vos, Bridget Barker, Chris Stevenson, Lucy Stanley and Alan D. Lopez. "The Burden of Disease and Injury in Australia 2003," Australian Institute of Health and Welfare, 2007, http://hdl.handle.net/10536/DRO/DU:30046702
2. Institute of Urban Indigenous Health. Annual Report, 2015/2016: 4.
3. Noted in a presentation to Practice Managers by Adrian Carson, 2016.
4. Institute of Urban Indigenous Health.
5. Ibid.

Bibliography

Begg, Stephen, Theo Vos, Bridget Barker, Chris Stevenson, Lucy Stanley, and Alan D. Lopez. "The Burden of Disease and Injury in Australia 2003." Australian Institute of Health and Welfare. (2007). Retrieved from http://hdl.handle.net/10536/DRO/DU:30046702
Institute of Urban Indigenous Health. Annual Report, 2015/2016.

6   Financial Sustainability Through Leadership

David Knowles and Chris Wilson

Introduction—a Brave New World

The non-profit sector is a significant contributor to Australian life in a community, cultural and environmental sense. It is easy to appreciate this contribution to Australian life, yet overlook the non-profit sector's enormous contribution to our economy. According to the Australian Bureau of Statistics (ABS), non-profits contributed $57.7 billion (3.8%) to Gross Domestic Product (GDP) and employed over one million Australians (9.27% of the workforce at the time) in 2012–13.[1] Volunteers alone contributed 521 million hours of work, equating to $17.3 billion of value-added. As the table below shows, between 2006–07 and 2012–13, the sector and its contribution to the economy and Australian civil society grew considerably.

As well as experiencing a period of significant growth, the non-profit sector is also in the midst of a paradigm shift. Life for non-profits is changing rapidly, and in many ways dramatically. Non-profit leaders face a future that looks nothing like the past—one in which they must deal with changes in government policy, increased regulation and accountability, rising costs, higher funder expectations, the need to prove impact, systemic change, tougher competition and the impact of digital innovation.

Adapt or perish is not an exaggeration for many non-profits given what they face in terms of competition and change. Standing still is not an option.

It is worth noting that the recent significant growth in Australia's non-profit sector has been achieved without a proportionate rise in income or workers, suggesting the sector may have begun to operate on a more efficient basis.[2] While non-profits should constantly look for ways to increase their efficiency, building and increasing financial sustainability is perhaps the highest priority for non-profit leaders. The importance of securing adequate funding has certainly been reflected in numerous leadership surveys in recent years and there is plenty of evidence to suggest this issue will continue to be of critical importance. For example, in the Australian Institute of Company Directors (AICD) 2016 NFP Governance and Performance Study, 45% of respondents described their income in the next financial year as highly variable or uncertain.[3]

Table 6.1 Contribution of the non-profit sector to the Australian economy

	2006–07	2012–13	% Change
Contribution to Gross Domestic Product	$34.66 billion	$57.71 billion	67%
Income	$75.99 billion	$107.48 billion	41%
Assets	$138.06 billion	$175.98 billion	26%
Employees	889,900	1,081,900	22%

(Source: Australian Bureau of Statistics)

Australian non-profits increasingly operate in a dynamic environment populated by a plethora of new competitors and funders who demand results as well as evidence of need and intent. To adapt and thrive in this new world, organisations must evolve and leaders must change the way they think and work.

To build a sustainable funding base in this environment, non-profits must adopt an *enterprising mindset*. An *enterprising mindset* is not a for-profit mindset, although making a profit or operating a for-profit business may be an effective way to achieve mission-based goals. Rather, it reflects an astute, dynamic and commercial approach that recognises non-profits are subject to market forces and must compete just as hard for support as they strive to help those they represent. The dictionary defines *enterprising* as 'having or showing the ability or desire to do new and difficult things' and 'having or showing initiative and resourcefulness'. These words sum up the *enterprising mindset* non-profits must adopt.

What This Means for Leaders

Embracing and adopting an *enterprising mindset* requires a different way of thinking and acting.

To begin with, non-profit leaders must first of all understand and accept that they work for a social enterprise, in the broadest sense of this term. Social enterprises, in this context, come in many forms. They include charities, non-profit groups and a plethora of for-profit groups with either a clear social purpose or a commitment to shared value. In essence, regardless of form, a social enterprise is *a revenue-generating business with primarily social objectives, whose surpluses are reinvested for that purpose in the business or in the community, rather than being driven by the need to deliver profit to shareholders and owners.*[4] Respondents in the AICD 2016 NFP Governance and Performance Study confirmed that their top two priorities over the next twelve months are responding to changes in their operating environment and diversifying their income sources.[5]

Leaders play a critical role in securing the financial future of their organisations. With so much competition from an ever-increasing number of socially-motivated enterprises, non-profit leaders looking to achieve financial sustainability will need to be proactive, enterprising and results-focused. They need to adopt a performance-based social enterprise mentality without compromising their values or their true purpose as a mission-based organisation. While this may be a real challenge for some, it is actually a natural and necessary response to the paradigm shift currently playing out. In this context, leaders need to question how their method needs to evolve in order to achieve their mission. The method is merely a means to an end.

While non-profit leaders do not need to trade mission or values for financial sustainability, they will need to be brave. To be strong and effective, non-profits—like other businesses—need investment in people, systems, infrastructure, brand and marketing. They will need to demonstrate their impact and overcome entrenched ideas about the way non-profits should be funded and how they should allocate their expenses. If leaders are to secure sustainable funding for their organisations they will at some point need to argue for investment that reflects the true cost of their operations. This is just one of the many challenges and opportunities they face.

Funding Sources

While adequate funding has long been an issue for organisations in the non-profit sector, a lack of funding options is not the problem. It is important to remember that the non-profit sector is vast and diverse and consequently the availability and suitability of individual funding sources will vary considerably from organisation to organisation. The rest of this section is given over to describing the most common sources of funding and some of the contemporary sources non-profits are beginning to tap.

Governments

The relationship between government and the non-profit sector is integral to the idea of a strong civil society. Government has long been a major funder of the non-profit sector in Australia.

In recent times, the non-profit sector's reliance on government funding grew from 33.5% of total income in 2006–07 to 38% in 2012–13, according to the ABS. Charities also become more reliant on government funding as they scale. 'The Australian Charities Report 2014' released by the Australian Charities & Not-for-profit Commission (ACNC) reported that 41% of large charities received more than half their total income from government sources, compared with just 9% of small charities.[6]

With an ageing population and other factors likely to put future administrations under significant budgetary pressure, all levels of government are paying close attention to spending. Many Australian government agencies are reviewing the extent to which they fund non-profit institutions and the manner in which they fund social issues in a broader sense.

New 'funding' thinking is manifesting itself in a number of different ways. Examples include:

Social Impact Bonds & Pay-for-Success Contracts

As governments look to maximise the social and economic benefit of their funding, they are examining how to transition funding from activity-based block funding to an 'outcomes-based' or 'pay-for-success' model. This is evident in the introduction of Social Impact Bonds (also known as Social Benefit Bonds) by numerous state governments.

User pays/Individualised Funding

It is now common for governments to use their funding to stimulate efficiency, create competition in the marketplace and give individual beneficiaries greater choice. An example of this is the National Disability Insurance Scheme (NDIS), which replaces block funding of disability organisations with individualised funding for people with a disability.

Government Contracts

Competitive tenders open to for-profits as well as non-profits are another common means by which governments allocate funding. In recent years, governments in Australia have been increasingly willing to award contracts for social programs to for-profit entities, where historically such work would have been given to non-profit organisations.

While financial support is highly valued by receiving non-profits, it is worth noting that the importance of government funding extends beyond purely financial considerations. For example, funding can provide a seat at the table, which, in turn, can help an organisation influence policy and advocate for those they support.

Philanthropy

Many of our great non-profit and charitable institutions are steeped in a rich philanthropic history. Many more institutions were founded by and are run with the help of significant gifts made by generous benefactors. While some believe Australia does not have a culture of philanthropy, others see reasons to be more positive:[7]

> "*The practice of giving on this continent is eons old. The rich traditions of the indigenous Aboriginal and Torres Strait Islanders honour*

> *reciprocity and relationships with ancestral lands, nature and clan, and an assumption that wealth is distributed.*"

More recently, private philanthropy in Australia got a significant boost, with the introduction of Private Ancillary Funds (PAFs), then called Prescribed Private Funds, in 2001. PAFs have since become a popular structure for individuals and families looking to structure their giving in a tax-effective manner. In the 2013–14 Tax-Year, donations *to* PAFs represented 19.8% of all tax-deductible gifts claimed and donations made *by* PAFs to charities equalled $300 million. By the end of the same year, PAFs had already donated $1.78 billion back into the charity sector.

In addition to PAFs, PuAFs and Community Foundations offer Australians the chance to commit to philanthropic activity in a planned, structured way. The advent of structured giving in Australia has given rise to a new breed of engaged philanthropist, who operates with a focus measureable impact. While the philanthropic dollar is hotly contested by grant-seeking charities, philanthropy should be seen as a two-way exchange of value. The philanthropist can offer time, talent and treasure, and in return, charities can offer donors the opportunity to be involved in something important, while making a meaningful difference. This also means charities are in a position to offer donors and their families opportunities for education and self-fulfilment.

Other Fundraising Sources

The Australian fundraising landscape is becoming more competitive. A person need only walk down the street, look at their email in-box, check their mail or answer their home phone to realise that charities are competing hard and investing heavily to win funding. The giving landscape is also challenging for fundraisers. In 2013–14, tax-deductible giving increased 11.7% to $2.6 billion. However, on closer inspection, giving outside of gifts *to* PAFs and PuAFs fell 6.1%. And 102,751 fewer tax-deductible claims were made than the year prior. In addition, the overall proportion of taxpayers claiming a tax-deductible gift fell slightly to 35.1%, well below it its recorded high of 47.9% in 1985–86.[8]

The Australian fundraising landscape is evolving thanks to competitive pressure and broader societal changes, like the digital revolution and the rise of social enterprise. Some of the more popular fundraising methods employed by non-profits include:

Regular Giving

Regular giving, where individuals are signed up to make ongoing donations, often by direct debit on a monthly basis, has become integral to the sustainability of many of Australia's leading charities. The attraction for charity leaders is a reliable and predictable income stream that is largely untied. The downside of regular giving is evident in aggressive donor acquisition methods employed in practices like face-to-face fundraising and telemarketing. The practice of face-to-face fundraising, carried out by third party fundraisers (sometimes referred to in a derogatory way as 'chuggers' or 'charity muggers') has become particularly controversial, with participating charities now beginning to question their reputational exposure.

Community Fundraising and Events

Community, or peer-to-peer fundraising, has been very popular in recent years, to the point where the market appears saturated. Like face-to-face and telemarketing, many non-profits are outsourcing activities, such as sporting challenge events, to for-profit event management businesses. Like regular giving, this can prove lucrative, efficient and good for brand-building. However, non-profit leaders need to work increasingly hard to stand out from the crowd and even successful events can be criticised due to high event management costs and slim margins. Event fatigue is also a factor, particularly for organisations targeting affluent individuals who are likely to receive multiple invitations each year.

Bequests

Back in 2005, the Giving Australia report found that *"an estimated 58% of the adult population have made a will and of these 7.5% have included in their Will a bequest to a charity or other nonprofit organisation."*[9] With an aging population and strong property valuations, bequests represent a significant opportunity for charities, particularly when they are Willed without any restrictions or conditions. Some bequests also form the basis of a perpetual endowment. We need only look at Paul Ramsay's incredible $3 billion bequest to The Paul Ramsay Foundation, as a reminder of the transformative power a bequest can have. Building a profitable bequest programs is a challenge for non-profit leaders as the return can take several years and outcomes are difficult to predict. However, delaying investment in a bequest program only delays the return.

Crowdfunding and Online Giving

For many years charities have seen the opportunities that exist online, but many have lacked the knowledge and experience to successfully harness its potential. In Australia, we are now starting to see organisations that have invested in digital and mobile fundraising rewarded with success. Building or using an effective fundraising platform is one of the critical tasks facing charity leaders. While there is often a case for outsourcing platform management, crowdfunding, where members of the public are invited to contribute to a community fundraising target usually tied to a specific project, has shown the value of controlling an effective and efficient digital fundraising platform. As we have seen in the for-profit world with businesses like Uber and Apple, the owner of a digital platform usually has a significant degree of control over users of the platform.

Membership Fees

Sustainably financing membership-based organisations has historically been less complex than other non-profit institutions due to the recurring and relatively predictable revenue they generated through membership fees and flow-on events. However, as the digital revolution gathers pace, would-be members have found access to information and each other easier, quicker and cheaper than ever before. Building a compelling value proposition has become harder for many membership organisations.

Corporate Philanthropy and Sponsorship

Over the last decade, the corporate sector has moved away from 'cheque-book philanthropy' towards a more strategic and commercial approach to corporate social responsibility. This has seen charity leaders go from building key relationships with single decision makers (typically the Chair or CEO), to building relationships across boards, committees, leadership teams and divisions. These relationships are now more likely to be based on an alignment of strategic interests, rather than just passion for a cause.

Income from the Sale of Goods and Services

The non-profit sector in Australia has a proud history of innovation. What has been largely missing is the ability to turn that innovation into a sustainable, untied income stream. As the line between for-profit and non-profit continues to blur and non-profit leaders explore new avenues for sustainable funding, the social enterprise model becomes increasingly attractive. Economically-meaningful non-profits currently generate 41% of their income from the sale of goods and services and this figure will surely rise if leaders choose to adopt an *enterprising mindset*.[10]

Social Enterprise

Social enterprise has the capacity to deliver significant impact and permanently alter the non-profit landscape. There is an enormous power in tying social impact to consumption and procurement. Social enterprises offering quality goods and services whilst simultaneously delivering significant social and environmental impact will prosper. Whether they prosper at the expense of traditional charity fundraisers remains to be seen, but this is a distinct possibility.

Property

Two thirds of all assets owned by non-profit organisations are invested in Property, Plant and Equipment. Yet, rental income represents less than 2% of all income earned by non-profits, suggesting that property is not generally seen as an income earning investment, but as a working asset used for core operations.[11]

Interest Income and Endowment Income

After property, cash is the main item on the Australian non-profit sector's balance sheet.[12] Interest income can be significant and vital in helping to offset operational costs. In recent years, falling interest rates have impacted many non-profits, forcing some to review their decision to invest in cash.

In this environment, non-profits with surplus cash are considering the merits of investing it in other asset classes. With existing property exposure so high, many organisations moving out of cash are making endowment-style investments that provide a reasonably steady and reliable income stream in excess of that available to the cash investor. Some go further and invest in the hope of growing their capital base as well. Regardless, all those looking to invest for a better return must regularly ask two questions: *"Is it better to spend money now or invest for the future?"* and, *"How much is enough when it comes to building a reserve or endowment?"*

Debt and Equity Financing

There is an increasing awareness among funders that adequate capital is needed to help scale non-profit organisations and that core organisational infrastructure investment is critical if non-profits are to fulfil their potential and achieve their mission. This awareness is still in its infancy, but it can be increased quickly if leaders in the sector begin to advocate for it strongly. In his 2001 book, *Third Sector—The Contribution of Nonprofit and Cooperative Enterprises in Australia*, Mark Lyons remarked that *"capital is harder to raise (for non-profits) than for the equivalent for-profit organisations. It might come from borrowings, but in the case of public-serving nonprofit organisations it will often come from donations gathered in a capital appeal."*[13] There are indeed challenges for non-profits wanting to access debt and capital markets. Legal structures often prohibit a non-profit organisation from offering equity investments. Many organisations are not in a position to take on debt, which is often subject to lender restrictions in any event.

In recent times, impact investing has emerged as a possible solution to the question of attracting capital. The current reality is though, most non-profits are simply not in a position to structure a compelling impact investment product. Most are not even in a position to repay investors who expect to be adequately compensated (in a financial sense) in return for making their investment.

Challenges, Opportunities and Realities

The biggest challenge facing many non-profit leaders is perhaps changing the way they think about their work. To adopt an *enterprising mindset* a leader needs to move away from the traditional *non-profit* mindset, which can be quite limiting, without adopting a purely *commercial* mindset, which is inappropriate in a mission-based context. This is a balancing act that requires leaders to fiercely protect mission and values while being more open to new realities and new ways of working. The backdrop for this challenge is as follows.

Rising Funder Expectations

Funders of all type expect more than they have in the past. In an interconnected world, members are harder to please. Governments and major philanthropic donors increasingly expect evidence of impact. Even small donors want direct engagement and input with the organisations they support. Demonstrating impact is very important and useful and it can also be hard and expensive. Leaders need to strike a balance between proving their impact in order to attract support, using evidence of impact to better direct available funding, and simply getting on with the job.

Government Funding and Policy

Non-profits that are heavily reliant on income from government may need to adjust their business models in the face of government funding pressures and a general policy shift towards outcome-based funding.

Philanthropy Limitations

Non-profits cannot rely on philanthropy to meet funding shortfalls, because in most cases philanthropy will be unable to fill the gap. As shown below in Figure 6.1, only small charities derive a significant portion of their income from donations, while overall, donation income accounts for just 8% of charitable income in Australia. Obviously, philanthropic support is likely to be even more challenging for non-profits operating without charitable status. Donation income is valuable—leaders just need to be realistic about

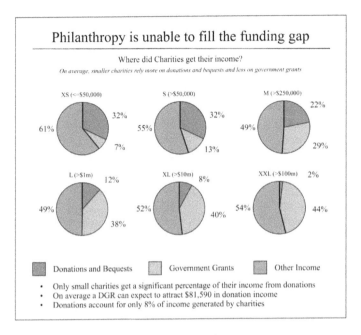

Figure 6.1 Philanthropy is unable to fill the funding gap.[15]

how much they can attract. The need to be realistic is especially important as giving growth in Australia becomes more concentrated and reliant
on structured philanthropy vehicles like Private Ancillary Funds (PAF) and
Public Ancillary Funds (PuAF) that can be challenging to connect to and
engage with. The 2016 Koda Capital Giving Snapshot revealed that while
tax-deductible giving rose 11.7% in dollar terms, 25% of all giving was to
PAFs and PuAFs, while giving outside of PAFs and PuAFs fell by 6.1%.[14]

Intermediary Risk

Managing intermediary risk is a challenge for non-profit leaders, particularly in the digital age. Few non-profits will identify as mere intermediaries,
standing between funders and beneficiaries, yet the description fits many,
to some degree. Intermediary risk in this context is the risk of rendered
partially or completely redundant by the creation of an alternative platform
that is able to connect people more efficiently and/or effectively. An example
of this risk can be found in the rise of digital crowdfunding platforms like
Chuffed, platforms that connect funders with communities in need, while
facilitating funding of community projects.[16]

Building Capacity Without Adequate Funding

Non-profits should be diversifying their income streams, seeking alternative revenue sources and taking steps to reduce their overall dependence on external funding. In a competitive environment, where there is uncertainty around government funding and philanthropic support is in short supply, every leader should be engaged in building a sustainable and reliable financial position. Building capacity while being funded on an activity basis is one of the main challenges for anyone facing this task. In this regard, the Australian Charities and Not-for-Profits Commision (ACNC) guide 'ACNC FAQ: Charities and administration costs' is a useful resource.[17] Growing self-generated and/or untied revenue has to be a very high priority for leaders seeking to build their overall capacity.

Presently, just thirty five percent of non-profit revenue comes from 'Income from Services', 6% from 'Sale of Goods', 2% from 'Rent, Leasing & Hiring' and 2% from 'Investment' & 'Royalties'.[18] These forms of income are invaluable to the non-profit sector and there must surely be a focus on growing them in years to come as leaders look at the sustainability of their business models.

Sweating Existing Assets

While seeking to grow revenue, leaders also need to ensure they are getting the most out of their existing assets. Two thirds of all non-profit assets are held as property, plant & equipment, while cash accounts for a further 19%.[19] In a low interest rate environment the decision to hold surplus cash needs to be reviewed and existing property commitments also need to be questioned. If a property asset is not contributing strongly to a mission-related goal or activity, the question of whether the capital tied up in it can be better applied must be asked.

Capitalising on the Digital Revolution

The digital revolution is an opportunity and a threat. Whether looking at availability of information via the ACNCs new portal or the proliferation of mobile apps revolutionising service delivery in sectors like health and education, it is clear technology is a major catalyst for change in the non-profit sector. Non-profits can't afford to get left behind. For many organisations, digitisation will play a critical role in terms of effective stakeholder engagement. Digital capability can engage supporters far and wide and it can also help manage reputational risks arising from greater transparency and immediacy in the age of social media. Of course, digital capability can also help non-profits address social issues, quickly and efficiently.

Valuing Intellectual Property

Non-profits are beginning to understand the value of their intellectual property (IP) and, with the help of technology, the potential to realise this value across traditional geographic boundaries. Potentially, IP is a source of self-generated income. Thanks to the global reach of digital technology, it is also possible to leverage IP for mission-related activities in a way that has not been considered possible before.

Fundraising

In most industries, individuals earning the revenue representing an organisation's lifeblood are among the best trained, best paid and best supported people in the organisation. Yet, in the non-profit sector this is rarely true. The Australia Post/GiveEasy 2015 Innovation Index of the Australian NFP Sector highlighted that people working in marketing and fundraising roles felt the least empowered in their jobs compared to other functions.[20] The bottom line is that most non-profits need to change their approach to fundraising if they want to get better at it. The role of the fundraiser must be respected, responsibilities must be clearly assigned and understood, and the role of the board must be addressed.

Building A Better Board

The non-profit board of the future is strong, skilled and active. Now, more than ever, non-profits cannot afford the luxury of a passive board, yet passive boards and passive board members are both common in the sector today. Building a better board and a board that is as focused on its own performance as it is on the performance of the CEO and the organisation is a huge challenge and an equally huge step towards creating an organisation capable of building financial sustainability.

Leveraging Available Talent

The future requires non-profit leaders to develop different people, skills and attitudes. Demand will increase for people who understand branding, people who, regardless of their official role, consider themselves as part of the sales and marketing team, people who understand technology, strategic thinkers and good communicators, people suited to collaborative work, people comfortable with transparency, those who are well-connected and, people comfortable with targets and a culture based on results. Although non-profits have several levers to pull (lifestyle, fringe benefits, purpose, etc.), for-profit organisations have always had the advantage of attracting talent with the promise of better pay. A challenge going forward for the sector will be how to attract and retain talent. If the talent isn't readily accessible, then the focus should be on how an organisation can unlock the expertise held within its support network (e.g. its board, donor base, etc.) to equip the organisation for this new environment.

Working in Collaboration

Demand for collaboration is growing among funders as newly-available data highlight duplication of effort and expense. While recent attention has been focused on merger activity, most non-profits will favour collaboration that preserves independence. There appears to be scope for much greater collaboration in the sector. The AICD 2016 NFP Governance and Performance Study reported that while 70% of respondents collaborate to advocate, only 26% share resources and just 15% share back office functions.*

The greater opportunity is to unlock the whole sector's potential by getting the other key players in society to work alongside it. For too long, social issues have been assigned to governments, corporations, non-profits and philanthropic organisations individually and tackled by them in isolation. There is plenty of evidence this approach has not worked. Now is the time for the principal players in Australian society to realise they share responsibility for creating the Australia we want to live in and can best create it by working collaboratively on the challenges and opportunities of our time.

Building a Strong Brand

In a crowded and competitive market, there is both an opportunity and a need to develop a strong brand identity to attract support from potential funders. There is real benefit in brand development, recognition-building and professional marketing, but for many non-profits investment proves challenging. For some, lack of money is an issue, while for others—ironically—spending available funds on this type of activity risks upsetting supporters. Winning internal support for this type of expenditure can also be challenging, with many non-profit decision-makers still uncomfortable with spending money on professional consultants and advisers.

Leveraging Good Governance

Many non-profits have worked hard to lift the standard of their organisational governance in recent years. Too often, governance is relegated to passive oversight, window dressing and box ticking, but it can be a powerful tool. The opportunity for leaders is to leverage recent improvements by

* See www.chuffed.org.

making good governance a source of competitive advantage when attracting funders.

What Leaders Need to Do to Secure Financial Sustainability

This section covers a number of things leaders should consider doing to deal with emerging challenges and to take emerging opportunities. Leaders will find some more relevant than others.

It is important to note that there is no blanket response applicable to all leaders. This is because there are many different types of non-profit, in different circumstances, at different stages of development. The path to financial sustainability will be very different for a small dance company, an operator of aged care facilities and a professional membership association. That said, broadly speaking, there are three things all leaders need to focus on, all of which fit with the concept of developing an *enterprising mindset*:

1. Forward thinking—embracing change and altering the way they think and work. This starts by spending more time looking at the world out-side to understand what the organisation needs to do to remain relevant and achieve its mission
2. Aligning people and practices—ensuring the organisation is ready and able to deal with a very different set of challenges and opportunities
3. Creating a platform for engagement—building the organisation's ability to successfully engage with funders and stakeholders in a connected world.

Specifically, non-profit leaders will need to:

Demonstrate Impact

The true contribution of the non-profit sector cannot yet be measured—as the saying goes, not everything that counts can be counted. That said, many things that count can be counted and measuring impact is a critical challenge the sector must accept. Non-profits must also dedicate resources to proving their impact. It is no longer enough to be engaged in a worthy cause, it is necessary to demonstrate how you make a positive difference. Adopting a framework to measure and communicate impact should be a high priority, as should building an organisation's evidence base. Simply accept that this is important to funding relationships and outcomes.

Invest in Their Capacity to Engage Critics and Supporters

In order to attract financial support and protect that support in the face of reputational challenges, leaders should focus on engagement, transparency, reputation and risk management. They must prepare their organisations for greater transparency and immediacy. The public increasingly demands it. Similarly, funders great and small increasingly want and expect to engage directly with those they support. The issue of engagement is such an important one that it may make the difference between an effective non-profit's success and failure. At a minimum, it is necessary to adopt an approach based on continually increasing organisational transparency. This might involve many changes and a focus on preparation, to ensure the organisation is ready to respond to external scrutiny. External scrutiny is increasingly likely in the future and speed of response will be almost as important as the response itself. Leaders should take steps to prepare for media scrutiny and trial by social media. For example, boards might examine key policies, positions and programs. Likewise, assets, liabilities and other commitments can be examined to ensure they fit with the organisation's mission and within acceptable ethical limits. To prepare for media scrutiny and test their responsiveness, leaders should role-play a scenario based on a real risk they have identified. Conducting an online audit to assess an organisation's online presence is another prudent activity to complete on a regular basis. What do others see and does it present the organisation in the best possible light?

Invest in Digital Capability

Technology is now so powerful and pervasive that 'switching to digital' is no longer a choice, but a necessity for the vast majority of non-profits. Consumption and communication are both going digital at a rate of knots. Investment in technology—and its application—must be considered not so much a strategy, but as something essential to remaining viable in the medium-to-long term.

For a non-profit, it is a case of 'your website is your shop front' and it is important to make an ongoing investment in making a good first impression. This investment extends beyond the organisation's website to its overall online presence. By way of example, potential funders are now almost as likely to assess charities using the ACNC's online portal as they are a charity's own website.[21]

To compete, non-profit leaders should first of all build digital competency into all levels of their organisation, so that they are well equipped to exploit technology, create cost savings and efficiencies and seize opportunities to extend their organisational reach and engagement.

Sweat Existing Assets

A lazy balance sheet can compound funding issues and reduce an organisation's ability to achieve its mission. Non-profit leaders should regularly review their organisation's balance sheet to ensure they are making the most of their existing assets. As 85% of Australian non-profit assets are held as either 'cash' (19%) or 'property. plant and equipment' (66%), it makes sense for leaders to start by reviewing these two asset classes.[22] Cash position reviews are particularly urgent given the current low interest environment. Many organisations are looking at how to redeploy surplus cash and some are now also starting to question their property positions. Some are beginning to utilise non-essential property assets more efficiently by deriving alternative income streams via redevelopment, renting or running mission-aligned social enterprises out of under-utilised space. Other charities are selling their non-mission related holdings to establish endowments that are invested across diverse asset classes, thereby reducing concentration risk, while generating a reliable income stream and capital growth over time, to fund mission related activity.

When moving away from cash, it is common for non-profits to establish an investment portfolio. Managing an investment portfolio is a task best suited to experienced professional. However, the BDRC Jones Donald March 2015 White Paper: The Challenge of Sustainable Funding for the NFP Sector reported that when it comes to management of investment assets 79% of non-profits use in-house expertise.[23] Furthermore it reported that only two in five have a documented investment strategy and only 42% have a written investment policy. It seems there is considerable scope for non-profits to make more of their investable assets and it seems a reluctance to pay for professional advice may be holding them back.

Leverage Intellectual Property

With an *enterprising mindset*, Australian non-profits need to build, protect and commercialise IP like never before. They need to think about the commercial and social value of their products and services in a global as well as local context. As technology reduces the tyranny of distance, information becomes more valuable to non-profits and leaders who realise this will inevitably focus more and more on the value of their own IP.

One final investment to consider in the digital sense is an investment in IP and data storage. Non-profits generate IP and often collect data with a social and/or commercial value. Thanks to digital innovation, non-profits now have more opportunity to build and leverage this value than ever before. Data and IP that might have been shared locally can now be shared globally. This fact alone has the potential to help non-profits advance their mission far beyond traditional boundaries and it also represents a new opportunity to generate much needed revenue.

Non-profits are now finding ways to selling their intellectual property to governments, corporates and other non-profit groups around the world. Leaders looking to follow this path care conducting IP audits to establish the potential value of IP produced by their organisations, actively building high potential databases, packaging and selling programs and identifying 'markets' outside traditional boundaries, where they might be able to advance their mission.

Mobilise Talent

Aligning *people capability* to the demands of the emerging external market is a critical task for non-profit leaders and one that again requires the adoption of an *enterprising mindset*. Sometimes this task means recruiting and sometimes it means upskilling or re-focusing people already working for the organisation. Retaining talent might have to involve spending more on training and development—not easy for non-profits but likely to be necessary.

Talent often resides outside an organisation, but within its support base. The next generation of philanthropists and supporters want to be far more hands on and engaged than their predecessors. Non-profits should be ensuring that they are ready to tap into this desire, using supporters for their skills, intellect and networks, as well as their dollars.

If non-profits are going to bring their full resources to bear—as they must—boards need to reflect on their own contribution. A skilled, well-connected, active and hard-working board is one of the biggest competitive advantages a non-profit can have. As boards focus on the performance of the CEO and the organisation, so should they focus on their own performance.

Getting the most out of board members is an issue for many organisations. The future simply does not support the idea that non-profit directors can act as passive overseers.

Building a more effective board can be challenging and is not usually an overnight task. The following advice can help frame a non-profit's approach to this critical process:

- Approach the whole task with an *enterprising mindset*
- Develop a matrix of valuable skills and perspectives matrix to help with recruiting and professional development
- Base this matrix on what market analysis and strategic planning needs over the next three-to-five years
- Agree a set of principles governing board performance and communicate expectations to new directors early in the recruiting process
- Create clear performance expectations for individual board members to drive good performance and establish clear accountabilities
- Create a comprehensive on-boarding process for all new directors
- Place a higher value on board vacancies. Be confident and present vacancies as a privilege and an opportunity
- Look in different places for passionate, hard-working board members. High profile candidates with distinguished corporate careers and full dance cards may not offer the most value in return for their involvement.

Review Their Approach to Fundraising

Non-profit leaders need to re-evaluate their approach to fundraising.

Non-profits should also rethink the relationship with major funders. Leaders should view all major funders as investors who need to be convinced and they should spend time with individual funders, to understand what a return means to them.

Re-evaluating the traditional approach to fundraising should also involve adopting a professional approach to every aspect of fundraising. Research conducted by leading US non-profit development group, Bridgespan, confirmed that non-profits who had successfully built large-scale funding programs did so by applying a professional structure to their funding model.[24]

Re-evaluating the role of fundraising also involves understanding and supporting fundraisers. In May 2016, the AICD, in its *Company Director* magazine article "*Good governance demands good fundraising*" article, reported on research conducted by QUTs Australian Centre for Philanthropy & Non-Profit Studies, which presented the two greatest challenges facing fundraisers as being lack of board understanding and leadership, in relation to fundraising, and lack of resourcing to undertake successful fundraising.[25]

It is very important to define and clarify fundraising responsibilities within a non-profit. Leaders must accept they have not just accountability for fundraising, but responsibility for it as well. Leaders need to work as and with fundraisers. This involves directly and heavily involving themselves in fundraising and relationship development. For many board members in particular, this will be an uncomfortable truth, given the passive role Australian non-profit directors have traditionally played.

The role of the board in fundraising is a particularly important and contentious one for many non-profits. Getting this role agreed, if necessary by establishing a set of principles to work towards, is likely to be a key task for leadership teams. Boards need to play a more active role for several reasons. For example, the kind of high-level skills and experiences needed for successful relationship building and deal-making are often in short supply outside of the board, and major funders typically expect, or at least respond well to, peer-to-peer interactions and engagement with people in 'positions of power'.

There is no single role for board members to play in fundraising and what is needed may change from time-to-time. Table 6.2 lays out different fundraising strategies and the role a board might play in supporting them:**

Diversify Their Income

Non-profit leaders faced with funding pressures and heavily dependent on a single source of funding need to look at alternative sources of revenue and consider the benefits of funding diversification. An effective way to begin

---

** See www.acnc.gov.au/ACNC/FindCharity/QuickSearch/ACNC/OnlineProcessors/Online_register/Search_the_Register.aspx?noleft=1

Table 6.2 Fundraising strategies and the supporting role played by the Board.[26]

Philanthropy or Donations Strategy	Role of the Board
Build the organisation's donor case	Contribute to and critique the case
Review projects likely to be attractive to donors	Bring objectivity to the selection of projects (e.g. those with evident social or cultural benefits)
Research the donor market by individuals and families likely to be interested in your organisation and its projects (linkage and interest and ability)	Use your knowledge of the community and your contacts to enhance the non-profit organisation's data and connections
Allocate team champions to pursue the relationship	Volunteer to play a lead role, where you have appropriate connections; inform the team's thinking on building key relationships
Build the relationships and enhance your knowledge of the potential donors, through regular communications and special events	Host/ attend social occasions, previews, first nights, work-in-progress events— any activities where potential or actual donors are being cultivated and board members can help
Build hypothetical donor cases for prospective good fit donors	Contribute to and critique the cases
Develop marketing materials directed to prospective donors— both for the organisation and for each project	Contribute to and critique the materials especially if you have relevant marketing, PR, fundraising or other experience
Make the approaches and hold initial discussions with prospective donors	Help to set up meetings, where you have connections
'Make the ask' or work closely with the appropriate person to make the ask e.g. Chair or CEO	Preferably as a peer of the donor, propose the specific amount and purpose (previously agreed with the staff); attend the ask meeting; personally make the ask on a peer-to-peer basis
Follow-up and confirm donation with a commitment	Ensure the follow-up occurs
Record any recognition or other 'benefits' agreed	Ensure that there is appropriate recognition of donors, and that this is handled systematically and in a manner consistent with the Tax Code (e.g., don't compromise a gift by negotiating unacceptable benefits in return)
Portfolio management	As a volunteer leader, manage an agreed portfolio of prospective donors
Confidentiality	Keep confidential any private information concerning prospective donors

Philanthropy or Donations Strategy	Role of the Board
Monitor progress and report regularly on performance	Require periodic reports to the board on progress, and on the review of progress with donors
Nurture the donor relationship—set the scene for future donations	Attend activities where donors are being cultivated or appreciated, and consider creative ways in which the relationship can be furthered

this process is to conduct a review of their funding mix—what is happening to it, what is growing and what is under threat?

These leaders should, with an *enterprising mindset*, actively and creatively search for opportunities to create new revenue streams and access capital. One way leaders are already doing this is in the nascent field of impact investing. More and more non-profits are sizing up potential opportunities to raise capital while trying to ascertain whether they are in a position to put together an impact investment product. The following questions will help a non-profit leader assess how well-positioned their organisation really is:

- Does an impact investment fit with and support your mission and your strategic plan?
- Do the leaders of your organisation understand the nature of impact investment?
- Do your key supporters and stakeholders have an appetite for investment and risk?
- Can you design an investment product that delivers a financial return for investors?
- Can you show investors how this return will be produced, after accounting for costs?
- Can you identify a discrete program or activity the investment will fund?
- Can you produce robust financial measurement reporting for this program or activity?
- Do you have access to advisers, brokers and intermediaries to help you access the impact investing community?
- Is there a reasonable prospect that offering existing supporters an impact investment will cannibalise your donor base?

Focus Their Philanthropy Effort

Non-profits relying on philanthropic support can better focus their efforts by paying attention to two trends—growth in structured giving and the increasing influence of women donors.

Structured giving vehicles (principally PAFs and PuAFs) are beginning to dominate the Australian philanthropic landscape and their continued growth should ensure they become more and more significant. Growth will come from donors contributing to them in the future and—because many of them operate as perpetual endowments—it will be accelerated by tax-exempt investment returns that compound over many years. To attract attention and support from the individuals controlling PAFS and PuAFs, non-profit leaders should focus on four things:

- Establishing personal contacts—relationships with founders and managers are crucial and often the only way to reach decision-makers
- Building relationships—philanthropy is relational, not transactional. Commitment, understanding and patience will be rewarded
- Communicating a clear value proposition—fundraisers need one to turn their appeal for support into a compelling proposition
- Helping donors—to give is to receive and most philanthropists are exploring. It is critical to take time to truly 'know your funder' and what can you do for them

Traditionally, philanthropy has been male dominated. Think of the great philanthropists: Carnegie, Rockefeller, Buffett, Gates and Feeney, for example. Women have long been a strong force in the non-profit sector and, as society evolves, they are now starting to become more influential in the philanthropic sector. The 2016 Koda Capital Australian Giving Snapshot revealed that a higher proportion of women than men made a deductible gift (36.5% compared to 33.8%).[27] Women also gave a higher proportion of their income than men (0.38% compared to 0.34%). Yet women are often overlooked as givers and as major donors, in favour of their male partners. This makes little sense, especially in a world where women are increasingly becoming asset owners, are earning higher incomes and are likely to outlive their male spouses. Moreover, because women are statistically more likely to inherit assets from their spouses they are also be more likely to make charitable bequests. This all means that there is a strong strategic argument that charities should focus more on women donors and should work hard to cultivate support from women in general—or else risk missing out on vital funding from the most generous 50% of Australia's population.

Collaborate and Partner

The case for collaboration and partnership is partly based on increasing demand from funders and partly based on the logic of experience. Numerous social problems have proved intractable, despite the best efforts of governments, charities and other non-profits. It is now easier than ever to obtain data on the non-profit sector and this visibility casts light on issues like duplication, concentration of effort and inefficiency. It is also making it easier for funders to see where collaboration can and should happen.

The non-profit sector cannot and should not be expected to address the social issues facing Australia on its own. Australia needs all the major participants in society to work together. This need obviously involves going beyond collaboration between NFPs to collaboration with other groups in society like business and government. NFPs need to drive this collaboration, not expect others to initiate it. Others might lead, but non-profits can't and shouldn't wait. Within the non-profit sector, leaders are exploring merger opportunities. Many more are exploring opportunities for genuine collaboration, to improve efficiency, resilience or impact. Everything, from consolidating back-office functions to joint fundraising and advocacy is on the table. This is work that needs to be undertaken in a strategic and well-thought-through manner, and with an *enterprising mindset*. A sensible approach to undertaking collaborative work looks like this:

- Get very clear on your desired outcomes
- Find partners with similar goals and values
- Identify the synergy
- Agree a common goal
- Confirm you have the resources and budget and that you can commit them
- Establish a clear framework for engagement and joint decision-making
- Accept you will have to adapt, learn and compromise
- Then make a commitment to the goal and each other

Conclusion

Significant change is coming to the non-profit sector and non-profit leaders must respond, in order to prepare their organisations for the future.

Leaders must quickly change the way they think and work in order to survive and succeed in a highly competitive sector that is evolving quickly.

Leadership will be critical to the financial sustainability of non-profit organisations and to drive good outcomes leaders must adopt an *enterprising mindset*, combining the best of traditional non-profit and commercial thinking.

Non-profits need skilled, and highly engaged boards that, inter alia, actively support fundraising in all its forms.

Acknowledgement: Portions of this chapter have been adapted from "2015 Koda Capital Non-Profit Review," "2015 Koda Capital Australian Giving Review," the "Koda Capital 2016 Giving Snapshot," and Koda's paper, "Preparing for the Future: Do or Die for Non-Profit Boards."

Notes

1. Chris Wilson. "The 2015 Koda Capital Non-Profit Sector Review," 2015, https://kodacapital.com/docs/the-2015-koda-capital-non-profit-sector-review_3.pdf
2. Ibid.
3. Australian Institute of Company Directors. "2016 NFP Governance and Performance Study: Raising the Bar," 2016, http://aicd.companydirectors.com.au/advocacy/research/2016-nfp-governance-and-performance-study-raising-the-bar
4. BC Centre for Social Enterprise. "What Is Social Enterprise?" www.centreforsocialenterprise.com/what-is-social-enterprise/
5. Chris Wilson. "The 2015 Koda Capital Non-Profit Sector Review," 2015, https://kodacapital.com/docs/the-2015-koda-capital-non-profit-sector-review_3.pdf
6. Australian Charities and Not-for-profits Commission. "Australian Charities Report 2014," 2014, www.acnc.gov.au/ACNC/Pblctns/Rpts/CharityReport2014/ACNC/Publications/Reports/CharityReport2014.aspx
7. Philanthropy Australia. "Philanthropy How to Guide: Effective Grant-Seeking," 2016, www.philanthropy.org.au/images/site/misc/Tools__Resources/Publications/Effective_Grant-Seeking_Guide.pdf
8. Koda Capital. "The 2016 Koda Capital Australian Giving Snapshot," 2016, https://kodacapital.com/docs/the-2016-koda-capital-giving-snapshot.pdf
9. Commonwealth of Australia. "Giving Australia: Research on Philanthropy in Australia," October, 2005, www.ourcommunity.com.au/files/GivingAustralia-Summary.pdf
10. Chris Wilson. "The 2015 Koda Capital Non-Profit Sector Review," 2015, https://kodacapital.com/docs/the-2015-koda-capital-non-profit-sector-review_3.pdf
11. Ibid.
12. Ibid.
13. Mark Lyons. *Third Sector: The Contribution of Nonprofit and Cooperative Enterprises in Australia* (Allen & Unwin, 2001).
14. Koda Capital
15. Ibid.
16. Australian Charities and Not-for-profits Commission. "Charities and Administration Costs," 2015, www.acnc.gov.au/ACNC/FAQs/FAQ_Charities_and_administration_costs.aspx
17. Chris Wilson. "The 2015 Koda Capital Non-Profit Sector Review," 2015, https://kodacapital.com/docs/the-2015-koda-capital-non-profit-sector-review_3.pdf
18. Ibid.
19. GiveEasy Pty Ltd and Australia Post. "Innovation Index—The Australian Not-for-Profit Sector," March 2015, http://ourneighbourhood.com.au/media/documents/Innovation-Index-Australian-NFP-Sector-2015.pdf
20. Australian Institute of Company Directors
21. Chris Wilson. "The 2015 Koda Capital Non-Profit Sector Review," 2015, https://kodacapital.com/docs/the-2015-koda-capital-non-profit-sector-review_3.pdf
22. BDRC Jones Donald. "The Challenge of Sustainable Funding for the NFP Sector," March 2015, www.sfg.com.au/__data/assets/pdf_file/0019/205705/FINAL_White_Paper.pdf
23. William Foster and Gail Fine. "How Nonprofits Get Really Big," 2007, www.bridgespan.org/bridgespan/images/articles/how-nonprofits-get-really-big/How-Nonprofits-Get-Really-Big.pdf?ext=.pdf

24. Daryl Kibble. "Good Governance Demands Good Fundraising," *Company Director* 32, no. 4 (2016): 50.
25 BoardConnect. "The Board's Role in Securing Philanthropic Support," 2015, http://boardconnect.com.au/component/rsform/form/146-lh1gthe-boards-role-in-securing-philanthropic-supportlh1g.html
26. Ibid.
27. Koda Capital

Bibliography

Australian Charities and Not-for-Profits Commission. Australian Charities Report 2014. 2014. Retrieved from www.acnc.gov.au/ACNC/Pblctns/Rpts/CharityReport2014/ACNC/Publications/Reports/CharityReport2014.aspx
Australian Institute of Company Directors. 2016 NFP Governance and Performance Study: Raising the Bar. 2016. Retrieved from http://aicd.companydirectors.com.au/advocacy/research/2016-nfp-governance-and-performance-study-raising-the-bar
BC Centre for Social Enterprise. What Is Social Enterprise? Retrieved from www.centreforsocialenterprise.com/what-is-social-enterprise/
BDRC Jones Donald. The Challenge of Sustainable Funding for the NFP Sector. March 2015. Retrieved from www.sfg.com.au/__data/assets/pdf_file/0019/205705/FINAL_White_Paper.pdf
BoardConnect. "The Board's Role in Securing Philanthropic Support." 2015. Retrieved from http://boardconnect.com.au/component/rsform/form/146-lh1gthe-boards-role-in-securing-philanthropic-supportlh1g.html
Commonwealth of Australia. "Giving Australia: Research on Philanthropy in Australia." October, 2005. Retrieved from www.ourcommunity.com.au/files/GivingAustraliaSummary.pdf
Foster, William, and Gail Fine. How Nonprofits Get Really Big. 2007. Retrieved from www.bridgespan.org/bridgespan/images/articles/how-nonprofits-get-really-big/How-Nonprofits-Get-Really-Big.pdf?ext=.pdf
GiveEasy Pty Ltd and Australia Post. Innovation Index—the Australian Not-for-Profit Sector March 2015. 2015. Retrieved from http://ourneighbourhood.com.au/media/documents/Innovation-Index-Australian-NFP-Sector-2015.pdf
Kibble, Daryl. "Good Governance Demands Good Fundraising." *Company Director* 32, no. 4 (2016): 50.
Koda Capital. The 2016 Koda Capital Australian Giving Snapshot. 2016. Retrieved from https://kodacapital.com/docs/the-2016-koda-capital-giving-snapshot.pdf
Lyons, Mark. *Third Sector: The Contribution of Nonprofit and Cooperative Enterprises in Australia*. Allen & Unwin, 2001.
Philanthropy Australia. Philanthropy How to Guide: Effective Grant-Seeking. 2016. Retrieved from www.philanthropy.org.au/images/site/misc/Tools__Resources/Publications/Effective_Grant-Seeking_Guide.pdf
Wilson, Chris. The 2015 Koda Capital Non-Profit Sector Review. 2015. Retrieved from https://kodacapital.com/docs/the-2015-koda-capital-non-profit-sector-review_3.pdf

Leadership in Practice: YWCA Queensland

The recent history of the YWCA in Queensland shares familiar themes with many NFPs. It is the story of transforming a collection of small, dispersed and dissimilar entities—all with shaky long-term outlooks—into a single, more dynamic organisation that:

- is strategically focused;
- will drive broader and deeper impact;
- is sustainable in the long term; and
- is relevant and suited to the current operating environment.

The YWCA is one of the largest and oldest women's organisations in the world. Established as the Young Women's Christian Association in England in 1855, the YWCA in Australia is now a largely secular organisation. It has a federated structure, and YWCA Queensland is one of its Member Associations.

During the last century, there were dozens of YWCAs all around Australia: charitable, grassroots, membership organisations that performed a hugely valuable volunteer role in the communities they served. By early this century these had followed the course of so many community-based organisations—they had either ceased to exist, or they had morphed into service provider organisations with paid staff.

In 2009, there were three YWCAs still operating in Queensland. While an outsider might assume that—with a global parent providing guideposts—these would be very similar, in fact this was far from the reality.

- One YWCA was a membership group that had been meeting for decades but, without renewal, was by then ageing and rapidly shrinking. It owned some real estate, and the members were considering donating this to another (non-YWCA) charity, and then disbanding.
- The second YWCA, based in Brisbane, was living off the rent of a CBD property and running some minor programs and women's engagement events that would not have sustained the organisation on their own.

- The third, based in the regional centre Toowoomba, was the most active and delivered a broad range of programs and services. However, it had succumbed to serious mission drift and was largely reliant on disparate buckets of government funding. Much of its activity did not look at all like YWCA work. It looked like what it was: moderately successful efforts to keep the doors open.

An amalgamation occurred in March 2011, and the CEO commenced in May. Her task was to transform this mash-up into a cohesive, value-creating, state-leading women's organisation.

Challenges Diagnosed

As it happened, the new board comprised mostly former management committee members of the city-based, engagement-focused YWCA, while almost all of the staff (approximately 20) had worked for the former regional, community service-focused entity. In early engagement with staff and board, the CEO quickly observed that the organisation the staff thought they were now working for was not the same organisation as the directors thought they were now governing; there was an alarming disparity in expectations and aspirations.

This reflected the fact that governance efforts up to that point had been focussed on the mechanics of amalgamation, in hindsight at the cost of both genuinely strategic thinking and anything more than rudimentary change management. There was at that point no strategic plan, nor even an articulation of vision or purpose, or a statement of strategic intent. The CEO saw that—even before considering external stakeholders—YWCA Queensland was already an organisation with an identity crisis.

Alongside this fundamental issue, she diagnosed that while certain parts of the new-from-old organisation did some great work with profound impact on the lives of a small number of individuals, it had the following challenges.

- No articulated vision or strategy with employee buy-in
- No real plan for long-term financial sustainability
- Too many diverse activities for its size
- Low reach and impact
- Limited management capability
- Low brand recognition and profile

There was also a lack of clarity about the ongoing role of membership. While this was not so much a viability challenge, it did increase the fuzziness and add a layer of complexity regarding how the organisation could honour the legacy of its forebears *and* engage new members/supporters.

Leading Transformation

So, how to address this nest of challenges? The CEO recognised that her task was to produce cohesion and coherence out of what felt at times like chaos; for this she would need buy-in from all key stakeholder groups: staff, members and their representatives (the directors), and external parties. She knew it would be a long and at times painful process, but it was do-able.

The identified challenges needed to be addressed together; there was not the luxury to address one at a time. The ensuing transformative work can be viewed in three parallel streams: strategic focus, staffing, and purposeful activity.

Strategic Focus

Alongside financial sustainability, which is a given, the CEO considered that one of the key responsibilities of the role is to be the custodian of the narrative. Every organisation needs a succinct, credible and compelling narrative about why it exists and how it prosecutes its mission, and a CEO needs to be able to articulate and 'sell' this better than anyone.

The CEO knew immediately that if *she* struggled to present the new YWCA Queensland (YWCA) in a coherent narrative, let alone in an 'anchovy statement', then every other stakeholder—internal and external—would struggle to articulate or even understand what YWCA was there for.

What the board of the time *wanted* the narrative to say was that YWCA did lots of great work to enhance women's leadership; indeed, this was their aspiration in amalgamating. What the organisation *actually* did at that time was provide community housing, disability services, a volunteer visiting service for people in aged care, a financial literacy program for school students, some training and employment programs, and also ran an 'op shop'—*none* of which were targeted exclusively or even predominantly at women.

The CEO commenced the long process of transformation with a visioning exercise, asking staff and directors: what would we *like* the narrative to be in five years' time? And in 15 years? What would we *like* people to say about YWCA?

The responses were tested, tweaked and retested until YWCA settled on a 15-year roadmap, a set of high-level five-year goals, a three-year Strategic Plan and a one-year Operational Plan. These documents articulated aspirations, prioritised current activities, and flagged divestments.

Even at this stage, the CEO was aware that this would be a stepped process. There is a limit to how much change is sensible to capture in a single Strategic Plan; while all such plans should be aspirational, they need to have some anchor points in current reality, and to not frighten the horses (primarily staff) with over-reaching ambition about a future they can't yet envisage.

So, the second step came later, in a 'strategic reorientation' halfway through the term of the original Plan. After a lot of consultative work with staff, directors and other stakeholders, YWCA was finally ready to commit to paper its intent to focus its activities on women and girls. The refreshed Plan that came out of this process will take YWCA through to its five-year and longer-term goal to be Queensland's leading women's organisation.

Staffing

There is no question that, upon amalgamation, the activity spread was way too broad. The reason this was a problem was the size of the organisation— the spread of activity did not match its scale. It was still a small organisation (approximately 20 staff and $1.5M turnover), which could afford little in management staffing. While there were some good service delivery staff, management expertise was spread way too thin. And while a CEO may have capability across many areas, they can't actually 'do it all'.

This is a very common scenario in NFPs: there is a single key manager appointed (e.g. CEO or Executive Director), who then discovers that there is a management vacuum between them and the next tier of 'managers'—often senior (and sometimes excellent) practitioners who have been elevated to supervisory roles with little or no management capability or training. In such a case, a CEO can very easily end up doing all operational management and very little strategic leadership—not the job they signed up for. Certainly this was the case at YWCA for the first 2–3 years.

Thus, a key driver for growing the organisation was developing the capacity to afford good, capable managers in both service delivery and back-of-house roles. This has been achieved through a combination of up-skilling and hiring. When an organisation is in expansion mode, adding new management hours is always a balancing act—there is a need to add and support new and emerging leaders, but also the need to have enough business to underpin these largely non-income-producing roles. An increase in turnover several-fold now provides a bank of management capability that was simply not possible before.

Over its first five years, YWCA undertook other significant workforce restructuring to align workforce capability with its planned future. As anticipated, this has not been without pain and has required probably the most critical change management process. The reality is that there will always be the early adopters, the later adopters and then those who may need encouragement to see that it's time to get off the bus. Willingness to embrace change is often in inverse proportion to length of service; however, some of the organisation's longest-serving staff are now some of its most capable and committed managers. The change process has honoured their existing expertise while harnessing it to a more strategic purpose.

Purposeful Activity

Activity that's not in the service of a clear strategy is just stuff.

Once YWCA *had* a strategy, it was easy enough to see which activities— however valuable to the individuals involved—were not a fit. Several long-standing programs were marked as exits, while others could be reoriented with a new focus on women and girls.

For example, the board had often wondered aloud why YWCA was involved in a (non-gendered) disability service; the CEO had observed that if it simply ceased offering disability services, financially the organisation would likely fall over. The win:win solution was to refocus this as a service primarily for women and girls with disability and looking particularly at their housing needs—a solution that aligns tightly with the articulated strategy, harnesses the organisation's considerable expertise in both housing and disability, fills a gaping area of need in the community, and contributes to YWCA's sustainability.

It was also easy—once a strategy was in place—to see where the organisation had high aspirations but little or no activity; this was especially evident in the (not immediately income-producing) areas of engagement and advocacy.

Once time permitted, the CEO set about devising some initiatives that would help position YWCA as the leading women's organisation in the state, *and* would result in income-producing work. Ideally, this would have happened sooner but the reality was that the CEO had insufficient bandwidth until some of the other matters discussed above had been dealt with, and there was additional capability in the management team.

From the start, the board had (not unreasonably) pressed for engagement and fundraising activities, particular in the corporate sector. However, as well as the issue with staffing capacity, in its first few years the organisation had neither the profile nor the products to make it an attractive partner for corporates—it couldn't yet deliver the goods. There were some successful events and engagements, but without staffing to follow-up, opportunities to capitalise were missed.

In truth, in terms of its positioning endeavours, in its first years the reality lagged perception. YWCA—through no dishonesty on its own part, but simply through public perception—was often believed to be bigger and more influential than it was. For the CEO, it sometimes felt like a case of 'fake it till you make it' or, in the words of a business advisory colleague, 'perception-led reality'. However, through purposeful and strategic relationship-building and related activity, the organisation now enjoys a justified and enviable reputation among key influencers and as a trusted partner of government.

Bringing It All Together

Turning the ship is a long, slow process . . . but it is turning.

Five years after amalgamation, YWCA has cemented its presence in Queensland. It is included in consultations, asked for media comment, and is well on its way to being the go-to women's organisation in the state. It hosts sell-out events and has a very popular fortnightly e-newsletter, which is a valuable conduit for remaining connected to its ever-growing supporter base.

In programming, it is building its reputation as a quality provider with particular expertise regarding women and girls. It has developed some valuable partnerships and, importantly, has developed 'product' that it is set to commercialise.

Its day-to-day work is now overseen by a highly capable General Manager, allowing the CEO the bandwidth to focus on longer-term strategic objectives. For example, YWCA has a lazy balance sheet, and is now investigating how to leverage this for long-term sustainability and growth.

The road to here from amalgamation in 2011 has required considerable investment, fortitude and a certain tolerance for failure; not every initiative has been a success. Commitment by the board, and its faith in the CEO, have allowed YWCA to stay the course it plotted in its 15-year roadmap. The future is looking bright.

Kate Tully
Chief Executive Officer
YWCA

7 Your People, Your Volunteers

Amanda Roan

Introduction

Building sustainable Not-for-profit (NFP) organisations is critical to society due to the social value they create including in countries such as Australia.[1] Over one million paid employees worked in Australian charities in 2014 while almost half of charities have both paid employees and volunteers.[2] Almost half of these charities reported that they had at least one paid employee and one volunteer.[3] The Australian Productivity Commission estimated that 4.5 million persons contributed volunteer labour.[4] Almost half of all paid employees in Australia's charities/not-for-profit sector were found in education (31.6) and aged care (15.3%). Social services and hospital services and rehabilitation accounted for a further 8.1% and 7.3% respectively. This sector breakdown indicates that not-for-profit employees include a large number of professional employees. In contrast, this survey showed that 44.3% of charities employed no paid staff.[5] Added to this is the managing of the estimated 6.1 million people who at some time take part in formal volunteering in Australia.[6]

These numbers reveal the importance of the sector in the labour market, a diverse workforce made up of heterogeneous working arrangements and, therefore, a considerable challenge for leaders and people managers. Human Resource Management (HRM), as opposed to the clerical function of personnel, emerged as a discipline in the early 1980s. With the growth in service and knowledge industries, the more sophisticated practices developed through HRM aim at improving the productivity of the workforce and fostering innovation and alignment with the organisation's strategy and operational environment. With much of the research and development of HRM being undertaken in the for-profit and public sectors, an important question for the not-for-profit sector has been *to what extent the principles and practices of HRM are relevant for the not-for-profit (NFP) sector?* This chapter will review some of the enduring principles of good HRM and examine the extent they are aligned with and challenged by working with employees and volunteers in the not-for-profit sector.

As HRM has the maximising of productivity and commitment of its staff as one of its main aims, the next section will briefly outline some of the motivational theories and accompanying research as applied to NFP employment. This will be followed by a review of some key HRM functions in relation to NFPs: attraction and retention; learning and development; and recognition and reward.

People, Motivation, Passions and Purpose

With the growth of service and later knowledge industries where the command and control approaches of scientific management were no longer considered appropriate, a great deal of research has focused on what motivates people to produce effort in the workplace. One outcome of this vast body of research and the multiple theories of leadership and work motivation is a realisation that what motivates people at work differs from person to person and can change over time. Hartel et al. summarise by stating that people are motivated at work by intrinsic factors such as friendly enjoyable work environment, challenging tasks and a genuine desire to help others as well as extrinsic factors such as money, status and other more materialistic items.[7] For leaders, understanding the balance of these factors is important.

Paid Employees

Although there is some evidence that employees of NFP organisations tend to be paid less than their counterparts in the for-profit sector, to an extent this reflects the industries where the NFP sector is concentrated such as educations and social services.[8] In countries such as Australia, industrial laws often determine wage levels although market forces can mean that the private sector is more attractive to certain groups. Answering the question as to whether some of those who work in NFP organisations have a distinct set of motivations is a difficult. Word states that there is mounting evidence to suggest that NFP employees are motivated by intrinsic rewards or a motivation to serve the community and the common good.[9] Quoting Light (2002), Word highlights a set of differences found between the responses between NFP, for profit and public sector workers.[10] Light's survey confirmed that not-for profit employees were significantly motivated by the common interest.[11] The survey also found that "about 75% of nonprofit employees disagreed that their work was boring in comparison to 46% of public and 54% of private employees" and "nonprofit employees were also less likely to believe that their jobs were dead end with no future, compared with public and private sector employees."[12] Although this is one snap shot, it points to the importance of the work environment in non-for-profit organisations for motivating employees.

This development of a positive organisational climate is supported by Holloway (2012) whose research supports the notion that leaders need to develop a close relationship with employees of NFPs if commitment to the organisation is their goal.[13] Kluvers and Tippett (2011) found "the success of the client" a strong motivator for staff in NFPs and this, and the organisation's mission, remained strong motivators even after the introduction of cash bonuses.[14]

Volunteers

But what motivates those who are not any-way-dependent on an organisation for their livelihood? Although it is easy to simply nominate intrinsic rewards, Worth (2009) reminds us that we need to consider the motivation of volunteers in two ways—"What motivates people to become volunteers in the first place and, second, what factors motivate them to perform at a high level and continue in their volunteer roles?"[15] At the beginning of this section I pointed out that people are motivated by a range of factors and taking away the need to earn money does not diminish the variety of needs and goals among the volunteer workforce.

Understanding why people freely give their time and effort is complicated. Batson and colleagues (2002) report four motives for community involvement.[16] Briefly outlined these are:

- **Egoism:** Increase one's own welfare. These authors state that this is the most obvious in acting for the common good and provide examples of the philanthropist who might endow a hospital or university to gain recognition and a student who may volunteer to add community service to their resume.
- **Altruism:** Aims at increasing the welfare of one or more individuals other than oneself. Commonly based in empathic emotion and the valuing of other people's welfare, a volunteer is motivated towards relieving the needs of the other person. Batson et al. report that empathy induced altruism appears to be directed towards specific others, it may not be possible to feel empathy towards abstract social categories such as the homeless or people with AIDS. It may also be short term such as when parents volunteer to organise sporting events while their own children are involved in these events.
- **Collectivism:** Motivation with the ultimate goal of increasing the welfare of a group or collective. Batson et al. state that these groups might be as small as a family or as large as humanity. They may be one's race, religion or political party. Although it may not be necessary to belong to the group to be motivated to help, we are more likely to be motivated to take action for a group with whom we identify, potentially leading to the existence of outgroups. However, unlike *egoism* and *altruism, collectivist* motivations can be removed from self-interest.
- **Principleism:** Motivation with the ultimate goal of upholding some moral principle such as justice. Batson et al. note that calls to act for the common good are often appeals to principle such as a duty to give our 'fair share' or care for our local environment. Although principles can be seen to transcend self-interest, the problem however is that knowing

when and how a given principle applies, as humans we are prone to conveniently forgetting or rationalising away principles such as accepting inequalities in society or forgoing the extra effort required to recycle.

Given this rather complex array of motivations and the broad range of circumstances and situations where volunteers provide valuable and essential labour, the question leaders need to ask is—does it matter what motivates volunteers? Pearce (2001) notes that with no direct monetary reason for joining or staying with the organisation the reliance on volunteer labour "creates unique pressures both for the volunteers and for the organisation."[17] For example, a substantial number of volunteers are recruited through personal contact meaning that volunteers are significantly more likely to report that friendly co-workers are important in their decision to stay in an organisation. Volunteering can often only commit 'spare' time as opposed to work time and family time. Overall, Pearce (2001) concludes that volunteering appears to be a less behaviourally committing act than taking on a paid job.[18]

A further example of the necessity of understanding the motives of volunteers can be found in sports organisations. Schultz (2005) notes the potential for volunteers to question the primary motivation of paid staff.[19] This can be particularly important when collectivism is involved as with a sporting club or when upholding a moral principle as in a religious organisation.

Regardless of these distinctions, as Worth (2009) points out "a considerable body of research on volunteers suggests that the factors leading to motivation and satisfaction are similar to those of paid staff."[20]

Managing the Relationship Between Paid and Unpaid Staff

Balancing the needs of paid and unpaid staff and diversity of working arrangements found in the NFP sector poses a challenge to leaders. As noted above, in Australia almost half of all charities have at least one paid staff member. Schultz (2005) points to research that shows the introduction of paid staff can lead to the change in the social structure of an organisation.[21] For Scheier, this change from volunteer-based occupations and organisations has been a historical phenomenon recalling that teachers and even police were once volunteers.[22] With regard to human services he notes that:[23]

> *It's difficult or impossible to do the job with just volunteers. It's equally difficult or impossible to do the job just with paid staff. Therefore, we are going to have to find the right mixture of staff and volunteers and make it work.*

For example, Schultz shows how there has been a trend towards professionalisation of management in sports clubs.[24] On the positive side this has been to overcome inadequacies and efficiencies deemed to occur in volunteer systems and a dwindling supply of volunteers. In Canada and Australia professionalisation has been linked to the political mileage gained by successful international competitions. Others report the creation of new jobs and professions.[25] Schultz's small study of differences between paid executives and volunteer managers highlighted different attitudes to the mission of the organisation.[26] Volunteers believed the organisation existed for the benefit of the members whereas the paid staff focussed on goods and services. He also found potential clashes in the spare-time/reaction perspective of volunteers and the boundaries around paid staff working time. Volunteers and paid staff also had different perceptions around the management of the organisation particularly the command structure and delegation.

Also in the context of sporting organisations, Taylor et al. (2006) found differences in the expectations and perceptions of paid staff and volunteers.[27] Using psychological contract theory, they found that club administrators had substantial expectations of volunteers "In relation to adherence to professional, legal and regulatory standards" whereas "volunteers were primarily concerned with doing rewarding work in a pleasant social environment that was able to fit within their often-tight restrictions."[28] Although much of the research highlights differences between paid-staff and volunteers, there is controversy in the literature around the extent of differences in HRM policies and practices required across NFP organisations. The next section will examine key HRM practices for both groups.

HRM Practices in Not-For-Profit Organisations

Attraction and Retention—Paid Staff

Staffing an organisation with people with the right skills, a high level of engagement and who contribute to a positive culture has long been acknowledged as one of the key objectives of HRM. As already stated, examinations of the NFP sector generally show that NFP employees tend to be paid less than they counterparts in private industries.[29] Being tied to short-term government funding and grants leads to temporary contract-based employment which may be unattractive to many employees.[30]

Research continually points to salary and conditions not being the first consideration of seeking work in NFP organisations.[31] Indeed, O'Loughlin states that "individuals who really want to work in the non-profit sector will do so regardless of higher salaries elsewhere."[32] The section on motivation above pointed to intrinsic motivation as the primary force in determining that person's work for NFPs. O'Loughlin found the importance of a 'defining moment' and the dual realisation both of the need for change and of the potential attractiveness of the NFP sector.[33] Leaders, therefore play a vital role in attracting and retaining staff and research points to two important areas for consideration: mission attachment and aligned values.

For some time now, various commentators have identified the organisation's mission and accompanying mission statements as an important management tool in NFP organisations.[34] When used effectively a mission statement can identify organisational objectives, give staff goals and directions and specify performance standards. Staff whose own values align with the organisations mission and values are more likely to enact these values in the services they provide thus upholding the organisation's public image.[35] This concern for image reflects current HRM concern for 'employee branding' defined as "the process by which employees internalise the desired brand image and motivated to project the image to customers and other organisational constituents" including future employees.[36] Indeed, commitment to a cause, being able to uphold personal values and to work for something in which they truly believe and the opportunity to do so in a community of like-mined others are strong attractors.[37]

Being attracted to an organisation does not mean a person will remain, particularly when circumstances do not support an employee's commitment to a cause. The support of leaders through difficult times and consultation and empowerment are critical.[38] The question then becomes what can HRM offer when pay, conditions and a sense of employment insecurity often undermine even strong commitment. Colleran et al. quote Hudson's employment survey as identifying the following activities as most frequently used initiatives for retaining staff in NFP organisations:[39]

- Flexible work (the capacity for staff to work when and how they want)
- Financial packages (the provision of tax-effective remuneration packages, thus increasing the remunerative value of otherwise uncompetitive packages)
- Leadership development (the provision of opportunities for training and experience—e.g. acting roles—to prepare for leadership roles)
- Succession-planning (utilising career planning and staff development to achieve retention)
- Mentor program (the provision of advice and support by an experienced person)
- Formal coaching (the provision of external coaching services for the development of staff)
- High-potential program (the identification of those staff likely to become leaders in the organisation, and the provision of leadership development support)

Attracting and Retaining Volunteers

Brundy argues that successful use of volunteers in an organisation rests on a deliberate consideration by the organisation of the rationale for volunteer involvement and that prior to recruiting volunteers, organisational leaders should decide on the appropriate goals for volunteer involvement.[40] It follows that volunteer-only organisations need to draw on the rationale for their existence in designing recruitment programs. The literature is generally in agreement that the intention to start, stay and leave amongst the volunteer population is highly variable and influenced by motivations, age, culture, role expectations and family situation.[41] To add to this volunteering can be ad hoc or arise spontaneously to meet a need on a short-term basis, may be an agency wide structured programs and may even be sought through a contracting agency that matches volunteers to organisations.

Hagar and Brudney state that there is no one size fits all prescription for recruitment of volunteers. Analysing the problems faced when recruiting volunteers, they identified a number of factors to take into consideration when recruiting volunteers.[42] Briefly, these are:

- Volunteer intensiveness or the number of and hours of volunteers influences ease of recruitment.
- Volunteer resource managers or an organisation's top management team have a degree of control over the culture and strategic management and can take steps to address volunteer management capacity (screening and matching volunteers, developing written policies and training etc.), broader organisational culture and specific recruitment strategies.
- A commitment to a volunteer resource manager paid or unpaid.
- The cultural tone set by staff who interact with volunteers
- The need to concentrate on only the most effective recruitment strategies in terms of methods and advertising.[43]

In their research into public charities in the United States Hagar and Brundey found that increasing the scale of intensiveness of volunteer usage helps to attenuate recruitment problems suggesting that organisations that use fewer volunteers do need to work harder to recruit their volunteers as they do not have mechanisms in place to find them. They also found that volunteer resource manager capacity may lessen recruitment problems where they can put in place specific management strategies aimed at enhancing the volunteer experience such as the recognition activities discussed below. This can be effective as potential volunteers must judge the organisation from what they can see rather than what they experience. Finally, they emphasise that using more and more ways to recruit volunteers may be counter-productive advising non-profit organisations to use the strategy they find works best.[44]

Although volunteer recruitment is complex and varied, it is not meant to suggest that sound HR recruitment practices should not be applied to volunteers. There is general agreement in the literature that the job description for the volunteer role needs to meet the organisational goals and the unique capabilities of the volunteers.[45]

Volunteers' attachments are sometimes described as precarious. Although some turnover is unavoidable as people relocate or other life factors interfere with their ability to volunteer, two factors stand out in the literature: the organisational environment including interpersonal relationships and recognition of service which will be dealt with in a section below. Lipp quotes the UPS Foundation research on volunteer retention as stating, "two out of five volunteers have stopped volunteering for an organisation at some time because of one or more poor volunteer management practices."[46] Proper management in Lipp's assessment includes competently designed jobs for volunteers; proper onboarding including welcoming and mentoring of volunteers; learning and development including ongoing training and support; and a culture of appreciation where volunteers and paid staff feel respected and valued (89–90).[47]

Of course, while the emphasis will differ depending on context the type of activity carried out by the volunteers, an investigation into volunteering in Emergency Services, Baxter-Tompkins and Wallace found connectedness and a sense of family were important as well as loyalty to the mission of the organisation.[48] Importantly, they ask the questions—what would make a volunteer leave the organisation? They found internal friction and conflict, issues of leadership style of paid employees and perceived lack of equipment were the major issues raised.[49] Along with managing conflict, listening to and asking for feed-back from volunteers, and saying thank-you, Lipp points to management factors such as not wasting volunteers time, understanding that the organisation is not the volunteer's number one priority in life and that volunteers may get overloaded and need on-going support.[50]

Learning and Developing Employees and Volunteers

Given the diversity of occupations, tasks and job status in the NFP sector the topic of training and development (T&D) is vast. As the discussion of retention illustrated, providing adequate training and learning and the opportunity to develop are tools for staff retention. The enduring problem is not only the development of a sustainable organisation but viewing learning, training and development as an investment and not just a cost.

Training and Development—Employees

Learning and development activities aim to develop and maintain competence in an organisation. Nankervis et al. maintain that although the desired level of performance "may be accomplished on an informal basis, better results are usually obtained through a well-organised formal training or a comprehensive on-the-job development program."[51] For all organisations, but particularly for NFPs, the delivery of cost effective programs is critical.[52]

Quoting Pynes, Blackmar and LeRoux list five key questions related to NFP training and staff development.[53] These are:

(1) 'How can we develop a comprehensive training plan to address the needs of managers . . . support staff, volunteers and board members?'
(2) 'What methods can we use to assess our agency's training needs?'
(3) 'How can we design and implement the training program?'(4) 'What

training delivery methods will we use?' and (5) 'How will we demonstrate that the training budget was well spent?'[54]

Those familiar with T&D will recognise that these questions are equally important in for-profit organisations. What is different for NFPs is that public accountability stresses demonstrating the benefit of HR activities for the mission and goals of the organisation—often within a short time frame.[55] This may be difficult as showing the benefits of investing in staff development requires a long-term perspective whereas programs may be short-lived.

Training and Development—Volunteers

As outlined above, the attachment of volunteers to the organisation can be tenuous with volunteers often needing to respond to other priorities in life when it comes to commitment to the organisation. At the same time, properly trained volunteers are important to maintain the organisation's performance and image. Despite loose attachments, the training of volunteers might be 'life or death' as in volunteers in emergency services or simply important for the satisfaction and retention of volunteers. One of the most important elements of the training of volunteers is the orientation program. Numerous commentators confirm that well-designed orientation programs reduce stress on volunteers, make them feel welcome and can reduce turnover.[56] Volunteers need to understand the job they will be expected to do, and have the necessary training, tools, and information to complete the job.[57]

Providing effective training in the volunteer sector goes beyond job performance. Costa et al. argue that creating a sense of community which is important for volunteer job satisfaction and commitment to the organisation can be enhanced through training activities.[58] Examining sports events volunteering, they observed:[59]

> *Event volunteers come together early in their volunteer experience (and sometimes for the first time) in the context of their training prior to the event. The opportunity to share opinions and experiences during training may enhance volunteers' sense of community because it is an early and tangible basis for interaction and indication of support from peers and supervisors.*

In sum, although the use of volunteer skills development covers a spectrum from executing basic tasks to leadership development for the voluntary board's members, the processes of needs assessment, careful consideration of method and expectation and evaluation as appropriate will enhance the organisation's capacity to deliver its mission.

Remuneration, Recognition and Reward

Pay and Rewards—Paid staff

Although employment relations regulations in many countries ensure a degree of parity between private sector and NFP salaries, material benefits are generally less for NFP employees. Indeed, a study in the United States by Yan and Sloan found that when salaries are above the medium it is unfavourable for donations overall.[60] The discussion above also emphasised the importance of intrinsic rewards, but it also outlined survey research that listed tax effective remunderation packages as a tool of attraction. In Australia 'salary sacrificing' as it has become known in Australia, "is used to increase the net value of employees' wages by providing them with access to their pre-tax earnings for a wide range of benefits."[61] Examining the Australian NFP community sector, Charlesworth and Marshall are critical of this reliance on tax concessions finding that it reinforces under-funding by government, nevertheless they confirm that it is a popular attraction strategy in the Australian NFP sector, although they dispute its effectiveness as a retention strategy.

Regardless of the influence of intrinsic rewards on working in NFPs equity remains an important consideration when designing a remunderation scheme. A long-standing principle based on Adam's equity theory is that staff will evaluate their salary and rewards compared to others and that this comparison may influence their behaviour and effort.[62] Although belief in mission and intrinsic motivation might partly mitigate comparisons with what is achievable in the private sector, fairness in calculating and distributing rewards remains an important principle in NFP management.[63]

Benefits such as flexible work arrangements and a positive workplace culture have largely been covered in the section on retention above. The research indicates that leaders must see salary and rewards as a package making sure that the benefits of working for an NFP are fair and adequate.

Recognition and Reward—Volunteers

The very definition of a volunteer means working without financial reward. The rewards from volunteering may be intrinsic but non-monetary recognition is also important. Recognition methods range from daily saying thank you, through certificates and Facebook posts to volunteer events such as luncheons and Christmas parties.

Cuskeley et al. clearly outline some of the problematic nature of managing volunteers as the lack of monetary reward means that a volunteer is not dependant on the organisation and so may be less subordinate to the organisation. They state:[64]

"Having volunteers recruited, orientated and trained for the job they are expected to do does not necessarily guarantee job performance."

Writing about sports volunteers, they note that the personal benefits of volunteering include work experience, tapping into community networks or assisting their child to participate in sport. Affective benefits include developing interpersonal relationships and friendships, group identification and associated group status.[65] Rewards may include job skills and the building of a CV.

However, the complex and somewhat self-serving nature of volunteer motivation does not exclude the notion that a powerful motivation for volunteering is the achievement of worthwhile and visible results.[66] Award ceremonies etc. reinforce desired performance and should be tailored to the individual volunteer's wants and needs. Brudney states "A heart-felt "thank-you" [emphasis in the original] can be all the acknowledgement many volunteers want or need."[67]

Conclusion

This chapter began by emphasising the workforce and organisational diversity in NFP organisation and the challenge facing leaders as people managers. Understanding motivation with an emphasis on intrinsic motivation is important. Although employees and volunteers may be attracted to working in an organisation because of its mission and goals, the staff and volunteers need to be recruited who have the ability to, or can be developed to achieve, appropriate organisational outcomes. Overall, in the absence of competitive extrinsic rewards, the organisation climate, often driven by leaders, is vital in retaining employees. Good HRM has a role in enhancing the NFP workplace.

Notes

1. J. Weerawardena, R. E. McDonald and G. S. Mort. "Sustainability of Nonprofit Organizations: An Empirical Investigation," *Journal of World Business*, 45, no. 4 (2010): 346–356.
2. Australian Charities and Not-for-profits Commission (ACNC). "Australian Charities Report 2015," Australian Government, 2015, www.acnc.gov.au/ACNC/Pblctns/Rpts/CharityReport2014/ACNC/Publications/Reports/Charity-Report2014.aspx
3. Ibid.
4. Australian Productivity Commission. *Contribution of the Not for Profit Sector* (Canberra: Australian Government, 2010).
5. Australian Charities and Not-for-profits Commission (ACNC).
6. Volunteering Australia. "Key Facts and Statistics About Volunteering in Australia," 2015, www.volunteeringaustralia.org/wp-content/uploads/VA-Key-statistics-about-Australian-volunteering-16-April-20151.pdf

7. C. E. Hartel, Y. Fujimoto, V. E. Strybosch and K. Fitzpatrick. *Human Resource Management: Transforming Theory into Innovative Practice* (Australia: Pearson Education Australia, 2006).

8. J. K. A. Word. "Human Resource Leadership and Management," in *Leadership in Nonprofit Organizations: A Reference Handbook*, ed. A. Agard Publishing Company (Thousand Oaks, CA: Sage, 2011).

9. Ibid., 402.

10. Word; P. C. Light. "The Content of Their Character: The State of the Nonprofit Workforce," *The Nonprofit Quarterly* 9, no. 3 (2002): 6–16.

11. Ibid.

12. Word, 400.

13. J. B. Holloway. "Leadership Behavior and Organizational Climate: An Empirical Study in a Non-Profit Organization," *Emerging Leadership Journeys* 5, no. 1 (2012): 29.

14. R. Kluvers and J. Tippett. "An Exploration of Stewardship Theory in a Not-for-Profit Organisation," *Accounting Forum*, 35, no. 4 (2011): 282.

15. M. J. Worth. *Nonprofit Management—Principles and Practice* (Los Angeles: Sage, 2009), 198.

16. C. D. Batson, N. Ahmad and J. A. Tsang. "Four Motives for Community Involvement," *Journal of Social Issues* 58, no. 3 (2002): 434–441.

17. K. P. Pearce. "Volunteers at Work," in *Understanding non-profit organizations—Governance, Leadership and Management*, ed. J. S Ott (Boulder: Westview Press, 2001), 327.

18. Ibid., 328.

19. J. Schultz. "Paid Staff in Voluntary Sporting Organisations: Do They Help or Hinder?" in *Volunteers in Sports Clubs* (Eastbourne: LSA, 2005), 40.

20. M. J. Worth. *Nonprofit Management—Principles and Practice* (Los Angeles: Sage, 2009), 199.

21. Schultz, 39.

22. I. H. Scheier. "Building Staff and Volunteer Relations," in *Understanding Non-Profit Organizations—Governance, Leadership and Management*, ed. J. S Ott (Boulder: Westview Press, 2002).

23. Ibid., 339–340.

24. Schultz, 37.

25. R. Baka. "Australian Government in Sport: A Delayed Elect Approach," in *Sport and Politics*, ed. G Redmond (Champaign, IL: Human Kinetics Publishers, 1984).

26. Schultz.

27. T. Taylor, S. Darcy, R. Hoye and G. Cuskelly. "Using Psychological Contract Theory to Explore Issues in Effective Volunteer Management," *European Sport Management Quarterly* 6, no. 2 (2006): 123–147.

28. Ibid., 23.

29. P. Cohen. "Non-profit salaries: Achieving Parity with the Private Sector," *Nonprofit Quarterly*, 17, no. 2 (2010), https://nonprofitquarterly.org/2010/06/21/nonprofit-salaries-achieving-parity-with-the-private-sector/

30. K. Akingbola. "Staffing, Retention, and Government Funding: A Case Study," *Nonprofit Management and Leadership* 14, no. 4 (2004): 453–465.

31. J. B. Bullock, J. M. Stritch and H. G. Rainey. "International Comparison of Public and Private Employees' Work Motives, Attitudes, and Perceived Rewards,"

Public Administration Review 75, no. (3) (2015): 479–489; J. O'Loughlin. "The Internal Market for Non-Profit Organisations: Considerations for Marketing, Recruitment and Motivation of Non-Profit Executive Employees," *Third Sector Review*, 12, no. 1 (2006): 57.

32. O'Loughlin, 63.
33. Ibid., 57.
34. E. Angelica. *The Wilder Nonprofit Field Guide to Crafting Effective Mission and Vision Statements* (Fieldstone Alliance, 2001); B. Glasrud. "Your Mission Statement Has a Mission," *Nonprofit World* 19, no. 5 (2001): 35–37; J. A. Pearce and F. David. "Corporate Mission Statements: The Bottom Line," *The Academy of Management Executive*, 1, no. 2 (1987): 109–115.
35. William A. Brown and Carlton F. Yoshioka. "Mission Attachment and Satisfaction as Factors in Employee Retention," *Nonprofit Management and Leadership* 14, no. 1 (2003): 5–18.
36. S. J. Miles and W. G. Mangold. "Positioning Southwest Airlines Through Employee Branding," *Business Horizons* 48, no. (6) (2005): 535; R. Wilden, S. Gudergan and I. Lings. "Employer Branding: Strategic Implications for Staff Recruitment," *Journal of Marketing Management*, 26, no. (1–2) (2010): 56–73.
37. D. Foote. "The Question of Ethical Hypocrisy in Human Resource Management in the UK and Irish Charity Sectors," *Journal of Business Ethics* 34, no. 1 (2001): 25–38.; O'Loughlin, 57.
38. I. Cunningham. "HRM in the Voluntary Sector" in *Human Resource Management in the Nonprofit Sector: Passion, Purpose and Professionalism*, eds. R. J. Burke and C. L. Cooper (Cheltenham: Edward Elgar, 2012).
39. N. Colleran, D. J. Gilchrist and C. L. Morris. "Staff Retention Factors in the Non-Profit Sector: An Examination of a West Australian Community Organisation," *Third Sector Review* 16, no. 3, 43 (2010): 46–47; Hudson Report. "Australia, Employment and HR Trends, Part Two: HR Insights, Engaging and Retaining Talent within a Complex Employment Landscape," 2007, http://au.hudson. com/documents/AU-Hudson-Report-Nov07-HR-Insights.pdf
40. J. L. Brudney. "Volunteer Administration," in *Understanding Non-Profit Organizations—Governance, Leadership and Management*, ed. J. S Ott (Boulder: Westview Press, 2001), 330–331.
41. T. Taylor, S. Darcy, R. Hoye and G. Cuskelly. "Using Psychological Contract Theory to Explore Issues in Effective Volunteer Management," *European Sport Management Quarterly* 6, no. 2 (2006): 123–147.
42. M. A. Hager and J. L. Brudney. "Problems Recruiting Volunteers: Nature Versus Nurture," *Nonprofit Management and Leadership* 22, no. 2 (2011): 137–157.
43. Ibid., 141–143.
44. Ibid., 142.
45. Brudney; E. G. Clary, M. Snyder and R. Ridge. "Volunteers' Motivations: A Functional Strategy for the Recruitment, Placement, and Retention of Volunteers," *Nonprofit Management and Leadership* 2, no. 4 (1992): 333–350.
46. A. L. Lipp. "Keeping the Volunteers You Have," in *Volunteer Engagement: Ideas and Insights Changing the World*, ed. R. J. Rosenthal (Hoboken, NJ: John Wiley and Sons, 2015), 89.
47. Ibid., 89–90.
48. T. Baxter-Tomkins and M. Wallace. "Recruitment and Retention of Volunteers in Emergency Services," *Australian Journal on Volunteering*, 14, no. 39 (2009).

49. Ibid., 6.
50. Lipp, 93–95.
51. A. R. Nankervis, M. Baird, J. Coffey and J. Shields. *Human Resource Management— Strategic and Practice* (South Melbourne: Cengage learning, 2017), 289.
52. Jeanette Blackmar and Kelly LeRoux. "8. Enhancing Learning and Skill Development Among paid Staff and Volunteers in Nonprofit Organizations," *Human Resource Management in the Nonprofit Sector: Passion, Purpose and Professionalism* 178 (2012).
53. Blackmar and LeRoux; Joan E. Pynes. *Human Resources Management for Public and Nonprofit Organizations: A StrategicApproach* (San Francisco, CA: Jossey-Bass, 2009).
54. Jeanette Blackmar and Kelly LeRoux. "8. Enhancing learning and skill development among paid staff and volunteers in nonprofit organizations." Human Resource Management in the Nonprofit Sector: Passion, Purpose and Professionalism 178 (2012): 182; Pynes, 310.
55. Kevin P. Kearns. "Private Sector Strategies for Social Sector Success," *San Francisco: Jossey-Bass Publishers* 15 (2000): 44–45; Blackmar and LeRoux.
56. G. Cuskelly, R. Hoye and C. Auld. *Working with Volunteers in Sport* (Oxon: Routhledge, 2006); Elizabeth R. Harp, Lisa L. Scherer and Joseph A. Allen. "Volunteer Engagement and Retention: Their Relationship to Community Service Self-Efficacy," *Nonprofit and Voluntary Sector Quarterly* 46, no. 2 (2017): 442–458.
57. Harp, Scherer and Allen.
58. C. A. Costa, L. Chalip, B. C. Green and C. Simes. "Reconsidering the Role of Training in Event Volunteers' Satisfaction," *Sport Management Review*, 9, no. 2 (2006): 165–182.
59. Ibid., 178.
60. W. Yan and M. F. Sloan. "The Impact of Employee Compensation and Financial Performance on Nonprofit Organization Donations," *The American Review of Public Administration*, 46, no. 2 (2016): 243–258.
61. S. Charlesworth and H. Marshall. "Sacrificing Workers?" *International Journal of Public Sector Management*, 24, no. 7 (2011): 674. doi: 10.1108/09513551111172495.
62. J. S. Adams. "Inequity in Social Exchange," *Advances in Experimental Social Psychology*, 2 (1965): 267–299; R. Kramar, T. Bartram, H. De Cieri, R. A. Noe, J. R. Hollenbeck, B. Gerhart and P.M. Wright. *Human Resource Management in Australia: Strategy, People, Performance* (North Ryde: McGraw-Hill Australia Pty Limited, 2014).
63. N. E. Day. "Compensation: Towards Rewards Programs in Non-Profit Organisations," in *The Jossey-Bass Handbook of Nonprofit Leadership and Management*, eds. D. O. Renz and R. D. Herman. Jossy (John Wiley & Sons, Inc: Wiley online library, 2016).
64. G. Cuskelly, R. Hoye and C. Auld. *Working with Volunteers in Sport* (Oxon: Routhledge, 2006), 86.
65. Ibid., 89.
66. Brudney, 335.
67. Ibid., 336.

Bibliography

Adams, J. S. "Inequity in Social Exchange." *Advances in Experimental Social Psychology* 2 (1965): 267–99.

Akingbola, K. "Staffing, Retention, and Government Funding: A Case Study." *Nonprofit Management and Leadership* 14, no. 4 (2004): 453–65.

Angelica, E. *The Wilder Nonprofit Field Guide to Crafting Effective Mission and Vision Statements.* Fieldstone Alliance, 2001.

Australian Charities and Not-for-Profits Commission (ACNC). *Australian Charities Report 2015.* Australian Government, 2015. Retrieved from www.acnc.gov.au/ACNC/Pblctns/Rpts/CharityReport2014/ACNC/Publications/Reports/CharityReport2014.aspx

Australian Productivity Commission. *Contribution of the Not for Profit Sector.* Canberra: Australian Government, 2010.

Baka, R. "Australian Government in Sport: A Delayed Elect Approach." In *Sport and Politics*, ed. G. Redmond. Champaign, IL: Human Kinetics Publishers, 1984.

Batson, C. D., N. Ahmad, and J. A. Tsang. "Four Motives for Community Involvement." *Journal of Social Issues* 58, no. 3 (2002): 429–45.

Baxter-Tomkins, T., and M. Wallace. "Recruitment and Retention of Volunteers in Emergency Services." *Australian Journal on Volunteering* 14, no. 39 (2009).

Blackmar, Jeannette, and Kelly LeRoux. "8. Enhancing Learning and Skill Development Among Paid Staff and Volunteers in Nonprofit Organizations." In *Human Resource Management in the Nonprofit Sector: Passion, Purpose and Professionalism*, edited by Ronald J. Burke and Cary L. Cooper. Cheltenham, UK: New Hortizons in Management, Edward Elgar, 2012.

Brown, William A., and Carlton F. Yoshioka. "Mission Attachment and Satisfaction as Factors in Employee Retention." *Nonprofit Management and Leadership* 14, no. 1 (2003): 5–18.

Brudney, J. L. "Volunteer Administration." In *Understanding Non-Profit Organizations—Governance, Leadership and Management*, ed. J. S Ott. Boulder: Westview Press, 2001.

Bullock, J. B., J. M. Stritch, and H. G. Rainey. "International Comparison of Public and Private Employees' Work Motives, Attitudes, and Perceived Rewards." *Public Administration Review* 75, no. 3 (2015): 479–89.

Charlesworth, S., and H. Marshall. "Sacrificing Workers?" *International Journal of Public Sector Management* 24, no. 7 (2011): 673–683. doi: 10.1108/09513551111172495.

Clary, E. G., M. Snyder, and R. Ridge. "Volunteers' Motivations: A Functional Strategy for the Recruitment, Placement, and Retention of Volunteers." *Nonprofit Management and Leadership* 2, no. 4 (1992): 333–50.

Cohen, P. "Non-Profit Salaries: Achieving Parity With the Private Sector." *Nonprofit Quarterly* 17, no. 2 (2010). https://nonprofitquarterly.org/2010/06/21/nonprofit-salaries-achieving-parity-with-the-private-sector/

Colleran, N., D. J. Gilchrist, and C. L. Morris. "Staff Retention Factors in the Non-Profit Sector: An Examination of a West Australian Community Organisation." *Third Sector Review* 16, no. 3, 43, 2010.

Costa, C. A., L. Chalip, B. C. Green, and C. Simes. "Reconsidering the Role of Training in Event Volunteers' Satisfaction." *Sport Management Review* 9, no. 2, (2006): 165–82.

Cunningham, I. "HRM in the Voluntary Sector," In *Human Resource Management in the Nonprofit Sector: Passion, Purpose and Professionalism*, eds R. J. Burke and C. L. Cooper. Cheltenham: Edward Elgar, 2012.

Cuskelly, G., R. Hoye, and C. Auld. *Working With Volunteers in Sport*. Oxon: Routhledge, 2006.

Day, N. E. "Compensation: Towards Rewards Programs in Non-Profit Organisations." In *The Jossey-Bass Handbook of Nonprofit Leadership and Management*, eds. D. O. Renz and R. D. Herman. Jossy John Wiley & Sons, Inc: Wiley online library, 2016.

Foote, D. "The Question of Ethical Hypocrisy in Human Resource Management in the UK and Irish Charity Sectors." *Journal of Business Ethics* 34, no. 1 (2001): 25–38.

Glasrud, B. "Your Mission Statement Has a Mission." *Nonprofit World* 19, no. 5 (2001): 35–7.

Hager, M. A., and J. L. Brudney. "Problems Recruiting Volunteers: Nature Versus Nurture." *Nonprofit Management and Leadership* 22, no. 2 (2011): 137–57.

Harp, Elizabeth R., Lisa L. Scherer, and Joseph A. Allen. "Volunteer Engagement and Retention: Their Relationship to Community Service Self-Efficacy." *Nonprofit and Voluntary Sector Quarterly* 46, no. 2 (2017): 442–58.

Hartel, C. E., Y. Fujimoto, V. E. Strybosch, and K. Fitzpatrick. *Human Resource Management: Transforming Theory Into Innovative Practice*. Australia: Pearson Education, 2006.

Holloway, J. B. "Leadership Behavior and Organizational Climate: An Empirical Study in a Non-Profit Organization." *Emerging Leadership Journeys* 5, no. 1 (2012): 9–35.

Hudson Report. Australia, Employment and HR Trends, Part Two: HR Insights, Engaging and Retaining Talent Within a Complex Employment Landscape. 2007. Retrieved from http://au.hudson. com/documents/AU-Hudson-Report-Nov07-HR-Insights.pdf

Kearns, Kevin P. "Private Sector Strategies for Social Sector Success." *San Francisco: Jossey-Bass Publishers* 15 (2000): 44–5.

Kluvers, R., and J. Tippett. "An Exploration of Stewardship Theory in a Not-for-Profit Organisation." *Accounting Forum* 35, no. 4 (2011): 275–84.

Kramar, R., T. Bartram, H. De Cieri, R. A.Noe, J. R. Hollenbeck, B. Gerhart, and P. M. Wright. *Human Resource Management in Australia: Strategy, People, Performance*. North Ryde: McGraw-Hill Australia Pty Limited, 2014.

Light, P. C. "The Content of Their Character: The State of the Nonprofit Workforce." *The Nonprofit Quarterly* 9, no. 3 (2002): 6–16.

Lipp, A. L. "Keeping the Volunteers You Have." In *Volunteer Engagement: Ideas and Insights Changing the World*, ed. R. J. Rosenthal. Hoboken, NJ: John Wiley and Sons, 2015.

Miles, S. J., and W. G. Mangold. "Positioning Southwest Airlines Through Employee Branding." *Business Horizons* 48, no. 6 (2005): 535–45.

Nankervis, A. R., M. Baird, J. Coffey J. Shields. *Human Resource Management—Strategic and Practice*. South Melbourne: Cengage learning, 2017.

O'Loughlin, J. "The Internal Market for Non-Profit Organisations: Considerations for Marketing, Recruitment and Motivation of Non-Profit Executive Employees." *Third Sector Review* 12, no. 1 (2006): 57.

Pearce, K. P. "Volunteers at Work." In *Understanding Non-Profit Organizations—Governance, Leadership and Management*, ed. J. S. Ott. Boulder: Westview Press, 2001.

Pearce, J. A., and F. David. "Corporate Mission Statements: The Bottom Line." *The Academy of Management Executive* 1, no. 2 (1987): 109–15.

Pynes, Joan E. *Human Resources Management for Public and Nonprofit Organizations: A StrategicApproach*. San Francisco, CA: Jossey-Bass, 2009.

Scheier, I. H. "Building Staff and Volunteer Relations." In *Understanding Non-Profit Organizations—Governance, Leadership and Management*, ed. J. S. Ott. Boulder: Westview Press, 2002.

Schultz, J. "Paid Staff in Voluntary Sporting Organisations. Do They Help or Hinder?" In *Volunteers in Sports Clubs*. Eastbourne: LSA, 2005.

Taylor, T., S. Darcy, R. Hoye, and G. Cuskelly. "Using Psychological Contract Theory to Explore Issues in Effective Volunteer Management." *European Sport Management Quarterly* 6, no. 2 (2006): 123–47.

Venzin, M. "Inexpensive and Creative Volunteer Recognition Ideas." *The Volunteer Management Report* 20, no. 8 (2015): 4–4.

Volunteering Australia. *Key Facts and Statistics About Volunteering in Australia*. 2015. Retrieved from www.volunteeringaustralia.org/wp-content/uploads/VA-Key-statistics-about-Australian-volunteering-16-April-20151.pdf

Weerawardena, J., R. E. McDonald, and G. S. Mort. "Sustainability of Nonprofit Organizations: An Empirical Investigation." *Journal of World Business* 45, no. 4 (2010): 346–56.

Wilden, R., S. Gudergan, and I. Lings. "Employer Branding: Strategic Implications for Staff Recruitment." *Journal of Marketing Management* 26, no. 1–2 (2010): 56–73.

Word, J. K. A. "Human Resource Leadership and Management." In *Leadership in Nonprofit Organizations: A Reference Handbook*, ed. A. Agard Publishing Company. Thousand Oaks: SAGE Publications, Inc, 2011.

Worth, M. J. *Nonprofit Management—Principles and Practice*. Los Angeles: Sage Publications, 2009.

Yan, W., and M. F. Sloan. "The Impact of Employee Compensation and Financial Performance on Nonprofit Organization Donations." *The American Review of Public Administration* 46, no. 2 (2016): 243–58.

Leadership in Practice: Sharing the Load at the Top—Peer Leadership at The CEO Institute

Introduction

There are many opportunities and challenges which come with being a CEO. Along with the sense of satisfaction that can come from major achievements, there can also be frustrations, uncertainties and fears when the going gets tough. Very often it is not appropriate for the CEO to share these concerns with others in the organisation. Furthermore, depending on the structure or personalities of the Board, it may not be realistic to share such concerns at that level either.

All of this can lead to a real sense of loneliness at the top. This is especially true for CEOs new to the role, and for those in organisations with less well-established governance arrangements, which can include many NFPs.

CEOs exist in a huge variety of contexts across public and private companies, NFPs and public sector entities, and across different sizes and types of organisations. However, there are striking similarities in the opportunities and challenges most CEOs face.

An initiative which has proven successful in connecting CEOs to lighten their load by sharing experiences and learning from each other is the CEO Institute.

The author has had the privilege of chairing a Brisbane based syndicate of the Institute for some six years. This comes after a career, primarily in the public sector, starting as a civil engineer, then transitioning through different roles to include some twenty-two years as CEO of major Queensland Departments. While most of the members of the CEO syndicate are from the private and not-for-profit sectors, the challenges they face are remarkably similar to the challenges which the author used to face in government.

The Institute

The CEO Institute has been operating for over twenty years as a membership organisation for Chief Executives. It is based in all Australian mainland state capitals and Auckland. Its prime focus of activity is based on meetings of syndicates of CEOs through which members connect with like-minded leaders to learn from each other in a supportive and confidential environment.

Each syndicate has approximately fifteen members drawn from different industry sectors and types of organisations. Members are matched so that there are no competitors within a syndicate and conflicts of interest are avoided. This is to ensure that the paramount principle of confidentiality is maintained so that members will feel encouraged to bring issues openly to the table for discussion. Chatham House Rules apply at all times.

Each syndicate meets monthly. While there is flexibility in meeting arrangements, the usual pattern is a morning meeting at a central city location, starting with a buffet breakfast, followed by a guest speaker addressing a topic previously raised by members, and then moving on to a round table discussion of business issues amongst members.

Some meetings have no guest speaker but instead workshop a particular issue, drawing on members' own experiences. On occasions, meetings are held at a particular member's workplace so that others can gain a better understanding of that business and its challenges. There have been some fascinating workplace meetings which completely changed members' views of what the business being visited was all about!

There are also other Institute activities, such as business lunches and social functions, where members can mix across syndicates to widen their networks. There are activities for 'emerging CEOs' as well.

Relevance to NFPs

The similarities of challenges facing CEOs from different types of organisations have already been noted, and this certainly includes NFP CEOs. In fact, an observer of syndicate meetings would be hard pressed to identify, on the basis of discussion around the table, which sectors members came from.

A notable feature of many members' backgrounds is the movement they have made between sectors over time. Overseas experience is another common feature. All this brings enrichment to the syndicate, especially for NFP members.

NFP members are always encouraged to join. Current and past NFP members have come from a wide range of fields, including education, health, disability services and church organisations.

Topics of Focus

The topics chosen to be addressed by guest speakers or by workshopping are based on members' interests. All members are regularly canvassed for their ideas on topics and potential speakers. It is usual for guest speakers to be leaders in their fields, often with high profile backgrounds.

Recurring themes the syndicate has addressed include:

- Executive/Board relationships, in particular CEO/Chair relationships.
- Business opportunities, including opportunities through digital disruption.

- Mergers and acquisitions.
- Achieving culture change to promote high performance.
- Managing poor performance.
- Effective engagement with the community, including crisis management.
- Examples of other topics which arise from time to time include:
- Changes to legal requirements, e.g. WH&S.
- Forthcoming elections and impacts of political change.
- Impacts of technological change.
- Developments in particular industry sectors.

The Personal Dimension

Probably the most valuable part of syndicate meetings comes from open communication around the table when members freely share their successes, failures and challenges and bring their wisdom to bear on each other's challenges.

These can cover a wide range—for example, from operational matters, through staff performance and culture, to merger/acquisition strategy, to relationships with board members and personal career questions. Recently, there has been quite a focus on promoting innovation, identifying opportunities for and threats from digital disruption, and balancing commercial objectives with wider responsibilities to the community.

A key role for the syndicate chair is to encourage members to feel free to talk honestly about personal challenges in their work life. It is a privilege to be part of discussions which help members to deal with the sometimes quite vexed dilemmas facing them.

It is also pleasing to see members follow up one-on-one outside of meetings to help each other on more specific opportunities.

Conclusion

A common experience of CEOs is that it is easy to become engulfed by the many challenges of the job. It can be ironic that, while addressing the development needs of their staff, a CEO can easily lose sight of the need to attend to their own development.

Membership of the CEO Institute is a very effective way to stay in touch with what your peers are doing and to learn from them and from great speakers, in a confidential and collegiate forum.

Bruce Wilson
CEO Institute

8 Non-Profit Marketing Strategy

Jay Weerawardena

Opening Vignette: Mirabel Foundation

Mirabel is an Australian Children's Charity that was established in Victoria in 1998 to help children of drug-addicted parents and it now operates in New South Wales as well. Mirabel is the vision of Jane Rowe, who served as a drug and alcohol counsellor for over twenty years and in her work witnessed the devastating effects that drug use has on the children of drug users and the cycle of abuse that repeats itself through generations if action is not taken. Mirabel has been the first in the whole world to establish a charity to look after the children of drug addicted parents.

Since this time, under Jane's guidance and leadership, Mirabel has provided vital assistance and support to thousands of children and currently supports over 1500 children and young people, the most profoundly overlooked casualties of substance abuse in our society.

Mirabel's programs achieve positive results for children and they carefully target and manage their funding to deliver the best outcomes for the targeted community. Being a small NFP primarily depending on donor funding, Mirabel has been cautious in its investing in new projects. Jane believes that remaining financially viable is critically important for Mirabel to continue to deliver its services. Mirabel was recognised as an example of best practice by the Australian National Council on Drugs (ANCD) and they were also honoured by being chosen as a finalist for Excellence in Prevention at the 2007 National Drug and Alcohol Awards and were awarded the Victorian Children's Charities Award in the category of Drug and Alcohol.

Like many other conventional Non-profits, Mirabel relies on public donations. Faced with increased competition for donor dollar, Mirabel has been forced to be innovative in all its operations, particularly in fund-raising. From the beginning, Mirabel has seen the value of marketing in educating the public and positioning its cause to differentiate from competition. Over many years Mirabel has used the Melbourne Comedy Festival to reach potential donors where they are strongly supported by comedians to educate audiences of their cause which Mirabel knows pays off in the long run. Interestingly, every year they engage in a different activity as successful fund-raising ideas are always imitated by others. Mirabel operates as a niche-marketer and adopts innovative entrepreneurial marketing strategies to build its public image, raise much needed funds for its projects and attract volunteers who provide much needed human resources to serve Mirabel's targeted community—the children of drug addicted parents.

Overview

Marketing, as defined by the American Marketing Association (AMA) is "the activity, set of institutions, and processes for creating, communicating, delivering, and exchanging offerings that have value for customers, clients, partners, and society at large."[1] The 'marketing concept' is at the core of the marketing discipline and it proposes that in order to satisfy its organisational objectives, an organisation should understand the needs and wants of consumers and satisfy these more effectively than competitors. This view differentiates marketing from several other orientations that are widely being confused with marketing such as the product, production, or sales orientation which pays lesser attention to customer needs.

Market Orientation

With the marketing concept gaining popularity, many organisations have assigned a prominent place to customers in their mission statements and adopted slogans such as 'customers first' and 'customers are our greatest assets'. This created much confusion, as there was no way of determining if a firm was truly dedicated to their markets. Addressing this need, after many industry consultations, academics developed 'market orientation'—a managerial tool which allows truly market-oriented firms to be determined. Market-oriented firms are those that actively collect information (marketing research) about markets (customers and competitors), share such information among all the functional departments of the firm and mobilise all such functions to satisfy customer needs.[2]

STP Framework

Conventional marketing strategy follows the STP framework of *segmentation* (segmenting markets, in terms of criteria such as demographic, geographic etc.) *targeting* (identify a specific customer segment or multiple segments on which the firm decides to focus all its marketing efforts) followed by *positioning* of its products and services in the minds of consumers to highlight its advantages over those of competitors' products.

Marketing Mix

Marketing mix is the mix of strategies that the marketers adopt to effectively take their products and service to the intended market segments. Whilst the conventional marketing mix strategy entails the 'Four P's' of Product (products/services), Place (distribution channels), Promotion (communicating the value of product and services) and Price, with the growing recognition of services, this mix now includes three additional Ps, namely People (humans involved with service delivery), Physical evidence (tangible elements of services), and Processes (procedures, mechanisms and flow of activities by which services are delivered).

Marketing and Competitive Advantage

Marketing's contribution to firm competitive advantage through innovation is well established and considered the primary source of firm competitive advantage. Innovation takes multiple forms of product, service, marketing and managerial innovation. It enables the firm to gain positional advantages in competitive markets in three ways—namely, cost advantage (adopting strategies to achieve least cost strategies), differentiation (adopting strategies to develop superior features in product and services), and niche-focus or targeting a marketing segment that fits with firm's resources and capabilities. Niche strategy, which is predominantly adopted by resource constrained small firms, involves specialisation and penetration of a chosen market segment which enables the firm to build an entry barrier to competitors.

Emergence of the Entrepreneurial Marketing Concept

Over the last few decades the concept of entrepreneurial marketing has gained prominence. Entrepreneurial marketing basically argues that marketers must be entrepreneurial if they are to make a differential contribution to a firm's competitive advantage. This view originated from the work of a group of academics led by Gerald Hills at the University of Illinois, Chicago, which later led to an annual symposium titled 'Research at the Marketing/Entrepreneurship Interface'. Following this view many researchers have found that resource-constrained small firms that are headed by entrepreneurial leaders adopt innovative marketing strategies to reach their target markets effectively in competitive markets.[3]

The most common features of entrepreneurial marketing include innovation, risk taking, and being proactive. Entrepreneurial marketing campaigns try to highlight the firm's greatest strengths while emphasising their value to the customer. One such strategy is 'resource leveraging'. With limited advertising budgets, entrepreneurial NFPs use resource-leveraging strategies such as the use of publicity or deliberately creating publicity around their product, services or the cause to gain the attention and persuade targeted audiences.[4]

Many of these concepts and frameworks s can be equally adapted to non-profits. However, the unique characteristics of NFPs require substantial modifications of for-profit marketing tools. We find that non-profit marketing strategy is shaped by two factors.

Non-Profits Are in a Transition: Shifting to Income Generating Strategies

Non-profits now operate in an increasingly competitive and constrained environment which is attributed to government favouring competition, privatisation and efficiency in the delivery of public services, and the exponential increase of NFP numbers. This challenging environment has threatened the sustainability of NFPs and forced them to move beyond purely relying on philanthropic and grant funding, towards a mix of funding sources supplemented with earned income.[5]

In Australia the main source of income is shifting from philanthropic gifts to government grants and contracts (38%) and sale of goods and services (34%).[6] This mirrors a global trend of NFPs moving in the direction of earned income strategies. Broadly, many conventional NFPs have pursued business model innovation incorporating more and more income generating activities. As a result the NFP field now has three types of NFPs with overlapping operational characteristics; 'conventional NFPs' that still rely on donor and government funding, 'social enterprises' that have income-generating businesses that support the overall social mission and 'social businesses' where business takes priority to deliver the social mission.

With this shift towards income generating activities the importance of marketing is felt more than before which is evident in all these organisational forms. For example, the conventional NFPs, which substantially rely on donor funding, channel all their marketing effort towards differentiating their cause from competitors for which they extensively pursue innovative fund-raising campaigns. Building a highly visible brand is at the core of this strategy. Classic examples are Surf Life Saving Australia (SLSA) and Mirabel Foundation, Victoria. Similarly, many social enterprises rely on their marketing campaigns to differentiate their causes and promote their business arms. For example, the Bawrunga Aboriginal Medical Practice, a self-funded GP service primarily established to deliver specialised medical services to indigenous Australians, now serves other communities as well for which they rely on various forms of marketing communications.[7]

At the extreme end of this NFP organisational formats continuum, we find 'social businesses' that are similar to for-profits where the sole operation is selling a product or a service to support a social issue. The well-known Grameen-Danone Shokthi Doi yoghurt factory in Bangladesh is a social business. It was initiated by Professor Mohammed Yunus, Nobel Prize winning economist and founder of Bangladesh's Grameen bank—one of the great leaders in the social value creation arena with the investment support of Franck Riboud, the CEO of Groupe Danone in Switzerland. The project was aimed to develop and market a nutritious yoghurt to alleviate malnutrition of Bangladeshi children. Their aim is to build more factories to address widespread children's malnutrition from the surplus generated from the first factory. Therefore, they assign a greater importance to their marketing effort and their campaign, to a great extent, is similar to that of a commercial firm. However, Shokthi-Doi yoghurt is mainly sold through door-to-door sellers as they cannot afford to use established retail channels with their low profit margins.

In this chapter, our focus will be more on conventional NFPs and social enterprises which form a somewhat homogeneous group, and we exclude social businesses as their marketing campaigns are similar to those of commercial organisations.

NFPs and Their Marketing Constituents?

In for-profit marketing, 'markets' are defined as comprising customers and competitors. However, with their social mission remaining the defining factor, NFPs view their markets as comprising a broader set of stakeholders. In the NFP context 'customers' are replaced by the 'beneficiaries'. While in the for-profit context customers have 'voting power' through their purchase choices across different competitive brands, in the NFP context they are humble 'beneficiaries' who may be disabled children receiving housing support, a poor farmer in drought affected sub-Saharan Africa receiving a water pump or the homeless looking for daily food, shelter and a warm water shower. Of course, understanding their needs is important in designing appropriate support schemes for them. However, there are other stakeholders who are viewed by NFPs as exerting a stronger influence on NFP operations of which donors and volunteers are prominent. While donors provide much needed funding, volunteers provide much needed human resources without which NFPs cannot implement their projects effectively. Similarly, as in commercial organisations competitors are important.

Implications for NFP Marketing

The two issues discussed above have important implications for NFP marketing. Whilst the 'market-driven' view in commercial marketing emphasises the importance of understanding the expectations and behaviours of market constituents for business success, the same is equally applicable to NFPs. However, as noted earlier, NFPs have to respond to the expectations of a broader set of stakeholders beyond customers and competitors, namely, donors, volunteers and beneficiaries. In regard to competitors, NFPs compete with them for donor dollars but at the same time are compelled to collaborate in many situations such as joint bidding for large community service projects offered by local government or government institutions which cannot be shouldered by a single NFP. Of all these stakeholders, donors and volunteers are the primary focus of NFP marketing campaigns. With this focus NFP innovation efforts are mostly directed towards fund raising and attracting more and more volunteers.

NFP Marketing Process

Using the commercial marketing process discussed above we first discuss how NFPs can benefit by adapting the STP framework—Segmentation, Targeting and Positioning process. Then we will move on to discuss the marketing mix strategy as applicable to NFPs.

Market Segmentation

Market segmentation is the process of dividing a broad consumer or business market, normally consisting of existing and potential customers, into sub-groups of consumers (known as segments) based on some type of shared characteristics.[8] The fundamental logic of this process is that markets consist of buyers and they differ in terms of their wants, resources, locations, buying attitudes and buying practices. Segmenting is therefore aimed at identifying high yield segments or segments that will provide the biggest return to the marketing effort of the firm and having growth potential. These segments later provide the basis of targeting the firm's marketing effort.

Broadly, segmentation allows the firm to identify prospective stakeholders within a large mass market and then to develop cost-effective marketing campaigns to reach such segments. This is truly relevant to many NFP that are operating under severe resource constraints. Interestingly, NFP are founded with a particular beneficiary in mind. For example, Mirabel Foundation started with the objective of looking after the children of drug-addicted parents and the RSPCA was founded to reduce the abusive treatment of animals and to operate rescue centres where abandoned pets can be temporarily housed pending adoption or euthanasia. Therefore segmentation mostly applies to donor and volunteer markets.

Segmenting Donors

Moving beyond the initial beneficiary-based segmentation, NFPs can benefit by segmenting donors and volunteers whose contributions are critical for NFP survival and growth. NFPs have many donors and volunteers with whom they must communicate to solicit donations, acknowledge such donations, and maintain good relationships with donors. In a recent survey of small-to-medium sized non-profits in the US by Bloomerang it was found that over 80% of NFPs are familiar with segmenting, and 60% of them are segmenting their marketing communications to donors.[9] Of those segmenting, the majority had five or more segments. For example, donors were segmented mostly in terms of donation amount and action history. Other criteria were donation type, communication preference, age, gender, and income or net worth. The donor's communication preference is another widely used criteria where NFPs segment donors in terms of email versus direct mail. The benefit of segmenting by communication channel is cost savings. For example, if donors do not respond well to direct mail, spending on postage and mail matter any more will not make sense.

Segmenting Volunteers

Many NFPs rely on volunteers to staff programs, sit on boards, raise money and fill support roles. Therefore, recruiting and retaining volunteers is considered a continual challenge for NFPs which require a segmentation-based approach as volunteers are motivated by different life-style factors.

There are many ways of segmenting a volunteer market. Randle and Dolnicar find that segmenting volunteers as high and low contributors is popular among NFPs.[10] There are significant differences between these two segments in terms of their socio-demographic characteristics and their motivation to volunteering. They are likely to be married or living with a partner, not working or in part-time employment, have children, and be over 35. They are motivated by a range of altruistic and egoistic motivations means. They seek out information on volunteering opportunities themselves, which means NFPs need to make sure that information on their particular cause is readily available, clear, and concise. These findings enable NFP leaders to develop a profile for this segment which will guide their marketing communication efforts. By targeting this group NFPs can minimise the costs of advertising, recruitment, and training which are associated with new volunteers.

The overall benefit of segmenting NFP markets is that it is more economical to group individuals with similar needs who are likely to respond in a similar way to a marketing message, and then address their needs with one marketing mix. Any organisation, NFP or for-profit, cannot afford to spend their limited resources on an unfocused marketing campaign which will lead to waste coverage. However, NFPs with high resource endowments can target more than one segment with multiple marketing mixes or try to capture all segments which is known as mass marketing. For example, Surf Life Saving Australia (SLSA) targets all those that appreciate the value of beach safety for their donor focused marketing campaigns. However, their marketing campaigns to attract volunteers will focus on age-based segmentation.

Once a segment or segments are identified, the next step is to evaluate them using the following criteria.

- *Measurability*: The size and the potential of the segment. For example, if a NFP decides to target wealthy donors, how many of them live in a given locality?

- *Substantiality*: Is the particular segment large enough in terms of cost involved to reach that segment?
- *Compatibility*: Is the segment compatible with the mission of the NFP? For example, a charity supporting young children may not be willing to seek sponsorships from alcoholic beverage manufacturers.
- *Accessibility*: Can the segment be easily reachable? For example, what sort of TV programs/newspapers/magazines are watched/read by the people in the segment, or can they be reached by a particular social media?

Positioning

As well-known positioning 'Gurus' Ries and Trout state, positioning is about gaining a space for your brand in the mind of the customer which is crowded with many other brands.[11] It is also about how you distinguish your brand from competitor's brands so that the customer will remember it when it comes to a purchase decision. Positioning is therefore one of the most powerful marketing concepts for NFPs. The NFP sector is crowded with many claiming to be the most worthy, and therefore beyond having a noble sounding mission statement the NFP must actively pursue marketing communications to build a reputation for its cause (brand) which will differentiate competitors' brands.

A product/brand can be positioned by using a variety of approaches and the most popular ones are positioning on product attributes and positioning against a competitor. Ries and Trout suggest the latter as the most effective as it makes a direct comparison of your brand with the competitor's brand.

Before embarking on positioning a brand, the NFP must determine where the brand is currently placed in the mind of donors/volunteers compared to the NFP's competitors. Perceptual maps are the most popular technique for this purpose which is a diagrammatic representation of consumers' mental representations of the relative place various brands have within a category. In a perceptual map NFPs can select two variables that are relevant to donors such as high social impact and highly efficient use of resources and then ask a sample of the donors to explain where they would place various NFP brands in terms of the assigned two variables. Results are plotted on a graph to indicate how the average member of the population views the brand that make up a category and how each of the brands relates to other brands within the same category. This map facilitates the NFP to locate where they are in terms of the two criteria and take appropriate action to move the brand to a preferred higher block in the consumer evaluations.

Developing a Marketing Mix (Extended Mix (6ps) to Cover Services)

Similar to their for-profit counterparts, NFPs have at their disposal a marketing mix-asset of marketing tools that can be appropriately mixed to reach their intended markets—primarily donors and volunteers. As identified earlier, they are the primary stakeholders who exert a strong influence on the survival and growth of conventional NFP. However, with many NFPs now moving into income generating activities such as selling of goods and services at a fee the marketing mix needs to cover them as well.

We now discuss the expanded Seven Ps marketing mix which covers both products and services. Many NFPs are service providers or a mix of products and services or services bundled with tangible product elements.

Products/Services

As Vignette 2 illustrates, NFP market offers to its beneficiaries are mostly services, sometimes bundled with physical products. People who benefit from non-profit products and services often are provided them free of charge or at a highly subsidised rate. The shortfall is typically made up from funds secured from donors.

Vignette 2:   Marketing Offers in Non-profit Organisations

Orange Sky Laundry, based in Brisbane is the world's first free mobile laundry service for the homeless. Started in 2016 by young social entrepreneurs Nic Marchesi and Lucas Patchett who were honoured as 2016 Young Australians of the Year for their efforts—the mobile laundry service has now grown to 11 services across Australia in Brisbane, Canberra, Gold Coast, Melbourne, Sydney, Sunshine Coast, Perth, Adelaide, SE Melbourne, Wollongong and Hobart. It now does over 6.9 tonnes of laundry every week. Beyond providing laundry services, their primary mission is to positively connect communities, and facilitate the homeless to find employment and a shelter. The founders are about to take their laundry concept overseas, with a rollout planned for the US next year.

Lentil As Anything Inc. (Lentil) is a group of not for profit vegetarian and vegan Australian restaurants. Patrons are asked to "pay what they feel" the meal, service and beverages are worth by contributing an amount of their choice into a box at the counter. Restaurants are located in Melbourne and Sydney, and its multiple missions are: caring for people; provide a wholesome and nutritious meal where money is not a concern; promoting multiculturalism; fostering an environment of inclusion and not exclusion, reforming Society; acting on the structures of society to restore justice; and extending/spreading its ethos and values: hiring volunteers, the long-term unemployed and the marginalised. The restaurants wholly rely on the generosity of their patrons, volunteers and suppliers to operate, without which the sustainability of the NFP will be at risk.

The Salvation Army is one of the world's largest Christian social welfare organisations. They are committed to their mission of supporting the most marginalised and disadvantaged members of the community. In Australia each year they extend care to more than one million Australians facing crisis through the provision of more than 700 social programmes, activities and centres.

The Salvation Army Australia is dedicated to alleviating the suffering of people through assistance provided to people affected by homelessness, crisis, family violence, emergencies and natural disasters, as well as drug, alcohol and gambling addictions and a range of other issues. They seek to be there for people during their times of need. The Couch Programme in Melbourne is one such program which is a safe, welcoming space for international students to socialise and interact with others, as well as access support services and information. The Couch is a vitally needed service as many international students can't afford the basics like food, travel and accommodation. More than 100 international students gather each night to share a meal and participate in a range of activities run by volunteers. The activities, like English conversation classes, barista training, movie nights, Spanish classes, yoga sessions and live music nights, aim to build a sense of community.

All these are non-profit organisations. The first two are relatively young and founded by young, entrepreneurial leaders who believed they can make a difference in the social value creation arena. The third is an established globally known NFP leader that has built a large global organisation to continue to deliver its social mission. These NFPs are different in size, age and most importantly in terms of their product/service offers. Whilst Orange Sky offers a service—laundry services to the homeless, Lentils offers a wholesome nutritious meal to support multiple social objectives and Salvation Army provide a large array of services and products to a large number of needy in the community.

However, some of the NFP products are 'persuasive ideas' that are inherent in social marketing campaigns such as 'Conserve energy', 'Save the planet', 'quit smoking', etc. However, as NFP marketing campaigns are targeted at a broader set of stakeholders of which donors and volunteers are prominent, the mission of the NFP serves the role of the core product. For example, the World Wildlife Fund (WWF) is selling to its donors the idea to get involved in the protection of the animals threatened with extinction, and encourages them to contribute to the preservation of eco-system and the protection of the environment. Some of these species include the giant panda, which can only be found in the bamboo woods of China, and the tigers (of whom 90% have been lost during the 20th century and are threatened with extinction). The same applies to the NFPs indicated in Vignette 2.

Branding in NFPs and Brand Vulnerability

The American Marketing Association defines a brand as: a name, term, sign, symbol or design, or a combination of them, intended to identify the goods or services of one seller or group of sellers and to differentiate them from those of a competitor.[12] As indicated, the strength of a brand lies in its identification of the brand elements that can be used together to facilitate the formation of strong favourable and unique brand associations. The brand of a non-profit represents its mission

While branding has received little direct attention in NFP until recently, it is acknowledged that the non-profit sector has strong brands, many of which are even global brands such as Greenpeace, Red Cross, Medecins Sans Frontieres, World Wildlife Fund and Amnesty International. These brands are more trusted by the public than the best-known for-profit brands.[13]

Today many NFPs, large and small, assign a broader and more strategic role to their brand in their core performance. As in for-profits, the NFP brand has an internal role in expressing an organisation's purposes, methods, and values. NFP branding strategy therefore involves proactively and deliberately trying to shape or influence perceptions of its targeted audiences—primarily donors and volunteers. As discussed at the beginning of this chapter under NFP positioning strategy, doing so requires the NFP to understand how the NFP is perceived, defining how you want to be perceived, clarifying how you communicate to make sure it's heading in the right direction, and communicating consistently. As noted earlier, perceptual mapping is one of the popular tools for this purpose.

However, NFPs are faced with distinct brand challenges, which include issues related to multiple stakeholders in managing the brand and the need to negotiate partnering and sponsorship arrangements. These challenges make the NFP brand vulnerable to external forces that are beyond the NFP's control and internal factors that require careful management. For example, the NFP's decision to associate with a sponsor not compatible with the NFP mission will adversely impact its brand. Newly established non-profit organisations can begin their organisational development with strong branding strategies. However, many established non-profit organisations have a strong brand heritage, which requires special preservation, continuous renewal and extension strategies.

Mini case 1:   Managing a Heritage Brand: The Surf Life Saving Australia[14]

Surf Life Saving Australia (SLSA) is a leading water safety and rescue authority in Australia. It has a national headquarters based in Sydney with governing bodies in each state of Australia.

In 2007 SLSA celebrated the 100th year of saving lives on Australian beaches, signifying its heritage as one of the most iconic images in Australia. After being founded in 1906 at Bondi Beach, Sydney over the subsequent decades it has become an essential part of the Australian culture and its attachment to the 'sun and sand'. Its services are valued at more than $1.6 billion each year and if SLSA was not on duty on our beaches, 485 people would drown each year.

In terms of competition, SLSA enjoys a unique advantage of being the only organisation that provides beach safety and other beach-related social activities. However, SLSA faced a critical time in the 1960s and 1970s with membership declines, which was unexpected as more and more people were coming to the beach. SLSA felt that there was possibly some confusion about what the organisation stood for: serious activities of safety or fun sport activities. At that time surf life-saving was only for men and the organisation was "almost military."

With a view to understanding stakeholder perceptions about SLSA brand, a marketing research firm was hired to undertake a formal brand audit and marketing research. It was specifically aimed at better understanding the SLSA brand asset and its dimensions so as to formulate better branding strategies with the aim of ensuring financial sustainability and the overall ability of the organisation to sustain its mission.

The audit found that SLSA brand personality was highly positively regarded by both the corporate sector and the general community stakeholders. Interestingly, the corporate perceptions of the brand were focussed on functional aspects of the brand and the organisation, namely *safety, Australian, healthy, community focussed and wholesome*. However, the general community identified the key values of the SLSA brand as *trustworthy, honesty, honourable, friendly, efficient, responsive, dedicated and reliable*. On a seven-point scale, they rated the brand at 6.5–6.6 on all values, higher than most other organisations. The general community tended to see the brand in more emotional terms and to identify human characteristics of the brand.

Encouraged by the findings of the audit, SLSA quickly moved on to refocus its marketing campaigns to strongly reinforce in the minds of stakeholders the SLSA mission—what it stands for.

A TV campaign 'Heroes', was undertaken to reinstate the core SLSA values of safety and selflessness and a definite heroic stance, providing a coherent image. This was repositioning, but it was not about taking on new values for commercial gain as in the traditional for-profit approach. Instead, it was a move back towards core, historical, heritage values, when there had been a drift of image towards more fun and commercial attributes for surf life-savers.

The SLSA brand name was also associated with higher recall of advertised benefit claims—an obvious competitive advantage. Surf Life Saving Australia's current logo of the human head/face in profile wearing the distinctive life saver's cap in the life saver's colours of red and yellow on a blue background with text identifying the organisation was specifically designed as a result of the brand audit to better reinforce the brand image in the minds of donors and volunteers.

At the same time the tag line/slogan 'The life of the beach' was also developed and 'it underpins everything we do'. The prime communication message of the organisation concerning beach safety 'Swim between the flags' was found to have a 99% recognition rate in the brand audit. The red and yellow colours were strongly and consistently associated with both the Surf Life Saving brand and the swim-safe beach flags. All of these suggest that the Surf Life Saving organisation pays consistent attention to the tangible elements of the brand.

Overall, as a result of the brand audit the organisation learnt that 92% of people thought that SLSA was worthy of support, but only 2% of people had supported them. Encouraged by that untapped goodwill, the Surf Life Saving Foundation was repositioned for fundraising and a much stronger donor/fundraising program was undertaken which resulted in 20% increase of income and increased competitiveness in the Australian NFP domain.

Pricing Strategy

Pricing is one of the most critical components of the marketing mix. For consumers, it helps them with determining if they are receiving value for money from a particular product or service. Price is a surrogate indicator of quality, and there is a general belief among consumers that high-priced products are of higher quality. Along with the price, the product brand provides the needed cue on the reliability of the product. For the firm, it's the only way to recover the costs they incurred in making and marketing the product. The firm will use pricing to recover both its fixed and variable costs.

In a for-profit firm, pricing strategy will be influenced by several factors. First, the availability of substitutes in the market—the Internet has made this easier for consumers. Second, the competition within the market again will determine the maximum price that can be charged. Whilst many firms still compete on pricing using discounts and value-deals to achieve higher sales and increased market share, others opt to compete on non-price elements of the marketing mix such as improved services. There are many pricing strategies, of which 'contribution margin-based pricing' or 'mark-up' pricing has remained as a popular way of pricing as it not only recovers the costs incurred but also a profit margin.

While the role of pricing in for-profit is very clear (which is to recover the unit cost of the product and earn a margin) such a practice will be seen as inappropriate where pricing will be more complicated. By definition, NFPs have a social mission of creating social value to the targeted communities which differs from creating shareholder value in for-profits. However, with NFPs increasingly shifting towards 'earned income' strategies, we can see many of the for-profit pricing tools creeping into the NFP domain.

As noted earlier, many NFPs provide services to the disadvantaged free of charge, and the cost of delivering the service is met by donor funding or government grants. For example, the cost of running the mobile laundry facility by Orange Sky Laundry is met through public donor contributions.

Many large and well-established NFPs which provide such services now rely on a mix of donor funding and charging fees to their clients. For example, as noted earlier RSPCA's mission is to prevent cruelty to animals by actively promoting their care and protection. For this, RSPCA runs 40 shelters and employs around 1,000 staff, which costs more than $100 million each year. Most of this comes from public donations and fundraising initiatives, as well as business partnerships, grants and RSPCA patrons. In this setting, RSPCA has a variety of donation schemes which address different donor needs and flexibility sought by many donors. For example, its workplace giving program allows employees to make regular donations from their pay to RSPCA that has Deductible Gift Recipient status. This allows employees to claim an immediate tax deduction. Employers can also match an employee's contribution dollar for dollar and sometimes even double donations to help make an even bigger impact. Similarly, their Pet Legacies scheme provides for when the pet owners pass away.

On the other hand, following an increasing trend, RSPCA runs a store to sell its pet care accessories and pet food at their head office at Wacol, Queensland and these products can be purchased online as well. In addition, RSPCA provides a variety of services at a fee such as dog training, pet insurance, pet cremations, etc.

Today, many non-profit organisations derive a significant portion of their revenues through fees from constituents who consume their services. Examples include universities that charge students tuition, hospitals that charge patients based on length of stay, tests, treatments and medicines received and facilities utilised, or museums that may charge admission, particularly to special exhibitions.[15]

Vignette 3: Innovative pricing to serve the poor at Aravind Hospital, India[16]

The Aravind Eye Care System in Madurai, India is the largest provider of eye care services in the world, which was primarily founded to serve poor people in India who cannot afford essential eye surgeries. Although it performs almost 350,000 eye operations a year, 60 percent of them are delivered at low or no cost. The quality of its services are well-known and its surgical complication rate, for example, is lower than many Western hospitals achieve. All of this has been achieved through rigorous performance management, highly standardised care delivery, extremely high staff productivity, and most importantly, willingness to innovate in everything from how to source supplies to who can deliver services.

The success of Aravind Hospital is attributed to the entrepreneurial leadership of its visionary leader Dr. Venkataswamy who was determined to eradicate needless blindness in India. Cataract related blindness was a major health issue among the poor in India with at least four million cases every year, contributing nearly a quarter of the world's blind. In this effort, Dr Venkataswamy was inspired by the service efficiency of McDonald's fast food delivery system and he sought to adapt it to the eye care system to cope with the increasing numbers of patients treated.

At that time, hospitals in India typically fell into two categories; private hospitals that served the small, wealthy segment of the population with state-of-the-art facilities and public or charitable hospitals that served the poor, the vast majority of which had inadequate, out-dated, overcrowded facilities. In addition, most of the poor living in rural areas away from big cities were unable to access most hospitals.

Dr Venkataswamy's desire was to provide eyesight to the blind, regardless of ability to pay. However, to make this scheme financially viable, he introduced an innovative three-tier pricing scheme where both the rich and poor will receive the state-of-the-art cataract surgery but the rich patients will pay a fee above the cost of operation, middle income patients will pay a fee equalling the cost and poor patients will receive the same service free of charge where that cost is recovered from other fee-paying categories.

Place (Distribution) Strategy

Distribution is the process of making a product or service available to the consumer, and this can be done directly by the marketer (manufacturer or service provider) or using indirect channels with intermediaries such as wholesalers or retailers. In the NFP context, distribution decisions are influenced by several factors. First, NFPs cannot afford to provide discounts to retailers who would normally in a for-profit context play a leading role in enhancing the value of the offering. Second, most NFP offerings are services and therefore are determined by the service location decisions. Third, some NFPs have to be purposely located in areas where there is no institutional support such as reconciliation programs in post-war/conflict countries such as Rwanda or providing basic food and sanitation to Syrian refugees in Jordan. A classic Australian example is the Royal Flying Doctors Service, which delivers emergency medical services in the outback.

Many large NFPs such as Surf Life Saving Australia (SLSA) and Salvation Army have their own channels of direct distribution using multiple service outlets. SLSA's services are delivered by 313 affiliated Surf Life Saving clubs that are located across all states of Australia. These clubs are equipped with all the equipment needed such as Red & Yellow Patrol Flags, power crafts, stretchers etc. However, small organisations may not have their own channels, such as Mirabel Foundation which has primarily operated in Victoria where it was first founded but now operates in NSW as well.

Promotion (Marketing Communications) Strategy

Promotion or marketing communication is about raising customer awareness of a product, service or brand of the firm with the aim of persuading potential customers to buy the product generating sales, and creating brand loyalty. The promotional mix or promotional plan includes personal selling, advertising, sales promotion, direct marketing, and publicity. The promotional mix specifies how much attention to pay to each of these five components, which will be largely determined by the budget. However, in situations where a firm decides to launch an aggressive marketing campaign to gain larger market share from others in the market, the communication mix will take prominence in the firm's budget.

Obviously, marketing communications play a critical role in NFP fund-raising campaigns. However, NFPs—in particular smaller resource-constrained ones—can't afford to spend on advertising. Most such NFPs operate in a local area serving local communities. For them, national or regional level TV or newspaper campaigns are not really necessary. In contrast, large NFPs such as SLSA and Salvation Army use the national TV when they make nation-wide appeals such as the 'Red Shield Winter Appeal' of Salvation Army.

Out of the five-component promotional mix indicated above, NFPs widely use publicity or public relations. The advantage of publicity over advertising is it has high credibility compared to advertising as it is generally known that advertising is paid for by the marketer. Also, as noted earlier, publicity is an entrepreneurial marketing strategy where small start-ups use it to reach their potential customers. For example, annual childrens' hospital appeals are normally launched with the support of a national TV channel or a newspaper which generates much publicity resulting in substantial donations.

With the emergence of digital social media, NFPs are increasingly using social media to convey their marketing messages effectively. One such communication approach that has gained immense popularity is content marketing. Content marketing means attracting and transforming prospects into customers by creating and sharing valuable free content. In a NFP context, it involves the creation and sharing of valuable but often free-to-use content in "webpages, blogs, e-newsletters, podcasts, videos, white papers, apps, virals, tweets, Facebook communications, online magazine or TV, etc."[17] It is a multichannel device through which charities may attempt to intervene in situations in which members of the public participate in conversations with or about a charity's operations.[18] In 2014, an average of 500 million tweets was sent every day (i.e., 6,000 every second); 300 hours of videos were uploaded to YouTube every minute, and 4.75 billion pieces of content were shared on Facebook every 24 hours.[19] Out of these, Facebook is the social media platform NFP marketers use most often, and also the one they say is most effective. While the effectiveness ratings for Facebook (+7%) and Instagram (+3%) increased over the last year, those for all of the other social media platforms decreased.[20]

People

People or human resources are an important ingredient in the marketing of services. People are a defining factor in a service delivery process, since a service is inseparable from the person providing it. For example, in for-profit service organisations such as hotels, restaurants and medical centres front-line staff play a key role in defining the customer perceptions of the service quality. Customers make judgments about service provision and delivery based on the people representing the organisation and the way service was delivered. The praise received by the volunteers for the Sydney 2000 Olympics and Paralympics demonstrates the powerful effect people can create during service delivery. Many organisations spend a lot of time and resources for training.

As many NFPs deliver services, the people who deliver such services and their knowledge and ability to deliver such services is important. However, NFPs predominantly rely on volunteers to deliver their services and therefore NFP leaders must pay adequate attention for the acquisition, training, motivating empowering and retaining volunteers. For example, with 169,633 members and 313 affiliated Surf Life Saving clubs, SLSA represents the largest volunteer movement of its kind in the world. Volunteers are individuals who serve in a NFP without being paid and they can be broadly classified as episodic volunteers who serve on an as-needed basis or who serve during special events or on projects of limited duration and regular volunteers who work regularly. The latter is the most important category for the NFP as their contribution is critically important to maintain their programs and regular activities. As indicated by Wymer, Knowles and Gomes (2006), volunteers fill many roles in NFPs and they fall into one of the following categories:[21] (a) board member or managerial, (b) fund-raising, (c) general support, and (d) direct service. Understanding the various roles is important because each attracts different types of people.

For example, board members or managerial volunteers are responsible for overseeing the various functions of the organisation in fulfilment of its mission. They are more likely than other types of volunteers to have higher levels of education, higher levels of income, and higher-status employment.[22] On the other hand, fund-raising volunteers' primary tasks involve raising money by soliciting contributions. These volunteers may also be responsible for writing proposals for grants. For many organisations, fund-raisers may be the most difficult volunteers to recruit. Fund-raising volunteers are more likely to be outgoing and socially oriented. Fund-raising involves setting challenging goals, working in a team, and feeling energised by a challenge. Fund-raisers also serve a public relations role because they represent the nonprofit to the community and influential persons.

Process

Services are inherently intangible processes. For example, a visitor staying at a hotel will be served in a processual pattern starting from making a booking on line, arriving at the hotel, greeted and taken to the reception by bell-captain's staff, check-in, bell staff taking visitors baggage to the room etc. This process is continued even after the visitor leaves the hotel where the hotel will seek the visitor's feedback about service quality during his/her stay at the hotel.

The 'front-room' and 'back-room' interplay is a crucial element of this service process. In a hotel, the front-room is represented by the front-office staff and the back-room represents support services which enables the front-office staff to deliver services. For example, in a hotel context, the backroom includes IT services, laundry, kitchen, airport shuttle vans etc. that the customer does not see. However, any failure by backroom staff will be immediately felt by the visitor. For example, when the visitor orders room delivery of breakfast the kitchen must have processes in place to deliver such orders within a reasonable time frame, and any substantial delay will be viewed as unsatisfactory.

These processes are equally evident in many non-profit services such as museums, public libraries and social security services where the efficiency in service delivery process is valued by clients. In a recent documentary, it was reported that a large refugee camp in Jordan for Syrian refugees has a bakery which makes and delivers 15,000 Syrian breads every morning to the whole camp. Service operations of such magnitude require well-developed processes with adequately skilled and motivated staff. Most of the bakery staff are refugees in the camp who are experienced in bakery work and they are paid a nominal salary by the UN.

The 'service blue-print' is the technique that is widely used by large-scale service organisations which delivers the same service with the same standard of service. A service blue print is a detailed flow-chart which provides the details of the service delivery process, often going down to even defining the service script and the greeting phrases to be used by the service staff. A blueprint enables managers to determine 'customer touchpoints' and how the front-room and back-room interplay occurs. A customer touch-point can be a 'pain point' when there are delays or services are not delivered to the satisfaction of service recipients in such touchpoints. For example, if there are long delays in serving meals at a cafeteria in a museum it can be a pain point which requires immediate attention by museum administrators.

Physical Evidence

Since services are intangible in nature most service providers strive to incorporate certain tangible elements into their offering to enhance customer experience. Booms and Bitner (1981) describe it as 'the environment in which the service is delivered and where the firm and customer interact, and any tangible components that facilitate performance or communication of the service'.[23] In a NFP context, service centres, social security offices, museum premises, and university student centres would be good examples for physical evidence. In a for-profit setting, it is important that the physical environment is consistent with the other aspects of the marketing mix and the physical environment has to feel right and be in line with their expectations. This is the case simply because the physical environment communicates to potential customers the service quality that can be expected. Given the intangible nature of services, consumers often rely on the physical evidence to evaluate service quality

In a for-profit context, service marketers must manage the physical evidence, which includes any element of the service environment which impacts on one or more of the customer's five senses—the sense of smell, taste, hearing, sight and touch. Key elements are ambience (the look and feel of a restaurant); layout (mostly applicable in retail settings) and general interior (flooring and carpeting) as well as interior displays (posters, signs, cards etc.). In a museum setting, the use of these atmospherics reflect the educational objectives of the museum—normally by their relatedness to the collection—and are seen as educational tactics. For example, the physical appearance of the Museum, including signage, fixtures, and displays, provides clues to orientation in their content, design, and process of development.[24]

However, the elements that are aimed at creating an aesthetic and appealing environment may not be really important in many NFP settings where the priority is to deliver a service that is urgently needed. In such situations functionality derived through the store layout will be important. For example, many medical services during the Ebola epidemic were delivered in makeshift hospitals. Here again the service location will be important. For example, SLSA, State Office in South Brisbane, Queensland, has a mix of aesthetics and functionality at the reception where published material such as annual reports are on display. However, its life saving outlets at beaches are temporary shelters with clearly visible signage and life-saving equipment.

With the emergence of digital marketing, digital tools and techniques now play an important role in providing physical evidence that can either support or detract potential customers from the other elements of the marketing mix. For example, websites, blogs, and social media are now an important part of the physical evidence element of the extended marketing mix. Many NFPs, as we saw above, use digital media to engage in content marketing practices where physical evidence derived through digital platforms cannot be ignored.

Concluding Thoughts

As noted throughout this chapter, the importance of marketing for NFPs cannot be underestimated in spite of the fact that NFPs are predominantly dedicated to delivering a social mission. With increased competition and internal resource constraints, NFPs are compelled to adopt an entrepreneurial leadership posture in managing all their strategic initiatives. As this chapter suggests, most of the marketing tools that are used by for-profit firms are equally applicable to NFPs. With the increased shift to earned-income activities, and the fact that NFP products are predominantly service, the importance of the extended seven Ps framework is clearly evident. However, the unique characteristics of NFPs which differentiate them from their for-profit counterparts require a somewhat different approach where NFP marketing constituents—such as donors and volunteers—require greater attention.

Notes

1. American Marketing Association, www.ama.org/AboutAMA/Pages/Definition-of-Marketing.aspx Retrieved on 13–06–17.
2. A. K. Kohli and B. J. Jaworski. "Market Orientation: The Construct, Research Propositions, and Managerial Implications," *The Journal of Marketing* 54, no. 2 (1990): 1–18.
3. G. Hills, C. Hultman and M. Miles. "The Evolution and Development of Entrepreneurial Marketing," *Journal of Small Business Management* 46, no. 1 (2008): 99–112.
4. G. S. Mort, J. Weerawardena and P. Liesch. "Advancing Entrepreneurial Marketings: Evidence from Born Global Firms," *European Journal of Marketing* 46 (2012): 542–561.

5. J. Weerawardena and G. Sullivan Mort. "Investigating Social Entrepreneurship: A Multidimensional Model," *Journal of World Business*, 41 (2006): 21–35; J. Weerawardena, R. E. McDonald and G. Sullivan Mort. "Sustainability of Non-profit Organizations: An Empirical Investigation," *Journal of World Business*, 45, no. 4 (2010): 346–356.
6. Australian Bureau of Statistics. Non-profit organizations, 2006–07 ABS Canberra, 2008.
7. Bawrunga Aboriginal Medical Centre. http://bawrunga.org.au/
8. Philip Kotler, Linden Brown, Stewart Adam, Suzan Burton and Gary Armstrong. *Marketing*, 7th edn (Australia: Pearson, 2007).
9. Steven Shattuck. "New Data Reveals How Nonprofits Are Segmenting Their Communications," 2017, https://blog.hubspot.com/marketing/data-how-nonprofits-segment-communications#sm.000017zqq32olmcttvnwk70hy tna4
10. M. Randle and S. Dolnicar. "Understanding the Australian Environmental Volunteering Market: A Basis for Behavioural Change in Sustainable Future," *Australasian Marketing Journal* 17, no. 4 (2009): 192–203.
11. Al Ries and Jack Trout. "Positioning," in *The Battle for the Mind* (McGraw-Hill Education; 2000).
12. American Marketing Association. "The American Marketing Association Dictionary," 1960.
13. Edelmen Trust Barometer. "Annual Global Opinion Leaders Study," 2011.
14. Based on Mort G. Sullivan, J. Weerawardena and B. Williamson. "Branding in the Non-Profit Context: The Case of Surf Life Saving Australia," *Australasian Marketing Journal*, 15, no. 2 (2007): 108.
15. McDonald, Weerawardena, Madhavaram and Sullivan Mort. "From 'Virtuous' to 'Pragmatic' Pursuit of Social Mission: A Sustainability-Based Typology of Non-Profit Organizations and Corresponding Strategies," *Management Research Review* (2015): 970–991.
16. Tracey Vickers and Ellen Rosen. *Driving Down Cost of High-Quality Care* (McKinsey and Co., 2011).
17. K. Hilpern. "How to Make Content Marketing Work for You," *The Marketer* (January/February 2013): 38.
18. R. Bennet. "Relevance of Fundraising Charities' Content-Marketing Objectives: Perceptions of Donors, Fundraisers, and Their Consultants," *Journal of Non-profit and Public Sector Marketing* (2017).
19. Barry, F. *Nonprofit Marketing Content in 2016* (New York: NpEngage, 2015), http://npengage.com
20. Content Marketing Institute. "Benchmarks, Budgets, and Trends—North America," 2016.
21. Walter W. Wymer, Patricia Knowles and Roger Gomes. *Nonprofit Marketing: Marketing Mfor Charitable and Nongovernmental Organizations* (Thousand Oaks, CA: Sage, 2006).
22. Ibid.
23. B. H. Booms and M. J. Bitner. "Marketing Strategies and Organizational Structures for Service Firms," in *Marketing of Services*, eds. J. H. Donnelly and W. R. George (Chicago: American Marketing Association, 1981), 47–51.

24. S. Mottner and J. B. Ford. "Measuring Non-Profit Marketing Strategic Performance: The Case of Museum Stores," *Journal of Business Research* 58 (2005): 829–840.

Bibliography

American Marketing Association. The American Marketing Association Dictionary. 1960.

American Marketing Association. Retrieved from www.ama.org/AboutAMA/Pages/Definition-of-Marketing.aspx Retrieved on 13–06–17

Australian Bureau of Statistics. Non-Profit Organizations, 2006–07 ABS Canberra, 2008.

Barry, F. *Nonprofit Marketing Content in 2016.* New York, NY: NpEngage, 2015. Retrieved from http://npengage.com

Bawrunga Aboriginal Medical Centre. Retrieved from http://bawrunga.org.au/

Bennet, R. "Relevance of Fundraising Charities' Content-Marketing Objectives: Perceptions of Donors, Fundraisers, and Their Consultants." *Journal of Nonprofit and Public Sector Marketing* 2017.

Booms B. H., and M. J. Bitner. "Marketing Strategies and Organizational Structures for Service Firms." In *Marketing of Services*, edited by J. H. Donnelly, W. R. George., 47–51. Chicago: American Marketing Association, 1981.

Content Marketing Institute. Benchmarks, Budgets, and Trends—North America. 2016.

Edelmen Trust Barometer. *Annual Global Opinion Leaders Study.* 2011.

Hills, G., C. Hultman, and M. Miles. "The Evolution and Development of Entrepreneurial Marketing." *Journal of Small Business Management* 46, no. 1, (2008): 99–112.

Hilpern, K. "How to Make Content Marketing Work for You." *The Marketer*, (January-February 2013): 38–41.

Kohli, A. K., and B. J. Jaworski. "Market Orientation: The Construct, Research Propositions, and Managerial Implications." *The Journal of Marketing* 54, no. 2 (1990): 1–18.

Kotler, Philip, Linden Brown, Stewart Adam, Suzan Burton, Gary Armstrong. *Marketing.* 7th Edition, Australia: Pearson, 2007.

McDonald, Weerawardena, Madhavaram and Sullivan Mort. "From 'Virtuous' to 'Pragmatic' Pursuit of Social Mission: A Sustainability-Based Typology of Non-Profit Organizations and Corresponding Strategies." *Management Research Review* (2015): 970–91.

Mort, G. S., J. Weerawardena, and P. Liesch. "Advancing Entrepreneurial Marketings: Evidence From Born Global Firms." *European Journal of Marketing* 46, no. 3 (2012): 542–61.

Mottner, S., and J. B. Ford. "Measuring Non-Profit Marketing Strategic Performance: The Case of Museum Stores." *Journal of Business Research* 58 (2005): 829–40.

Randle, M., and S. Dolnicar. "Understanding the Australian Environmental Volunteering Market: A Basis for Behavioural Change in Sustainable Future." *Australasian Marketing Journal* 17, no. 4 (2009): 192–203.

Ries, Al, and Jack Trout. "Positioning." *The Battle for the Mind.* New York: McGraw-Hill Education, 2000.

Shattuck, Steven. *New Data Reveals How Nonprofits Are Segmenting Their Communications.* 2017. Retrieved from https://blog.hubspot.com/marketing/data-how-nonprofits-segment-communications#sm.000017zqq32olmcttvnwk70 hytna4

Sullivan Mort, G., J. Weerawardena, and B. Williamson. "Branding in the Non-Profit Context: The Case of Surf Life Saving Australia." *Australasian Marketing Journal* 15, no. 2 (2007): 108–19.

Vickers, Tracey, and Ellen Rosen. "Driving Down the Cost of High-Quality Care: Lessons From the Aravind Eye Care System." *Interview With Dr. Srinivasan, Health International* 11 (2011): 23.

Weerawardena, J., R. E. McDonald, and G. Sullivan Mort. "Sustainability of Non-profit Organizations: An Empirical Investigation." *Journal of World Business* 45, no. 4 (2010): 346–56.

Weerawardena, J. and G. Sullivan Mort. "Investigating Social Entrepreneurship: A Multidimensional Model." *Journal of World Business* 41 (2006): 21–35.

Wymer, Walter W., Patricia Knowles, and Roger Gomes. *Nonprofit Marketing: Marketing Management for Charitable and Nongovernmental Organizations.* Boston: Sage Publications, 2006.

Leadership in Practice: Youngcare—Leadership in a Not for Profit

Introduction

Youngcare is a high profile Not for Profit organisation focused on assisting young Australians to avoid or exit aged care by providing facilities and programs across Australia. Youngcare receives no recurrent government funding.

Youngcare's mission is focused on the 7000 young people with high care needs living in aged care in Australia today. But with another 700,000 living at home being cared for by loved ones—the real issue is 707,000 strong.

The heart and soul of Youngcare is about changing lives, creating impact and giving Young People with High Care Needs (YPWHCN) a life with choice, independence and dignity.

Leadership in any sector presents challenges. But perhaps, the challenges and rewards of leadership in the not-for-profit balance differently.

There is certainly a view that working for a not for profit is easier. I can say with conviction, having worked in the private sector, in education and having run a small business, that the not for profit sector is as challenging, as demanding, and requires as broad a range of skills and experience.

New team members at Youngcare would often give feedback that they were working harder than they ever had in previous roles. We believe that the rewards merit the effort.

I believe that experience from different sectors is an important asset in any not for profit leader. As a CEO in this sector you have to manage relationships across a broad scope of backgrounds, corporate partners, government, legislation, donors, suppliers and importantly those we're here to support, which with Youngcare was our current and potential residents and grant recipients. Understanding their pressures and their language is a considerable strength.

My Passion for Youngcare

My son was 19 when he acquired a brain injury in a traffic accident. As we struggled through the weeks and the months of intensive care and recovery towards rehabilitation, the options available to young people with high care needs became frighteningly clear. Specialist facilities or financial support to allow these young people to live independently or with loved ones are rare and extraordinarily hard to come by. The most likely option for a young person who needs long term constant care is admission into an aged care facility. As a mother, this was not acceptable. It was inconceivable.

My son's recovery has allowed him to live a full and independent life. We have been fortunate. However, the experience opened my eyes to the fact that 7000 young people are living in aged care facilities in Australia today. Another 700,000 are living at home, at high risk of entering aged care because of the cost of specialist equipment, or because their loved ones can no longer care for them.

My eyes were open to a situation and a need for change. It has been my driver every single minute of each day as CEO of Youngcare.

A personal commitment to social change is common in people who work in the not-for-profit sector. They may have experienced illness, loss or hardship first-hand and are committed to putting a situation to right, or they are motivated by a sense of social justice and empathy.

The risk is, when a leader is driven by personal passion, boundaries between work and self can become blurred. Personal commitment may make the leader work longer hours, set extraordinarily challenging targets for themselves and for the team, or take on too many separate projects.

The commitment to making a difference may be why a not-for-profit leader takes a particular role. Their job, however, is to show leadership by balancing that passion with strategic vision, operational effectiveness, financial clarity, team leadership qualities and stakeholder management abilities.

Setting the Vision and Making It Real

Leadership starts with vision: vision for what the organisation represents and what it wants to change in the world in which it operates.

For Youngcare the vision is of a future where young people with high care needs are housed in age appropriate accommodation that meets their physical and social needs and those of their carers:

> Youngcare's vision is for a future where all young people with high care needs live the young lives they deserve.

An organisation's vision becomes meaningful when it is interpreted into a strategy for the organisation—how we'll achieve this vision—and a series of goals achievable over time.

Not-for-profits like Youngcare operate in shifting regulatory environments. Government policy can be unpredictable in timing and impact. The disability sector has been particularly fluid in recent years with the introduction of the National Disability Insurance Scheme (NDIS). Constant uncertainty can make setting a coherent strategy that motivates the team and moves the organisation towards its goals, a challenge for the board and the CEO.

At Youngcare we had an annual three-step strategic planning review to keep our activities relevant to stakeholders, and relevant to our vision:

- **Step one: high level strategic plan:** Each year the Youngcare board, the CEO and key leadership team members reviewed progress over the past 12 months, what had been achieved and lessons learned, and brainstormed appropriate objectives for the coming year. Risk analysis was an important aspect of setting new directions. The process was facilitated by an external consultant.
- **Step two: strategy on a page, 'SOAP':** the outcomes of the high level strategic plan are presented as the annual 'strategy on a page', or *soap* for the whole organisation and external stakeholders. This captured the strategic goals and core activities that would drive the Youngcare strategy forward.
- **Step three: the operational plan:** From the *SOAP*, the CEO and team leaders developed a specific, coherent plan of goals and activities that would be actioned to support the strategy and the vision, including financial targets, resources, specific, measurable goals and time frames for delivering them.

Building a Culture of Passion and Excellence

Culture is crucial to not-for-profit organisations. The culture embodies the values the organisation represents, and the impact it believes it can have. Culture is often why talent is attracted to an organisation. It is a key reason people stay.

At Youngcare we aimed for a culture of passion and excellence. We built this through collaboration, cooperation, recognition and mutual support.

We started from a low base. At the beginning of my tenure as CEO, there were clear signs of disengagement. The organisation was siloed. Staff turnover and absenteeism were high.

How We Built the Youngcare Culture

Organisational Restructure

Eight months into my tenure I led a full restructure of Youngcare. The goal was to align skills with focus areas, and with the overall strategy and create the basis of the culture of passion and excellence. Restructures are complex and leaders must work with clarity, vision and conviction, focusing on the desired outcomes. Two roles became redundant which was significant in a small organisation. The team had the opportunity to apply for their own or other roles at Youngcare. The legal aspects of the significant organisational change were managed with the pro bono support of Herbert Smith Freehills. Leaders should not forget to finish the restructure process with an opportunity for the team to give feedback on how it went and how they feel about the outcome. It was important to me that the Youngcare team found the restructure professional and fair.

Leadership Style

I work to achieve a leadership style that is open, approachable and informal. Above all, I believe in being authentic to myself and to the team. Part of this was to reflect openly about what I was learning and what I could improve on.

Buzz Meetings

Our weekly whole-of-team 'Buzz' meetings were an important way to ensure communication across the whole organisation, preventing siloed behaviour, and reinforcing the idea that each division was important in delivering its part of the overall strategy. The meetings encouraged people to articulate what they needed from the Leadership team or CEO. Everyone was asked to talk about their 'win' from the previous week. We took the opportunity to connect the day-to-day back to Youngcare's overall strategy and vision.

One-On-One Check Ins

Approximately every six months each team member had a 20-minute check in with the CEO. It is an important way of feeding ideas up the chain, checking in with the culture and ensuring everyone understands that they were important to the organisation.

Youngcare Events

Youngcare events support the organisational culture, as well as being vehicles for fundraising and brand building. Many of our activities (fun runs, the Simpson Desert Challenge) were physical fitness events. Training together is a team building experience. We included stakeholders and Youngcare's residents and grant recipients. Sharing these activities and the responsibility for our fundraising creates a culture in which young people with high care needs and their families and loved ones are truly contributing, as peers, to the solutions that Youngcare seeks to create.

Culture of Excellence

To encourage and promote excellence we worked with clear position descriptions for each team member, supported by individual and team KPIs. We reviewed these KPIs every three months with a focus on transparent, two-way feedback. I set high personal standards for myself and for the leadership team. Feedback on issues that reflected missed goals or under-performance emphasised the learnings and opportunities to address things differently next time around.

Inclusivity and Diversity

Inclusivity and diversity are part of the fabric of any successful organisa-tion. Youngcare works with people with disability and has staff members with first-hand knowledge of the challenges they and their families face. We are fortunate to have people with disability on staff and as volunteers. The benefits are enormous for increasing the team's understanding of residents/ grants recipients working *with*, not just *for*, people with high care needs. It also improves our service. People in need of support are able to talk to Youngcare staff who truly understand their issues, and who more easily identify the kind of support required. Youngcare expresses its commitment to diversity through a statement that we publish online and refer to in all our hiring literature.

What Makes an Excellent Leader of a Not-For-Profit Organisation?

A CEO is only as good as the people that surround them. A strong CEO of any organisation is aware enough to recognise their strengths as well as gaps in experience or capability. They are not afraid to sur-round themselves with a team that complements those capabilities and fills the gaps.

Any individual CEO will have some, but not all, of the skills for the job they do. Recognising this, being open to learn and to support from those around, is important.

As CEO of Youngcare, the skills I brought to the organisation were stake-holder engagement, marketing, branding and communications, with an in-credible passion for a cause that was so dear to my heart. As a leader, my style is one that finds a way to make things happen. This is suited to an organisation like Youngcare, where meeting urgent needs of people in diffi-cult circumstances often means simply finding a way to make things happen, often against the odds.

People are effective at work—and as leaders—when they have support in their personal lives. My husband Richard was a source of knowledge, experience and support. He was able to provide honest commentary and feedback—sometimes on difficult topics that were hard to hear. I especially valued his take on behaviours, language and how to manage challenging situations.

I believe women often have a particular leadership style. We can be more reflective than perhaps our male counterparts. I believe women in the not-for-profit sector have to work harder at bringing the Board with them.

Working with a Board

The CEO sits between the Board and the team. The CEO's job is to make the Board's vision happen, to work within their parameters, and to deal with the operational elements of delivering outcomes. The CEO is responsible for relationships with the staff, for staff performance and for any disciplinary issues that arise.

The board must set the agenda, create a realistic and relevant vision and be enablers that support the daily operations with big-picture insight, expertise and continuity. It is important that they recognise and observe boundaries of their responsibility.

In the book, 'Leading the Board—The Six Disciplines of World-class Chairmen' by Andrew Kakabadse & Nada Kakabadse, they say:[1]

> "*The CEO drives the car, while the Chair of the Board is responsible for "road worthiness of vehicle and safety of all those on board—stakeholders, employees and customers.*
>
> *The Chair must ensure CEO (driver) is carrying out the necessary safety checks on the car, enough rubber on the tires, petrol, oil in the engine, water in the wipers. Chair must also ensure necessary licences are up to date and that paperwork is all in order if they are pulled over.*
>
> *But—and it is an important but—the CEO must be allowed to operate the accelerator and steer the car—Chair sits in passenger seat—there to stamp on brakes or grab the wheel IF required. Chair and board should be consulted on the destination, but must not interfere while CEO is driving, and should leave the actual route to leadership team. . . . "*

Lord Clive Hollock says, "*You've got to stand back and let the CEO get on with it.*" He promotes a "*boss of the business versus boss of the board*" distinction between Chair and CEO.

Defining the relationship between the Board Chair and the CEO is the basis for any successful relationship. A strong understanding between the two strengthens the whole organisation. This is not always an easy undertaking. Knowing how to make it work, to enable the Chair and CEO to stand shoulder-to-shoulder to the full benefit of the organisation, can take time and practice.

In not-for-profits the role of Chair is usually an unpaid role. To ensure that the organisation can work effectively and meet its regulatory and strategic requirements, this may be a weakness. The role of Chair is so crucial to success, and there is an argument that it should be paid and accountable.

Because of the nature of the not-for-profit sector, much of the work done is through the good will of volunteers. This extends to the board, and one downside might be that the roles and expectations of each board member may not be clearly defined, or appropriately accounted for.

Managing the Stakeholders

Not-for-profit organisations—like any business are responsible to a complex range of stakeholders. For Youngcare we focused on the following.

- **Young people:** Residents, Grants Recipients, Families and loved ones, and those we're here to serve and support
- **Charities:** Other organisations working in the sector, with whom we collaborate
- **Care Providers:** Wesley Mission Brisbane who provide the care at Sinnamon Park, Coomera and the Wooloowin Share House. Plus MS Queensland, who will provide the care at Albany Creek.
- **Government (State and Federal level):** Youngcare has received land and capital grants from state level government. We work at federal level lobbying and informing policy, etc.
- **Donors:** We have a range of donors, from multinational finance institutions to local bridge clubs who support us regularly. It is important to keep them informed about the impact of their donations, and the progress we are making.
- **Corporate Partners:** Youngcare's largest corporate supporter is Suncorp. We also receive a lot of in kind support from corporates, including legal firms, management consultants and media companies.
- **Volunteers:** Volunteers are crucial to Youngcare's activities, from supporting us at events, to providing expertise in their particular skills areas.

Remembering That Not For Profits Are Businesses Too

A not for profit might not need commercial success, but they still are financially accountable. The financial function and division of responsibilities, reporting, etc., is key to success, to transparency and to viability.

Our annual turnover was $4.75 million. To create a transparent system, we upgraded our systems to provide appropriate reports and analysis.

Managing the division of labour between the finance function and the board can be challenging. Drawing clear lines of responsibility and ensuring appropriate flow of information and feedback can ease the process and make sure everyone feels confident that this is strong and rigorous.

Samantha Kennerley
Former CEO, Youngcare
With Kirsten Lees
Principal, ThinkFirst

Note

1. Andrew Kakabadse. "Leading the Board: The Six Disciplines of World Class Chairmen," *Strategic Direction* 26, no. 8 (2010).

Bibliography

Kakabadse, Andrew. "Leading the Board: The Six Disciplines of World Class Chairmen." *Strategic Direction* 26, no. 8 (2010).

9   Leadership and Governance Issues in Faith Based Organisations

Susan Dann

Introduction

In recent times, as governments world-wide have reduced their direct role in welfare provision in favour of funding external organisations to deliver services, faith based organisations (FBOs) have become a key player in the highly-contested health and social welfare space. Whilst the vast majority of issues facing FBOs are identical to those facing secular NFPs, the history and fundamental rationale for the existence of FBOs means that these organisations will face some very specific and complex dilemmas.

The governance and leadership challenges facing faith based organisations, and many responses to these challenges, are similar across different faith traditions and across different manifestations of the same faith base. Due to size, formal organisation and level of international engagement, the focus of the FBO literature tends to be on those organisations from the Christian, Islamic and Judaic traditions.[1] This does not, however, mean that other faith traditions are absent in this space nor should there be any assumption that multiple organisations from the same faith base will operate in the same way. Specific responses to challenges will vary not only as a consequence of the faith tradition and faith based governance of the organisation in question, but also how that faith is interpreted and manifests in practice. Intra-faith differences between FBOs are at times greater than those which exist between secular and faith based organisations.[2]

Responses to issues are also moderated by the societal and governmental structures within which the organisation operates. In broad terms, where welfare provision is considered predominantly the role of the state, there will be a lesser role for FBOs than in societies where a conservative model of welfare operates and in which the primary responsibility for welfare falls to non-governmental bodies.[3]

In this chapter, issues will be considered at a broad faith level. However the focus will be on how FBOs respond to the challenges of being based on a faith tradition in economies and societies which are predominantly secular in their approaches. This excludes, therefore, any discussion of FBOs in theocracies where there is no clear separation between public and faith based institutions. Where possible, broad-based examples will be used—however, specific examples will be taken predominantly from the Australian context, and within the Australian context, on how the Roman Catholic Church* has responded to the increasing regulation and reporting requirements facing all NFP and FBO governance bodies.

Nature of Faith Based Organisations

Whilst participation in formal religion has declined in Australia, the US and in Europe, religion continues to be a major force in politics and society throughout the world, with more than 80 per cent of the world's population reporting a religious faith.[4] Religious based organisations with the purpose of providing services, including health, education and social services and which are derived from specific faith traditions are common throughout the world. There are more than 3,000 NGOs that the United Nations engages with and which have been afforded 'official' UN status. Of these, approximately 10 per cent can be classified as FBOs.[5]

The full scope of faith based organisational activities is very broad, however there is a preponderance of organisations in the broad charity and social sectors. A central characteristic of those attracted to FBOs tends to be faith as a motivating force to engage in compassionate pursuits regardless of faith tradition.[6] In particular, FBOs are very prominent in the fields of health, education and social welfare, although the exact extent of engagement is difficult to determine due to difficulties in data collection. Estimates relating to the impact of FBOs in the provision of health services in Africa, for example, vary widely from 30 to 70 percent.[7]

The rise of the FBO in service delivery, particularly in the United States, has resulted in a plethora of publications around the nature of FBOs including attempts to define and categorise FBOs. If there is one consistency in the definitional literature, it is that there is no accepted definition of what constitutes a faith based organisation.[8] At the simplest level, FBOs can be seen as being similar to secular NGOs in that they are independent, not for profit and altruistic, but differentiated by their affiliation with a religious structure, doctrine or community.[9]

Rather than focus on definitions, a number of authors instead have identified common characteristics of FBOs in an attempt to capture the diversity of foci and activities. Two such attempts are those presented by Jeavons (1997) and Sider and Unruh (2004).[10]

Jeavons' (1997) defining characteristics of FBOs are commonly cited in the literature and can be summarised as follows:[11]

1. The organisation self identifies as a religious organisation and displays this identity through its name, mission etc.;

---

* The terms Catholic or Catholic Church in this paper will be used to refer to the Roman Catholic Church rather than all Catholic traditions unless otherwise stated.

2. Employees, volunteers and clients of the organisation have a religious orientation;
3. Material resources are provided primarily by religious people or organisations;
4. Organisational goals, products and services are religious in nature and performed on the basis of religious values;
5. Decision-making relies on religious values, beliefs, activities or experiences in information processing and decision making;
6. Leadership tends to be vested either in a member of the clergy or requires that leaders have a theological education and/or that leaders are active in the life of a congregation; and
7. The organisation interacts predominantly with other religious organisations.

Since the recent increase in FBO and governmental interaction a number of these characteristics are less defining than at the time of publication however, most remain important differentiators between secular and faith based not for profit organisations. The extent to which characteristics 2, 3 and 6 are essential also depends on social and governmental context, with all three being less relevant to the Australian context, where faith based organisations have a long history of government funding and engagement, much of which is tied and so comes with the requirement to adhere to a range of related legislative restrictions.

Sider and Unruh (2004) propose a more complex six-fold classification system of FBOs.[12] Their system categorises organisations on a continuum based on the centrality of faith to organisational identity and programs or activities, and names the different types of organisations as follows:

1. Faith permeated
2. Faith centred
3. Faith affiliated
4. Faith background
5. Faith secular partnership and
6. Secular.

The typology further provides guidance on the classification of the organisation and its programs with the classification of the organisation based on:

1. Mission statement and other self-descriptive text;
2. Origins and foundations;
3. External affiliation(s);
4. Selection of board/directors, managers and staff;
5. Resourcing both financial and nonfinancial; and
6. Inclusion of religious practices

The classification of programs is based on:

1. Religious identity of the physical environment;
2. Religious content of programs;
3. Integration of religious content with other program components; and
4. Expected connection between religious content and desired outcomes.

Faith permeated, centred and affiliated organisations, for example, all have explicit religious references in their mission and self-descriptive texts. In comparison, faith background organisations may have historical ties to religious groups which are no longer active, and references to religion tend to be implicit rather than explicit (e.g. references to 'values'). Whilst the typology has its critics (see, for example, Jeavons 2004), it does provide a means by which organisations can be broadly categorised on a relative basis depending on the contemporary influence and impact of religion and faith on activities, governance, culture and leadership.[13]

For the purposes of this chapter, the focus is on FBOs which have a clear and overt link to a specific religious or faith tradition i.e. those which are faith permeated, centred or affiliated. It is important that to be considered an FBO the organisation should have an ongoing and living link with the religious base of its origins, and that the values and beliefs of that religious foundation continue to inform strategic intent including the development and implementation of programs within the organisation.

For the link to be overt it should include reference to its religious origins or purpose in the name, environment, branding, mission or statement of purpose. This would preclude, therefore, faith background organisations which, while they may have originated from within a specific faith base, have consciously and strategically moved away from contemporary engagement with the faith tradition via processes such as secular re-branding with no religious reference in name or iconography and a lack of mention of God, religion or faith in mission or purpose.

Faith Based Organisations in the Australia

FBOs as service providers, and the debates around their appropriate contribution, came to prominence in the US with the welfare reforms of the 1990s and the introduction of programs such as Charitable Choice.[14] In Britain the debate resurfaced in the context of the short lived Big Society Agenda.[15]

In contrast, the role of FBOs in providing education, health and welfare services in Australia is well established, embedded within the social structure and policy environment and consequently relatively, although not totally, uncontroversial. Swain traces the history of faith based welfare in Australia from its origins in the colonial era through to the present.[16] In so doing she demonstrates clear historical links between poverty alleviation and the welfare activities of FBOs.

Models of welfare delivery in Australia and co-operation between state and FBOs developed over the course of the 20th century to a point where there is an expectation that church organisations will, like state organisations, provide services to people regardless of faith affiliation. State funding for welfare programs in Australia requires that programs be "secular at the point of service delivery and open to all members of the community irrespective of religious belief" or nonbelief.[17] As a result, the role of religion and FBOs in welfare and social service delivery in Australia, in many ways, has been "normalized to the point where it was taken for granted."[18]

The Australian Charities and Not-for-Profits Commission (ACNC) estimates that, in Australia, there are approximately 9,500 religious based charities in Australia. These organisations employ more than 132,000 staff and engage over 500,000 volunteers. Over a third of these charities (38 per cent) have multiple purposes with advancing education, relief of poverty, sick or the needs of the aged being predominant amongst these alternative foci.[19]

Within the general classification of faith based organisations in Australia, there are multiple institutions founded in the Catholic faith tradition which provide education, health and social welfare services. The peak bodies representing these organisations are Catholic Health Australia and Catholic Social Services. In addition, the National and state Catholic Education Commissions are responsible for the Catholic schools sector.

As an indication of the approximate size and reach of these organisations, Catholic Health Australia represents over 75 hospitals and 550 aged care facilities operated by different arms of the Catholic Church in Australia. This accounts for approximately 19,000 residential and aged care beds, 9,500 beds in health care facilities, 14,000 community or home care service recipients and 35,000 employees.[20]

Catholic Social Services represents "a national network of 53 Catholic social service organisations that provide direct support to hundreds of thousands of people in need each year on behalf of the Catholic Church."[21] These services include assisting women and children escaping family violence, housing and homelessness support, mental health and disability services, refugee and asylum seeker support and various partnerships delivering services to indigenous communities. It is estimated that Catholic social welfare organisations provide services to more than a million Australians each year, arguably collectively forming the largest provider of welfare services in Australia.[22]

Catholic Education employs approximately 91,000 to teach 765,000 students, of whom 30 per cent are not from a Catholic faith background. The number of students has been growing steadily and it is anticipated that the number of students will increase to around 950,000 within 10 years. The number of Catholic schools is also anticipated to continue to grow, with an extra 200 expected to be built over the next five years to add to the existing 1,700.[23]

Despite the overall secular nature of Australian society, it is clear that FBOs have a significant social and economic impact in Australia. It is important then to better understand the challenges facing these organisations with respect to their governance and leadership responsibilities.

Governance and Leadership Issues Facing Faith Based Organisations

On one level, FBOs are no different from other NFPs in relation to the challenges they face. Increasing demands for service, competitive and non-guaranteed income streams, extensive and complex reporting requirements and complex social problems are stretching the resources of all NFPs. It is not the intent of this chapter to focus on these commonalities, although in practice these outweigh the differences, but rather to shed some light on key specific issues facing FBOs in addition to those facing secular NFPs.

On the surface many FBOs can appear to clients and outside bodies to be secular in terms of the services provided and even the name or branding of the organisation. In examining the differences between secular NFPs and FBOs Ebaugh et al. posed the question, "Where's the religion?"[24] Their response is 'everywhere'—in self-presentation, staff and volunteers, resourcing approaches and decision-making processes. It is at these points of difference and their interactions with the wide community and funding bodies, including government, that FBOs are facing particular challenges.

Service Provision

One of the key challenges for all NFPs including FBOs is for the leadership of the organisation to re-orient staff toward a service mindset that is inclusive of strategic business perspectives. Much of the discussion about mission versus business has been resolved as a result of external pressures, and in particular the operational requirements and reporting obligations faced by all NFPs in receipt of government funding. With the entry of large scale for profit enterprises into traditional NFP fields such as community and aged care, the need for demonstrably high quality systems and service delivery is essential across the sector.

With respect to whether FBOs provide a service which is commensurate with those provided by other NFPs, in an analysis of existing studies Bielefeld and Cleveland found that the quality of service provision by secular and religious NFPs was perceived as similar, with some studies finding service to be perceived as superior in FBOs.[25] The reason for this, however, is likely to be accounted for by self-selection of staff and clients attracted to a faith infused environment at times of crisis.

In contrast, Amirkhhanyan et al. undertook a quantitative analysis of service quality indicators in the aged care sector and found no evidence to support the common perception that FBOs provide higher quality services when compared to secular NFPs. Overall secular NFPs provided a wider range of services when compared with FBOs indicating that FBOs tend to be more specialised in their practical application of mission.

The challenge for both FBOs and other NFPs is to maintain and exceed the quality of services in light of the increasingly competitive market.

Funding

FBOs "derive their identity and purpose from religious or spiritual traditions but state funding can place restrictions on organisations with respect of religious expression."[26] This quote highlights a key challenge for FBOs when competing with other NFPs for state funding. Some researchers such as Amirkhanyan et al. raise the question as to whether or not faith focused organisations in receipt of government money should be allowed access to that money without having to lose their mission or change their mission.[27]

In the Australian context, and given the size and integration of FBOs in the overall delivery of health, education, and social welfare services, a significant withdrawal of funding to FBOs arguably would create significant negative repercussions.

Where conditions related to the receipt of funding focus on reporting or compliance to safety standards and so on, the impact is felt equally across all NFPs due to the increased costs of compliance. It is when there are additional requirements which may conflict with religious views that hard decisions need to be made.

There are increasing concerns amongst contemporary agencies that by becoming over-reliant on government funding FBOs may be constrained in their faith driven advocacy roles, especially around issues related to the "poor and dispossessed" including refugees.[28] The pressures of funding are such that some groups may choose to forgo funding for specific programs or overall, to maintain their independence in determining models of service delivery.[29]

A related challenge for large FBOs operating in multiple sub-sectors of social welfare provision is that government funding for services in one area may see the organisation assisting people who another program within the organisation is sanctioning. For example, the move of a number of FBOs into employment service provision means that one arm of the broad faith group is responsible for reporting breaches of conditions which may result in government sanctions. At the same time another arm of the organisation is funded to provide welfare services to assist those whose benefits have been removed or reduced as a result of such sanctions.[30]

While funding restrictions impact on all NFPs, there is a strong potential for funding conditions to undermine the core religious and spiritual purpose of FBOs. As Bielefeld and Cleveland (2013 p. 452) succinctly summarise the issue, "government funding and market forces are powerful secularising forces."[31]

Impact of Charism and Maintenance of Religious Purpose

Central to the authentic longevity of FBOs is the capacity of the organisation to sustain its fundamental faith focused organisational purpose, particularly in light of changing regulatory and financial circumstances. Competitive external factors can result in NFPs and FBOs changing their strategic direction, however the constraints on FBOs which are founded in faith traditions can be particularly complex.

Within the Catholic tradition institutions often draw on the *charism* of the founder or founding religious congregations to guide strategic direction. Charism is defined as "a gift given by the Holy Spirit to a person or group for a particular work in the world."[32] Seven characteristics of charism have been identified i.e.:[33]

1. "Special gifts that equip the faithful for a way of life or specific ministry in the Church;
2. Originate with the Holy Spirit;
3. Are given to founders of religious congregations;
4. Are subsequently transmitted from founders to followers;
5. Are authenticated by the Church's pastors, who share responsibility with the religious congregations for preserving them;
6. Are distinctive; and
7. Should be used for the ongoing renewal of the Church."

The charism of a particular order or religious community determines its identity, way of life, spirituality and structure. It is through adherence and commitment to specific charisms that Catholic institutions are able to differentiate themselves not only from secular organisations or other FBOs but also from each other within the Catholic faith tradition.[34] The concept of charism, or divinely inspired works, is not unique to Catholicism but rather is common across faith traditions.

One of the key leadership and strategic decisions facing FBOs is how to maintain and appropriately communicate the charism in an increasingly secular and regulated operational and competitive environment. One of the key challenges for the laity involved in the management of faith based organisations is appreciating and maintaining the charism given the decreased presence of the religious in daily engagement with the ministries.

Whilst many FBOs have embraced this challenge and have used the works of the founders and associated charism as a central plank for defining operational purpose, some institutions have retreated from their religious identity in the face of government and market forces. Evidence of such retreats comes in various forms including the secularisation of mission statements and de-emphasis of religious identity. These actions are often driven by the need to access and secure stable funding in an increasingly competitive environment.[35]

Ebaugh et al. report that despite external pressure, the vast majority (>80 per cent) of faith based organisations retain religious references or symbolism in their external communications via branding, name and imagery.[36] Consequently it is usually relatively easy to identify FBOs from the public presentation of the organisation.

Fidelity to the charism or equivalent religious purpose is a significant challenge facing contemporary FBOs.

Attracting and Retaining Staff

Although in the same market for labour resources as commercial enterprises, FBOs, like many other NFPs, tend to pay less. They also have a higher reliance on volunteers.[37] Like other NFPs in the Australian context however it is possible for FBOs to offer attractive overall packages due to tax incentives.

Overall in the literature, there is considerable evidence that employees are attracted to work in, or volunteer with, FBOs for reasons other than financial remuneration. Bassous (2013) found that the main incentives attracting and retaining staff into FBOs were leadership style, organisational culture, mission and job meaningfulness.[38] Practices such as pay incentives for performance were considered of limited or no value in motivating staff.

A contentious issue for all faith based organisations is the extent to which FBOs may enact or apply for exemptions to anti-discrimination laws with respect to employment and client service. While many staff may self-select into a compatible faith based environment this cannot be assumed.

There is a delicate balance which needs to be maintained between organisational performance needs and regulatory requirements and the desire to maintain a distinctive faith based culture.

Again while this dilemma has a specific manifestation in FBOs, it is present in other organisations in the NFP space where organisational objectives and values have the potential to influence hiring and management decisions. For example, some health-related NFPs have a preference to employ staff who model their health behaviours such as not smoking, maintaining an appropriate weight, and exercising.

Responding to Leadership Challenges

As outlined in the introduction, a number of the specific examples as to how FBOs respond to the challenges of operating in increasingly regulated secular environments will be drawn from the experience of the Roman Catholic Church in Australia.

The Catholic Church is arguably one of the oldest continuously functioning international entities in the world, with an organisational culture and history stretching back 2,000 years. Worldwide there are currently estimated to be 1.3 billion Catholics which accounts for around 17.5% of the world's population.[39] An organisation with such a long history and large membership inevitably has complex internal governance structures which have developed over the centuries to respond to changing contexts over time.

It would be a mistake however to conceptualise the Catholic Church as a monolithic body with a rigid approach to all social, political and governance issues and with a single response to all issues. Within the Church many different religious orders operate, each of which has its own internal structures and focus. All are bound however by core principles of Church teaching and Church (canon) law.[40]

Maintaining the Charism or Organisational Purpose

As previously outlined a significant challenge facing the leadership of FBOs is to maintain the charism of the founder and stay true to the purpose of the organisation. Hall (2005) quoted in Bielefeld and Cleveland (2013) argues that organisational values "once institutionalized, have a taken for granted status and are unlikely to be altered unless changing circumstances lead people to question them."[41] While the founding religion or order provides an identity reflecting the way that religion views service, maintaining that identity is not automatic and requires ongoing management.

Most contemporary Church based organisations have embedded their religious values in programs and organisational culture and conceptualise their welfare work as modelling their values rather than preaching them.[42] The practice of living faith helps to connect spiritual nurturing to organisational activities. This integration and embodiment of religion into daily activities helps to maintain the organisational identity of the FBO.[43]

Charism however extends beyond a simple definition of values and provides a stable point of reference over time as an aid for discernment and decision-making. While the charism provides constancy, the manifestation of the charism in specific works changes over time. Consequently an in depth understanding of the charism is required to be able to maintain its dynamism in a changing world. Changed manifestations may take the form of expanding to new areas of endeavour in response to a new manifestation of need or alternatively withdrawal from established ministries where there is no longer a need or where the need is being serviced by alternative means e.g. governmental programs.[44]

Strategically embedding and maintaining the charism is the responsibility of senior staff including board directors. The mechanisms for doing this are often embedded in education and formation activities.

Governance Structures

In order to separate the spiritual and corporate governance/legal accountabilities of religious based organisations, one option is for it to adopt a dual governance structure. An approach which has been used by some entities within the Catholic Church to provide a governance structure around the maintenance of the founder charism in the face of declining congregational numbers and active congregational participation in management and governance is the creation of entities known as *Public Juridic Persons (PJP)*.

A Public Juridic Person (PJP) is a legal entity under canon (Church) law that allows the Church's ministries to function in the name of the Catholic Church. PJPs are formally defined as "aggregates of persons or things which are established by the competent ecclesiastical authority so that, within the limits allotted to them in the name of the Church, and in accordance with the provisions of law, they might fulfil the specific task entrusted to them for the public good."[45]

Whilst in practice this is a complex process, and each case will vary, a simple explanation below highlights some of the key principles. The first step in this process is usually to restructure the relevant ministry, whether it is a school, health facility or other organisation, as a company. The purpose of this process is to separate civil accountabilities from canonical responsibilities. The company manages programs and services and engages with government and other funding bodies using standard reporting process as required by law. The management of the company reports to a board of directors.

Membership of the company typically is the organisation (PJP) created to maintain the mission of the founding congregation. The PJP in turn is generally managed by a board of trustees whose underpinning purpose is to ensure the continuance of the charism. The company provides a report to the member on all issues, including mission related issues, annually at an AGM in the same way that companies report to shareholders. Trustees are predominantly, and in some cases exclusively, members of the laity. The Trustees also typically appoint the board(s) of directors of the company(ies).

Reporting of the PJP will vary according to which competent ecclesiastical authority it is set up under. These two tiers of governance allow the FBO to fulfil civil responsibilities but also provide, through canon law structures, a clarification of the relationship between the organisation, Church and sponsoring congregation.[46]

An example of a large PJP which has multiple ministries reporting into it is Mary Aikenhead Ministries, created to carry on and expand the health, aged care, education and welfare ministries previously conducted by the Sisters of Charity. The Trustees in turn report annually to the Holy See's Congregation for Institutes of Consecrated Life and Societies of Apostolic Life.*

Decision Making and Discernment

In order to maintain the essential nature and purpose of the organisation, faith based organisations engage a final filter of decision making which explicitly refines decisions in light of the ministry of the organisation and the charism. It is insufficient in the context of strategic decision making for the Board or Trustees of an FBO to simply consider those financial, legal and marketing analyses which are integrated into a business plan or proposal without also explicitly considering the spiritual and mission dimensions.

* www.maryaikenheadministries.org.au

While both secular NFPs and FBOs rely on similar secular expertise and decision-making models, FBOs supplement these models with spiritual exercises to reach decisions.[47] This may include something as simple as prayer, which is typically used to open decision-making meetings as a way of focusing discussion or more complex models. It may simply be the final question, "How does this action further the vision of the founder?"

Discernment, as the term is used within Christian faith communities, refers to a decision-making process whereby the decision-makers engage in spiritual exercises in an attempt to align their will with God's. Discernment is an essential tool for decision-making in faith based organisations. It is also an ongoing process whereby once made, decisions are constantly reviewed in light of the fruits or outcomes of the decision and adjusted as necessary.

Gallagher and Goodstein, for example, outline the complex mission discernment process used by the Holy Cross Health System in the US.[48] Not all decisions are subject to this process, but rather it is reserved for key strategic decisions that affect the organisation's identity or impacts on the capacity care of the poor and vulnerable or other key mission elements.

The process adopted by Holy Cross Health System enables a broadened discussion of ethical implications, responsiveness to the interests of key stakeholders and the positive or negative impact on the organisation's commitment to care of the poor. Discussion is driven by issues of integrity, self-identity, empowerment, stewardship and human dignity as expressed through the mission of the organisation.

Education, Formation and Employees

While many people who work in faith based organisations have a prior affiliation with that faith tradition, increasingly FBOs employ staff of other faiths or no faith background. The challenge for both organisation and employee then is how to transmit the mission, vision and charism of the organisation in a way which is meaningful and appropriate.

As a general rule, FBOs have no requirement that employees are members of the foundational religion but rather that they support and enact the mission and values of the organisation in the workplace. Often employees are attracted to and support the values of the FBO even where they do not subscribe to the religious foundation.[49] With respect to volunteers, however, there is some evidence to indicate that volunteers tend to be attracted to the specific faith base, not just the values.[50]

Within the context of Catholic social welfare organisations, for example, which are based on the principles of Catholic social thought,* non-Catholics are often attracted by values such as human dignity, preferential

---

* Catholic social thought or teaching is the body of doctrine developed by the Catholic Church on matters of social justice. While precise definitions vary, the core principles of Catholic social thought are: human dignity, the common good, solidarity, subsidiarity, stewardship, dignity of work and preferential option for the poor.

options for the poor, and stewardship (sustainability). Recruitment is generally based around commitment to mission and values rather than religious orientation.[51]

To ensure a common understanding of the charism and values, FBOs will generally undertake a combination of education and formation programs. Education provides the information about the history of the organisation, founders' stories and definition of values whereas formation activities allow employees to explore these themes in more depth from a spiritual development perspective.

Staff induction programs provide the ideal opportunity to introduce the religious ethos and heritage.[52] For many staff from different backgrounds, the narrative of the founder is an engaging way to introduce the complex concepts of charism as well as the foundational values.

Conclusions

Faith based organisations are major contributors world-wide in the fields of health, education and social welfare. Despite their prevalence, however, relatively little academic work has been undertaken on FBOs. That which has been undertaken is generally focused on issues impacting on Christian based organisations.

Many of the issues which face FBOs are common to all not for profits, however by the nature of being founded in a religious context or faith base these organisations face additional challenges with respect to governance and leadership. This chapter has highlighted some of these issues, particularly those around maintenance of mission in light of increasingly competitive and condition-based funding. In discussing how these issues are being addressed by FBOs the main focus has been on the Catholic Church in Australia, although the same issues are being addressed in a similar way across faith traditions.

Notes

1. Jeffrey Haynes. "Faith-Based Organisations at the United Nations," 2013.
2. Michael Barnett and Janice Gross Stein. "Introduction: The Secularization and Sanctification of Humanitarianism," in *Sacred Aid: Faith and Humanitarianism*, eds. Michael Barnet and Janice Gross Stein (Oxford: Oxford University Press, 2012).
3. Beth R. Crisp. "Social Work and Faith-Based Agencies in Sweden and Australia," *International Social Work* 56, no. 3 (2013): 343–355.
4. Pew Research Center. "The Global Religious Landscape," 2012, www.pewforum.org/files/2014/01/global-religion-full.pdf, Retrieved on 15-01-17.
5. Haynes.
6. Ipsita Mitra. "The Politics of Faith and Space: A Study of Faith-based Organizations," *Asian Journal of Multidisciplinary Studies* 3, no. 7 (2015).
7. Jill Olivier, Clarence Tsimpo, Regina Gemignani, Mari Shojo, Harold Coulombe, Frank Dimmock, Minh Cong Nguyen et al. "Understanding the Roles of Faith-Based Health-Care Providers in Africa: Review of the Evidence with a Focus on

Magnitude, Reach, Cost, and Satisfaction," *The Lancet* 386, no. 10005 (2015): 1765–1775.

8. Thomas H. Jeavons. "Religious and Faith-Based Organizations: Do We Know One When We See One?" *Nonprofit and Voluntary Sector Quarterly* 33, no. 1 (2004): 140–145.

9. Matthew Clarke and Vicki-Anne Ware. "Understanding Faith-Based Organizations: How FBOs Are Contrasted with NGOs in International Development Literature," *Progress in Development Studies* 15, no. 1 (2015): 37–48.

10. T. H. Jeavons, "Identifying Characteristics of "Religious" Organizations: An Exploratory Proposal," in *Sacred Companies: Organizational Aspects of Religion and Religious Aspects of Organizations*, ed. J. Memerath III, P.D. Hall, T. Schnitt and R.H. Williams (New York: Oxford University Press, 1997), 79–95; Ronald J. Sider and Heidi Rolland Unruh. "Typology of Religious Characteristics of Social Service and Educational Organizations and Programs," *Nonprofit and Voluntary Sector Quarterly* 33, no. 1 (2004): 109–134.

11. Jeavons.

12. Sider and Unruh.

13. Jeavons.

14. Wolfgang Bielefeld and William Suhs Cleveland. "Defining Faith-Based Organizations and Understanding Them Through Research," *Nonprofit and Voluntary Sector Quarterly* 42, no. 3 (2013): 442–467.

15. Steven Kettell. "Thematic Review: Religion and the Big Society: A Match Made in Heaven? Steven Kettell," *Policy & Politics* 40, no. 2 (2012): 281–296.

16. Shurlee Swain. "A Long History of Faith-Based Welfare in Australia: Origins and Impact, " *Journal of Religious History* 41, no. 1 (2017): 81–96.

17. Beth R. Crisp. "Challenges to Organizational Spirituality as a Consequence of State Funding," *Journal for the Study of Spirituality* 5, no. 1 (2015): 48.

18. Rose Melville and Catherine McDonald. " 'Faith-Based' Organisations and Contemporary Welfare," *Australian Journal of Social Issues* 41, no. 1 (2006): 69.

19. P. Knight and D. Gilchrist. *Australia's Faith-Based Charities 2013: A Summary of Data from the Australian Charities 2013*, 2015.

20. Catholic Health Australia, 2017, www.cha.org.au

21. Catholic Social Services Australia, 2017, www.cssa.org.au

22. Crisp.

23. National Catholic Education Commission, www.ncec.org.au, Retrieved on 20-01-17.

24. Helen Rose Ebaugh, Paula F. Pipes, Janet Saltzman Chafetz and Martha Daniels. "Where's the Religion? Distinguishing Faith-Based from Secular Social Service Agencies," *Journal for the Scientific Study of Religion* 42, no. 3 (2003): 411–426.

25. Wolfgang Bielefeld and William Suhs Cleveland. "Faith-Based Organizations as Service Providers and Their Relationship to Government," *Nonprofit and Voluntary Sector Quarterly* 42, no. 3 (2013): 468–494.

26. Crisp, 48.

27. Anna A. Amirkhanyan, Hyun Joon Kim and Kristina T. Lambright. "Faith-Based Assumptions About Performance: Does Church Affiliation Matter for Service Quality and Access?" *Nonprofit and Voluntary Sector Quarterly* 38, no. 3 (2009): 490–521.

28. Swain.

29. Crisp.

30. Swain.
31. Bielefeld and Cleveland, 452.
32. Catechism of the Catholic Church, 799, www.vatican.va/archive/ENG0015/_ INDEX.HTM, Retrieved from 20-01-17.
33. Susan M. Sanders. "Charisms, Congregational Sponsors, and Catholic Higher Education," *Journal of Catholic Higher Education* 29, no. 1 (2010): 5.
34. Timothy J. Cook and Thomas A. Simonds. "The Charism of 21st-Century Catholic Schools: Building a Culture of Relationships," *Journal of Catholic Education* 14, no. 3 (2011).
35. Bielefeld and Cleveland, 468–494.
36. Ebaugh et al.
37. Crisp.
38. Bassous, Michael. "What Are the Factors that Affect Worker Motivation in Faith-Based Nonprofit Organizations?" *VOLUNTAS: International Journal of Voluntary and Nonprofit Organizations* 26, no. 1 (2015): 355–381.
39. Pew.
40. Canon Law Society. *The Code of Canon Law* (Bangalore: Theological Publications, 2010).
41. Bielefeld and Cleveland. Peter Dobkin Hall. "The Rise of the Civic Engagement Tradition," *Taking Faith Seriously* (2005): 59.
42. Swain.
43. Bielefeld and Cleveland.
44. Sanders.
45. Canon Law Society, 116.
46. Sanders.
47. Ebaugh et al.
48. John A. Gallagher and Jerry Goodstein. "Fulfilling Institutional Responsibilities in Health Care: Organizational Ethics and the Role of Mission Discernment," *Business Ethics Quarterly* 12, no. 4 (2002): 433–450.
49. Crisp.
50. Ebaugh et al.
51. Crisp.
52. Ibid.

Bibliography

Amirkhanyan, Anna A., Hyun Joon Kim, and Kristina T. Lambright. "Faith-Based Assumptions About Performance: Does Church Affiliation Matter for Service Quality and Access?." *Nonprofit and Voluntary Sector Quarterly* 38, no. 3 (2009): 490–521.

Barnett, Michael and Janice Gross Stein. "Introduction: The Secularization and Sanctification of Humanitarianism." In *Sacred Aid. Faith and Humanitarianism*, edited by Michael Barnet and Janice Gross Stein. Oxford: University Press, 2012.

Bassous, Michael. "What Are the Factors That Affect Worker Motivation in Faith-based Nonprofit Organizations?" *VOLUNTAS: International Journal of Voluntary and Nonprofit Organizations* 26, no. 1 (2015): 355–81.

Bielefeld, Wolfgang, and William Suhs Cleveland. "Faith-based Organizations as Service Providers and Their Relationship to Government." *Nonprofit and Voluntary Sector Quarterly* 42, no. 3 (2013): 468–94.

Bielefeld, Wolfgang, and William Suhs Cleveland. "Defining Faith-based Organizations and Understanding Them Through Research." *Nonprofit and Voluntary Sector Quarterly* 42, no. 3 (2013): 442–67.

Canon Law Society. *The Code of Canon Law*. Bangalore: Theological Publications, 2010.

Catechism of the Catholic Church. 1994. Accessed 20 January 2017. Retrieved from www.vatican.va/archive/ENG0015/_INDEX.HTM

Catholic Health Australia. 2017. Retrieved from www.cha.org.au

Catholic Social Services Australia. 2017. Retrieved from www.cssa.org.au

Clarke, Matthew, and Vicki-Anne Ware. "Understanding Faith-based Organizations: How FBOs Are Contrasted With NGOs in International Development Literature." *Progress in Development Studies* 15, no. 1 (2015): 37–48.

Cook, Timothy J., and Thomas A. Simonds. "The Charism of 21st-Century Catholic Schools: Building a Culture of Relationships." *Journal of Catholic Education* 14, no. 3 (2011).

Crisp, Beth R. "Social Work and Faith-based Agencies in Sweden and Australia." *International Social Work* 56, no. 3 (2013): 343–55.

Crisp, Beth R. "Challenges to Organizational Spirituality as a Consequence of State Funding." *Journal for the Study of Spirituality* 5, no. 1 (2015): 47–59.

Ebaugh, Helen Rose, Paula F. Pipes, Janet Saltzman Chafetz, and Martha Daniels. "Where's the Religion? Distinguishing Faith-Based From Secular Social Service Agencies." *Journal for the Scientific Study of Religion* 42, no. 3 (2003): 411–26.

Gallagher, John A., and Jerry Goodstein. "Fulfilling Institutional Responsibilities in Health Care: Organizational Ethics and the Role of Mission Discernment." *Business Ethics Quarterly* 12, no. 4 (2002): 433–50.

Hall, Peter Dobkin. "The Rise of the Civic Engagement Tradition." *Taking Faith Seriously* (2005): 21–60.

Haynes, Jeffrey. Faith-Based Organisations at the United Nations. 2013.

Jeavons, Thomas H. "Religious and Faith-Based Organizations: Do We Know One When We See One?" *Nonprofit and Voluntary Sector Quarterly* 33, no. 1 (2004): 140–5.

Jeavons, T. H. "Identifying Characteristics of 'Religious' Organizations: An Exploratory Proposal." In *Sacred Companies: Organizational Aspects of Religion and Religious Aspects of Organizations*, edited by J. Memerath III, P. D. Hall, T. Schnitt and R. H. Williams. New York: Oxford University Press, 1997, p79–95.

Kettell, Steven. "Thematic Review: Religion and the Big Society: A Match Made in Heaven? Steven Kettell." *Policy & Politics* 40, no. 2 (2012): 281–96.

Knight, P., and D. Gilchrist. Australia's Faith-Based Charities 2013: A Summary of Data From the Australian Charities 2013. 2015.

Melville, Rose, and Catherine McDonald. "'Faith-Based' Organisations and Contemporary Welfare." *Australian Journal of Social Issues* 41, no. 1 (2006): 69.

Mitra, Ipsita. "The Politics of Faith and Space: A Study of Faith-based Organizations." *Asian Journal of Multidisciplinary Studies* 3, no. 7 (2015).

National Catholic Education Commission. Accessed 20 January 2017. Retrieved from www.ncec.org.au

Olivier, Jill, Clarence Tsimpo, Regina Gemignani, Mari Shojo, Harold Coulombe, Frank Dimmock, Minh Cong Nguyen et al. "Understanding the Roles of Faith-based Health-Care Providers in Africa: Review of the Evidence With a Focus on Magnitude, Reach, Cost, and Satisfaction." *The Lancet* 386, no. 10005 (2015): 1765–75.

Pew Research Center. The Global Religious Landscape. 2012. Accessed 15 January 2017. Retrieved from www.pewforum.org/files/2014/01/global-religion-full.pdf

Sanders, Susan M. "Charisms, Congregational Sponsors, and Catholic Higher Education." *Journal of Catholic Higher Education* 29, no. 1 (2010): 3–18.

Sider, Ronald J., and Heidi Rolland Unruh. "Typology of Religious Characteristics of Social Service and Educational Organizations and Programs." *Nonprofit and Voluntary Sector Quarterly* 33, no. 1 (2004): 109–34.

Swain, Shurlee. "A Long History of Faith-Based Welfare in Australia: Origins and Impact." *Journal of Religious History* 41, no. 1 (2017): 81–96.

Churches of Christ Care

Introduction

Churches of Christ in Queensland, under the banner of Churches of Christ Care, is one of Australia's largest providers of care, accommodation and community services targeting those most in need. In this case study, we consider what drives this faith based not-for-profit, and gain an understanding of its approach to strategy, leadership, public policy and brand management. We will also reflect on some of the obstacles that it has encountered along the way.

History

Churches of Christ Care (then known as Churches of Christ in Queensland Social Service Department) was established in 1930. The organisation started in response to social needs identified by a group of the faithful who reached into their own pockets, funding services that the government didn't or couldn't fund. Starting with a single aged care service in Brisbane, today the organisation cares for over 27,000 people in need across in excess of 150 services in the States of Queensland, Victoria, and the Pacific nation of Vanuatu. Its geographical footprint is larger than 93% of the nations of the world; employs around 3,500 paid staff and 1,500 registered volunteers; and its financial turnover is around $240 million per annum, with a $600 million asset base.

Churches of Christ in Queensland is constituted under Letters Patent, an ancient (and little understood) legal instrument issued to the organisation under royal decree. While a useful and flexible means of incorporation, it is poorly understood in other jurisdictions. Given this, the organisation has pursued other forms of recognition/incorporation for the organisation, or parts of the organisation, including an Australian Company Number, permitting easier cross border trade, and creating (ASIC recognised) companies limited by guarantee for special purpose vehicles/dedicated service streams.

Governance

The organisation is governed by a skills based and remunerated board who are accountable to the membership of Churches of Christ in Queensland,

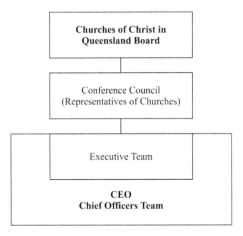

Figure 9.1 Governance structure of Churches of Christ in Queensland

represented by a group (the Conference Council) elected from the membership of the churches (Figure 9.1). The board appoint the CEO, who is part of a four person Chief Officers Team (also including the Chief Operating Officer, Chief Mission Development Officer, and Chief Financial Officer). The Chief Officers together are the key decision makers of the organisation, responsible for day-to-day leadership and management of Churches of Christ in Queensland, including all wholly owned entities.

The Chief Officers also form part of a 15 person Executive Team. This broader group is responsible for developing and disseminating organisational policy, and ensuring achievement of organisational strategy.

Focus and Mission

Churches of Christ Care is principally focused on the areas of: Children Youth and Families (including early childhood services, family based early intervention, and out of home care for children/young people who have been abused or neglected); Community Housing; and Seniors and Supported Living (including community care, residential care, and retirement living). It also provides a range of discrete services in response to identified local community needs, including for example: a medical clinic and rural health outreach, rural chaplaincy, drop in centres/cafes, social enterprise activities, and men's sheds.

There are certainly larger organisations in particular service streams, especially listed aged care providers. And as the population ages, and there continues to be a dollar made out of aged care in Australia, the number and size of players in this space will grow. However, such organisations would never entertain managing a 10 bed aged care service in Cunnamulla, nine hours' drive from Brisbane (as close to the 'Outback' as you can get), or in many other rural and remote communities that Churches of Christ operates. It is also a fact that the *raison d'être* of many such operators is shareholder return, not necessarily social return for the client and the broader community.

This driving focus on a social return, personal uplift, or community benefit, however you would like to express it, is summed up in the organisation's unifying mission statement: "Bringing the light of Christ into communities." Its mission is very much focussed on its understanding of the character of Christ: a person who loved unconditionally, was driven by a strong sense of justice, preached compassion, and demonstrated an unwavering desire to improve the world around him for the lost, hurt, hungry, unclean or unloved. And this is what drives the organisation and has done so for the past 85 plus years. It's also what has driven similar faith based organisations stretching back millennia.

At their best, faith-based community services organisations are capable of demonstrating great compassion that is very difficult for governments to replicate. Their mission compels them to go where government and others don't or won't, and their commitment often extends way beyond election or funding cycles.

But the organisation doesn't just step out in blind faith to do "good works" across the countryside, void of strategy or discipline. This may, to an extent, characterise the approach of some not-for-profits, but as with our for-profit cousins, it's not a recipe for success or longevity.

Values and Biblical Principles

Churches of Christ in Queensland (the parent entity of Churches of Christ Care) promotes three core values, also well steeped in biblical principles: modelling unconditional love; being good stewards; and behaving with integrity.

The first value, or a similar variant, is what you might expect coming from a faith based organisation. While you may expect to see 'unconditional love' written, it is actually very difficult to practice. Without doubt, it is the first amongst the organisation's values. However, if it were the organisation's only value or guiding principle, the organisation may well risk going the way of the dinosaur. For unconditional love to be practised sustainably requires a framework of good stewardship and integrity.

The notion of good stewardship is particularly key to the organisation's financial success. It is a truism that where there is no margin there is no mission. All successful organisations effectively manage their resources, and the most effective employees (including managers) are firstly good stewards of themselves.

By and large, the organisation has exercised sound stewardship, exponentially increasing its reach and impact over the past fifteen years. It has also made its mistakes along the way. In an attempt to be good stewards, it

established commercial activities with the intent of generating profits to subsidise activities of high missional benefit/low return. While this is a sound
principle, in its zeal the organisation purchased businesses such as tourist
ventures, and a motel in a mining town. A downturn in tourism, and some
years later a downturn in the mining industry, respectively turned income
generators into cost centres! The moral to this story: know what your core
business is, play to your strengths, and learn from your mistakes.

Exercising stewardship has also meant making tough decisions to close
whole service streams in areas that the organisation has not had sufficient depth of skill to run as optimally as it should (e.g. drug and alcohol
services; and residential disability care), recognising that there are other
organisations eminently better qualified and resourced. Similarly, while it
has acquired many individual services over the years, it has also decided
to close a number, determining that cost of operation outweighed missional benefit. Knowing when and how to exit something is as important
as recognising the right acquisition. For many not-for-profits, (including
churches) the asset becomes a millstone around their neck and they forget
their reason for being—which is rarely about buildings. For still others,
existence has become their primary reason for being: community needs
may have changed, government and other organisations may have stepped
in where once they had no presence, but the board may continue to hold
onto the reason for their initial incorporation, and the habit of monthly
meetings!

For Churches of Christ in Queensland, it has continued to respond to
the environment in which it exists: mostly driven by community need, but
well informed by government regulation, and market dynamics. It has also
developed a diversified funding model: ensuring scale across various service
streams (e.g. seniors care and accommodation, and community housing)
and diversification of service types that promotes vertical integration within
each stream (e.g. community care, retirement living and residential aged
care within the seniors care service stream). Furthermore, it has ensured sufficient resourcing and staff specialisation within each service type.

As a faith based organisation that receives a large amount of public funding, as well as donations from individuals and organisations, and in occupy-
ing what some would see as a position of moral authority, it has a lot to lose
if it doesn't conduct itself in a manner consistent with public expectation.
Enter the pillar of Integrity. The organisation has earned universal respect
from its funders and government partners as one that will strive to meet and
more likely exceed standards, and proactively manage poor performance.
This hasn't always been the case however. In the past it, like other faith
based not-for-profits, has put up with poor performers. Managers haven't
wanted to offend them, thinking it somehow wouldn't be Christian to do
so. This misplaced grace can affect an organisation like cancer, conferring
an acceptance of mediocrity and thereby pulling others down to the lowest
common denominator.

While treating staff with respect, the organisation is under no misapprehension as to who it exists to serve. It is cultivating a client-centric approach, moving away from an entitlement-based, staff-centric culture that can ironically characterise some 'community services' organisations.

If the above focus on the organisation's Christian heart seems sanctimonious, it's certainly not intended to be. Rather, it is intended to explain much of what is to follow. The leaders of Churches of Christ in Qld truly believe in the organisation's mission and attempt to uphold its values, as lofty as they are. At its base, there's not a lot more complexity to the organisation than that: knowing its mission and staying close to its values.

Demonstrating the Mission and Values in Practice

In being very public about its mission and values, and actually demonstrating them in practice, the organisation has attracted like-minded leaders, staff and volunteers. At a time when we are told that it is impossible to attract volunteers, the organisation has tripled the number of registered volunteers from 500 to 1500 in three years. It has attracted government funding, including capital grants, at a time of government fiscal constraint. It has received critical acclaim from government departments and industry contemporaries, and registers consistently high satisfaction levels from clients and staff. It is increasingly seen as a go-to organisation in communities and industries that it is a part of.

So what's the difference here: why have some NFP's struggled, and even contracted, while Churches of Christ in Qld has expanded?

As highlighted earlier, Churches of Christ Care, like other contemporary faith-based service providers, was founded by conviction and contribution by folks who had 'skin in the game': donating money, skills, time, or prayerful support to make a difference in the lives of other people in a community where they were personally connected. The early growth of this and other organisations was based on these initial foundations, replicating the model of service development with strong input from folks in local church congregations and communities: it's a story played out across the country. Such folks invariably responded to local need where they saw it, engaging government where possible but not being limited by their ability to do so. If there was a will, and no government support, there would still more often than not be a way.

But over the later 20th century the government established itself as principal funder in a number of social and community services areas. Increasing legislation and the related compliance burden, including the cost of non-compliance and possible litigation, forced a consolidation of services under a corporate umbrella, separating care services from their local (church) leadership.

In more recent times the increase in regulation (and in some cases extreme regulation) and contractual obligations has also meant that previously self-determining organisations have started to march by the beat of someone else's drum. What's more, the funding source and government stipulation has actually begun defining why the organisation exists and what services they provide.

A recent graphic example of this was a previous state government's insertion of a clause in funding contracts that limited community organisations' ability to advocate for legislative change: a fundamental right and some would say responsibility of community organisations. Fortunately, a change of government, and significant community response, saw this clause removed. Actions such as imposing these sort of clauses serve to enforce notions in government circles that community organisations that receive public funding are simply branch offices of the government, albeit cheaper to run and easier to control!

While Churches of Christ Care has had many strong and visionary leaders over the years, the desire for funding, and compulsion to follow the crowd (being other organisations within industry segments) has at times propelled the organisation away from its mission and towards a homogenised response to what the government of the day saw as desirable. This behaviour has resulted in a number of faith based social service providers taking on the look and feel of secular counterparts, to the extent that some have pursued separate incorporation and objects apart from their parent entity (the Church). Some parent entities have responded by effectively discontinuing whole divisions of activity altogether, and re-investing into other forms of ministry. For others, the complete legal and/or constitutional separation of the subordinate agency has left the parent powerless to recover missional control.

Governance, Change, and the Member Base

For Churches of Christ Care, the issue of missional drift and parent entity control came to a head around 2008. This was a very difficult time for the organisation and for many good people who were doing the best they could within their own context. But the context was never going to propel the organisation to where it is today. There were separate boards with separate executives each pursuing their own separate agendas.

What followed was a fundamental restructure of the parent entity, Churches of Christ in Queensland, and multiple subordinate agencies, their boards and constituent documents. This resulted in the affirmation of one organisation (Churches of Christ in Queensland) with one mission, one board, one CEO, rowing in the one direction. The integrated entity still has many faces, largely in responses to nonsensical government policies. For example, the Public Benevolent Institution (PBI) of Churches of Christ Care still exists, and a separate housing company has been created in order to appease federal government requirements of large community housing providers (i.e. to be companies limited by guarantee). But now, the one board can manage multiple entities, or rather the same directors can constitute different boards as required, and subordinate entities can act for the best interests of the parent.

The leadership challenge set for the new CEO and Board of Churches of Christ in Queensland was principally to bring together all aspects of the organisation in what it means to be a 'church': to integrate what had become a fairly fractured organisation. The major structural/constitutional changes effected in 2009 may have set the foundations, but the real work still lay ahead.

Many individual care services had been founded by individual churches as their expression of mission in the local community, but over time these services had been effectively handed over to the corporate entity to manage, disenfranchising local churches (the voting members of the parent entity) along the way. The challenge was how to re-connect with the local church's vision for mission, whilst maintaining the benefits of professional management of what had become a very regulated environment, where margins were increasingly being squeezed.

The organisation took a multipronged approach to reconnecting with its member base, including:

- Creating region focused Strategic Action Leadership Teams (SALTs). These teams bring together senior Churches of Christ (care, church, and corporate support) leaders, along with community leaders passionate about bringing uplift to their community, to discern the needs of a local community. They then work together to develop and deliver a regional Mission Action Strategy;
- Building the role expectations of the Chief Mission Development Officer, and their direct reports, in promoting the organisation's mission in all it does;
- Better pooling of the overall assets of the organisation (as far as legally and ethically permissible), and using the resource base to support growth and development of churches, and church leadership. This included re-diverting the treasury functions of the PBI from a commercial bank to the parent entity's own Church Development Fund: generating an income stream for non-PBI activity while honouring the letter and spirit of PBI law;
- Promoting shared training and development events across the leadership of the entire organisation (not just churches, or care services); and
- Giving all parts of the organisation (including churches) better access to the specialist skills and services that resided in central support functions.

With all of the above, the organisation's Chief Officer's Team has maintained clear oversight of all aspects of planning and service innovation, ensuring alignment with the organisation's mission and strategic direction.

While all change is a work in progress, the above and other initiatives have given the organisation's members greater control over their organisation, and individual churches increased opportunity to pursue their mission in the local community.

At the same time, and contrary to what some may expect, the organisation's core systems have been becoming more commercial (i.e. focused on efficiency, productivity, professionalism, and customer service). Where once the organisation may have pursued commercialisation at the expense of its mission, improved commercial practices are in fact permitting a greater focus on work in and through churches and in the community.

Representation and Involvement

While the organisation is subject to much regulation (in excess of around 200 discrete pieces of legislation and multiple quality frameworks), it certainly does not just accept those that it doesn't agree with. Rather, it (or its senior staff) actively lobbies for the changing of public policy, regulation, contracting arrangements, and so forth.

The organisation has also been very deliberate around encouraging its senior leaders to become members of Boards and industry peak bodies, or other government or industry reference groups in areas relevant to its mission or areas of service delivery. At last count, senior staff have held board level positions on seven peak organisations or similar directly relevant to the work of Churches of Christ.

Furthermore, where the power dynamics are such that there is no industry voice in an area of need, and where there needs to be balance to the government's voice, the organisation will actively support creation of a forum for such a voice. Over the past several years, the organisation has supported the creation of four industry, peak or community organisations: the Community Services Industry Alliance, The Queensland Community (community organising) Alliance, Community Housing Providers for Queensland, and Pastoral and Spiritual Care of Older People (PASCOP). Senior staff are serving on the boards of each.

At the same time, where it has seen a proliferation of industry voices (e.g. multiple 'peak' bodies in the aged care space, separately incorporated in each state) which weakens the position of industry around the government table, it has actively advocated for consolidation or at very least cooperation.

This representation and involvement isn't just about influence, it is also about obligation. And this is where the value of stewardship, founded in biblical principles, reappears: *"from those that are given much, much will be expected"* (refer Luke 12:48). The organisation very much sees that contributing to improving public policy and industry development isn't just a nice to do, it is fundamental to who it is. Why just improve the lot of thirty thousand, as important as that work is, when you can positively impact the lives of another three million?

To come to where it is today, over recent years the organisation has transformed the conversations that it has internally, with co-providers, and with government. Its leaders no longer see themselves as being beholden to government, as too small, or too diversified to be useful. Furthermore, and perhaps more significantly, it has moved beyond being sensitive about the identity 'Churches of Christ', fearing it may repel potential customers with what may be seen as an overly 'religious' label.

Its leaders now stand in the place as equals around the table with government and industry colleagues, who understand that each service or service stream is part of a large and strong organisation, where its diversity is an incredible strength. And when other organisations have moved away from religious language in their titles, acquiring non-descript names or meaningless acronyms, Churches of Christ has celebrated its roots and used its name and the lessons of Christ as a rallying point.

The organisation is seeking to trade on its reputation, to make Churches of Christ in Queensland synonymous with unconditional love, quality care, and community uplift. Recognising that this brand has been in development for 86 years, why give that away?

Churches of Christ in Queensland is not content to just respond to funding rounds and the like—rather, it is more likely to lead industry discussions, initiate dialogue with government, and propose service responses and commensurate funding models.

Leadership and Management

The organisation hasn't relied on just one person to bring it to where it is today, with the inherent risk that all will come crashing down if or when they move on. It's true that tone is set from the top, and certainly Churches of Christ has solid, credible, and authentic leadership at the chief officer level. But its senior executives have also gone about devolving leadership, empowering managers to advocate for and lead change within their communities or industry segments, all the while well connected with the direction of the whole. A meeting of the organisation's Executive Team represents more a gathering of the Knights of the Round Table where all voices are equal, than a typical command and control structure.

Churches of Christ in Queensland has invested much in leadership and management development over the years. Its earlier leadership development program was grounded on the principles of servant leadership. This work has also informed a more recent development program for managers, built around several modules, variously titled: powerful conversations; leadership compass; and contagious leadership. Targeting the top 300 managers of the organisation, the program helps participants to identify and develop the leadership traits and potential in themselves and others.

Other recent leadership/management development initiatives of note include: all Board members and Chief Officers being supported to undertake a company directors course; supporting senior executives to undertake University of Queensland Business School's Leadership in the Not-For-Profit Sector course; and creating a range of leadership and development initiatives for frontline staff, tailored to their area of work/practise.

The organisation is more likely now to look globally for examples of best practice for the organisation, and for the best learning experiences for its leaders. Leaders have participated in, and presented at international conferences and undertaken study trips to leading organisations in various countries, and its Chief Operating Officer has recently completed the Advanced Management Program at the Wharton School of the University of Pennsylvania.

Notwithstanding all the management development, strategic planning and sheer hard work, the leadership of Churches of Christ in Queensland will also tell you that where it is today is made possible through the work of those who have gone before, and furthermore if God wasn't in it the organisation would have folded before now.

The approach to and from management, combined with strong quality frameworks and organisational communication systems, have ensured a level of consistency in message and service delivery throughout the organisation. This has contributed to many years of unbroken accreditation, licensing or equivalent across all services, and sustained levels of compliance across multiple compliance frameworks.

A Caring and Cared-for Workforce

In order to successfully pursue the organisation's mission, and achieve its strategic goals, requires an appropriately aligned and engaged workforce, whether paid or voluntary. As a society we have over-complicated delivery of all manner of social/human services. At its core, Churches of Christ in Queensland have realised that the greatest thing that we can offer someone in need is another person who really does care. Of course technical skills are important (e.g. knowing how or what to teach, what medicines to administer, how to navigate a government system), but they are required episodically, whereas care, personal connection and commitment to/from others are core and universal needs.

The organisation is in an ongoing quest to develop a workforce (and broader community) that is both caring and cared for. Some of the organisation's initiatives around workforce recruitment and development include:

- Recruiting with a particular focus on values, currently using a campaign of "imagine making a difference";
- Engendering a focus on the organisation's mission and values through the on-boarding process;
- Developing close links with universities and TAFE, facilitating student placements and internships;

- Using bulk-purchase ability to offer staff discounts on all manner of things from health insurance, to gym membership and car repairs;
- Providing a significant amount of work related, leadership, and career development training and support, including access to a central Study Assistance Scheme to encourage career advancement;
- Supporting clients (e.g. young people exiting care or long term unemployed housing tenants) and others looking to develop job skills or gain employment through a social enterprise program;
- Expanding the range of opportunities for volunteering: basically tailoring volunteering opportunities to individual skills, qualities and capacity. Volunteers are engaged across hundreds of roles, from simply collecting rubbish, to providing social support to elderly residents, to providing research and legal support;
- Facilitating a scheme for staff to contribute to a fund for other staff who are experiencing difficult circumstances. This fund (as well as other organisational contributions) is particularly used to support those that are impacted by natural disasters;
- Providing opportunities for support service/head office staff to connect with frontline mission: for example, by working alongside direct care staff, or spending time with clients.

Through the above types of strategies, and by developing the overall reputation of the organisation, Churches of Christ in Queensland is increasingly being approached by qualified and values-driven people looking for a role in the organisation, whether advertised or not.

As good as the above and other organisational strategies may be, they do not guarantee a perfect match between person, position, and organisation. The organisation is only one contributor in a larger industry, drawing most staff from the industry. In addition, in many geographical areas in which it operates, the community and hence the organisation's needs are often high and the choice of candidates limited.

Given this, and the fact that we work in human services, dealing with people at their most vulnerable times and at times exhibiting their most extreme behaviours, things do go wrong. And when they do, the organisation responds swiftly and transparently. It views those regulating its various activities as inherently good, and who it's better to work with than against. The organisation is quick to disclose any adverse events, and is open in outlining its proposed course of action, or actions already undertaken. When faced with the likelihood that a staff member has harmed a client, but a lack of evidence to prove it, the organisation will unashamedly err on the side of protecting the client.

In doing so, it has developed a high level of trust from various regulators, whereby some have remarked that they don't need to be involved further because they trust that Churches of Christ in Qld will be thorough and appropriate in its response. Such reputational and relational capital is invaluable for if and when things really do go wrong.

Brand, Reputation, and Success

Brand and reputation is as important to Churches of Christ in Queensland as it is to any organisation. This case study should be conveying the impression of an organisation that is more interested in substance over spin. And it's in the substance that its reputation and brand is built. While current market changes, particularly in the community care space, will result in the need to spend on marketing campaigns, it is almost embarrassing to admit that for most services the organisation has spent very little on marketing because of the word of mouth referrals that emanate from existing clients, their relatives or treating professionals. This is most exemplified in the organisation's Retirement Living area, a highly contested market, consisting of many large players with massive marketing budgets. Year after year, CofCQ underspend its marketing budget for this area, and its occupancy remains around a credible 98%.

While only one indicator of organisational success (and a poor one given the organisation's mission), Churches of Christ in Queensland's annual revenue has doubled (to circa $240m) between 2009 and 2016, with every indication that that level of growth will continue. The revenue growth indicates the growth of services through acquisition, success in tenders and the like.

Conclusion

In this case study, we have used convenient labels such as community housing, retirement living, or residential aged care, however Churches of Christ Care is actively seeking to remove barriers between service streams and types, at least internally anyway. The organisation holds the strong view that it should start by focusing on the needs of individuals and communities, and moving outwards to identify the best way of meeting same, rather than starting with a funding bucket and rules and finding someone to match to the funding. In doing so the organisation has provided leadership in developing products and services that better meet the needs of individuals. While still relatively young on the maturity scale of service innovation, the organisation has ambitious plans that if well executed will earn the interest of some funders and regulators, and likely the ire of others who like to think they are controlling the market.

And this flags some of the other challenges that the organisation has had along the way, such as: regulation that is written for small, single stream providers; paternalistic funding regimes that provide incentives for inefficient service delivery—where any surplus generated must be returned to the government (we don't do this in infrastructure projects, so why do it in community building projects?); being aligned with some NGO's that perpetuate a 'poor me' mentality, only moving if they're funded by government to do so; and some in government that perpetuate notions that the NGO (and particularly NFP) sector is poorly governed, managed, and rarely delivers effectively.

Above all, the polarisation of government and NGO has not served the community well in recent years. However, at least in Queensland anyway, a new conversation is starting that is more inclusive, seeing the industry as inclusive of all parts, including government and NGO. Churches of Christ is central to promoting a more inclusive rhetoric, in the hope of a more productive reality. The community we live in is of and for us all, and we should all take our respective responsibilities in developing the kind of society that we collectively want to live in.

David Swain
Chief Operating Officer
Churches of Christ in Queensland

10 Leading Through the Jungle of Legislation, Regulation and Reporting

Paul Paxton-Hall

Introduction—Focus on the 'Brand'

The measure of success for an NFP organisation will vary from one NFP to another because differing purposes will drive different outcomes. Also, the sustained delivery on purpose is only achievable over the medium to long term if there are sufficient financial resources at the disposal of an NFP. This would normally suggest that making a surplus or being 'not-for-loss' is a critical aspect for any NFP success.

However success for an NFP is measured, what is clear is that for an NFP (as with any business) a trusted reputation and sound brand recognition are crucial for sustained delivery on purpose.

Confidence in an NFP brand will have a direct correlation with that NFP's success. This is because good brand recognition means that an NFP's stakeholders can have confidence that the NFP's activities reflect the values essential to achieving the stated purpose or mission of the NFP.

So, a primary role for any CEO as he or she strives to ensure stakeholder confidence in the NFP's brand, is to ensure that the organisation's board, employees, volunteers and other stakeholders consistently live out the values of the NFP i.e. all stakeholders need to be 'on the same bus'.

Factors that Influence the Brand

There are a number of ways this fundamental objective of a good CEO can be met.

Getting the Strategy Right

Being clear about the strategic direction of the organisation is the new CEO's first challenge because it cannot be set just by the CEO; it necessarily involves input from all stakeholders. The CEO's role with the chairman is crucial in being able to guide the board towards the right strategy for the organisation to achieve mission.

Governance

An integral aspect of determining mission is fixing on governance arrangements. From a governance perspective, necessary factors include:

(1) getting the right board in place for the needs of the NFP at that time with the appropriate skill set required;
(2) ensuring there is a good balance between the strategic role of the board and its compliance function;
(3) promoting the need to be striving always to achieve corporate governance best practice in the NFP's internal operations;
(4) ensuring appropriate protocols and policies exist for recruitment, delegation, workplace health and safety and other HR policies more generally; and
(5) ensuring that values are lived out in the way employees, volunteers and other stakeholders are shown respect and treated with dignity at all times.

Ensuring Activities Meet the Mission

Another key ingredient to achieving a quality brand recognition is to ensure there is a regular review by the NFP of its activities. This is necessary because it is the NFP's activities that drive purpose; activities must remain relevant if the NFP's reputation is to be enhanced.

Consideration of Economic and Social Inputs

In addition to governance requirements and ensuring confidence in the currency of an NFP's activities, a CEO must, all the while, have a clear eye on necessary economic inputs in achieving the desired brand recognition. Those inputs will need to consider such things as:

(a) relevant funding and its sources;
(b) required employees and appropriate skills;
(c) the appropriate volunteer base if relevant;
(d) appropriate technology and, with it, necessary intellectual property and licensing arrangements; and
(e) physical assets such as premises, motor vehicles and other relevant plant and equipment.

In terms of necessary social inputs, the CEO of an NFP will need to be cognitive of historical relationships with government, private enterprise and others (perhaps major benefactors), the organisation's abilities as well as its capacity for risk in the way it carries out its activities.

The Regulatory Framework

Whilst any NFP CEO will need to be mindful of the drivers of a quality brand, he or she cannot avoid the real challenges that exist around the regulatory framework for NFPs. Getting this wrong dooms any NFP to certain failure.

The specifics of the regulatory framework for an NFP will differ depending upon a number of factors which include:

- whether the NFP is registered as a charity or not;
- the legal structure of the NFP;
- the relevant jurisdiction in which the NFP carries out its activities; and
- its size.

Irrespective of these specifics just mentioned however, all NFP's have consistent, overarching reporting requirements to government agencies which include:

- the corporate and financial reporting requirements associated with the legal structure under which the NFP is incorporated;
- fundraising legislation requirements;
- Tax Act endorsement requirements; and
- financial, governance and performance information required by most government agencies as a condition of government funding.*

Corporate and Financial Reporting

The bulk of NFP organisations are unincorporated entities. Unless they are registered as charities under the ACNC Act,[2] unincorporated entities have no reporting obligation. For charities registered with the ACNC, reporting obligations will differ depending on size. ACNC reporting obligations are consistent with the reporting obligations in the Corporations Act for companies limited by guarantee but differ yet again for incorporated associations under respective State-based association incorporation legislation.

Incorporated Associations

The current reporting obligations in Australia for incorporated associations are as follows:

Table 10.1 Reporting obligations for incorporated associations.

QLD	NSW	ACNC/VIC/WA
Level 1: assets or total revenue above $100,000		Large/Level 3: Revenue over $1 million

* Refer to paragraph 6.4 of Contribution of the NFP Sector; Productivity Commission Research Report January 2010 at page 129

QLD	NSW	ACNC/VIC/WA
Level 2: assets or total revenue between $20,000 and $100,000	Tier 1: Annual gross revenue over $250,000 or assets over $500,000	Medium/Level 2: Revenue greater than $250,000 but less than $1 million
Level 3: assets or total revenue below $20,000	Tier 2: Annual gross revenue less than $250,000 or assets less than $500,000	Small/Level 1: Revenue less than $250,000

Companies Limited by Guarantee

Corporate and financial reporting obligations for companies limited by guarantee (**CLG**) which are not registered as charities with the ACNC will differ depending upon the size of the company. A company is a small CLG in a particular financial year if:

- it is a company limited by guarantee for the whole of the financial year;
- it is not a deductible gift recipient at any time during the financial year;
- the revenue of the company is less than $250,000; and
- it is not a commonwealth company for the purposes of the *Commonwealth Authorities and Companies Act 1997*.

The *Corporations Act* enshrines a 3-tiered differential reporting framework for CLGs as follows:

Table 10.2 3-tiered differential reporting framework for CLGs

Tier	Nature of company	Obligations

1	Small company limited by guarantee	• No obligation to do any of the following unless required to do so under a member direction or ASIC direction:
		  • prepare a financial report;
		  • prepare a directors' report;
		  • have financial report audited;
		  • notify members of reports

2	Company limited by guarantee with annual revenue <$1,000,000	• must prepare a financial report; • must prepare a directors' report, although less detailed than that required of other companies; • need not have financial report audited but if not audited, then financial report must be reviewed; • must give reports to any member who elects to receive them.

(Continued)

Table 10.2 (Continued)

Tier	Nature of company	Obligations
3	Company limited by guarantee with annual revenue >$1,000,000	• must prepare a financial report; • must prepare a directors' report, although less detailed than that required of other companies; • must have financial report audited; • must give reports to any member who elects to receive them

Registered Charities

For organisations (however structured) registered with the ACNC, the ACNC Act distinguishes between small charities, medium charities and large charities in a manner consistent with the tiering of not-for-profit CLGs that are not registered as charities; namely:

1. **small charities**: annual revenue is less than $250,000;
2. **medium charities**; annual revenue is $250,000 or more but less than $1,000,000; and
3. **large charities**: annual revenue is greater than $1,000,000.

Size affects ACNC financial reporting obligations which are as follows:

Table 10.3 Size and ACNC financial reporting obligations.

	Small	*Medium*	*Large*
Annual Information Statement	• Must submit— Includes nine financial information questions	• Must submit— Includes 12 financial information questions	• Must submit— Includes 15 financial information questions
Financial report	• Can submit (optional)	• Must submit	• Must submit
Cash or accrual accounting	• Can use accrual or cash	• Must use accrual	• Must use accrual
Type of financial statement2	• Special purpose financial statement (optional) or • Reduced disclosure regime general purpose financial statement (optional) or • Full general purpose financial statement (optional)	• Special purpose financial statement (if not a "reporting entity") or • Reduced disclosure regime general purpose financial statement or • Full general purpose financial statement	• Special purpose financial statement (if not a "reporting entity") or • Reduced disclosure regime general purpose financial statement or • Full general purpose financial statement

	Small	*Medium*	*Large*
Review or audit	• No ACNC obligation for review or audit	• The ACNC requires your financial reports to be either reviewed or audited	• The ACNC requires your financial reports to be audited

Altered Reporting Obligations for CLGs Registered as Charities

For those charities which are structured as CLGs, there are altered reporting obligations now to ASIC meaning that charities structured as CLGs no longer have to file returns with ASIC but, rather, report to the ACNC. These altered reporting obligations can be depicted as follows:

Table 10.4 Altered reporting obligations for CLGs

Type of change	ACNC	ASIC
Register		
Apply to register a company	No	Yes
Apply to register a charity	Yes	No
Change details		
Notify change of name to a company	Yes	Yes
Remove word 'Limited' from name (without changing legal name) as long as meet s150(1) of the Corporations Act 2001	No	No
Apply to change the 'legal' name of a company to omit the word 'Limited'	Yes	Yes
Notify changes to: • registered office/address for service • directors (responsible persons) • constitution (governing documents)	Yes	No While it is not a requirement, you can choose to notify ASIC of these changes. Late fees do not apply.
Report annually		
Submit an *Annual Information Statement* for each reporting period	Yes	No
Submit financial statement for 2013 reporting period (period starting on or after 1 July 2012 but before 1 July 2013) (see *ASIC guidance on reporting obligations*)	No	Yes*
Auditor		
Notify of resignation or removal of an auditor	No	Yes
Notify appointment of an auditor	No	No

(Continued)

Table 10.4 (Continued)

Type of change	ACNC	ASIC
Close		
Request to revoke registration of a charity or notify of no longer being entitled to registration as a charity or if charity has closed (ACNC will advise ASIC in such cases)	Yes	No
Notify external administration of a company	Yes	Yes
Apply to deregister a company	Yes	Yes

Fundraising Legislation Reporting Requirements

At the Federal level, fundraising is controlled by three pieces of legislation, namely:

- the Corporations Act;
- the *Australian Securities and Investments Commission Act 2001*; and
- the Australian Consumer Law so far as it relates to misleading and deceptive conduct.[2]

State and Territory fundraising legislation and regulators are as follows:

Table 10.5 State and territory fundraising legislation and regulators.[3]

Jurisdiction	Legislation	Regulator
New South Wales	*Charitable Fundraising Act 1991 Lotteries and Art Unions Act 1901*	Office of Liquor, Gaming and Racing
Victoria	*Fundraising Appeals Act 1998 Gambling Regulation Act 2003*	Consumer Affairs Victoria
Queensland	*Collections Act 1966*	Office of Fair Trading
	Charitable and Non-Profit Gaming Act 1999	Office of Gaming Regulation
South Australia	*Collections for Charitable Purposes Act 1939*	Office of Liquor and Gambling Commissioner
	Collection for Charitable Purposes Act 1939—Code of Practice	
	Lottery and Gaming Act 1936	
Western Australia	*Charitable Collections Act 1946*	Department of Commerce
	Gaming and Watering Commission Act 1987	Office of Racing, Gaming and Liquor

Jurisdiction	Legislation	Regulator
Tasmania	*Collections for Charities Act 2001*	Consumer Affairs and Fair Trading
	Gaming Control Act 1993	Tasmanian Gaming Commission
Australian Capital Territory	*Charitable Collections Act 2003*	Office of Regulatory Services
	Lotteries Act 1964	ACT Gambling and Racing Commission
Northern Territory	*Gaming Control Act 1993*	Racing, Gaming and Licensing Division, Department of Justice

Fundraising Reform

The plethora of legislation affecting the fundraising challenges of a new CEO make this area of the law a practical challenge to say the least. An example of the challenge is the fact that the Queensland *Collections Act* uses definitions for the term 'charity' and 'charitable purpose' which have really been unchanged since 1966. In other words, the Collections Act does not reflect the fact that we now have a Commonwealth Act, the *Charities Act 2013*, which provides a modern statutory definition of charity for Commonwealth legislative purposes. Clearly it is in the interests of all not-for-profit CEOs that statutory reform be made in the area of fundraising—ideally in a manner that is consistent across State boundaries.

The fact that State fundraising legislation applies both to charities and also to those organisations which may not be registered as a charity but which have a community purpose makes for a dual reporting obligation.

The need for corporate reporting obligations for not-for-profit organisations and separate fundraising reporting obligations, makes it clear that there is need for reform of the law around reporting to avoid unnecessary and inefficient duplication if the notion of 'report once-use often' is to be realised. Whilst some States and Territories have taken the initiative of recognising reports lodged with the ACNC in relation to charities, this area of the law has still a long way to go. Apart from anything else a busy CEO needs to be mindful of community expectations around the transparency of giving as an important issue for some stakeholders.**

Conduct of Charitable Fundraising

For those CEOs who rely on fundraising, they will need to have regard to the practical reality that charitable fundraising has been under a public cloud in the UK since early 2015 because of certain unprofessional practices entered

** South Australia, ACT and Tasmania have all initiated reform for the reporting obligations of charities to State-based regulators.

into by fundraising organisations in the UK. Indeed, a UK journalist at the time expressed the view that *"the core of the problem is that the public image of charities has become dominated by their means, not their ends."*[4]

The use of commercial fundraising operators and paid collectors has become more commonplace and, with that trend, more sophistication and commercially-orientated fundraising practices have been developed—not all of which serve the NFP sector well.

The role of the Australian Consumer Law (**ACL**) in dealing with fundraising problems is being considered as part of the March 2016 discussion paper on a review of the ACL. As well, the Queensland government is considering other aspects of fundraising reform at the present time.

Administration Costs Associated with Fundraising

Frequently commentary will be published in media outlets about the cost ratios for certain charities and the amount in each dollar of funds raised which go to charitable purpose as distinct from administrative costs.

For CEOs, decisions around cost ratios and fundraising disclosure need to be considered. In Queensland, written agreements between a charity and a third party fundraiser must be lodged with and approved by the Minister.*** The Office of Fair Trading provides guidance to charities seeking to lodge a third party agreement which specifies that an agreement must contain a number of provisions including monetary consideration. However, a minimum return to the charity is not specified.

Victoria and New South Wales do have standards in this area. In Victoria, the registration of a commercial fundraiser is subject to public disclosure conditions if less than 50% of fundraiser proceeds will be distributed to beneficiaries. If less than 35% of fundraising proceeds will be distributed, then the commercial fundraiser must justify their registration to the regulator. In New South Wales, the total expenses payable must not exceed 50% of the gross proceeds obtained.

Online Fundraising Challenges

These days the CEO of a charity wanting to fundraise publically will need to consider what role, if any, social media will play as part of that process given the growing use of social media such as Twitter and Facebook to facilitate fundraising and crowd funding.

Fundraising appeals conducted online or via social media are difficult to regulate because of the borderless nature of the internet. Just what controls might be set by government have yet to be determined but reform in the area cannot be too far away.

*** Collections Regulation 2008 (Qld) section 33

Tax Endorsement Requirements

The Importance of Tax Concessions

All not-for-profits, whether registered charities or not, would struggle to remain viable without government tax concessions.

Relevant tax concessions are as follows (and are dependent upon the status of the organisation concerned):

Input tax concessions:

(a) fringe benefits tax rebate or exemption;
(b) GST concessions, payroll tax, stamp duty and gambling tax concessions.

Income tax exemption:

Wealth tax concessions: land tax exemption; and
Tax deductibility: the ability to deliver a tax deduction for anyone gifting money or property to the organisation.

The advantages of the various tax concessions have been at the forefront of a number of high profile charity tax cases[†] in recent times. A CEO needs to be mindful of relevant tax concessions available and, as part of that process, mindful of what needs to be done to retain appropriate tax concession status. This is because endorsement, when given, does not apply automatically throughout the life of the organisation. Indeed, the Tax Office has an ongoing role to play in assessing an organisation's continued entitlement to claim tax concessions.[‡]

Determining Concessional Tax Status

The requirements for tax exemption or tax deductibility will vary depending upon the status of the NFP. Suffice to say that the ACNC is now the gate keeper for appropriate charity registration, including associated sub-group registration,[$] which in turn informs endorsement entitlement with the ATO.

For other NFPs, tax exemption may be afforded by way of self-assessment e.g. community service organisations or the doctrine of mutuality may apply for mutual associations such as co-operatives and clubs.

[†] *Commissioner of Taxation v Word Investments* [2008] HCA 55 and *The Hunger Project Australia v Commissioner of Taxation* [2013] FCA 693

[‡] See TR2015/1—Income Tax: Special Conditions for various entities whose ordinary and statutory income is exempt.

[$] Refer to the 12 headings of charitable purpose as defined in section 12 of the *Charities Act 2013*

Government Funding Acquittal

Requirements for funding conditions acquittal will differ from State to State and government department to government department. The NFP sector as a whole is facing the challenges of diminished government funding as demands on the public purse grow. It is this economic reality that is instrumental in the move towards consumer directed care models in disability services and aged care that have occurred in overseas jurisdictions in recent times and have commenced in Australia with the reforms to aged care in 2014 and the National Disability Insurance Scheme.

The challenge for the new CEO is the recognition that under the traditional, direct government funding model, governments have tended to see the not-for-profit sector as part of its broader community services strategy rather than appreciating the mission/strategy of the individual organisation. With that reality the sector as a whole has had a relatively weak bargaining position in determining government funding contract terms with governments traditionally taking a view of 'take it or leave it' in determining terms of funding.

Now the new paradigm sees not-for-profit organisations competing for the consumer dollar. This is starting to present challenges to CEOs around internal administration because of things like the need to market, be competitive, watch cash flow and watch debtor recovery as opposed to a world where once upon a time an amount of money would be given to the organisation to spend in the way government generally wanted.

The economic strength of an organisation is going to drive a new behaviour but the more market savvy CEOs are recognising that long term sustainability will depend upon a diminished reliance on the government/taxpayer dollar. These are key strategic issues for any CEO in the third sector today and a reason why mergers or joint ventures are occurring in the sector.

The Leadership Challenges and How to Respond

The regulatory demands and changing face of government and community expectations of not-for-profit organisations has probably never been as challenging as it is today. Those community expectations are exacerbated by demographic challenges, particularly an ageing population and a greater percentage of GDP being spent by government on health care. Yet all the while, the CEO must, through all these challenges, remain positive and focused on mission. The importance of compliance must never be trumped by the strategy to deliver on purpose.

To achieve this focus on strategy, a CEO must be cognisant of the regulatory and community challenges in getting the basics right; namely:

- ensuring he or she has the right board which is able to focus on strategy development;

- keeping an eye on margin vs mission; and
- developing a considered business plan that recognises community and economic challenges and ensure it is reviewed regularly.

Notes

1. *Australian Charities and Not-For-Profits Commission Act 2012.*
2. Productivity Commission Report at page 136.
3. Productivity Commission Report at page 137.
4. J. Baggini. "Charities Risk Losing Our Goodwill with Aggressive Fundraising Tactics," *The Guardian*, 10 June 2015 referred to at p22 of the discussion paper.

Bibliography

Australian Taxation Office. TR2015/1—Income Tax: Special Conditions for Various Entities Whose Ordinary and Statutory Income Is Exempt. 2015.

Baggini, J. "Charities Risk Losing Our Goodwill With Aggressive Fundraising Tactics." *The Guardian*, 10 June 2015.

Productivity Commission. "Contribution of the NFP Sector: Productivity Commission Research Report." January 2010.

Stories from the Field:
The Smith Family

Introduction

Australian charities have changed in number, size and focus dramatically over the past century. The dominance of the larger, established charities, and the emergence of thousands of new ones, is an interesting story of the scale of problems facing us, the inability of governments to address this scale alone and to keep pace with the public's desire to see societal change, and the charities changing focus in light of these challenges.

Philanthropy and the Not-for-profit Sector

The scale of the many issues facing us is important to contemplate in thinking about the role that the not for profit space plays in advancing society and solving or salving its ills. Consider the pace of current advances being made. HIV AIDS is no longer prevalent enough to warrant being a notable disease in Australia (sadly not in all parts of the world). Contemplate the speed in which this disease has been eradicated due to the resources that were mobilised to remove it as a threat. The Australian public were mobilised as the grim reaper advertising dramatically raised public consciousness and significant resources flowed into the charities and medical research facilities that were treating and researching the disease worldwide.

Contemplate that each year, 123,000 new cases of cancer will be diagnosed in Australia, and so many Australians are dealing with cancer.[1] Yet in recent years, medical research has made such huge advances that many previously incurable cancers are now treatable with medication.

The not for profit sector spent $960m on research in 2012/13 while the Australian Government spent $1,275m. The increased collaboration between research institutions globally has been lubricated by the funds that those individuals and their families suffering from cancer, and/or supporting cancer research have provided to ensure other families do not face the same devastation.

Yet against this track record of the public being increasingly involved in social change, the percentage of Australians who give has dropped, from 87% in 2005 to 81% in 2016. Australians are giving more, however, with

$210 per annum more in real terms than in 2005, which is seeing the overall funding pie grow from $10.1 billion given by individual Australians in 2005 to $12.5 billion in 2016.[2] Is this sustainable, given that the average Australian who does give currently supports seven charities each?[3] Are there structural issues to giving we need to see for the sector to continue to improve Australians lives?

It is no accident that the most significant month for giving in Australia is June, the end of the financial year as people look to minimise their tax through supporting their important causes. The introduction of private ancillary funds in Australia, coinciding with the largest wealth bubble in our history as the baby boomer generation matures and looks to how they will distribute their wealth has seen a sustained period of major philanthropy and bequests that will continue for many years to come and underwrite some significant societal impacts. The taxation system is critical in underpinning a much greater partnership between public and private funding in areas of greatest need yet has had minimal reform in recent years.

Many people look at the US as a leading philanthropic light, with both the shift to social entrepreneurship and the overall level of philanthropy in the US. As a percentage of income, Americans give 1.9% versus Australians at just 0.34%, and the fact that the US has death taxes creates a significant motivation for the wealthy in the US to distribute their wealth to charities.[4]

Not that there hasn't been tremendous leadership in philanthropy outside of these structural drivers. One of the strongest proponents of 'giving while you are living' is Chuck Feeney, an American of Irish descent who set up, as Bill and Melinda Gates and Warren Buffett have done, a foundation from which the majority of his wealth will be given away in his lifetime. Chuck Feeney's Global Philanthropic Fund has funded causes as broad as Ian Frazer's vaccine to present cervical cancer in Australia and the rights movement for gay marriage in Ireland, creating significant societal benefits and change.

It is this combination of leadership, the public's appetite for societal change and the ability to mobilise resources to scale that are so critical to the biggest issues we have, and continue to face. This case study focuses largely on the leadership challenges for the sector, using one of Australia's oldest charities, The Smith Family, as an example of these challenges.

Leadership Challenges

There are some sectors of the non-profit world that are currently facing what academics have termed a 'starvation cycle', that is, the reduction in spend by organisations on key infrastructure as funding for their cause declines or in response to the constant misguided focus on where charities should spend their funds, as if somehow those who work for the poorest should do so somehow without all the overheads of any organisation operating in today's world.

With the rise of globalisation in the 1970s and a consciousness of the world and its issues driven by the ubiquity of television and the media, the public supported famines in Africa and natural disasters world over like they never had before. International development was growing in the public's consciousness as a legitimate means of reducing suffering and stabilising third world economies. The Rockefeller family recognised that the Vietnam War was driven from extreme poverty and inequality amongst the world's poorest people, largely living in rural areas and involved in agriculture. The thought leadership in setting up the international research institutes (e.g. International Maize and Wheat Improvement Center— CIMMYT, International Rice Research Institute etc.) to lift third world agrarian based economies out of poverty as a means of creating a stronger peace was inspiring.

Against this backdrop of public support for overseas aid and development, the leadership of organisations like World Vision to boldly make child sponsorship and the 40-hour famine a rite of passage for every young person and family in Australia made them one of Australia's most significant charities. With dramatic pictures of starving, emaciated children whose plight was championed by global pop stars Bob Geldof and Bono beamed into our lounge rooms, we dug deep to make global poverty a thing of the past.

Forty years on and the scale of the issue facing billions of people living under hundreds of corrupt and poorly led regimes remains enormous yet the Australian public has not made it an election issue for successive Federal Governments as they have systematically reduced the size of Australia's aid budget as a percentage of Gross National Income. Today the Australian taxpayer contributes 0.22% of GNI to overseas aid development, less than half what it was at 0.47% in 1975.

Those charitable organisations whose focus is on third world poverty have also struggled to maintain the public's attention on their cause just as Government funding is also diminishing. Are our international development agencies and charities now in a starvation cycle and is this issue peculiar to the issue of overseas development agencies, or is this the beginning of a broader malaise that may beset the entire Australian charity sector moving forward? Both these scenarios will demand a lot of the leadership in the not for profit sector moving forward.

The Smith Family

A good case study of strong leadership combined with a cause aligning with the public's concerns and underlying trends is The Smith Family. While the charity has remained focused on children living in disadvantage, it is unrecognisable from the charity that was started by five Sydney businessmen in 1922.

As poverty has stubbornly remained a reality for one in ten Australian children, the organisation has continually refined its focus to increase its impact on this issue. The two most significant shifts have been a shift from welfare handouts to proactive educational support for children and their parents over the past two decades, and more recently, the development of a very rigorous measurement of the organisation's societal impact. This case study is the story of those transitions.

A Children's Charity since 1922, the founding of The Smith Family is a very Australian story. In December 1922, during a period of relative prosperity post World War 1 and before the Great Depression had taken hold, five businessmen on their way home from a successful business trip met in the Woolpack Hotel in Parramatta. In the course of conversation about their upcoming Christmas celebrations with their families, they questioned whether everyone was as fortunate and if poverty was a reality for many Australians. They undertook to come back together having looked into this issue in and around Sydney. Upon regrouping, the businessmen were quite shocked at what they had uncovered, and were compelled to do something about it.

The action that the men took was to donate toys and sweets to the Carlingford Home for Boys that Christmas. When the matron asked who to write to thank for the donation, in keeping with the anonymous nature of philanthropy of the day, the first man answered that his name was Smith, a very common Australian name. "What about the others?" the matron asked. "They're Smiths too," replied the man. "We're all Smiths. We're The Smith Family."

And so, The Smith Family was born and the tradition of making Christmas a special time for children, and putting disadvantaged children at the centre, has remained the focus of the organisation.

In recognising that this single generous gesture would not have a lasting impact on disadvantage in Australia, the men drew up a set of guidelines for what would become The Smith Family. The focus on impacting the lives of children and those living in disadvantage, a national, sectarian approach and embracing the goodwill of Australians were all, and remain, central tenets of the modern Smith Family.

During the Depression of the late 1920s and early 30s, The Smith Family assisted with the food and clothing needs of thousands of Australians as unemployment soared, and responsibility for the care of children and families fell to organisations such as The Smith Family which set up hospitals and orphanages. The organisation was founded on volunteers and during this time thousands of Australians were also helping provide food and clothing packages through The Smith Family. Today the organisation has some 8,700 volunteers supporting its work.

Since 1963, the sale of used clothes in The Smith Family retail stores have helped generate surpluses that offset our administration costs. This enduring social enterprise has expanded into clothing recycling also and ensures that the majority of funds raised through donations from supporters can be spent directly on programs for disadvantaged students.

The 1970s saw The Smith Family react to the needs of refugee families fleeing war in Vietnam and Timor, while also being one of the first emergency relief organisations that arrived in Darwin to help residents recover from the devastation inflicted by Cyclone Tracey.

In the late eighties the organisation undertook research with the families it was helping to support through its welfare approach. The findings were stark. Australians living in disadvantage wanted a better future for their children, and they saw that education was key to that better future. The results highlighted that children of families that The Smith Family had been helping were also receiving welfare. The cycle of poverty was not being broken through our support.

Organisational Focus

This research led to a fundamental rethink about the organisation's focus. The health sector was undergoing a transition from treating heart disease and other significant diseases to looking to prevention as cure: taking a proactive, early intervention approach, underpinned by public awareness raising.

The Smith Family decided to change its whole approach. It began the shift away from welfare payments and replaced them with education scholarships and local support through a new program called *Learning for Life*. This was a dramatic shift for an organisation upon which tens of thousands of Australians were reliant on for financial support. The CEO Elaine Henry, who, with the Board and Chairman Rick Turner, then CEO of Ernst and Young, led this shift in focus and had to take the organisation and its volunteers and supporters through this substantial change. Elaine had come from a background in health and understood the importance of early interventions, based on evidence. She also understood this would be a significant change for the established charity, its staff, volunteers and supporters.

And there was deep concern as many felt the organisation was abandoning so many needy people in making such a dramatic change in direction and Elaine spoke of holding sessions with concerned stakeholders for hours as they talked through why the change was deemed necessary.

This change in The Smith Family's organisational focus also took place decades before the importance of education and the focus on STEM (science, technology, engineering and maths) that pervades our media, job searching and conversations today was prevalent. At the time of this decision, manufacturing was still strong, the economy was travelling well and unemployment was low. The dramatic structural adjustment in our workforce that we are currently experiencing, creating demand for an increasingly highly educated workforce, was still 20 years away. For a charity to put its whole focus on the importance of education was somewhat radical for the time.

It is interesting to observe the impact that strong leadership and significant change have on the culture of an organisation. The organisation is now very proud of this significant change, and the relevance of its current direction. There is a strong desire to continue to innovate and change. There is an equally strong desire to stay very focused on what actually makes a difference in the lives of young Australians born into disadvantage and how to effect change. This desire for impact has led to a more recent set of fundamental shifts for the organisation.

A more proactive, early intervention approach in the support of children's education to alleviate poverty requires a longer-term view, as a charity, of your activities, and their impact. The Smith Family's *Learning for Life* program supports children from their first day of school to their last day of formal education, be that the end of their TAFE or university degree. In many cases, this requires a 17-year commitment for each and every student that is brought onto the *Learning for Life* program. The charity also recognised the emerging evidence over the past 20 years of the importance of the early years in a child's brain development and long-term educational achievements and today runs programs for nearly 38,000 children aged 0–5 nationally in Australia's most disadvantaged communities.

The *Learning for Life* program has been developed over the last twenty years to encourage school attendance, reduce social isolation and improve student's educational outcomes. The theory of change underpinning the program sees a combination of financial, emotional and practical supports through a locally based *Learning for Life* coordinator working closely with the family and providing support to the students. The families receive a small financial scholarship starting at $48 a month in primary school and increasing as education costs increase through to tertiary studies. They must spend this on educational items and the students must seek to achieve a 90% attendance rate across each year to remain on scholarship.

Evidence of Impact

Since the organisation's shift to supporting children's and young people's education, a series of evidence-based programmatic approaches have been tested across a place-based approach that sees these programs operating today in 94 communities nationally. These programs are the third facet of the *Learning for Life* program and focus on the educational needs of students as they transition into primary school, as they develop and move into more challenging aspects of secondary school and begin to choose their subjects for the last years of school and begin thinking about their career aspirations. The 17-year commitment comes to an end if and when the student completes up to four years of tertiary studies.

Four years ago the organisation invested substantially in ensuring that it could measure the impact of its work with the 33,195 students receiving a *Learning for Life* scholarship. While having a very clear idea of the effectiveness of each of its programs, the organisation began a journey of measuring the longitudinal outcomes for the *Learning for Life* students, and setting goals to improve these outcomes over time. These long-term outcomes formed the base of the organisation's new five-year strategy and focused around:

- improved school attendance, critical to achieving positive educational outcomes;
- improved advancement from Year 10 to 12, with each year of completed schooling enabling better outcomes; and
- improved post-school engagement, in work and/or study 12 months after leaving the Learning for Life program.

The organisation can now show that it is achieving 90.7% attendance rate for primary school students. While there is no data available nationally on attendance rates for students from different socio-economic backgrounds, the rate for Aboriginal and Torres Strait Islander students in Years 1 to 10 attending government schools was 83%, versus the higher rate of 86.1% for Aboriginal and Torres Strait Islander students on the *Learning for Life* program.

Advancement of students from Year 10 to Year 12 reached 68.2% in 2015, well above the 60.6% of young people from the lowest socio-economic backgrounds that have completed Year 12 or equivalent, and a 5% improvement on the years 2012–14.[5]

The third crucial measure of engagement as a measure of the success of the organisation's approach to supporting a student's education is the proportion of Learning for Life students who successfully transition from school to further education, training or employment. In 2015, The Smith Family students achieved 84.2%. Of the remaining 16%, four in five were actively seeking employment and one in six was volunteering. Of that 84.2%, 65.8% were fully engaged. By way of comparison, Lamb et al. (2015) report that the proportion of Australians aged 24 who are fully engaged in employment, education or training from Australia's most disadvantaged backgrounds is only 58.9%.[6]

This is The Smith Family's first set of longitudinal data that measures both the improvements in its effectiveness over time, and the worthiness of investing in Australian young people, irrespective of their socio-economic status. This data gives policy makers, researchers and donors a very clear picture of the impact of the *Learning for Life* program.

Rosie Simpson
Former Head of Fundraising
The Smith Family

Notes

1. Australian Cancer Research Foundation. "Cancer Statistics Australia," https://acrf.com.au/on-cancer/cancer-statistics-australia/
2. Australian Government. "Giving Australia 2016 Launched," 2016, www.communitybusinesspartnership.gov.au/giving-australia-2016-launched/

3. Pareto Fundraising. "State of the Donation 2016,," http://paretofundraising. com/2016/03/state-of-the-donation-2016/
4. Myles McGregor-Lowndes and Cameron J. Newton. "An Examination of Tax Deductible Donations Made by Individual Australian Taxpayers in 2006–07," 2009: 4–5. http://eprints.qut.edu.au/20579/1/CPNS_Working_Paper_Final.pdf; American Association of Fundraising Council. "Giving USA, 2011." (2011).
5. Stephen Lamb, Jennifer Jackson, Anne Walstab and Shuyan Huo. "Educational Opportunity in Australia 2015: Who Succeeds and Who Misses Out," *Centre for International Research on Education Systems, for the Mitchell Institute* (2015).
6. Ibid.

Bibliography

American Association of Fundraising Council. Giving USA, 2011. 2011.

Australian Cancer Research Foundation. Cancer Statistics Australia. Retrieved from https://acrf.com.au/on-cancer/cancer-statistics-australia/

Australian Government. Giving Australia 2016 Launched. 2016. Retrieved from www.communitybusinesspartnership.gov.au/giving-australia-2016-launched/

Lamb, Stephen, Jennifer Jackson, Anne Walstab, and Shuyan Huo. "Educational Opportunity in Australia 2015: Who Succeeds and Who Misses Out." *Centre for International Research on Education Systems, for the Mitchell Institute.* 2015.

McGregor-Lowndes, Myles, and Cameron J. Newton. An Examination of Tax Deductible Donations Made by Individual Australian Taxpayers in 2006–07. 2009. Retrieved from http://eprints.qut.edu.au/20579/1/CPNS_Working_Paper_Final.pdf

Pareto Fundraising. State of the Donation 2016. 2016. Retrieved from http://paretofundraising.com/2016/03/state-of-the-donation-2016/

Part III

New Journeys, New Horizons

11 Innovation Leadership

Mark Dodgson

Introduction

Napoleon said it was the job of the leader to define reality, then give hope. In the rapidly changing, highly unpredictable world we find ourselves in, buffeted as we are by 'wicked problems' and the powers of technological change and globalisation, defining reality in contemporary organisations can present even more challenging tasks than those confronting the French Emperor.* Household names in the corporate world go out of business almost overnight. A young man in his university dormitory invents a method for students to communicate with one another and uses it to create a company that within 10 years is worth more than the Bank of America. How is it possible to define reality when the world is so turbulent? Who could possibly have defined a reality where the success of Facebook was predictable?

The world, furthermore, is extremely complex in the sense of being highly integrated and interdependent, and where random events can have substantial multiplier effects. That is, the world of the modern organisation is not only *complicated*, with many systemic connections, but is *complex* in that those connections and influences can be erratic and volatile, and may not only be *unknown*, but could also be *unknowable*. The Fukushima nuclear disaster, a major event in and of itself, had massive and unforeseen consequences for a number of key industries—autos, LCD flat panel displays, lithium batteries, food—because its region was host to a number of critical suppliers in global supply chains. Because of the intricacy and complexity of these supply chains, many large multinationals were unaware of their exposure and vulnerability. Defining reality in these circumstances can be daunting, often requiring organisational leaders to be very bold or very brazen.

The leader then has to give hope to employees and stakeholders. Amongst all the turbulence and uncertainty, she or he has to develop a persuasive and reassuring narrative that their organisation knows where it is heading and how it is going to get there. In these circumstances, there is much to be said

---

* Wicked problems are so pervasive and complex that any solutions proposed are commonly conflicting and contradictory. (See H. Rittel and M. Webber. "Dilemmas in a General Theory of Planning," Policy Sciences 4 (1973): 155–169.

for the well-established virtue of KISS, keeping it simple, stupid. Or, in the more sophisticated interpretation of Sull and Eisenhardt, developing some simple rules for surviving and thriving in a world full of turmoil and confusion.[1] Sull and Eisenhardt argue that simple rules are short cut strategies that focus our attention and simplify the way we process information.[2] They allow us to act without having to stop and rethink every decision.[3]

> *"Simple rules work, it turns out, because they do three things very well. First, they confer the flexibility to pursue new opportunities while maintaining some consistency. Second, they can produce better decisions. When information is limited and time is short, simple rules make it fast and easy for people, organizations, and governments to make sound choices. They can even outperform complicated decision-making approaches in some situations. Finally, simple rules allow members of a community to synchronize their activities with one another on the fly. As a result, communities can do things that would be impossible for their individual members to achieve on their own."*

As someone who has been researching innovation for nearly 40 years, studying literally thousands of organisations, I am very aware of its difficulties and surprises. Innovation in many ways is an idiosyncratic process, differing across sectors and affected by individual organisational purpose, history, structure, capabilities and culture. Yet, in my experience, there are some simple principles, or rules, about innovation that broadly apply, and while their generality may preclude highly specific leadership strategies, they do provide a high-level guide which can be useful for leaders of not for profits and social enterprises.

Simple Rules for Innovation Leaders

Rule 1: TINA

Innovation is defined by the successful application of new ideas. It is not *having* ideas, which lie within the purview of discovery, creativity and inspiration, but putting those ideas to valuable *use*. It does not include those many ideas put into use that don't get anywhere, wither on the vine, and have no effect. Innovations *successfully* improve the performance of organisations and their ability to meet objectives. In a slightly adapted version of Joseph Schumpeter's schema, innovation is found in a wide range of areas, including new and improved products and services, processes, organisational structures, paths to market, and business models.[4] There is, therefore, a wide range of possible areas in which to innovate. The evidence shows that innovation delivers greater profit and market value, enhanced ability to survive downturns, and furthermore provides more attractive and exciting places to work.[5] When circumstances confronting organisations are uncertain and unpredictable, innovation importantly provides *the capacity to adapt.*[6]

British Prime Minister, Margaret Thatcher, had a favoured saying that "there is no alternative," and the acronym TINA became a well-used aphorism. It is highly appropriate to innovation. There is no alternative to innovation in most organisations. It is about the preparation, planning and implementation of novelty and change, without which few organisations can thrive and survive in a dynamic and evolving world. Without innovation, private sector organisations are put out of business by competitors, public sector organisations face scrutiny over whether they are making best use of tax payer's money, resulting in closure or movement of responsibilities to other portfolios, and NGOs and philanthropic organisations are superseded by those better at delivering value to supporters, donors and recipients.

As well as marshalling and accelerating the positive impacts of innovation, leaders also have to be aware of their, perhaps unforeseen, negative consequences, and attempt to negate them. Chernobyl, Thalidomide, and mortgage-backed securities were perceived as successful innovations at one time. These negative consequences may be unforeseeable, but just as organisations are increasingly held to account for their environmental impact, their leaders need to be conscious of the potential downsides of innovation. There is no alternative to addressing the social and environmental consequences of innovation.

Rule 2: Build the Innovation DNA

Biographies and autobiographies of great innovation leaders are rarely insightful and are often worthless hagiographies. All too often little account is taken of the fortuitous circumstances in which leaders succeed or the contributing efforts of those working with or for the person in question. Lou Gerstner's book on his time as the leader of IBM is an exception.[7] His book's title *Who Says Elephants Can't Dance* was a rebuke to those who hold that large bureaucratic organisations can't be responsive and flexible in the face of extraordinary challenges.[8] Gerstner took over IBM at a time when the New York Times had written the company's obituary, employment dropped by 125,000 and its share price plummeted 90 per cent. His approach was to make IBM more market facing, embrace open standards and collaboration, and to dramatically shift the company towards the provision of services. He recognised that the company was very technologically driven—its staff have won five Nobel Prizes—and that this was distracting attention away from the customer. Yet he realised that IBM's distinctive strength was its science and technology and he wanted to retain that focus, but at the same time inculcate innovation with a market facing approach that was engrained into the company's culture: into its DNA:[9]

> *I came to see, in my time at IBM, that culture isn't just one aspect of the game—it is the game. In the end, an organization is nothing more than the collective capacity of its people to create value. Vision, strategy,*

marketing, financial management—can set you on the right path and can carry you for a while. But no enterprise—whether in business, government, education, health care, or any area of human endeavor—will succeed over the long haul if those elements aren't part of its DNA.

When innovation is part of an organisation's DNA it encourages experiment, risk and tolerance of failure. When there is a high degree of uncertainty, clear and obvious solutions to problems are rarely immediately evident, so experimentation is important, and as it is often impossible to predict outcomes, risk taking is inevitable, and as a result some failure is unavoidable. Innovation leaders accept this and encourage innovation to become part of the culture and values of the organisation they represent.

Rule 3: Establish Supportive Voices

Although they may not be aware of specific efforts and instances, very little innovation occurs within organisations without the sanction of senior managers. Unless the CEO in particular is wholeheartedly supportive of the innovation agenda, much action in the area is half-hearted and highly incremental. In turn this requires the CEO to be supported by her or his Board of Directors, and the Chair of the Board has an especial role to play in protecting the CEO from short-term pressures and restrictions on any form of risk-taking. An actively supportive CEO, who continually extols the virtues of innovation, similarly gives his or her employees *permission to get excited*, to try new things without fear of retribution or recrimination if they don't turn out as expected.

In many ways, Thomas Edison might appear to be the innovation leader from hell. The inventor of the phonograph, electric light bulb, means of energy generation and distribution, and motion pictures, amongst numerous other world-changing inventions, demanded extraordinary commitment from his employees. His chief assistant, Clarence Dally, lost an arm and most of a hand during experiments with fluoroscopy during which Edison nearly lost his own eyesight. Nicola Tesla, one of Edison's most eminent employees (with whom he had a major falling out,) complained that in his first two weeks of work he only managed 48 hours sleep. Edison's work practices would challenge current workplace health and safety standards. Staff caught sleeping were exposed to the 'corpse reviver'—a terrifying noise beside the ear, or the 'resurrector of the dead'—which set them alight using a small explosive device. Yet Edison inspired great loyalty. One of his assistants said there was: "a little community of kindred spirits . . . enthusiastic about their work, expectant of great results, for whom work and play were indistinguishable." Edison provided the best equipment and made work interesting. He recognised the real value of his employees: "From his neck down a man is worth a couple of dollars a day, from his neck up he is worth anything his brain can produce," and liberated them from burdensome bureaucracy: "Hell, there are no rules here—we're trying to accomplish something."[10] Edison gave his employees permission to get excited, and they rewarded him with their extraordinary efforts.

A very effective leader of a major science organisation once explained to me that his overarching preoccupation was C^3: communication, communication, communication. The ability to articulate a clear and memorable message is one of the lessons of Sull and Eisenhardt's simple rules. The authors use the example of Professor Michael Pollan from the University of California, who summarises his years of research into diet and nutrition, which we all know can be highly confusing and contradictory, in this simple way: eat food, not too much, mainly plants. By 'food' he means proper food, recognisable by your grandmother, not processed rubbish. The innovation leader provides simple, consistent, memorable messages.

Rule 4: Negate the Antibodies

In their classic book from the 1960s, *The Management of Innovation*, Burns and Stalker distinguished between mechanistic and organic organisations.[11] The former are appropriate to stable, predictable circumstances, and are typified by high degrees of specialisation and organisation silos, the latter to those that are evolving and uncertain and are typified by decentralisation and cross-functional teams. There has therefore been long appreciation of the dangers of imposing too much formality and structure on organisations working in creative and fluid environments, and of having too little discipline and procedure in those that are ordered and predictable. Yet, despite, the obviousness of the need not to stifle innovation many organisations seem unable to resist the temptation to rely on mechanistic as opposed to organic approaches even when circumstances demand the latter.

Permission to get excited may be granted by an organisation's leaders, and may be enthusiastically embraced by many employees, especially those that are younger and more adventurous, but organisations develop strong innovation antibodies that destroy novelty. Reliance on rigid routines and procedures are an especial feature in large, complex organisations where bureaucracies develop that combat precedents. The emphasis is on centralisation of authority and compliance with policies and rules, and prescribed routines and procedures, reflecting a distinctive lack of trust in employees and fear of instability brought about by difference and diversity. Such process-driven organisations are anathema to innovation and creativity.

The innovation antibodies are often evident in middle layers of management, protective of their turf and whose responsibilities and incentives are directed towards delivery of highly defined operational objectives that leave no room for innovation. Antidotes to these innovation antibodies include regular affirmation of the importance of innovation by senior managers, and the balancing of incentives away from the immediate with weighting given to longer-term results. To protect innovation and initiative some organisations establish semi-sanctioned, separate organisations known as

Shunkworks where workers are liberated from everyday organisational constraints.

Innovation leaders recognise that innovative workers are often motivated by intrinsic rather than instrumental rewards—that is, by, for example, freedom to operate and peer recognition rather than remuneration—and whereas they might be perceived as being driven, stubborn and unresponsive to management fiat, in some circumstances these can be virtues. The analogy lies in the way the oyster can't make a pearl without a piece of grit: organisations that promote similarity and compliance are rarely capable of doing things out of the ordinary. Effective innovation leaders accept these characteristics of innovators and provide them focus and direction, building synergies between individual and organisational objectives.

Rule 5: Find the Balance

Innovation is a terribly imprecise word. On the one hand it refers to small, incremental changes: doing what you already do a little bit better. On the other it can mean massive, disruptive changes with profound consequences. Few organisations are capable of instigating transformational innovation, but the radical changes they bring about affect virtually all of them. The implication is that organisations need to engage with innovation in all its amplitude.

Jack Welch, the ex-CEO of GE once said that anyone can manage for the short term and anyone can manage for the long term, but the real challenge is to manage both at the same time. The balance innovation leaders seek can be seen in portfolios of innovation investments, decisions on what to do in-house, buy or partner in producing, and in choices of organisational structures. A portfolio approach recognises that the majority of innovation is incremental, for example in improving an existing product and expanding its market. At the other extreme would be a much smaller proportion of the portfolio that focuses on radical and transformational innovation. Such investments are made by the small number of organisations actually seeking to develop such innovations and by a larger number that take a position in order to keep an eye on potential future disruption and to possess the option to quickly respond to them should they choose to do so. In the middle of the portfolio are those innovations with medium scaled ambitions that move organisations into different, but related areas. The actual balance depends on strategic decisions on whether to be an innovation leader or follower, but few organisations can sustainably progress without investments across the portfolio.

In pursuance of their purpose, organisations have choices in whether to rely on buying in goods and services, doing things themselves, or partnering with others in collaborations and networks. Their decisions are influenced by factors ranging from concerns to reduce the costs of transactions to the building of core capabilities that give them distinctive advantages.

The balance in their choices influences their capacity to innovate. So buying rather than making, and indeed over-reliance on external partnerships, can reduce internal innovative skills and abilities.

Established practice is for organisations to try to move from *loose* (i.e. organic) structures and practices at early stages of innovation, when there are many unknowns and ideas are still experimental, to *tight* (i.e. mechanistic) when the configuration of innovations are established. The challenges for innovation leaders are to ensure that each form of organisation is not used in the wrong circumstances, preventing, for example, the incipient bureaucratisation discussed above, and to manage the balance between the two in the same organisation, requiring different incentives and reporting relationships. The challenge, in the modern parlance, is to be organisationally ambidextrous: to simultaneously reward playful adventurousness and cautious discipline.

Rule 6: Celebrate Successes

It is a sad indictment of the time poverty and busyness of modern work that successes often don't get the celebration they deserve. Innovation involves organisational and personal *risk* and its success should be recognised and appreciated commensurately. The organisational task is to clarify what success looks like. Innovation is a quintessentially *collaborative* activity involving people with different skills from different parts of the organisation. Innovation is furthermore *cumulative* over time, with advances built on past achievements. Attributing success to particular parts or groups can fail to properly appreciate the contributions of others. Success can be measured quantitatively and comparatively simply, for example using financial metrics, but conventional measures such as return on investment and discounted cash flow are highly imperfect and incomplete indicators of innovation achievements. Other measures may involve more qualitative complex assessments of how they have enhanced organisational capability, improved employee motivation, and improved the organisation's ability to respond to future challenges.

The celebration of success has to appreciate that returns to innovation are highly skewed. A small proportion of the population of innovations are responsible for the majority of the positive outcomes. Virtually impossible to predict *ex ante* which the most successful will be, the issue is how to balance rewards for all those contributing to the pool from which the most beneficial emerge.

Conclusions

Tolstoy, in *War and Peace*, observed "there is no greatness where there is not simplicity." There is no irony of seeking simplicity in the face of complexity. Innovation leadership is a difficult and challenging role, because innovation itself is beset with uncertainty and complexity. There are no manuals or blueprints for success (although there are legions of consultants prepared to sell you one). In the face of turbulent and unpredictable circumstances, detailed prescriptive strategies and plans are unlikely to be of great value. As the old military saying goes, no battle plan survives first contact with the enemy, or put more prosaically by the boxer Mike Tyson "everyone has a plan until they're punched in the mouth." An alternative approach to innovation leadership is the adoption and use of a number of simple rules to help guide behaviours and decisions. As Sull and Eisenhardt argue, simple rules work best when flexibility matters more than consistency, and innovation is an area where change is more important than stability.[12] The simple rules outlined here: *TINA, build the innovation DNA, establish supportive voices, negate the antibodies, find the balance*, and *celebrate successes*, provide a high-level guide to many of the issues to be confronted by innovation leaders.

As with all progress in life, it must be said, the possession of 'rules', and knowledge, insight and wisdom, only gets you so far. When asked about the virtue he appreciated most in his Generals, Napoleon answered "luck." There are many who claim that you make your own luck, but perhaps the best insight in this regard comes from Horace Walpole and his tale of the Princes of Serendip. The Princes set off on their adventures seeking particular riches, which they failed to find, but they found many other treasures, *simply because they were looking*. The effect of simple rules may lie not with their specific nature, but result from their very existence. Serendipity is a benefit of curiosity, and a common contributor to innovation, and reflects Pasteur's wise dictum that fortune favours the prepared mind.

Notes

1. D. Sull and K. Eisenhardt. *Simple Rules: How to Thrive in a Complex World"* (New York: Houghton Mifflin Harcourt, 2015).
2. Ibid.
3. Ibid., 6.
4. J. Schumpeter. *The Theory of Economic Development* (New Brunswick: Transaction Publishers, 1934).
5. M. Dodgson, D. Gann and A. Salter. *The Management of Technological Innovation: Strategy and Practice* (Oxford: Oxford University Press, 2008).
6. M. Dodgson, D. Gann and N. Phillips (eds). *The Oxford Handbook of Innovation Management* (Oxford: Oxford University Press, 2014).
7. L. Gerstner. *Who Says Elephants Can't Dance* (New York: Harper Collins, 2003).
8. Ibid.
9. Ibid., 182.
10. M. Dodgson and D. Gann. *Innovation: A Very Short Introduction* (Oxford: Oxford University Press, 2010).
11. T. Burns and G. Stalker. *The Management of Innovation* (London: Tavistock Publications, 1961).
12. Sull and Eisenhardt.

Bibliography

Burns, T. and G. Stalker. *The Management of Innovation.* London: Tavistock Publications, 1961.

Dodgson, M. and D. Gann *Innovation: A Very Short Introduction.* Oxford: Oxford University Press, 2010.

Dodgson, M., D. Gann, and N. Phillips (eds). *The Oxford Handbook of Innovation Management.* Oxford: Oxford University Press, 2014.

Dodgson, M., D. Gann, and A. Salter. *The Management of Technological Innovation: Strategy and Practice.* Oxford: Oxford University Press, 2008.

Gerstner, L. *Who Says Elephants Can't Dance.* New York: Harper Collins, 2003.

Rittel, H. and Webber, M. "Dilemmas in a General Theory of Planning," *Policy Sciences* 4 (1973): 155–69.

Schumpeter, J. *The Theory of Economic Development.* New Brunswick: Transaction Publishers, 1934.

Sull, D., and K. Eisenhardt. *Simple Rules: How to Thrive in a Complex World.* New York: Houghton Mifflin Harcourt, 2015.

Leadership in Practice: YGAP

Introduction

The desire to help others and make a difference is perennial but each generation approaches the goal in its own way. This is certainly true for YGAP, a highly innovative Not for Profit which believes that a world without poverty is possible; a world where everyone receives a quality education, can earn a fair wage and live in a good home, free from violence and preventable disease.

The foundation of YGAP's whole approach is entrepreneurialism. Rather than using traditional aid models, they operate in many countries throughout the world by finding and supporting local 'impact entrepreneurs' who are changing lives in some of the world's toughest communities. They believe local leaders have the solution to local problems. They express it this way:

> "Rather than imposing our perceived solutions on a foreign community, we support local leaders who live there and have developed their own. We believe that the best solutions are entrepreneurial, so we focus on early stage ventures that exist to improve access to education or healthcare, create jobs or build safer homes. We believe this is the most effective, sustainable means of tackling poverty because these local leaders understand the unique challenges of their communities. Our role is simply to help refine and scale their solutions."

The organisation has achieved remarkable success. Since their foundation in 2008, YGAP has significantly and measurably impacted the lives of 139,529 people living in poverty, and aims to back 1,000 entrepreneurs and impact one million lives by 2018.

The local leaders are supported in their home countries, through a professional 'Accelerator' development program tailored to their needs. It now follows what has been devised as an Impact Model which has four basic ingredients for the support of the local Impact Entrepreneurs:

- **Find:** National searches are conducted in each of the countries where YGAP works for local entrepreneurs with start up ventures that exist to change the lives of people living in poverty. Hundreds apply for each intake and the top 15 are selected.

- **Accelerate:** The selected start up entrepreneurs go through an intense entrepreneurship accelerator where they access a training curriculum devised by YGAP and rapidly improve their ideas to make them more scalable, sustainable and able to quickly impact hundreds of people in their communities
- **Support:** After the accelerator, they are provided with twelve months of support in the form of free lawyers, website and graphic designers, mentors, business advisors and small injections of $500 to help overcome barriers or test ideas.
- **Grow:** The entrepreneurs that build the most exciting, scalable, and sustainable ventures through the support phase move into the growth phase where they access rounds of $25,000 grants and investments as well as specific growth advice and support.

Fundraising—a Feast of Merit

The organisation's own operation, including fund raising, is also based on entrepreneurialism. Not for them the often heavy reliance of charities on conventional grants and donations. They are a true social enterprise owning and running profitable social ventures and fundraising campaigns.

Nowhere is this more evident than in their very successful flagship venture 'Feast of Merit', a lively restaurant in Melbourne, where both the enthusiasm of the staff and the food are bubbling. All profits go directly towards the impact work across Africa, Asia, and Australia. This is also where the leadership team meet regularly for breakfast. YGAP, as a profit- driven social enterprise, was designed to be replicated in any industry or organisation by anyone with a vision for social good.

The choice of the name for the restaurant is a lesson in itself. Feast of Merit stems from a community festival in Nagaland of North Eastern India. This celebration occurs when a person acquires a position of wealth and can choose to invite the whole community including the underprivileged to share the wealth. The ceremony is a celebration of humanity, a distribution of wealth and the empowerment of community. Within the Feast of Merit journey YGAP has continued to celebrate the Naga's culture, sense connection to land and language, as well as its rich history and tradition. Feast of Merit has become a hub for local community members to gather, feast, and experience the energy of YGAP.

Other innovative and fundraising YGAP approaches include '5 cents', a program which asks every Australian to collect small change to drive big change and ensure every child can receive a quality education and an equal start in life. When the idea came from one of their volunteers, there were calculated to be $150 million worth of five-cent coins in Australia. Another recent idea is 'Polished Man', a program which challenges men to paint one nail to help end violence against children.

YGAP also hosts many events as part of its fundraising. Their function space is open to all kinds of events with profits going towards helping projects. YGAP also hosts impressive events such as the annual Sydney and Melbourne vision dinners and the 2013 Bhalobashi (meaning 'love' in Bengali) Ball which celebrated five years of YGAP fundraising and raised a $75,000 profit on the night.

Leadership, Communication, and Engagement

Whilst there were a number of co-founders of YGAP, the spotlight invariably falls on Elliot Costello, who is often compared with his father Tim Costello—until recently the CEO of World Vision and a doyen of the Not for Profit movement in Australia. The comparison is interesting because Elliot has tended to eschew many of the traditional approaches adopted by international charities such as World Vision as he reaches out to a new, young audience who think and communicate in different ways. He explains that the current younger generation may have little in the way of money to donate but they are very willing to give of their time. They are also keen to suggest innovative ways to achieve the organisation's mission. However, to attract and retain young volunteers it is vital to use their language and tap into their ideals and their desire to contribute. Conventional methods and approaches of the Not for Profit sector are often irrelevant to this generation.

Indeed YGAP has a communications approach which is fine-tuned to the receptiveness of the younger generation. Its success has been attributed to a number of factors:

- Communication between YGAP and its supporters has always been through a fun, laidback and informal approach.
- YGAP was founded in 2008 with a young team and has since gained a huge number of young supporters. To ensure this audience continues this support, YGAP communicates with clear and succinct messages on what YGAP are doing, how they are achieving their aims and how supporters are helping YGAP achieve these goals.
- The issues that YGAP are tackling are disheartening topics; therefore it is important to maintain upbeat communications on how successful supporters have been in having an impact on lives as opposed to continuously distressing messages on the lives of impoverished communities.
- The communication used during the five-cent and Polished Man campaigns is designed to be very informative and clear about how getting involved will directly help YGAP support impact entrepreneurs around the world. YGAP feel it is important to have exciting and entertaining

communication during these campaigns to ensure a younger generation want to get involved.

Elliot Costello himself is cast as a social entrepreneur with a long held social conscience and a penchant for taking risks. He explains that YGAP came about by accident when he and a group of 12 socially minded friends wanted to combine their two loves of travel and volunteering, but faced the obstacle of exorbitant fees associated with most international volunteer programs which helped create change in developing countries. So they decided to cut out the middleman and fundraised within their own communities before packing their bags and flying to Africa to help build classrooms for schools in need. After realising that there was an appetite for these projects Elliott left his job as an accountant to start YGAP. The founders of YGAP realised that by partnering directly with NGOs whose work directly affects people in developing countries this would cut out the intermediary and associated fees. More importantly YGAP knew it was important that local leaders could serve their local communities and have solutions to their own problems.

As a leader he has always placed great stress on the fact that their results must be measurable and authentic, and this evidence-based approach has no doubt been a major contributing factor to the very long list of partnerships which YGAP has formed with corporates, community groups, and individuals. Partnerships have become a key element of the organisation's resourcing and activity. Elliot believes that every business should be socially minded and he prides YGAP in making philanthropy accessible to everyone. He points out that simply by choosing to dine at their restaurant or support their campaigns people are changing the lives of people living in poverty. Also people want to be able to make ethical decisions and it is YGAP's job to make that decision-making process an easy one.

It is clear that Elliot is a consultative and open leader who inspires his team by his own example of dedication and energy. He has revealed that he starts every day with 'morning pages', when he writes three pages that help him to set some clear intentions for the day ahead. This is often followed by team breakfasts at 'Feast of Merit' and then consultations with more members of the team at headquarters in Richmond, Melbourne. He considers it vital to touch base regularly as a group to ensure all projects are on track and to ensure that all team members are supporting one another.

The Appeal of YGAP

YGAP appeals to a young, innovative audience due to its unique impact model. Many young people have become angry and disheartened in recent years at the lack of impact of the big charities/NGOs and the lack of *real* change and prosperity within the developing countries in which they work. The YGAP model takes a unique bottom-up approach and by fostering impact entrepreneurs who have local solutions to local problems, tangible change can be seen in local communities. This clear and encouraging progress is a huge attraction for those wishing to drive true change.

Another attraction for young people is the speed at which YGAP is growing; having impacted 155,379 lives is immensely impressive. Also a passionate and dedicated team who are all united on the best approach to poverty alleviation is a big attraction for young people.

YGAP has an impressive young volunteer team because it is a pioneering organisation and young people want to show their support and become part of an incredibly growing movement. People want to feel they are part of a movement of change and while not everyone is able to contribute financially, YGAP allows everyone to feel part of a solution through volunteering or creating awareness.

YGAP appeals to potential partners who are attracted by the vision of empowering communities disadvantaged by poverty, enabling them to become self-sustainable. There is now a very long list of partners and donors including individuals, Trusts and Foundations, Non-Profit Partners, YGAP Board members, and Corporates encompassing some of Australia's largest organisations across the whole spectrum of commerce and industry.

The YGAP experience dispels many negative perceptions about the motivations and interests of younger generations. It also demonstrates that a social enterprise approach harnessing entrepreneurialism with a social conscience has immense potential for the engagement of future generations, given the right leadership.

Kenneth Wiltshire

12 Strategy, Leadership and Team Building

Karina Collins

Introduction

The roles of strategy and leadership are ever evolving, especially in today's fast moving and somewhat ambiguous digital world where certain approaches that have proven somewhat successful for decades are, in many cases, fast becoming obsolete.

Adding more complexity for non-profit organisations are the increasing demands to deliver on a complex organisational purpose whilst most likely suffering from considerable resourcing constraints.

So what does this mean for our leaders in non-profit organisations, both in terms of leadership and strategy? How must we adapt and transform to shift our prior style, approaches and practices into a new gear to deliver on these expectations?

The non-profit sector has been slower than its corporate counterpart to embrace the custom and practice of strategy and performance management. Whereas in the corporate sector the outcomes sought by strategy are generally increased market share, growth and shareholder return, for non-profit organisations the outcomes sought are individual and social. This in turn has tended to result in non-profits taking a more internal and reactionary approach (to deal with a specific issue or challenge) to strategic planning.

As non-profit organisations continue to face (among other things) ongoing crowding for donor dollars, technological advancements, member divergence, political and economic uncertainty and ongoing structural change to business models, traditional approaches must be challenged. Strategy has to shift from being a '2 day workshop with Leadership and Board', to being a well-considered, well informed, well planned and able-to-be-executed activity that is embedded into the day to day DNA of the organisation. This means we need to transition from a reactionary model of scrambling to develop a document that will 'sit on the shelf and gather dust' (until next year's retreat) to an analytical, evidence-based process that results in hard choices being made to compete differently within our chosen market(s).

Whilst seasoned leaders might argue that the contemporary challenges of today are new iterations of an already-experienced theme, there would arguably be wide consensus that the pace of change (and hence the need to rapidly respond) is new. Leaders are challenged like never before to ensure that they have the right blend of skills and approach to be successful in what they do. No longer can a leader stand solely on their technical skills or market connections—leaders need to complement these strong foundations with a wealth of accompanying strategic, social and interpersonal skills that allow them to rapidly assess and adapt to an ever changing environment.

So in practical terms, what needs to change?

For the past two decades I have worked with hundreds of public, private and non-profit organisations in the areas of strategy and leadership. I have seen a definite shift from having to 'convince' organisations (from any sector) about the need for well-considered and deliberate interventions in the areas of strategy and leadership to instead being sought out to 'educate and inform' organisations and leaders on how to improve and embed contemporary leadership skills and strategy practices into their organisations. In my experience, the priority areas to focus on are ensuring effective:

1. Leadership
2. Team Dynamics
3. Strategic planning, and
4. Implementation

The four priority areas are self-reinforcing. For example, in the absence of strong, committed and trusted 'leadership', it is near impossible to achieve an effective and functional 'team dynamic'. If the 'team dynamic' is dysfunctional, 'strategic planning' will be suboptimal, and so on.

Appreciating the self-reinforcing nature of each priority area is critical. Many times an organisation will want to jump straight to strategic planning—and will neglect to appreciate that in the absence of strong leadership and teams, strategic planning could be (depending on the unique circumstances) ineffective given the lack of alignment and probable inability to drive engagement towards execution.

Leadership

What is an ideal leadership profile for non-profit organisations? What are the behaviours you need to demonstrate every day to sustain an exceptional workforce that is absolutely, 100%, committed to you?

The ultimate role of a leader is to effect sustainable and positive change—whether that be in response to a defensive (responding to a threat) or offensive (taking advantage of an opportunity) strategy. I have used for a number of years the 'TRUE' Leadership Profile for non-profit organisations:

- (T): Be **Transparent** to stakeholders about the organisation and its operations
- (R): Be **Responsive** to new challenges and ideas
- (U): Embed **Unique** and critical thinking
- (E): Deliver outcomes through **Execution**

To consider and challenge your current leadership style against the TRUE model, ask yourself 'how do I demonstrate (or not) this trait or capability now?' and consider:

- Is there anything that you should **stop doing**?
- Is there a gap that highlights something you should **start doing**?
- Is there a gap that highlights things you currently do that you should do **more of**?
- What strengths have you reinforced as the things you should **keep doing**?

Table 12.1 'TRUE' Leadership Profile

Leadership Style	Description
1. T: Transparent	Engage in the open book philosophy of leadership—make available enough information and data to your employees so that they understand and can take ownership of the operations and how their action (or inactions) contribute to the overall performance of the business.
2. R: Responsive	Demonstrate initiative—be responsive to challenges and actively work to establish new, innovative solutions. Earn respect as someone that 'gets things done', 'anticipates opportunities', and 'embraces change'.
3. U: Unique	Provide unique insight that influences strategic choices to shape a clear vision, purpose, and strategy for the organisation. Embed critical thinking as an organisation capability—enabled through ongoing analytical processes and practices considering internal and external data.
4. E: Execution	Have a clear plan for execution. Translate goals and strategies into actions (activities or projects) with measurable timelines, allocated resources, and associated success measures, accountabilities, funding strategies and monitoring arrangements.

Team Dynamic

What are the unique challenges for teams in non-profit organisations? How can we improve the performance of our teams—from the Board and Leadership, through to external stakeholders and staff?

The Role of the Board

Clients often ask me 'who should be responsible for the development and execution of our strategy?' or 'who should be held accountable for the execution of our strategy and how?'

Ultimately, the Board is responsible for the organisation, and with that the effectiveness of its strategic planning processes, with Leadership and Management accountable for execution and monitoring.

Whilst not unique to non-profit organisations, the following constraints are often more prevalent:

- A tendency for the Board to become too involved in operations;
- The need to professionalise organisation structures, roles and operations; and
- A lack of formal governance arrangements and performance reporting.

For non-profit organisations, it is often a challenge to define the role of the Board. Leaders need to identify and apply a framework to how the role of the Board (areas of responsibility), works with and through that of the CEO as noted in Figure 12.1 below.

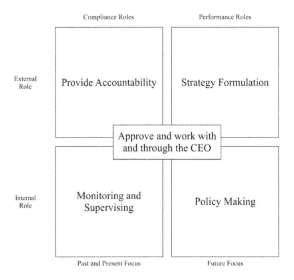

Figure 12.1 The Role of the Board.[1]

How do leaders go beyond understanding the role of the Board and effect change to improve the way in which the Board and Leadership work together? Often this can be a sensitive and complex area. A good starting point is being able to clarify the current arrangements in order to identify what is working, and where improvement is required.

Table 12.2 provides a framework for thinking about and analysing the style of your Board in relation to strategy and execution. An effective Board will be engaged within the parameters of its role.

To consider and challenge your current Board arrangements against the framework, ask yourself 'how does our Board participate in these areas of strategy and execution?' and consider:

- Is there anything that the Board should **stop doing**?
- Is there a gap that highlights something the Board should **start doing**?
- Is there a gap that highlights things the Board currently does that it should do **more of**?
- What strengths have you reinforced as the things the Board should **keep doing**?

Teams

Most often team outcomes are impacted by team dynamics.

For leadership and for strategy this means leaders must ensure they have effective, well-functioning teams in order to ensure 'readiness' to embark on strategy. A poor team dynamic will almost certainly have a negative impact on the organisation's ability to formulate and execute its strategy.

I have seen organisations achieve exceptional outcomes when teams have a positive team dynamic. Conversely, I have also seen situations where a poor team dynamic has resulted in a vicious cycle of mistrust, and ultimately such teams are driven by self-ego and personal agendas.

Figure 12.2 illustrates the cause and effect of dysfunctional team dynamics upon team outcomes, and how a robust tool can analyse team dynamics and develop targeted strategies to improve team performance.

Well-planned and carefully considered conversations and focus groups (facilitated by an independent third party) promote open and honest discussion of team dynamic amongst key stakeholders. Ideally, teams will identify behaviours that are causing dysfunction, and agree to a set of principles to transition to, to sustain a functional team. A Team Charter is an effective tool that will capture the decisions made, and symbolise the commitments made by the team to itself and each other.

Table 12.2 The style of the Board in strategy and execution.[2]

Area of focus in relation to Strategy and Execution: Level of Participation in Strategy Development

Passive	Engaged	Intrusive
CEO drives strategic direction, and keeps the Board informed at Board meetings.	Defines the role of the Board in Strategic Planning process, and understands how each Board member can contribute. Acts as a partner in the strategic planning process, and provides insight into relevant stages of the strategic planning process. Engages industry and specialist expertise to add value to the strategic planning process and decision-making.	Dominant personalities on the Board impose their will on the strategic planning process, rather than enabling management to contribute.

Area of focus in relation to Strategy and Execution: Decision-Making

Passive	Engaged	Intrusive
Reviews' CEO's recommendations and approves them without much further investigation.	Challenges the CEO's recommendations and assumptions to test the robustness of decisions. Engages industry and specialist expertise to add value to the strategic planning process and decision-making.	Board members get too involved in day-to-day management decision-making during execution. Holds up or overrules management's tactical operational decisions during execution.

Area of focus in relation to Strategy and Execution: Impact on the Organisation

Passive	Engaged	Intrusive
The organisation is denied the benefit of the skills and expertise of the Board. Over reliance on the CEO may result in unqualified and unchallenged risks to be taken.	The Board and management are working as a team to analyse, define and develop the strategy. Accountability for roles in the strategic planning process is clear.	Actual performance of staff is not as easily measured. Loss of time dedicated to Board level matters. Frustration amongst the management team.

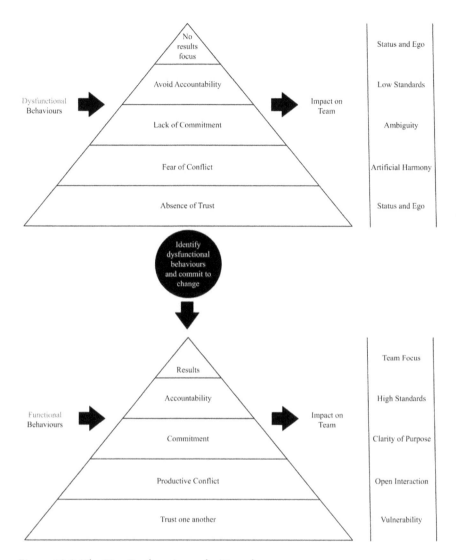

Figure 12.2 The Five Dysfunctions of a Team.[3]

Strategy Planning

"Strategy is the creation of a unique and valuable position, involving a different set of activities"—Michael Porter.

I have helped hundreds of organisations plan for, and execute on their strategies. I have seen organisations both over-complicate, as well as 'play down', strategy (usually through a fear of failure due in part to a lack of knowledge over process). I am convinced that just as leadership and teams (and the various dimensions thereof) are critical to the successful development and execution of strategy, so too is:

- The need to understand *what* strategy is, and be able to differentiate strategic planning from operational excellence;
- The need to inform the strategic planning process with data and insights; and
- The need for a well thought out, practical and achievable process for how the activity of strategic planning is to be orchestrated throughout the organisation.

Strategy versus Operational Excellence

Michael Porter notes the following as the five essentials of strategy:[4]

1. A unique value proposition compared to other organisations
2. A different, tailored value chain
3. Clear trade-offs, and choosing what not to do
4. Activities that fit together and reinforce each other
5. Strategic continuity with continual improvement in realising the strategy

Central to Porter's theories on strategy is the difference between 'operational effectiveness' and 'strategic positioning' (Figure 12.3). Organisations that fail to create a unique value proposition through clear choices and trade-offs will inevitably get 'stuck' in operational effectiveness—essentially mirroring their competitors to do the same things better. Operational effectiveness alone can often become a race to the bottom as organisations compete on best practices and simply doing the same things better.

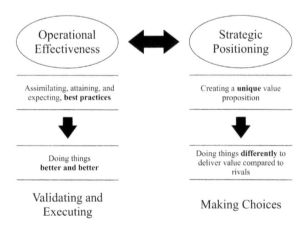

Figure 12.3 Operational Effectiveness versus Strategic Positioning [5]

Many organisations can get caught in a cycle of strategic plans that only ever capture operational effectiveness tasks. Whilst from a performance perspective they may continue to meet their improvement goals (of attaining or shifting further towards best practice), from a markets and growth perspective they fail to establish, grow or sustain a competitive position. Leaders stuck in this cycle need to make hard choices and shift their organisations from 'comfort and process', to 'risk, uncertainty and critical thinking' for longer-term gain and sustainability.

Data Analytics

> "What underlies the malaise of so many large and successful organisations worldwide is that their theory of the business no longer works"- Peter Drucker

It is critical prior to embarking on any strategic planning exercise that you have deep and informed insight of the business model, and that you understand the entirety of the organisation to help inform evidence based, strategic and operational thinking.

A survey into the strategic planning practices of non-profit organisations found that 39% of high performance non-profit organisations were highly successful at developing data-driven strategies.[6] With the continued emergence of data analytics tools and capability, this number should be expected to have increased considerably.

Data is everywhere—but how do we think about it in terms of its usefulness? A simple way to think about and characterise data sets and their utility is to consider:

- Volume—the quantity of data available
- Veracity—the accuracy of the data being received or generated
- Velocity—the pace of creation of the data or data set

For data to be useful, it needs to be collected, aggregated, cleaned and analysed. The power of data is in the statistical story it can tell us—the ability to show causality in scenarios that test strategic options. The real value is then in the people asking the questions—and shifting the thinking from the boundaries of today's business model.

To create sustainable value from data, organisations must transition from 'looking in the rear view mirror' (what happened?) to using insight (why did it happen?) to inform clear strategic choices (what should I do?).

Figure 12.4 is an example I use of extending information to insight, decision and action in the context of customer analytics. It demonstrates the transition from descriptive analytics to diagnostic, predictive, prescriptive and pre-emptive analytics.

Before embarking on your strategic planning exercise consider your data sets and their utility in your planning exercise. In practical terms—where does your organisation sit on the continuum of information, insight, decision and action?

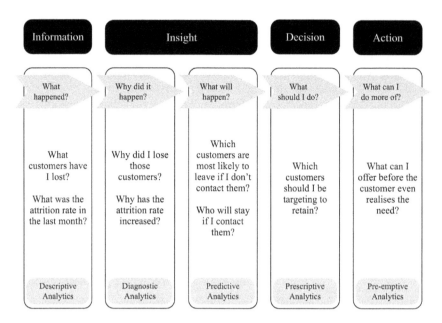

Figure 12.4 Data Analysis and Analytics.

Consider the example above in the scenario of a strategic planning workshop:

- Prior to the workshop, participants are provided the 'information and insights' along with some options for 'decision' and 'action'.
- In the workshop, informed participants will discuss and debate the options and agree on how to move forward.
- This is the power of data—shifting from assumptions to evidence-based decision-making.

Strategic Planning Process

Strategic planning typically has multiple stages, which come together to form an end-to-end process which usually starts with strategic review and analysis, and results in assessment of performance against the stated plan, with a continuing characteristic of review and redesign to ensure the plan stays flexible, agile and relevant. Figure 12.5 shows this process.

Organisations can get 'stuck' in review and planning without ever addressing strategy development. These organisations are in the cycle of 'operational effectiveness', and are yet to transition to consider 'strategic options' and clear strategic choices. Intervention is required to ensure the end result

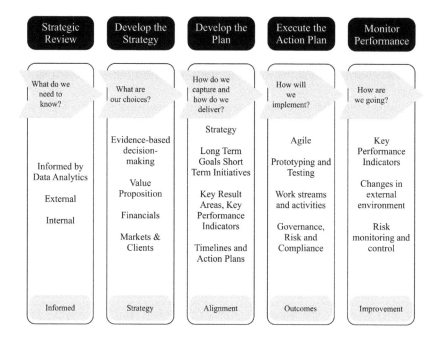

Figure 12.5 Strategic Planning Process

is not a plan that merely mirrors the business of today (reading more like a business plan of how to do the same things more efficiently).

The above mentioned survey conducted by the Association for Strategic Planning also found that larger organisations are more likely to invest time and resources on review activities that include external data gathering and analysis to inform strategic choices, whereas smaller organisations are more likely to turn to internal brainstorming and vision/mission discussions.[7] This is an interesting observation in the context of the strategic planning process and probable constraints of organisation capability (understanding contemporary analysis approaches) and capacity (having the resource and skills to conduct) within smaller organisations.

Following are a range of useful tools and methods for the review, development and planning stages.

Strategic Review Tools and Methods

There are a multitude of tools that can be used to ensure the robustness of the process. Some critical ones in the strategic review stage are the SWOT (Strengths, Weaknesses, Opportunities and Threats) and the VRIA (Valuable, Rare, Imitable, and Actionable).

SWOT Analysis

In strategy or business planning, the SWOT analysis can be used to assess factors internal or external to the team/organisation, and ensure that these are accounted for in the development of any plan. Whilst strengths and weaknesses are internal to the organisation, opportunities and threats are external.

To make sure that all relevant factors are considered in the SWOT analysis, you may choose to call upon different models to guide your thinking. Some of the more prominent options used to prompt thinking are the PESTLE model (Political, Economic, Social, Technological, Legal, Environmental), the SEEDTIP model (Social, Economic, Ecological, Demographic, Technological, International, Political) and the PROFIT model (Physical, Reputational, Organisational, Financial, Intellectual, Technological).

And finally—make sure you ask 'why?' and 'what is the action?' for any items captured in your SWOT. This step translates the data collected into strategic choices.

VRIA Analysis

The VRIA stands for Valuable, Rare, Imitability, and Actionable and is a measure of the relative strength of the capabilities and resources of the organisation in its ability to generate a real competitive advantage. You may also see this model referred to as the VRIO (Valuable, Rare, Imitability, and Organisation).

Real competitive advantage arises where an organisation is able to generate above normal profits using its specific capabilities and resources because they have an element of rarity or value that is difficult for a competing firm to duplicate quickly.

The matrix below (Figure 12.6) shows how capabilities and resources can be assessed using this model. Where any resource of the organisation

Is it Valuable?	Is it Rare?	Is it hard to Imitate?	Can we Action it?	Result
No	No	No	No	Competitive Disadvantage
Yes	No	No	No	Competitive Neutrality
Yes	Yes	No	No	Short Term Disadvantage
Yes	Yes	Yes	No	Unused Advantage
Yes	Yes	Yes	Yes	Long Term Advantage

Figure 12.6 VRIA assessment for competitive advantage in the marketplace you operate in.[8]

satisfies all conditions in the matrix, it represents a chance for true competitive advantage in a market:

Strategy Development Tools

Three Horizons of Growth

Originally developed by well-known management consultants Mehrdad Baghai, Stephen Coley and David White, the Three Horizons of Growth model (Figure 12.7) describes the need for any organisation to be continuously operating in and thinking about not only the business model of today, but also creating the business models of both the short and longer term futures of the organisation.

The underlying premise of the model in strategy is that operating in your core business is as important as devoting time and investment to uncovering future opportunities *and* making decisions to explore the best of these. Information and insight gleaned via internal and external review and data analysis will help to shape and inform your thinking about core and future business models.

Strategists and business planners will often refer to each of the horizons as follows:

- **Horizon 1:** Extending and defending your core business and current market position
- **Horizon 2:** Actively building the business of tomorrow (emerging business)
- **Horizon 3:** Designing viable options for the longer term and 'placing bets' on which options should be pursued further

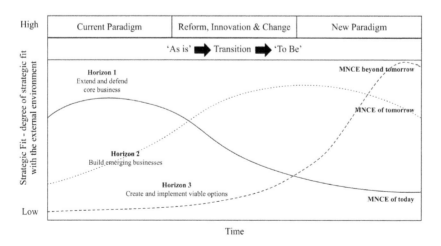

Figure 12.7 Three Horizons of Growth.[9]

Stating Your Value Proposition

Any model that seeks to capture your strategy in a simple way will require you to understand and be able to clearly explain your value proposition.

When stating your value proposition, it is critical to voice this in a manner that is relevant and completely accessible to your clients and contacts. You should avoid using jargon or technical terms and instead focus on understanding the job that a client requires to be completed.

Figure 12.8 demonstrates the link between the needs of your client and the products and services that you offer.

You must identify either the current 'pain points' or 'gains' that a prospective client may be looking to address and focus on how your products or services can provide the solution that is required.

As a simple example, the carer of a young man with an acquired brain injury may be seeking to access services for daily support under his NDIS plan. However, in their mind, the job that they require completed could be voiced as:

- Ensuring that my son is in safe hands
- Giving my son some independence to make him feel better
- Someone to help my son go shopping to the supermarket

Whereas, a mental health and disability support professional may describe the same service as 'daily living support meeting the requirements of your NDIS plan and offering sustainable independence solutions'

Developing and communicating a value proposition in this example requires the provider to identify the real problem at the heart of the client's thinking and to simply and clearly show the value they can provide in solving this core challenge.

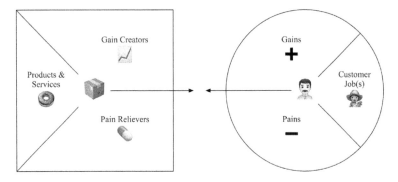

Figure 12.8 Voice of the client value proposition.[10]

Digital Value

There is no doubt that any strategic plan developed in today's organisations must consider digital. Boards and Leadership team must challenge their current business model and determine how digital technologies can be leveraged to create digital value.

For non-profit organisations, digital value can be realised through:

- **Digitisation of internal processes**—transforming operations using digital to standardise and automate workflows and processes;
- **Digitisation of client engagement and delivery**—using digital to connect with clients through social media and mobile technology; and
- **Digitisation of products and services**—reshaping the customer value proposition using digital technologies.

Whilst there is a natural relationship between them, there is not a dependency to take on each simultaneously. For most organisations, the constraints of funding, time, resource and capabilities will often influence priorities.

Any investment in digital client engagement must be augmented with data analytics capability to make sense out of, and glean insights from the new data sets generated. According to former Google CEO Eric Schmidt, in 2010 we were producing as much data every two days as existed up to 2003.[11] Given the exponential rise in social media and mobile technologies one can only assume that number is far greater today. In itself, the trajectory points not only to the complexity of harnessing and leveraging such large volumes of data, but in the opportunity that digital client engagement presents if we are able to gain insights from it.

For organisations embarking on digital transformation, it is likely that they are already participating in some capacity in digital. This may be via website activity, social media participation, client portal technology or similar. IBM suggest that determining the best path to transformation requires a thorough understanding and evaluation of several factors:[12]

- Where products and services are on the physical-to-digital continuum in the industry
- Mobility and social networking adoption levels and expectations of customers
- Strategic moves by other industry players
- The degree of integration at every stage of the transformation—between new digital processes and legacy, physical ones.

An organisation's path to digital transformation may follow one of the three paths shown in Figure 12.9.

Paths to digital transformation

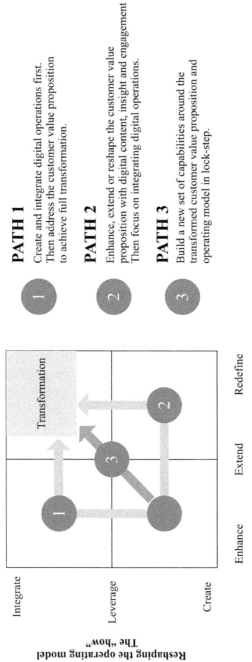

PATH 1

Create and integrate digital operations first. Then address the customer value proposition to achieve full transformation.

PATH 2

Enhance, extend or reshape the customer value proposition with digital content, insight and engagement Then focus on integrating digital operations.

PATH 3

Build a new set of capabilities around the transformed customer value proposition and operating model in lock-step.

Figure 12.9 Digital transformation requires strategic development of the value proposition and the operating model.[13]

But what does a 'project' to help organisations determine and navigate through their transformation path look like? Using models like IBM's to categorise and prioritise paths, leaders must establish digital transformation projects that have the following three core objectives:

1. Informing and engaging stakeholders
2. Confirming and communicating the Transformation Pathway
3. Embedding digital capability for ongoing, sustainable value creation

In my experience, typically the program of work within a medium sized organisation to deliver on these outcomes can be spread across Strategy & Design, and Deployment activities which incorporate prototyping concepts as noted in Figure 12.10.

Plan Development Tools

Strategy Map

One of the most popular methods of capturing strategy on a single page, and determining the actions to flow from this, is the Strategy Map, which is based on the Kaplan/Norton Balanced Scorecard approach.

The Strategy Map uses four perspectives to plot a long-term (3–5 year) direction and identify the short-term (1–2 year) resources and actions that will need to take place to achieve stated objectives.

An example Strategy Map is set out below (Figure 12.11), with a summary of the four perspectives as follows:

- **Financial Perspective:** Where will you seek to increase revenue and reduce costs to achieve your objectives? What assets can you leverage in pursuit of these objectives?
- **Market/Customer Perspective:** What is your value proposition? What markets will you trade in and what will you choose to exit?
- **Internal Perspective:** What processes will be required to achieve your objectives?
- **Learning Perspective:** What knowledge, skills and resources are required to compete?

A comprehensively completed Strategy Map will have defined goals and actions for each relevant component—including how success will be measured. These goals and actions are then drawn into plans for execution throughout the organisation.

Strategy Canvas

An alternative (and sometimes simpler) method of capturing the same strategic information is to use the Strategy or Business Model Canvas (developed

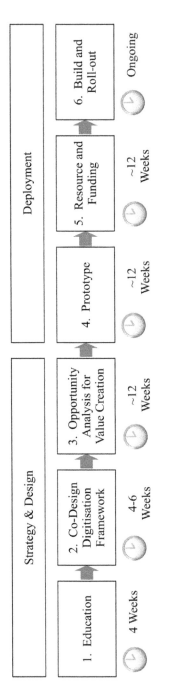

Strategy & Design

1. Education	2. Co-Design Digitisation Framework	3. Opportunity Analysis for Value Creation
4 Weeks	4-6 Weeks	~12 Weeks

Deployment

4. Prototype	5. Resource and Funding	6. Build and Roll-out
~12 Weeks	~12 Weeks	Ongoing

Identify pathway to digitisation:

- Adopt a case study based approach to educating key stakeholders about digital trends, threats, and opportunities
- Model the organisation's Digitisation Framework and identify the priority opportunities for value creation

Embed digital capability

- Validate model through prototypes
- Establish a centralised function to deliver digital capability across the organisation.

Figure 12.10 A sample program of work for Digital Transformation

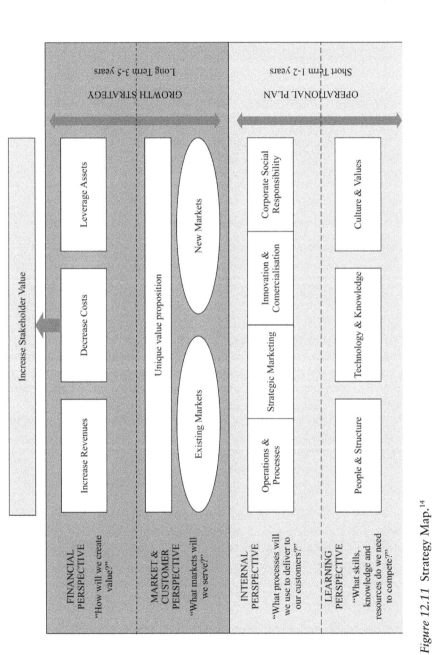

Figure 12.11 Strategy Map.[14]

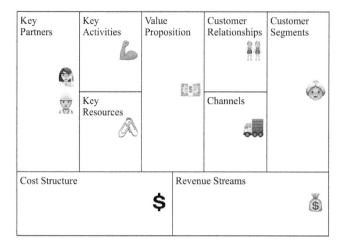

Figure 12.12 Business Model Canvas.[15]

by Strategyzer for the use of start-up organisations or those seeking a faster approach to documenting strategy) see Figure 12.12 for an example.

The Strategy Canvas uses the same approach as the Strategy Map to identify the revenue and cost structures that are relevant to your objectives, and to plot the resources, partners and relationships that will be required for you to succeed.

As with the Strategy Map, each element captured above must flow into an action plan to state who is responsible for each task and how progress towards longer-term objectives will be measured.

Implementation

Due in part to the pace of change, but also the impact of new technologies, organisations are being forced to rethink and reorganise their approach to strategy execution and how activities are organised, resourced, funded, prioritised, and communicated.

Agile Approach

The more traditional approaches of waterfall that were suited to a steady-state environment are not necessarily as effective for some organisations today, and need to be replaced or augmented with more contemporary models of agile and scrum to accommodate the fast pace of change, the need to assess and test many options, and the need to continuously demonstrate achievement of milestones.

Outsourcing Non-Core Activities

Similarly—leaders must understand the array of new outsourcing options available to today's businesses. Whether it is your graphic design, research, call centre, accounts or debt collection (to name just a few of the many options), the expansion of the outsourcing market to include offshoring means leaders can access comparable services for considerably more flexibility and lower costs.

Funding Execution

With this comes the added complexity of how leaders commit funding to the execution of strategic initiatives—in a less certain environment organisations are being asked to commit to funding where only time and effort are certain—not necessarily scope. The idea of prototyping chosen scenarios or options to a certain level of commitment to fail fast (accelerated change and innovation versus detailed planning and assessment) is an extremely different way of thinking and managing for most of today's leaders. The emergence of alternative funding models such as crowd funding also introduces new opportunities to engage with stakeholders and even involve employees with how organisations fund strategic choices—again, new concepts that today's business leaders need to be cognisant of to maximise how they best deliver on their organisation's vision.

Resourcing and Skills

Finally—the next biggest challenge facing organisations is resourcing, possibly more so in non-profit organisations where for a multitude of reasons long tenures (10, 15, 20 plus years) are common. Often this means that funds are tied to resources that lack the experience and skills to execute on our strategic choices. This is a sensitive and difficult issue that needs to be addressed. Leaders need to give staff the opportunity to upskill, or offer a respectable and workable exit solution that will ultimately offer them the opportunity to be purposeful in some other capacity whilst allowing the organisation to redirect its funds for the realisation of its stated purpose. There is no doubt this is one of the more difficult aspects of change to address (maybe the most difficult) as the rapid pace of change increasingly renders less meaningful a raft of roles that were critical no less than five or 10 years ago.

Specific to digital transformation, a new emerging set of capabilities are emerging that are required to reshape and transform organisations as noted in Figure 12.13.

Digital transformation capabilities

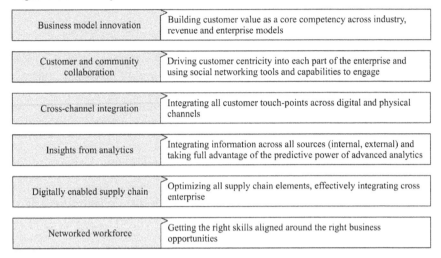

Figure 12.13 Reshaping the business and operating model requires a new set of capabilities.[16]

Barriers to Successful Execution

The Harvard Business Review (HBR) Advisory Council is a representative group of HBR readers that are regularly polled to gain insights into business. In March 2010, HBR conducted a survey of the Advisory Group, asking them about strategy and execution.[17]

Based on the 1,075 responses to the survey, HBR identified the following top five challenges to executing strategy (ranked by importance of the challenge and then the popularity of the response):

- Making strategy meaningful to front-liners, translating strategy to execution, and aligning jobs to strategy.
- Poor communication of strategy.
- Lack of clear and decisive leadership and leadership actions inconsistent with strategy.
- Lack of accountability or follow through, and inability to measure impact.
- Too focused on short-term results.

How can we overcome these barriers? Several barriers to effective strategy execution are listed in Table 12.3 from the HBR survey, along with some suggestions for dealing with these barriers.

Table 12.3 Strategies to address Barriers to Execution.

Barrier	Suggestions for addressing barrier
Making strategy meaningful to front-liners, translating strategy to execution, and aligning jobs to strategy.	Review the strategic plan and ensure that the long-term growth goals have been broken down into medium and short-term objectives. Review the organisational structure to ensure that it is aligned to the strategy. Develop clear and concise operational plans that link budgets, forecasts, targets and actions to the longer-term strategy. Ensure all strategically critical positions and teams have at least one Key Performance Indicator that can be tracked back to the strategy.
Poor communication of strategy.	Review the strategy to see if it is overly complex. The strategy should focus on no more than three strategic priorities—make sure that these are reinforced at all levels in the organisation.
Lack of clear and decisive leadership and leadership actions inconsistent with strategy.	Assess the incumbents in leadership positions—are they the right people for taking the strategy forward (regardless of what they have achieved in the past)? Ensure leaders understand and agree on the strategic plan and associated operational plans.
Lack of accountability or follow through, and inability to measure impact.	Review all positions, and ensure they are aligned to the strategic plan.
Too focused on short-term results.	Ensure that there is at least one person other than the CEO who is responsible for the strategic planning process, and keeping people accountable to implementing the strategic plan. Review the notes in relation to the Chief Strategy Officer below.
A lack of robust conversation around the strategy to see if the organisation is actually capable of implementing the strategy.	Review the strategy and challenge the assumptions being made about the competitive environment, customer responses, organisational capabilities and weaknesses. Gain clarity around objectives, targets and people.
A lack of agreement or poor alignment in relation to the strategy.	Use strategic planning as a creative process to tease out the differences in opinion, and get a better understanding of why people are not in agreement—does everybody have access to the same level of information? Are they the right people in the right jobs? Are there personal conflicts and political issues that need to be addressed first?

(*Continued*)

Table 12.3 (Continued)

Barrier	Suggestions for addressing barrier
Lack of clarity around how the strategic growth goals and financial objectives are linked to the operational business models, budgets, plans and forecasts.	Re-visit the long-term and short-term goals. Are they balanced? Is the long-term plan broken down into medium term chunks that relate back to shorter-term operation initiatives?
No buy-in to operational budgets.	Involve the people responsible for delivering the operational outcomes in the budgeting process. If their recommendations are to be overridden by management, give these people the opportunity to challenge your thinking—perhaps they have information that you do not have.
No connection between Key Performance Indicators (KPIs) and strategy growth goals and financial objectives.	Use the Balanced Scorecard and/or Strategy Mapping processes to align financial, market, operational, and learning and growth goals, and establish KPIs.

Notes

1. B. Tricker. *International Corporate Governance—Text, Readings and Cases* (New York: Prentice Hall, 1994), 149.
2. D. A. Nadler. "Building Better Boards," *Harvard Business Review* 82, no. 5 (2004): 102–111.
3. Adapted from Patrick Lencioni. *The Five Dysfunctions of a Team* (John Wiley & Sons, 2006).
4. Michael E. Porter. "What is strategy." Published November (1996).
5. Harvard Business School. "Operational Effectiveness vs. Strategy," *Harvard Business School Institute for Strategy and Competitiveness*, www.isc.hbs.edu/strategy/business-strategy/Pages/operational-effectiveness-vs-strategy.aspx Retrieved on 19-07-17.
6. Association for Strategic Planning. "Strategic Planning Successful Practices in Non-Profit Organisations," March 2012.
7. Ibid.
8. Adapted from J. B. Barney and W. S. Hesterly. "VRIO Framework," in *Strategic Management and Competitive Advantage* (Australia: Pearson, 2010), 68–86.
9. Mehrdad Baghai, Stephen Coley and David White. *The Alchemy of Growth: Practical Insights for Building the Enduring Enterprise* (New York: McKinsey & Company, Inc, July 2000).
10. Strategyzer. "The Value Proposition Canvas," https://strategyzer.com/canvas/value-proposition-canvas
11. M. G. Siegler. "Eric Schmidt: Every 2 Days We Create As Much Information As We Did Up To 2003," 2010, https://techcrunch.com/2010/08/04/schmidt-data/

12. IBM Global Business Services. "Digital Transformation," 2011, www-935.ibm. com/services/us/gbs/thoughtleadership/pdf/us_ibv_digita_transformation_808. PDF
13. IBM Institute for Business Value Analysis. "Digital Transformation," www-07. ibm.com/sg/manufacturing/pdf/manufacturing/Digital-transformation.pdf
14. R. Kaplan and D. Norton. *The Balanced Scorecard* (Boston, MA: Harvard Business School Press), 1996; R. Kaplan and D. Norton. *Strategy Maps: Converting Intangible Assets into Tangible Outcomes* (Boston, MA: Harvard Business School Publishing Corporation, 2004).
15. Strategyzer. "The Business Model Canvas," https://strategyzer.com/canvas/business-model-canvas?url=canvas/bmc
16. IBM Institute for Business Value Analysis.
17. Roger L. Martin. "How Hierarchy Can Hurt Strategy Execution," *Harvard Business Review* 88, no. 7–8 (2010): 74–75.

Bibliography

Baghai, Mehrdad, Stephen, Coley, and David White. *The Alchemy of Growth: Practical Insights for Building the Enduring Enterprise*. New York: McKinsey & Company, Inc., July 2000.

Barney, J. B., and W. S. Hesterly. "VRIO Framework." In *Strategic Management and Competitive Advantage*, 68–86. New Jersey: Pearson, 2010.

IBM Global Business Services. Digital Transformation. 2011. Retrieved from https://www-935.ibm.com/services/us/gbs/thoughtleadership/pdf/us_ibv_digita_transformation_808.PDF

IBM Institute for Business Value Analysis. Digital Transformation. Retrieved from https://www-07.ibm.com/sg/manufacturing/pdf/manufacturing/Digital-transformation.pd

Kaplan, R. and D. Norton. *Strategy Maps: Converting Intangible Assets Into Tangible Outcomes*. Harvard Business School Publishing Corporation, 2004.

Kaplan, R., and D. Norton. *The Balanced Scorecard*. Harvard Business School Press, 1996.

Lencioni, Patrick. *The Five Dysfunctions of a Team*. Hoboken: John Wiley & Sons, 2006.

Martin, Roger L. "How Hierarchy Can Hurt Strategy Execution." *Harvard Business Review* 88, no. 7–8 (2010): 74–5.

Nadler, D. A. "Building Better Boards." *Harvard Business Review* 82, no. 5 (2004): 102–11.

Porter, Michael E. *What Is Strategy*. Published November, 1996.

Siegler, M. G. Eric Schmidt: Every 2 Days We Create as Much Information as We Did Up to 2003. 2010. Retrieved from https://techcrunch.com/2010/08/04/schmidt-data/

Strategyzer. The Business Model Canvas. Retrieved from https://strategyzer.com/canvas/business-model-canvas?url=canvas/bmc

Strategyzer. The Value Proposition Canvas. Retrieved from https://strategyzer.com/canvas/value-proposition-canvas

Tricker, B. *International Corporate Governance—Text, Readings and Cases*. New York: Prentice Hall, 1994.

Leadership in Practice: GIVIT—Connecting those who have with those who need

Introduction

The idea began when a young mother was surprised at the struggle she endured when trying to donate second-hand baby clothes to someone else in need. Simply 'having something to give away' was not quite the same as what the charities 'needed to give away'. Most charities were reluctant to take items that increased their storage costs and did not help their clients. Juliette Wright instead found that local charities were desperately searching for essential and useful items such as sanitary products for women who had fled domestic violence, and steel-capped boots to enable unemployed fathers to secure work. Items that came in quickly, went out quickly, and made a difference.

Juliette quickly realised that charities did not need to be overloaded with items that the donor no longer needed. Rather, the charities needed items that addressed the recipient's specific needs. Charities needed gifts that helped pull their clients out of poverty. Juliette could see, though, that a real problem existed. Charities had no way of communicating their exact needs.

A natural social entrepreneur, Juliette decided to create an online platform, GIVIT. Although not a natural technologist, the idea to her seemed obvious. Through this innovative use of technology, every charity in Australia could communicate their needs to potential donors, and obtain exactly what they needed through the simple act of giving. Within six months, she had established the website and recruited 15 charities to request items. The website matched the donation to those that needed it. If no one needed the item, then the charities faced no extra storage costs.

The effectiveness of this arrangement was quickly apparent. A donated bike enabled a single mother to get to work. A donated microwave heated meals for a man who had recently lost his wife and was unable to cook. Within a few weeks, more than 80 charities were requesting items. On the basis of the adoption of this technological platform GIVIT, in 2009, quickly became a national network that connected thousands of Australians wanting to support hundreds of charities.

True to its roots, today GIVIT is a national not for profit that still connects those who have with those who need, in a private and safe way. The

GIVIT aim is to alleviate poverty by ensuring every community service provider has what it needs through the simple act of giving. GIVIT is free for the charity to use, and makes giving easy by allowing potential givers to see exactly what is required by vulnerable community members. GIVIT supports all agencies, services and charities in Australia that work directly with impoverished, marginalised and vulnerable people. The not for profits can empower their clients and improve quality of life by obtaining the items they require through the website at no cost. This unique virtual warehouse eliminates the need for organisations to store, sort and dispose of unwanted items, and in this way saving valuable time and resources, and better addressing needs.

The GIVIT website allows trusted charities to list their requests on the website where everyday Australians can donate in response to those requests. As an option, donors can also pledge their offer of donated items on the website. When a need is matched to a donation, the GIVIT portal sends an email to exchange contact details between the donor and the charity. Then the charity and the donor agree between themselves on a delivery option. Once the charity receives the item it is privately passed on to the recipient—the donor and recipient never meet as, above all, GIVIT aims to preserve the dignity and privacy of people accessing support. There is no fee to the charity or the donor.

GIVIT has changed the status quo by re-thinking the way in which donations may be made to those in need. As with many organisations that seek to innovate and change, the advantage of GIVIT's approach became apparent in a time of need. GIVIT's defining moment came during the devastating 2011 floods in Brisbane, Queensland, when that state's Premier contacted Juliette to ask if GIVIT could be the official website through which people could make donations. Queensland was not unfamiliar with flood events, but the flood was the first state crisis that required mobilisation of so many resources in the digital age.

In this crisis, GIVIT proved the effectiveness of its model. The GIVIT website received more than 1.8 million hits and matched 33,500 goods with those in need over a single three week period. GIVIT now has formal agreements with Federal and State governments to conduct their humanitarian support programs or large-scale natural disaster appeals, and this arrangement continues to prove effective.

GIVIT is a volunteer-based organisation with very low operational overheads—although *low* operational overheads are not *no* operational overheads. Consequently, GIVIT has had to take great care to ensure its sustainability at the same time as it used new technologies in novel ways. The Board is comprised of people with widespread experience in the private, public, and community sectors. The organisation now has established partnerships across the nation with corporates and governments and has a substantial funding donor base. GIVIT also uses its social media platform to engage with the donors that use their service. The GIVIT website was launched on Facebook, and GIVIT still actively respond to reviews on their

Facebook page.[1] Currently, Facebook reviewers rate GIVIT as '4.8 stars', and there are 2,500 followers on Twitter.

Through GIVIT, over 1,000 of Australia's most trusted charities have been assisted, over 315,000 items have been donated, and some 130,000 marginalised vulnerable and disadvantaged people have received support to date.

Local Hero and Citizen of the Year

That young mother frustrated by her difficulties in donating baby clothes refused to accept the way things were. Juliette Wright is still the dynamic CEO of GIVIT, and has been identified as an outstanding leader with some 14 awards to her credit including National Local Hero and Citizen of the Year. These awards invariably cite leadership qualities she exhibits. The awards acknowledge these qualities with words and phrases such as 'passion and inspiration', 'commitment to the underprivileged', 'social enterprise', 'entrepreneur', 'game changer', 'innovation', 'fun', 'fearless', 'community leader', 'world of difference', and 'resilience'.

But leadership is not about a thesaurus or vapid inspirational quotes on the Internet. In this case, leadership has required learning to make choices. She has learnt a great deal about the business of donations. A valuable early lesson was that some donations are more harmful than good, as occurs when donors think that people in distress will take any old thing even if it is not needed. So, Juliette has developed rules about donating—such as only accepting new or as-new items.

During crisis events such as floods and cyclones, though, Juliette also learned that donations of new items can unfairly compete with businesses in shattered towns still struggling to get on their feet. So, Juliette also makes sure that corporate donors spread offers of bulk donations widely throughout a community so as not to unduly impact a town's economy. GIVIT also recognises that for communities hit by disaster the 'end game' is the return to a normal life. So, in disaster situations as the community moves from 'survival mode' and looks for sustained recovery, it is essential for GIVIT to work with local services.[2]

Advice for Social Entrepreneurs

A charismatic figure, Juliette has an impish sense of humour. When asked if she had any advice for aspiring social entrepreneurs, she offered three pieces of advice. The first was to understand the risks, but to surround yourself with people who can help deal with the risks:

> "*If I listened to everyone who said 'no', or thought failure was a sign I was not supposed to be doing GIVIT, I would not have helped over*

126,000 people who are impoverished, marginalised or vulnerable. With every start up there is a risk. My advice is to do a risk register and get people who think you will fail to clearly articulate their argument (before you ignore them!). Then, enjoy hallucinating all the ways your business will fail! Then mitigate those risks with your wits and by surrounding yourself with people who are savvy and experienced in that area."

Juliette has been awarded for her resilience—and it is clear she has a knack of avoiding the nay-sayers—but she is very much aware of the potential legal issues any social enterprise faces. Her second piece of advice here is to get a pro bono lawyer:

"As social enterprises are always new and exciting, think about getting a law firm's support. When I started I was told I have the 'Terms & Conditions' of a hairdresser! Lawyers seem scary as a breed but I think they have been the most surprisingly warm and supportive group. I said I wanted to start a donation portal, and you know how risk averse they are! Get a pro bono lawyer, get their advice and solid terms and conditions—it determines business protocols."

Finally, Juliette has advice for social enterprises to clearly set out the goals of the social enterprise so that the volunteers understand why they are doing what they are doing:[3]

"Are you going to have volunteers? Everyone loves lots of encouragement and very clear goals. My advice is not to give them KPIs and numbers to achieve, but a clear goal of where you are heading as that keeps them on focus rather than running with every great idea that new businesses get . . . daily"

GIVIT Kids

In line with her natural bent as a social entrepreneur, Juliette has continued to innovate online and look for new outlets. One of Juliette Wright's most significant innovations has been the development of GIVIT Kids, a child friendly website empowering children to donate new and pre-loved items to meet the urgent materials needs of Australian families in a fun and safe way. The response has been incredible with children giving to children and families in need, particularly over the Christmas period. Also the learning tools incorporated in the program are now recognised in school curriculum as classroom resources for teachers of Civics and Citizenship in primary schools.

A leader's vision is important, and the effective leader has a clear vision and the drive to succeed. The goal in creating GIVIT in the first place was to make giving easy.[4] GIVIT has achieved this aim. Tellingly, Juliette's motivation in establishing GIVIT Kids was to help develop a philanthropic culture within Australia. Time will tell if the vision comes to pass.

Micheal Axelsen
and
Kenneth Wiltshire

Notes

1. Tess McGlone. "The Kindness of in-Kind Giving," *Giving Australia 2016 Blog*, 2016, Retrieved from http://blog.bus.qut.edu.au/giving-australia-2016/the-kindness-of-in-kind-giving/#more-234
2. Jessica Hinchliffe. "2011 Brisbane Floods: Juliette Wright, founder of GIVIT, Reflects on Generosity in Wake of Disaster," *ABC Radio Brisbane*, 11 January 2016, www.abc.net.au/news/2016-01-11/givit-juliette-wright-reflects-on-generosity-after-2011-floods/7076352?pfmredir=sm
3. Team Benojo. "We talk with Australia's Local Hero 2015 Juliette Wright." Benojo, February 2015, https://benojo.com/blog/we-talk-with-australias-local-hero-2015-juliette-wright
4. Jessica Hinchliffe

Bibliography

Hinchliffe, Jessica. 2011 Brisbane Floods: Juliette Wright, Founder of GIVIT, Reflects on Generosity in Wake of Disaster. ABC Radio Brisbane 11 January 2016. Retrieved from www.abc.net.au/news/2016-01-11/givit-juliette-wright-reflects-on-generosity-after-2011-floods/7076352?pfmredir=sm

McGlone, Tess. The Kindness of In-Kind Giving. Giving Australia 2016 Blog, 2016. Retrieved from http://blog.bus.qut.edu.au/giving-australia-2016/the-kindness-of-in-kind-giving/#more-234

Team Benojo. We Talk With Australia's Local Hero 2015 Juliette Wright. Benojo, February 2015. Retrieved from https://benojo.com/blog/we-talk-with-australias-local-hero-2015-juliette-wright

13 Successful Nonprofit Leadership In An IT World

Micheal Axelsen

Introduction

Information technologies in general, and social media and the internet more specifically, have transformed the way in which the nonprofit achieves its goals and communicates with its donors and important stakeholders. Fundraising, marketing, brand recognition and attracting volunteers are no longer about making phone calls at 7pm for two weeks a year or finagling free airtime on television. Innovations in information technology (IT) and the way in which it is used mean that these tasks have become more active, time-consuming, engaging, and ultimately more effective.

These points are raised clearly in several case studies discussed in this book such as GIVIT, The Smith Family, Australian Red Cross, and RSPCA. GIVIT's goal is to make giving easy, and this goal is achieved by innovative use of an internet platform to match donations to those that need it quickly in times of crisis, emergency, or urgent need. The Smith Family and the Australian Red Cross use IT to shape their fund-raising strategies and to maintain contact with donors. The RSPCA uses business analytics and digital dashboards to track many key performance indicators that are central to its mission. For example, at RSPCA each day key staff receive an email with information critical to managing the care of their animals such as their length of stay.

It is clear that IT is more relevant—and more of a leadership challenge—now and into the future for nonprofits. The leader in a nonprofit wants to make the right decisions at the right time with the right people so that the IT function works.

This book identifies some of the challenges faced by leaders in nonprofit organisations, and particularly those nonprofits that are transforming to a more stable and sustainable future. One challenge is meeting the demand for IT services. Meeting this demand is often problematic. The key concern addressed by this chapter is, "How can the leader best govern the nonprofit's demands on its technology?"

Technology innovations in social media have transformed the way non-profits communicate with donors and stakeholders, raise funds, and manage their brand and reputation. IT is important for all nonprofits—whether they have just started out or are a mature sustainable business. Nonprofits are under increasing pressure to innovate and change the way they use complex and interdependent technologies in reflection of current trends.[1]

This IT investment though can be expensive. The 'IT black hole' is a common source of frustration: large sums of money are spent on IT for no clearly identifiable return.[2] This frustration is compounded when no-one seems willing to take ownership of the problem and resolve it. The problem here is usually a 'people' rather than a 'technology' issue—the nonprofit's IT function is a 'socio-technical' information system (IS).[3] The technology needs to be considered in the social context in which it is used—the people and the organisation itself matter as much as the technology.

The temptation is to 'just fix IT', with the leader rolling up their sleeves and doing what needs to be done. The leader though should not be involved in the 'running of IT'—even if they are good at it. The leader's role is to build the framework that allows others to 'get IT right'. Leaders must not 'do the doing' themselves if they wish to make the nonprofit sustainable. The decision-making framework needs to consider the people and the organisation as well as the technology platform itself, and the circumstances of the nonprofit.[4]

Accordingly, in this chapter I provide insights into how the leader can 'get IT right'. These pragmatic insights develop from academic theory and insights from practice. The goal, though, is to provide the leader with a framework of IT governance principles and practices to apply to their own situation.

I address this goal as follows. First, I explore IT governance in the context of nonprofits and identify several core principles for IT governance. Second, I consider the nature of IT decision-making, the roles of those making the decisions, and the types of decisions to be made. Third, I present a set of practical IT governance practices (structures, processes, and relational mechanisms) used to support the decision-making framework, and consider how the nonprofit can match these mechanisms to their circumstance. Finally, I conclude by summarising the key points and identifying likely future challenges for IT governance in nonprofits.

Nonprofits and IT Governance

As with all organisations, the nonprofit often experiences the 'IT black hole' phenomenon. That is, despite large investments in IT, the returns on those investments are often meagre. This is a problem of IT governance. The core principles of IT governance provide a foundation for the leader to use in designing the IT decision-making framework to suit their situation.

The IT Black Hole

The 'IT black hole' is a conundrum with which many leaders are familiar: large sums are spent on IT but no returns ever seem to arise.[5] No matter the investment, the IT function remains a source of pain with few signs of progress. The black hole is most prominent in nonprofits that constantly spend money to 'put out fires'. Rather than being reactive, the nonprofit needs to effectively govern its IT.[6]

For the nonprofit, IT can be a particular problem due to the initial focus on tending to the mission. This task takes all the leader's energy, and often building a strong IT governance framework is a secondary consideration. Consequently, when the organisation is on a more stable footing, the leader discovers the pain that arises from a poorly directed IT function. Frustration arises when the promised benefits of IT investment never eventuate.

For the nonprofit just starting out, effective IT is important if the nonprofit is to become sustainable. Ineffective IT constrains the growth and sustainability of the nonprofit. The problems that arise are a real management distraction. IT staff might indicate that the users expect too much, or that the IT actually works 'just fine', while the users complain the IT staff do not listen to their needs. All the leader wants, though, is to just 'get IT right'—and for this headache to be resolved.

The 'right' IT, though, is elusive and varied. The importance of IT for nonprofits varies. For a very few, IT is not critical, but for many others the investment in IT is fundamental to success. New technologies provide opportunities to develop and implement new business strategies.[7] However, IT's complexity can also expose the nonprofit to risks such as cybercrime, fraud, errors and omissions.[8] For IT to deliver on the promised benefits as well as manage the IT risks, the leader must ensure there is an effective IT decision-making framework.

IT Governance

The role of the leader is to 'lead' (rather than 'do') and so the leader should not 'do the doing' when it comes to delivering IT services. The leader's role is instead to set up the governance framework for others to work within. Rather than focussing upon the investment made in technologies alone, the leader must consider IT as a 'socio-technical' information system (IS).[9] The leader has to create a framework that considers the people and the organisation that use the technology platform.[10]

Without an IT decision-making framework, the IT function operates without direction. People do the things they *think* they ought to be doing. Although done with the best of intentions, the result often is that IT does not deliver what is needed. Without leadership, IT staff often fill the vacuum by making the decisions that, in their view, need to be made. This is particularly so when those in the business disown the problem and 'just want IT to make it all work'. IT decisions made in this way are often poor as "IT can't estimate accurately what business cannot define precisely."[11]

There is no 'silver bullet' that ensures the nonprofit 'gets it right'.[12] However, good IT governance can help. At its core, IT governance is about the way in which the nonprofit makes decisions about its IT. De Haes and Van Grembergen provide a workable definition for this 'governance of IT':[13]

> "*Enterprise Governance of IT (EGIT) is an integral part of corporate governance, exercised by the Board, overseeing the definition and implementation of processes, structures, and relational mechanisms in the organisation that enable both business and IT people to execute their responsibilities in support of business/IT alignment and the creation of business value from IT-enabled business investments.*"

That is, IT governance aims to align the work of the IT function with the needs of the nonprofit, and this in turn allows the nonprofit to achieve business value from its investment. Figure 13.1 shows this relationship.[14]

Figure 13.1 The relationship between the enterprise governance of IT and business value.[21]

Fundamentally, this is a top-down approach. The leader and the board set the framework for making IT decisions. That framework ensures that business and IT make complementary decisions that address the nonprofit's needs. The leader does not, fortunately, have to establish the framework without guidance from practice. The COBIT IT governance framework from ISACA is popular.[15] Another useful perspective is the 'foundation for execution approach'.[16] Both of these useful perspectives are underpinned by several core principles of IT governance.

Principles of IT Governance

Between the COBIT framework and the foundation for execution approach, there are three common principles to consider:[17]

1. **Separation of management of IT from governance of IT.** Management plans, builds, runs and monitors activities to achieve the objectives set by those governing the non-profit.[18]
2. **IT governance builds upon corporate governance.** The IT governance framework builds upon and extends the corporate governance framework in place.[19]

3. **Alignment of Business and IT strategies.** Alignment is a strategic fit between internal and external components of the nonprofit, and a functional integration between the business and IT. The nonprofit looks for alignment between business strategy and IT strategy.[20]

These three principles have several implications. First, governance is different to management. This implies that the leader and the board set out the framework, and management plans, builds, runs and monitors IT activities. The framework sets out the decision-making authority and the means by which IT decisions are made.

Second, the standard of IT governance is closely related to the standard of corporate governance. This implies that it is difficult to have strong IT governance when corporate governance is weak. In general terms, any plan to improve the standard of IT governance needs to consider the standard of corporate governance as well.

Third, the business and IT strategies need to align for the business to derive value from its IT investment. This implies that the business and IT strategies are well articulated with each informing the other, and they have a role to play both externally and internally. Figure 13.2 shows this relationship.

These three principles provide a foundation to the leader in designing the IT decision-making framework. The IT decision-making framework identifies the role of different stakeholders in the nonprofit and their responsibilities for different types of IT decisions.

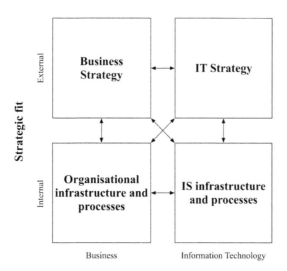

Functional Integration

Figure 13.2 Business and IT alignment.[22]

The Management of IT Decision-making

The principles of IT governance highlight the complex and inter-dependent nature of IT decision-making. Managing IT decision-making requires consideration of the roles in decision-making and the nature of IT decisions that need to be made.

Roles in IT Decision-making

IT decision-making is considered in terms of two high-level roles. First, there is the IT decision-making role of business staff that work in and on the business. These business staff work in non-IT areas. Second, there is the decision-making role of IT staff. IT staff work in the IT function.[23]

An IT decision ought to involve both the business staff and IT staff roles to at least some extent, although primary responsibility for the decision may lay with either (or even both). 'IT business' decisions are IT decisions that directly affect business capability, and 'wholly IT' decisions are IT decisions that directly affect IT infrastructure and capability. These IT decisions are not made in isolation. IT business decisions made by business staff affect the 'wholly IT' decisions made by IT staff, and vice versa. Figure 13.3 shows examples of how primary decision-making might be assigned.[24]

Defining business staff as 'all staff that are not in IT' and IT staff as 'all staff in IT' is a high-level simplification. COBIT separates business staff into 17 roles (including 'Human Resources', 'Chief Risk Officer', 'Business Process Owners', and 'Chief Executive Officer') and IT staff into nine roles (including 'Chief Information Officer', 'Head IT Operations', and 'Privacy Officer') that better reflect this complexity.[26]

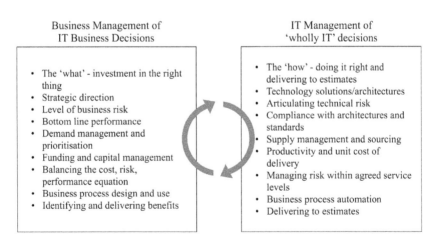

Business Management of
IT Business Decisions

- The 'what' - investment in the right thing
- Strategic direction
- Level of business risk
- Bottom line performance
- Demand management and prioritisation
- Funding and capital management
- Balancing the cost, risk, performance equation
- Business process design and use
- Identifying and delivering benefits

IT Management of
'wholly IT' decisions

- The 'how' - doing it right and delivering to estimates
- Technology solutions/architectures
- Articulating technical risk
- Compliance with architectures and standards
- Supply management and sourcing
- Productivity and unit cost of delivery
- Managing risk within agreed service levels
- Business process automation
- Delivering to estimates

Figure 13.3 Identifying who should make different types of IT decisions.[25]

Responsibility levels can also be considered more distinctly. These may be assigned according to the RACI ('Responsible, Accountable, Consulted or Informed') Chart approach for different roles.[27] A RACI chart identifies the roles that are responsible for getting the task done, accountable for the success of the task (the lowest appropriate level 'where the buck stops'), consulted about the decision, and informed about the decision. Table 13.1 provides an example RACI chart from COBIT.[28]

Table 13.1 Example RACI Chart for analysing and reporting performance.

Role	Analysing and reporting performance
Business Staff	
Business Executives	A(ccountable)
Business Process Owners	R(esponsible)
Project Management Office	C(onsulted)
Audit	I(nformed)
IT Staff	
Chief Information Officer	C(onsulted)
Service Manager	R(esponsible)

The RACI chart provides explicit guidance as to the responsibility level of the different types of business staff and IT staff in the decision-making framework according to the type of decision. The responsibility level changes according to the nature of the IT decision that is to be made. A responsibility level of 'informed' is the lowest level, and the level of 'accountable' is the highest level of responsibility.

IT Business Decisions, Wholly IT Decisions, and Responsibility Levels

At a high level, IT decisions consist of two broad types: 'IT Business' and 'wholly IT' decisions. Within these types, there are four domains of IT decision-making to consider: the planning, building, running, and monitoring of IT. These four domains draw, conceptually, from the familiar 'Plan-Do-Check-Act' Deming cycle, and are prominent in the process domains of several IT governance frameworks.[29] All IT decisions fall into one of the four domains.

For the domain of IT planning, the decision-making framework sets out the responsibility levels for the identification of how IT can best contribute to the nonprofit's achievement of its business objectives.[30] These decisions develop the IT strategy, the IT approach and architecture to be adopted, and consider how best to use IT for innovation. Other key concerns in this domain include more operational planning tasks such as budget management, human resource management, service agreements, risk management, and supplier management.[31] Principally, IT planning addresses the future of IT and how it is to be used in the nonprofit.

For the domain of IT building, the decision-making framework sets out the responsibility levels for the identification of IT requirements and project and program management of new IT capacity and capabilities.[32] These decisions implement the IT strategy, and focus on developing and managing IT capacity and organisational change. Other key concerns in this domain include the selection and implementation of new IT solutions and acceptance testing of the delivered outcomes.[33] Principally, IT building addresses how the nonprofit builds, acquires, and configures new IT investments.

For the domain that relates to the running of IT, the decision-making framework sets out the responsibility levels for the actual delivery of required IT services.[34] These decisions relate to the day-to-day management of IT operations, help desk requests and the resolution of more critical incidents. Other key concerns in this domain include IT security and business continuity and disaster recovery planning.[35] Principally, this domain is all about 'keeping the lights on', 'keeping IT running', and ensuring that IT works and delivers its operational services.

For the domain of IT monitoring, the decision-making framework sets out the responsibility levels for monitoring, evaluating, and assessing the decisions and processes relating to the other three domains.[36] These decisions relate to assessing the quality of these decisions and processes, and ensuring that the nonprofit addresses the regulatory framework that governs its activities. Other key concerns in this domain include performance management and monitoring of internal control.[37] Principally, IT monitoring addresses the need to provide feedback and make decisions about how to adjust activities to ensure that IT continues to meet the needs of the nonprofit as part of a continuous improvement process.

The responsibility levels for these decision domains vary according to the nature of the decision. For example, an 'IT business' decision might be whether to invest in an IT technology such as a new accounting information system, whereas a 'wholly IT' decision might be the design of the technology solution that supports the accounting information system. However, responsibility might be shared between business and IT staff for a particular decision. For example, the decision set out in Table 13.1 places responsibility for analysing and reporting performance with both business and IT staff.

The decision-making framework can be expressed as a RACI chart of decisions, roles, and responsibility levels. This framework may be formally written down as a policy, or simply communicated well to the relevant staff. The nonprofit then needs to implement the practices for decision-making that are appropriate for the nonprofit in making these decisions.

Practices in IT Decision-making

The IT decision-making framework requires a mix of IT governance practices to support and accommodate it. These practices can be categorised as structures, processes, or relational mechanisms.[38] Figure 13.4 provides examples of these categories of IT governance practices and how they relate to the governance of IT.

The nonprofit can implement structural, process, and relational mechanism practices across these categories in many different ways. Together these practices are a portfolio from which the nonprofit may choose. The nonprofit should choose to implement the practices for decision-making that are appropriate in light of its circumstances. The practices that will appeal to the leader of a nonprofit will depend on the practices themselves as

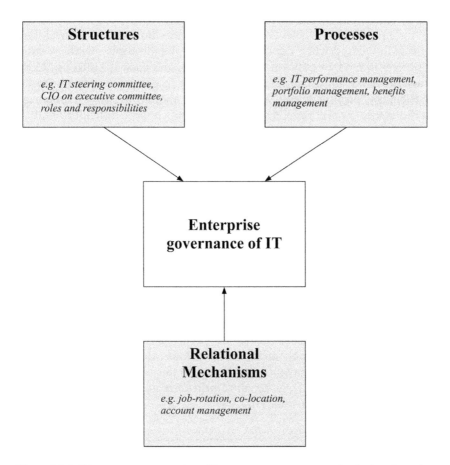

*Figure 13.*4 IT governance practices (Structures, processes, and relational mechanisms) and their relationship.[39]

well as whether the practice suits the nonprofit given the 'stage of growth' in the nonprofit's life cycle from the startup stage to maturity.[40]

In the discussion that follows I therefore define and examine each category of IT governance practices. In doing so, I relate these practices to the nonprofit's stage in the lifecycle. This provides a basis for considering the relevance of the practice to the nonprofit. I consider four separate stages in the lifecycle that are based upon a simple model designed specifically for the nonprofit context.[41] This simple model considers the 'startup stage', the 'angel stage', and the 'growth stage'. In line with other theorists in this field, I also consider a final 'maturity' stage.[42]

These stages have distinctive characteristics.

The initial startup stage is where the nonprofit exists to support the initial idea and shared vision of an individual or small team about the nonprofit's mission to benefit society.[43] At this stage, governance is usually negligible, with accountability ad hoc or even anarchistic.[44]

A nonprofit that survives past the startup stage moves into the angel stage. This is the period when the nonprofit seeks philanthropic investors—time, resources in kind, or cash—to invest in, share, and grow the mission. At this stage the nonprofit usually starts to formalise its governance arrangements. Particularly, documentation and compliance monitoring is very important at this stage—or else angel investors will be much more difficult to find.

Having secured investors, the nonprofit moves into the growth stage. In this stage, it seeks to grow and appeal to investors likely more interested in the business opportunity than the social benefit.[45] At this stage, sophisticated governance processes and systems are needed to monitor and manage the new operational complexities that arise as the nonprofit grows. Much more formal accountability and governance practices come into existence at this time.

Finally, the nonprofit matures and becomes sustainable and mature. In this stage, existence is usually assured and the business formalises so much that it becomes bureaucratic and stable. The maturity stage can be long or short—it is possible that the mature nonprofit loses touch with its mission and faces an existential crisis from which it may not survive. Maturity is stable and sustainable, but this stage has its own particular risks as well.

With these scenarios in mind, the discussion that follows is also illustrated with examples drawn from practice. In this way, I provide a decision-making framework of IT governance principles and practices that readers may apply to their own situation.

Structures

Structural practices are reflected in the organisational chart of the nonprofit. There are structural mechanisms—usually organisational units, forums or roles—that provide a basis for making collaborative IT decisions. That is, these structures provide a means for business staff and IT staff to interact and discharge their responsibilities according to the RACI chart.

Figure 13.4 identifies several examples of structural practices.[46] These include an IT steering committee, an executive committee that includes a Chief Information Officer (CIO), and defined roles (such as the CIO). Five structural practices are key practices in the governance of IT due to their ease of implementation and their overall effectiveness.[47] These five practices are discussed in turn:

- **IT strategy committee at level of board of directors:** This committee exists to ensure that IT is a regular agenda item for the board. Given the board focus upon IT, these issues are prominent and act to remind business and IT staff that IT is considered important.[48]

The structure is relatively easy to implement as board committees likely already exist as part of corporate governance, and are effective due to the prominent focus upon these issues.

In the early stages (start-up and angel stages), this practice is relevant for nonprofits that are heavily IT-dependent, but is more generally relevant to nonprofits in the growth and maturity stages. Nonprofits seeking to mature out of the early stages (particularly the angel stage) and become more sustainable would do well to consider creating this role as a way of indicating the seriousness of the nonprofit about its future.

- **CIO on executive committee:** Here, the CIO is a full member of the executive committee. This committee is the forum through which the nonprofit's members of the C-suite executives such as the Chief Executive Officer (CEO), Chief Operating Officer (COO), and the Chief Financial Officer (CFO) manage and direct the business. As with the board level IT strategy committee, the equal standing of the CIO and participation in this top-level forum highlights the importance of IT issues and ensures that the strategic direction has management support.

This practice is somewhat more difficult to implement than a board-level IT strategy committee as it requires the recruitment of a (potentially expensive) CIO to the nonprofit.

For this reason, this practice is most applicable to nonprofits in the growth or maturity stages. IT-dependent nonprofits may however benefit from this practice in the startup stage. Nonprofits seeking to grow quickly should consider this practice particularly given the likely future benefits for IT governance as the nonprofit becomes sustainable.

- **A CIO reporting to the CEO and/or COO:** Here, the CIO role has a direct line of responsibility to the CEO or COO rather than full membership of the executive committee. It is likely that the CIO role would have an *ex officio* liaison role on the executive committee if it exists.

Again, this practice is relatively effective in that a clear understanding of the importance of IT to the nonprofit is communicated and the CIO role is very important to ensure IT strategic success.

The need to recruit an expensive CIO role does make this practice difficult to implement, and again it is likely that this practice is most applicable to nonprofits in the angel, growth or 'mature' stages of growth. I note that a heavily IT-dependent nonprofit would be more likely to require a C-suite level CIO than a CIO in a more subservient role. Again, startup nonprofits should lay the foundation for adopting this practice if they wish the nonprofit to mature quickly. For example, a 'virtual CIO' such as an external part-time IS consultant to assist with strategy might be relevant to the startup nonprofit.

- **IT steering committee:** This steering committee provides a forum for the executive and senior management staff (that is, business staff) to evaluate and prioritise IT investment. Although its composition and responsibilities will depend upon the nonprofit's circumstance, this steering committee would likely consist mainly of business staff at the management level. The committee would also likely include any IT staff roles that are involved in IT strategy. A common error is for the steering committee to be directed and chaired by IT staff—such an arrangement often leads to the committee becoming a 'fiefdom' of the IT staff and not a forum for genuine discussion. Although it is important to have IT staff involved in the steering committee, the primary purpose of the committee is for business staff to make choices and provide direction to IT staff.

The steering committee is a strong practice to implement almost from the outset as it does not force IT staff to make choices and 'pick winners' on behalf of the business.[49] This is an effective practice to adopt when formulated correctly, and it is relatively easy to implement as it does not require recruitment of a specific IT leadership role.

Nonprofits in the startup stages may not greatly benefit from this practice but as soon as practicable an IT steering committee structure is an important practice for the nonprofit in the angel, growth, and maturity stages to adopt.

- **IT project steering committee:** This committee is similar to the IT steering committee in that it provides a forum for business staff and IT staff to coordinate, prioritise, and manage IT projects. It is important to note that this steering committee usually manages multiple projects and has stewardship over the nonprofit's entire portfolio of projects. Subcommittees or other liaison structures may exist. For example, a project that has a single process owner might have its own coordination meetings between business and IT staff and simply provide regular updates to the IT project steering committee.

As with the steering committee, this is a relatively easy to implement practice and it is very effective for a nonprofit with multiple complex projects to implement.[50]

For these reasons, this practice is probably most suited to nonprofits in the growth and maturity stages of growth. However, nonprofits in the startup and angel stages should consider adopting some of this discipline (e.g. formal governance structures) if they are undertaking relatively complex IT projects.

De Haes and Van Grembergen identify a further seven structural practices, but these are not considered as easy to implement or as effective as the five key practices they note. These practices though should be reviewed and considered for the circumstances of each nonprofit.

In reviewing these structures, the note should be made that the role of the CIO is fairly loosely defined. According to some views, the CIO role is a strategic role rather than an IT technical role. As used here, the CIO role extends to the more technical IT manager or Chief Technical Officer roles. The CIO role is an important one, and there needs to be a fit between the CIO role and the maturity of information leadership capability in relation to the criticality of information and technology to differentiate the nonprofit.[51]

The need for a CIO that fits the nonprofit is high, and further it is important to have a forum or at least some means for the business staff—rather than IT staff—to assess the business need for IT. For example, in one large nonprofit in the finance sector that I consulted to, the Chief Information Officer (CIO) could not understand the problem as the network availability and throughput were both of world standard.

This was true, but had been achieved by preventing users from adding any software or hardware to their systems and by constraining network throughput for functions deemed 'low priority' by the IT function. The IT environment was stable and reliable, but did not do what the nonprofit needed done. In this case, the network 'worked', but end users found the IT resources completely unusable for their tasks. The end users did not have a means or a forum to redress the imbalance—they 'took what they were given'. It was likely no coincidence that the CIO had been promoted from his former role as network administrator on the basis that he desired a salary increase.

Processes

Processes refer to the way in which the nonprofit performs its work. These IT governance processes are formal strategic IT decision-making and IT monitoring procedures. The aim here is that the nonprofit's policies have procedures for staff to follow for consistent behaviour, and to ensure that proper inputs (according to the RACI Chart) are provided into decisions that are made.

Figure 13.4 identifies several examples.[52] These include IT performance management, portfolio management, and benefits management. Four process practices are key practices in the governance of IT due to their ease of implementation and overall effectiveness. These four practices are discussed in turn:

- **Strategic IS planning:** This process creates the IT strategy document, and it is a defined and formal process. This process is important as it determines the quality of all IT planning in the nonprofit, and presents a clear view on the use and role of technology.

Formal and comprehensive strategic IS planning is difficult to achieve—particularly in an organisation where formal corporate governance is not high. However, a base level of strategic IS planning is relatively simple to achieve, and it provides a basis for later development of the process.[53] Strategic IS planning is though essential for any IT governance effort to be successful.

IS planning can be very complex and time-consuming. In this form it is likely ill-suited for the needs of the startup nonprofit. However, at least a basic level of strategic IS planning (e.g., a statement of IT goals and an IT budget) is needed for nonprofits in the startup and angel stages of growth. As the nonprofit moves to the more mature stages so too should the strategic IS planning process evolve to become more formal and potentially complex.

- **Portfolio management:** The portfolio management process is closely related to the project steering committee structure. Here, the process formalises the selection and acquisition of new IT assets in terms of business needs, existing IT assets, the standards for business cases, information economics, calculation of return on investment, and payback periods.

The decision to purchase new IT assets should have a level of formality and a sense of purpose. The absolute worst approach is to use the 'golf course' decision-making model (by basing the decision upon fads and hearsay) or the 'most recent salesperson' approach (where IT assets are purchased according to a salesperson's ability and desire for a sales commission).[54] It is important to buy IT assets that the nonprofit needs in light of its overall portfolio rather than acquiring IT assets piecemeal.

This approach is, on its face, relatively easy to achieve though strong portfolio management requires a collegiate culture at the management level. In more mature nonprofits this may be difficult due to established internal power structures.[55] However, it is precisely the more mature nonprofits that benefit the most from portfolio management as there is an established IT platform and coordinated IT investment is needed to ensure that IT is effective.

Accordingly, it is likely that the portfolio management process is most effective for nonprofits in the growth and mature stages if they have multiple IT assets that share data and/or are key to common processes. Startup nonprofits need to be sure that their investments in IT will support the nonprofit into its more mature stages, and work well or complement the existing investment in IT.

- **Project governance and project management methodologies:** This process sets out the processes and methodologies used to govern and manage IT projects.[56] There are common project management methodologies such as the Project Management Body of Knowledge and Prince2 that provide extensive details on project management.[57] This process is important for IT project success as IT project success is more likely when project management approaches are used.[58]

As with strategic IS planning, implementing complete methodologies is usually difficult, but even base methodologies offer distinct advantages in effectiveness.

Again, at least a basic level of project management process is required for nonprofits across the early stages of growth. A nonprofit in the startup or angel stage of growth is building systems to accommodate the future, sustainable, nonprofit. The leader of such nonprofits should ensure that project management is strong even if a 'lite' version of the management methodology is followed. As the nonprofit moves to the more mature stages so too should project management processes evolve to become more sophisticated.

- **IT budget control and reporting:** The budgeting process that controls and monitors IT investments and projects is a low-level control, but an effective one if corporate governance is at a reasonably high standard.

This process is relatively easy to implement and effective, though for effectiveness it is dependent upon strong standards of corporate governance and a culture of ensuring value for the nonprofit.

However, this process is effective for nonprofits across all stages of growth. The budget is the tool that demonstrates the actual choices made in IT investments. For the startup nonprofit it is key to understanding the investment made. For a nonprofit in the angel stage, an IT budget will be central to discussions with potential angel investors. In the growth and maturity stages the IT budget will very likely prove a valuable management tool.

De Haes and Van Grembergen identify a further seven process practices, but these are not considered as easy to implement or as effective as the four key practices they note.[59] These practices though should be reviewed and considered for the circumstances of each nonprofit.

Of the three categories of governance practices, processes are most dependent upon the maturity of the corporate governance in place. A nonprofit where staff rarely follow processes is unlikely to find these staff make an exception for IT governance processes. In line with the principles of IT governance, corporate governance and IT governance are inter-related.

Of the key practices, strategic IS planning is likely to be performed poorly by many nonprofits. For example, in one mature nonprofit in the aged care sector that I reviewed, the IT strategy was written by the CIO in isolation. The IT strategy included many of the CIO's 'wish-list' items where the business case for these items had not been established. Indeed, the CFO and CEO appeared perplexed as to what items were paid for, what was yet to be paid for, or whether the items were used (or even useful). The CIO also sought little external validation of the proposed direction of the IT strategy.

As one indication, the strategy was built upon adoption of cloud technologies whilst the nonprofit was located in an area with relatively poor and expensive internet access. The CEO in particular was concerned at the cost of the IT function, and this indicated misalignment between the IT strategy (focussed on adopting new technologies) and the business strategy (focussed on being a low-cost provider of health services). The strategic IS planning process was executed poorly on many levels in this instance. The amount spent on IT investment was relatively eye watering, and the 'IT black hole' was very much in evidence. For this mature nonprofit, stronger budget control and business staff responsibility for IT business decisions were implemented as part of the IT governance solution in this instance.

Relational Mechanisms

The governance practices of relational mechanisms aim to build resilient, collaborative, and constructive relationships amongst executives and managers amongst the business and IT staff. These practices aim to develop strong relationships before events conspire to sour relationships. It is much more difficult for 'bad blood' to develop between business and IT staff if a strong relationship already exists.

Figure 13.4 identifies several examples of relational mechanisms.[60] These include job rotation, co-location, and account management. The survey of experts conducted by De Haes and Van Grembergen identified the key relational mechanism as IT leadership due to its perceived ease of implementation and overall effectiveness.

IT leadership is the ability of the CIO to clearly outline their vision for IT in the nonprofit, and to communicate that vision to others in non-technical terms so as to be clearly understood. This practice is dependent upon the individual ability of the CIO, but has a high impact upon the success of the IT function. For their vision to have impact, the CIO needs to be able to speak in business-oriented terms at the 'C-suite' level. Otherwise, support of the vision by business staff is likely to be low.

As with other practices that rely upon the appointment of a CIO role, it is somewhat difficult to implement as it requires the recruitment of a (potentially expensive) CIO to the nonprofit. This practice is most applicable to nonprofits in the growth or maturity stages, although IT-dependent nonprofits will definitely benefit from strong IT leadership in the startup or angel stages as well. Nonprofits in the angel stage will also benefit from strong IT leadership in the search for an angel investor.

De Haes and Van Grembergen identify a further nine relationship mechanisms, but their research indicates that these practices are not as easy to implement or as effective as the four key practices discussed above.[61] These practices though should be reviewed and considered for the circumstances of each nonprofit.

An additional relational mechanism that is not explicitly addressed by De Haes and Van Grembergen includes practices that ensure a strong relationship with external service providers.[62] Such mechanisms are important given the increasing use of outsourcing and offshored service providers. Anecdotally, relationships with third parties commence well, but over the longer term can sour if the relationship is managed poorly.[63] In these cases, formal business/IT account management and informal meetings between business and IT staff with representatives of the service provider ensure strong relationships with key long-term service providers for the nonprofit across all stages of growth. Meeting with representatives of the service provider is important for all nonprofits in each of the different stages of growth. Startup nonprofits are likely to not have their own IT resources, and instead rely on external IT providers. The ability to manage that relationship is critical for the nonprofit that is keen to reach the maturity stage.

The relationship with external service providers is an important one, and over time the extent of its importance can be easily missed. For example, one nonprofit in the childcare sector that I reviewed had over time adopted a single 'private cloud' arrangement for all of its IT. It had also adopted various cloud-based technologies in key applications such as their childcare management IS, health and safety IS, and Office 365 (file, print, and email servers). The next versions of their accounting IS and payroll/HR IS promised cloud capability.

It was only after a year or so of these changing arrangements that the IT manager came to the realisation that the expensive 'private cloud' arrangement was providing an expensive gateway to its similarly cloud-based IS. In effect, the nonprofit was paying twice over for services it no longer needed, and for disaster recovery programs on data that simply no longer mattered. With more effective relationship management (they had not met with key service providers in over six months) this turn of events could likely have been avoided. In this case the nonprofit was mature, but the wasted resources would likely mean the end of a startup or an angel nonprofit.

Conclusion

This chapter has provided several key points as guidance to the leader in a nonprofit for leading IT for success, and although the current pace of change in this domain is daunting it seems that the future holds no fewer challenges to deal with. This leads me to make several final comments for the leader to contemplate.

Key Points

This chapter began with a consideration of the nature of the 'IT black hole'—that no matter how much is spent on IT, the returns from the investment seem meagre. Usually, the IT black hole is a result of reacting to IT problems rather than proactively planning and coping with these issues. Further, the problems usually arise from the social context in which the IT is used rather than the technology itself. That is, there is a problem of governance.

IT governance requires an understanding of how decisions are made, and this requires the leader to identify a decision-making framework that sets out the roles of business and IT staff in making decisions. Otherwise, a vacuum of decision-making will be filled with well-intended—but often misguided—decisions. The decision-making framework needs to set out which business or IT staff roles are responsible, accountable, consulted or informed in decision-making regarding the planning, building, running, and monitoring of IT services.

The leader also needs to consider how to support this framework by establishing key governance practices. These practices are structures (e.g. IT Steering Committee), processes (e.g. strategic IS planning) or relational mechanisms (e.g. job rotation). Gillies and Broadbent provide a good summary of governance mechanisms and their relationship to the organisation and their role in IT governance.[64] This summary includes most of the key practices identified by De Haes and Van Grembergen, and Figure 13.5 presents an adaptation of this discussion from Gillies and Broadbent.[65]

The leader needs to consider their own circumstances (and the stage of growth of the nonprofit) before implementing these practices and mechanisms. The different governance practices to choose will likely be affected by the nonprofit's stage of growth (startup, angel, growth, or mature stages). Getting IT to 'work' requires the leader to get the IT governance 'right' in support of the nonprofit's journey to becoming a social enterprise.

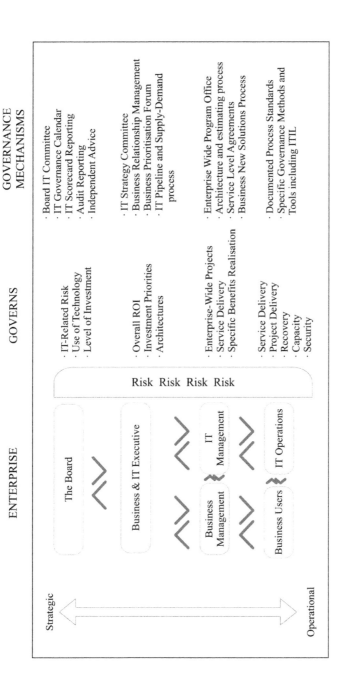

ENTERPRISE

Strategic

The Board

Business & IT Executive

IT Management

Business Management

Business Users

IT Operations

Operational

Risk Risk Risk Risk

GOVERNS

· IT-Related Risk
· Use of Technology
· Level of Investment

· Overall ROI
· Investment Priorities
· Architectures

· Enterprise-Wide Projects
· Service Delivery
· Specific Benefits Realisation

· Service Delivery
· Project Delivery
· Recovery
· Capacity
· Security

GOVERNANCE MECHANISMS

· Board IT Committee
· IT Governance Calendar
· IT Scorecard Reporting
· Audit Reporting
· Independent Advice

· IT Strategy Committee
· Business Relationship Management
· Business Prioritisation Forum
· IT Pipeline and Supply-Demand process

· Enterprise Wide Program Office
· Architecture and estimating process
· Service Level Agreements
· Business New Solutions Process

· Documented Process Standards
· Specific Governance Methods and Tools including ITIL

Figure 13.5 Prominent IT governance mechanisms showing structures, processes, and relational mechanisms (adapted from Gillies and Broadbent).[66]

The Future of IT Governance

IT governance is never 'set and forget'. Changes occur in technology and expectations, and the decision-making framework needs to adapt to these changing circumstances. The leader in a nonprofit needs to address five prominent challenges arising from recent IT developments.

First, nonprofits increasingly turn to the cloud to manage their IT services.[67] Cloud computing offers the potential to 'level the playing field' by accessing more technology for less in using shared infrastructure for a subscription. Cloud services offer the real potential that the nonprofit need not manage its own infrastructure and instead simply ensure that the internet connection is reliable and that cloud-based services comply with the regulatory framework. Such changes may have implications for the type of IT staff the nonprofit needs to employ.

Second, the use of online social media (Facebook, Twitter and so on) has increased exponentially. The impact of a bad Yelp or Google review on a nonprofit's can be positive or negative. Nonprofits manage their online reputation and increasingly communicate with their stakeholders through social media. This is apparent from the case studies in this book for RSPCA Queensland, GIVIT, and the Australian Red Cross.

Third, relatively recent mobile devices such as iPhones (2007), iPads (2010), and Android tablets (2011) have changed the nature of work in all organisations. These tools have allowed new innovations to be provided by nonprofits. For example, some nonprofits use mobile devices for timesheet data entry and as mobile fundraising tools. These innovations bring opportunities, but also potential challenges such as compliance with data privacy regulations.

Fourth, concerted ransomware attacks have become prominent. Ransomware is a virus with a commercial business model—data is encrypted with a secret key and held to hostage until a ransom is paid. The nonprofit needs to ensure that its data is cybersecure. In an increasingly inter-connected world, cybersecurity has become a key challenge.[68]

Finally, the regulatory environment continues to change. The nonprofit must constantly address its own compliance needs and monitor changes to legislation such as data privacy laws.[69] This requires a current IT strategy and arrangements with service providers that continue to address these changing business compliance needs.

Concluding Comments: Technology and the Journey to the Social Enterprise

This chapter aimed to address the question, "How can the leader best govern the nonprofit's demands on its technology?" In particular, the focus has been upon the nonprofit's journey through the different stages of growth to put itself on a mature and sustainable footing, potentially as a social enterprise.

The principles, roles, responsibility levels and practices outlined in the IT decision-making framework in this chapter can be very complex, or very simple. That is, the different elements of the framework scale to meet the needs of any size nonprofit. The broad points outlined here apply irrespective of scale but will require adaptation for smaller organisations.

For example, in the early stages most nonprofits are focussed on achieving their mission (and surviving day to day). However, the startup nonprofit that thinks seriously about its relationship with IT and how IT helps to deliver its services will provide a strong foundation for the nonprofit's future sustainability. An angel nonprofit that uses social media to clearly articulate its vision to its wider stakeholders, or ensures that its technology choices comply with regulatory requirements, will be able to build stronger relationships with the early investors and intermediaries.

This investment provides a platform for the nonprofit looking to grow and obtain broad support for its mission in the growth stage. Sophisticated corporate governance—including IT governance—is needed to cope with the increasing operational complexity and accountability demands on the nonprofit. After a period, the nonprofit's growth flattens out and the nonprofit enters a stage of maturity. Here, the IT investment is very important for the nonprofit to formalise its operations and encourage stability. It is also critical in this mature stage that the nonprofit continue to use technology to seek out opportunities to innovate and reinvigorate itself. IT is critical for this flexibility and development.

Overall it is apparent that IT leadership is important for nonprofits. As with all organisations, nonprofits are under increasing pressure to innovate by using complex and interdependent technologies. The quality of the nonprofit's leadership in this world of technology will have implications for the nonprofit's future success.

Notes

1. Fatemeh Rahimi, Charles Møller and Lars Hvam, "Business Process Management and IT Management: The Missing Integration," *International Journal of Information Management* 36, no. 1 (2016).
2. Steven De Haes and Wim Van Grembergen, "IT-Enabled Value (Chapter 4)," (Springer, 2015).
3. Enid Mumford, "Computer Systems and Work Design: Problems of Philosophy and Vision," *Personnel Review* 3, no. 2 (1974).
4. Rudy Hirschheim and Heinz K. Klein, "A Glorious and Not-So-Short History of the Information Systems Field," *Journal of the Association for Information systems* 13, no. 4 (2012).
5. De Haes and Grembergen.

6. Ibid.
7. Martin Hirt and Paul Willmott, "Strategic Principles for Competing in the Digital Age," *McKinsey Quarterly*, no (May 2014).
8. De Haes and Grembergen.
9. Enid Mumford, "Computer Systems and Work Design: Problems of Philosophy and Vision," *Personnel Review* 3, no. 2 (1974).
10. Rudy Hirschheim and Heinz K. Klein. "A Glorious and Not-So-Short History of the Information Systems Field," *Journal of the Association for Information systems* 13, no. 4 (2012).
11. Chris Gillies, *Business Management of Information Technology* (Melbourne, Australia: CPA Australia, 2008), 14.
12. Jerry Luftman. "Assessing IT/Business Alignment," *Information Systems Management* 20, no. 4 (2003).
13. De Haes and Grembergen, 2.
14. Ibid.
15 Ibid.
16. ISACA, *Cobit 5 Enabling Processes* (Rolling Meadows, IL: ISACA, 2012); Mauricio Marrone et al. "IT Service Management: A Cross-National Study of ITIL Adoption," *Communications of the Association for Information Systems* 34, no. 1 (2014).
17. Jeanne W. Ross, P. Weill and D. Robertson, "Chapter 2 — Define Your Operating Model," in *Enterprise Architecture as Strategy: Creating a Foundation for Business Execution* (Boston, MA: Harvard Business School Press., 2006).
18. Ross, Weill and Robertson; Peter Weill and Jeanne Ross, *IT Governance: How Top Performers Manage IT Decision Rights for Superior Results* (Boston, MA: Harvard Business School Publishing, 2004); ISACA, *Cobit 5 Enabling Processes* (Rolling Meadows, IL: ISACA, 2012). Mangalaraj, Singh and Taneja.
19. ISACA, *Cobit 5 Enabling Processes* (Rolling Meadows, IL: ISACA, 2012).
20. Ibid.
21. De Haes and Grembergen, 2.
22. J. Henderson and N. Venkatraman, "Strategic Alignment: Leveraging Information Technology for Transforming Organizations," *IBM Systems Journal* 38, no. 2&3 (1999); De Haes and Grembergen.
23. Chris Gillies, *Business Management of Information Technology* (Melbourne, Australia: CPA Australia, 2008): 14.
24. Ibid.
25. Ibid.
26. ISACA.
27. Kristin Weber, Boris Otto and Hubert Osterle, "One Size Does Not Fit All—A Contingency Approach to Data Governance," *ACM Journal of Data and Information Quality* 1, no. 1 (2009).
28. ISACA.
29. M. Best. "Walter a Shewhart, 1924, and the Hawthorne Factory," *Quality and Safety in Health Care* 15, no. 2 (2006); Hesham Bin-Abbas and Saad Haj Bakry, "Assessment of IT Governance in Organizations: A Simple Integrated Approach," *Computers in Human Behavior* 32, no. 0 (2014).

30. Wim Van Grembergen and Steven De Haes. *Enterprise Governance of Information Technology* (Springer, 2015).
31. ISACA, *Cobit 5 Enabling Processes* (Rolling Meadows, Illinois: ISACA, 2012).
32. Van Grembergen and Haes.
33. ISACA.
34. Van Grembergen and De Haes.
35. ISACA.
36. Van Grembergen and De Haes.
37. ISACA.
38. De Haes and Grembergen.
39. Ibid.
40. Jay Galbraith, "The Stages of Growth," *Journal of Business Strategy* 3, no. 1 (1982).
41. Marta Marie Maretich, Jed Emerson and Alex James Nicholls, "Governing for Impact: Managing Mission-Driven Organizations through Stages of Growth and Investment," (2016).
42. Danny Miller and Peter H. Friesen, "A Longitudinal Study of the Corporate Life Cycle," *Management Science* 30, no. 10 (1984); Robert Phelps, Richard J. Adams and John Bessant, "Life Cycles of Growing Organizations: A Review with Implications for Knowledge and Learning," *International Journal of Management Reviews* 9, no. 1 (2007).
43. Marie Maretich, Emerson and James Nicholls.
44. Peter Weill and Jeanne Ross, *IT Governance: How Top Performers Manage IT Decision Rights for Superior Results* (Boston, MA: Harvard Business School Publishing, 2004).
45. Marie Maretich, Emerson and James Nicholls.
46. De Haes and Grembergen.
47. Steven De Haes and Wim Van Grembergen, "An Exploratory Study into IT Governance Implementations and Its Impact on Business/IT Alignment," *Information Systems Management* 26, no. 2 (2009).
48. Chris Gillies and Marianne Broadbent, *IT Governance: A Practical Guide for Company Directors and Business Executives* (Melbourne, Australia: CPA Australia, 2005).
49. Chris Gillies, *Business Management of Information Technology* (Melbourne, Australia: CPA Australia, 2008), 14.
50. Gillies and Broadbent.
51. Joe Peppard, Chris Edwards and Rob Lambert. "Clarifying the Ambiguous Role of the Cio," *MIS Quarterly Executive* 10, no. 1 (2011).
52. De Haes and Van Grembergen.
53. Gillies and Broadbent.
54. Ibid.
55. Angela Liew. "The Use of Technology-Structured Management Controls: Changes in Senior Management's Decision-Making Behaviours," *International Journal of Accounting Information Systems* (2014).
56. De Haes and Van Grembergen.
57. Sandra Matos and Eurico Lopes, "Prince2 or Pmbok—a Question of Choice," *Procedia Technology* 9 (2013).
58. Amgad Badewi, "The Impact of Project Management (Pm) and Benefits Management (Bm) Practices on Project Success: Towards Developing a Project

Benefits Governance Framework," *International Journal of Project Management* 34, no. 4 (2016).
59. De Haes and Van Grembergen.
60. Ibid.
61. Ibid.
62. Ibid.
63. David Carter et al. "Outsourcing: Opportunity or Threat?" (2016).
64. Gillies and Broadbent.
65. De Haes and Van Grembergen; Gillies and Broadbent.
66. Gillies and Broadbent.
67. Kenji E. Kushida, Jonathan Murray and John Zysman, "Cloud Computing: From Scarcity to Abundance," *Journal of Industry, Competition and Trade* 15, no. 1 (2015).
68. Anthony P. Valach. "What to Do After a Ransomware Attack," *Risk Management* 63, no. 5 (2016).
69. Nick Abrahams and Jamie Griffin. "Privacy Law: The End of a Long Road: Mandatory Data Breach Notification Becomes Law," *Law Society of NSW Journal*, no. 32 (2017).

Bibliography

Abrahams, Nick, and Jamie Griffin. "Privacy Law: The End of a Long Road: Mandatory Data Breach Notification Becomes Law." *Law Society of NSW Journal* no. 32 (2017): 2017–18.
Badewi, Amgad. "The Impact of Project Management (Pm) and Benefits Management (Bm) Practices on Project Success: Towards Developing a Project Benefits Governance Framework." *International Journal of Project Management* 34, no. 4 (2016): 761–78.
Best, M. "Walter a Shewhart, 1924, and the Hawthorne Factory." *Quality and Safety in Health Care* 15, no. 2 (2006): 142–3.
Bin-Abbas, Hesham, and Saad Haj Bakry. "Assessment of IT Governance in Organizations: A Simple Integrated Approach." *Computers in Human Behavior* 32, no. 0 (2014): 261–67.
Carter, David, Micheal Axelsen, Tanya Titman, Dinesh Aggarwal, and David Fotheringham. Outsourcing: Opportunity or Threat? 2016.
De Haes, Steven, and Wim Van Grembergen. "An Exploratory Study Into IT Governance Implementations and Its Impact on Business/IT Alignment." *Information Systems Management* 26, no. 2 (2009): 123–37.
——— "Enterprise Governance of IT, Alignment, and Value (Chapter 1)." 11–43: Springer, 2015.
———. IT-Enabled Value (Chapter 4). 11–43: Springer, 2015.
———. Enterprise Governance of IT (Chapter 2). 11–43: Springer, 2015.
Galbraith, Jay. "The Stages of Growth." *Journal of Business Strategy* 3, no. 1 (1982): 70–9.
Gillies, Chris. *Business Management of Information Technology*. Melbourne, Australia: CPA Australia, 2008.

Gillies, Chris, and Marianne Broadbent. *IT Governance: A Practical Guide for Company Directors and Business Executives*. Melbourne, Australia: CPA Australia, 2005.

Henderson, J., and N. Venkatraman. "Strategic Alignment: Leveraging Information Technology for Transforming Organizations." *IBM Systems Journal* 38, no. 2&3 (1999): 44–44.

Hirschheim, Rudy, and Heinz K. Klein. "A Glorious and Not-So-Short History of the Information Systems Field." *Journal of the Association for Information systems* 13, no. 4 (2012): 188–235.

Hirt, Martin, and Paul Willmott. "Strategic Principles for Competing in the Digital Age." *McKinsey Quarterly* (May2014): 1–13.

Isaca. *Cobit 5 Enabling Processes*. Rolling Meadows, IL: ISACA, 2012.

Kushida, Kenji E., Jonathan Murray, and John Zysman. "Cloud Computing: From Scarcity to Abundance." [In English]. *Journal of Industry, Competition and Trade* 15, no. 1 (2015): 5–19.

Liew, Angela. "The Use of Technology-Structured Management Controls: Changes in Senior Management's Decision-Making Behaviours." *International Journal of Accounting Information Systems* (2014): 32–64.

Luftman, Jerry. "Assessing IT/Business Alignment." *Information Systems Management* 20, no. 4 (2003): 9–15.

Mangalaraj, George, Anil Singh, and Aakash Taneja. IT Governance Frameworks and Cobit-a Literature Review. (2014).

Maretich, Marta Marie, Jed Emerson, and Alex James Nicholls. Governing for Impact: Managing Mission-Driven Organizations Through Stages of Growth and Investment. 2016.

Marrone, Mauricio, Francis Gacenga, Aileen Cater-Steel, and Lutz Kolbe. "IT Service Management: A Cross-National Study of ITIL Adoption." *Communications of the Association for Information Systems* 34, no. 1 (2014): 865–92.

Matos, Sandra, and Eurico Lopes. "Prince2 or Pmbok—a Question of Choice." *Procedia Technology* 9 (2013): 787–94.

Miller, Danny, and Peter H. Friesen. "A Longitudinal Study of the Corporate Life Cycle." *Management Science* 30, no. 10 (1984): 1161–83.

Mumford, Enid. "Computer Systems and Work Design: Problems of Philosophy and Vision." *Personnel Review* 3, no. 2 (1974): 40–9.

Peppard, Joe, Chris Edwards, and Rob Lambert. "Clarifying the Ambiguous Role of the Cio." *MIS Quarterly Executive* 10, no. 1 (2011): 31–44.

Phelps, Robert, Richard J. Adams, and John Bessant. "Life Cycles of Growing Organizations: A Review With Implications for Knowledge and Learning." *International Journal of Management Reviews* 9, no. 1 (2007): 1–30.

Rahimi, Fatemeh, Charles Møller, and Lars Hvam. "Business Process Management and IT Management: The Missing Integration." *International Journal of Information Management* 36, no. 1 (2016): 142–54.

Ross, Jeanne W., P. Weill, and D. Robertson. *Chapter 2—Define Your Operating Model, in Enterprise Architecture as Strategy: Creating a Foundation for Business Execution*. 25–44. Boston, MA: Harvard Business School Press, 2006.

Valach, Anthony P. "What to Do After a Ransomware Attack." *Risk Management* 63, no. 5 (2016): 12–12.

Van Grembergen, Wim, and Steven De Haes. *Enterprise Governance of Information Technology*. 2015. doi:10.1007/978-0-387-84882-2

Weber, Kristin, Boris Otto, and Hubert Osterle. "One Size Does Not Fit All—a Contingency Approach to Data Governance." *ACM Journal of Data and Information Quality* 1, no. 1 (2009): 4:1–4:27.

Weill, Peter, and Jeanne Ross. *IT Governance: How Top Performers Manage IT Decision Rights for Superior Results*. Boston, MA: Harvard Business School Publishing, 2004.

Leadership in Practice: Staying Ahead of the Game

Three Key Ideas

Changing Times

> The organising idea is to explore how we start to take charge of our own destiny in these changing times.

The Community Services Industry faces unprecedented reforms, with a significant focus on the marketisation of the industry, through the application of competition policy. The most notable examples of this are in the areas of disability and aged care where consumer choice and individualised funding reforms are transforming the way organisations do business. These reforms, although not a surprise to an industry that participated in their development, have created an atmosphere of discontinuity that has thrown business models, financial sustainability and issues related to the nature of the workforce to the forefront of leaders and decision makers across the industry. The challenges arising from this must turn the leadership of the Industry to ask questions about how to engage in adaptive processes into the future that are built upon a scenario approach to planning. These reforms are not one-off occurrences; they represent examples of the application of competition policy which link back to a bigger imperative—productivity gains.[1]

At the centre of the introduction of these reforms are dramatic changes to funding that move away from funding organisations to funding individuals.[2] This approach is not problematic in and of itself, but it is being implemented without a policy approach that defines a commitment to industry transition. In the least marketised of all business environments we are witnessing an approach to industry transition that is patchy and without an overall framework. Perhaps at its worst it is completely *laissez faire*. Funding reform is not a comprehensive approach to transformation and will create change, but is a blunt instrument.

These examples of reform must lead us to contemplate the future, which is set in a continued narrative of fiscal constraint and budget cuts at state and federal levels of government. This rubs in an uncomfortable way against the business models of community service organisations, where dependence on government funding is high but the risks of this in the long term are still poorly articulated. A 'better outcomes' mantra has colonised the discourse in the absence of any investment in industry transition to new ways of working. The leaders of the community services industry must grasp the nettle and go about reframing this discourse from one of dependence and limited productivity to one that frames value in both social and economic terms.

To do this we must conceive of ourselves in terms of an industry rather than as a set of disparate sectors. Our strength in numbers is significant, literally.

Problems of Profile and Reputation

> Without a focus on the change the Industry makes (outcomes) and no verification, we are subject to the risk of poor reputation.

There has been a protracted discussion about moving to an outcomes approach in community services. Anecdotally at least leaders and practitioners alike acknowledge that it is critical to improved service delivery, however, we seem unable to achieve collective action on this across industry. In other western contexts such as the United States of America, they have also been having a long discussion about what this move means supported by a new generation of philanthropists who want to achieve more with the dollar they invest.[3] However, this discussion has now moved to tackle questions of implementation. Like in business all good strategies have often failed in implementation; so too has a move to outcomes failed in implementation.

That said, there are always risks in generalisations and there are many organisations that have tackled this shift successfully, designing and measuring service delivery through an outcomes lens. This provides us with some excellent lighthouse examples but is not sufficient to move a whole system where it needs to be to successfully transform service delivery to an outcomes approach. A lack of outcome reporting does not equal a lack of outcomes, but a lack of outcomes design and implementation at a system level equals rhetoric without reform.

The lack of evidence about the delivery of outcomes in community services is a limited and limiting analysis. Organisations already deliver outcomes; that is they deliver change in the lives of people that they work with. The questions that we need to consider are ones of direction and design. Who decides what services are to be delivered and how do they arrive at this view?

In this sense, it is generally true that the people for whom community service organisations deliver services are not in charge of direction or design, albeit this is changing in disability and aged care. The community organisations themselves are not often in charge of direction or design. In many cases direction and design originates in the investment specification documents of government, where throughputs and outputs dominate the procurement process. Here there is a tenuous at best link between these investment specifications and an outcomes approach. In child protection, we may pursue an outcome focussed on family reunification but the investment specification drives a child safety approach delivered through placement services. These real and challenging contradictions are the territory for ongoing dialogue and discussion between community service leaders and governments of all persuasions.

There is an incredible opportunity for the leadership of the community services industry to take forward a discussion that returns us to the disciplines of theory of change and program logics, placing the people that the Industry works for at the centre of this design work as a matter of course. This will require leadership from Industry that is proactive, rather than reactive. The problem is not whether we achieve outcomes but rather a lack of sophistication in understanding the relationship between inputs (the business dimension) outputs (the intervention dimension) and outcomes (the change dimension). This lack of sophistication in general terms leaves the Industry exposed to reform that demonises everything done before, while holding the new world order (whatever that will be) as a kind of nirvana.

If we take up the outcomes challenge we must also care about our performance across the Industry. Putting aside the fact that the investment framework to which the Industry is contracted is output focussed, a lack of verification about outcomes has now been equated to poor performance. Conflating these two ideas is dangerous for the reputation of a whole industry and leaves organisations open to extremes of criticism when things do go wrong, and they inevitably will.

The Big Picture

> We will remain a continued focus for reform because of fiscal constraint and the fact that we are the last frontier for productivity gains.

The community services industry has long been subject to the forces of competition through competitive tendering and more recently direct reforms to funding that place service users at the centre of the service delivery and choices about it. However, competition and debates about it in a 'mission' orientated context are a red herring; the real agenda lurking behind the application of competition policy is productivity gains. The industry has billions of dollars in public funds flow through it on an annual basis and very little of this investment is subject to reforms in the businesses themselves that are aimed at productivity gains. In fact the very nature of the 'not-for-profit business' precludes a focus on productivity, it is just not the point compared to the commercial world. The potential benefits of focussing on productivity—effectiveness and efficiency across the industry—is little understood but could have significant direct and multiplier economic and social benefits. The intergenerational report by the Federal Government and long term forecasts on national productivity show there is little to be gained from a continued focus on traditional productivity levers; new frontiers are required or declining productivity will have a major impact on our national economy. This agenda must be set by Industry as we move forward, in fact it is imperative if we are to be taken seriously in an economic as well as a social sense and this should be a major goal of Industry and its leadership. Otherwise, as is often the case, we will as recipients of government funding find ourselves subject to reforms that are outside our control and potentially unpalatable.

As a society Australia is a stable and well-governed democracy with a strong social safety net. This social safety net would not be as functional as it is (despite acknowledged limitations) without the significant contribution of the community services industry. However, as some of our most distressing and intractable problems of social disadvantage grow, community service organisations become trapped in the endless reform analysis and become in many ways part of the problem even while being the best solution we currently have. Returning to the roots of our mission, faith based, or otherwise is critical in these times.

This will require the leadership of the Industry to undertake two critical tasks. The first is to return properly to the reason for being by reconnecting with the strengths and weaknesses of the most vulnerable of our Australian population; to reignite advocacy in an emboldened way, but not because this fits funding trends, but because it matters for the future of Australian Society. The second thing we must do is to find unusual alliances crossing tradition boundaries to engage government and the private sector, and the institutions they are in charge of in new and creative ways. The Industry and its leaders must see themselves as core to this creative force and awaken a wave of action that draws on the very best of each sector's strength, with an eye firmly planted on the people that matter, the issues they face and collective action.

Conclusion

The community services industry faces many challenges into the future but there are also enormous strengths to draw upon as we collectively reshape our future. We must embrace the fact that we have and are reliant on government funding and read the changes to funding approaches as a trend, not one-off action. This will mean that we will have to recast value as we see it and approach investment and funding relationships with a view to leverage this investment. We are also going to have to care about our performance in terms of shifting the dial on entrenched or intractable social problems or risk irrelevance. This is a task well within our reach and one at which, with strong leadership, we can excel. Finally, we must become more productive and position the business of community service delivery at the forefront of competition reform, not only because it matters in economic terms but because in a fiscally constrained environment it may be a real way of increasing our effectiveness on the frontline.

The leadership of the community services industry faces a challenge that is truly exciting—to take charge of the future by understanding the issues beyond the task of service delivery. In accepting this challenge and tackling issues of reputation, performance and productivity we have the opportunity to rewrite the narrative and completely reshape the future of the Industry.

Belinda Drew
Chief Executive Officer
Community Services Industry Alliance

Notes

1. Commonwealth of Australia. "Competition Policy Review," 2015, http://competitionpolicyreview.gov.au/final-report/
2. Commonwealth of Australia. "Disability Care and Support," www.pc.gov.au/inquiries/completed/disability-support/report
3. Leap of Reason. "Leap of Reason," http://leapofreason.org; United Way. "A Guide to Developing an Outcome Logic Model and Measurement Plan," 2017, www.yourunitedway.org/wp-content/uploads/2015/12/UWGRP-Guide-to-Outcomes-and-Logic-Models-6-8-15.pdf

Bibliography

Commonwealth of Australia. Competition Policy Review. 2015. Retrieved from http://competitionpolicyreview.gov.au/final-report/
Commonwealth of Australia. "Disability Care and Support." 2011. Retrieved from www.pc.gov.au/inquiries/completed/disability-support/report
Leap of Reason. Leap of Reason. 2017. Retrieved from http://leapofreason.org.
United Way. 'A Guide to Developing an Outcome Logic Model and Measurement Plan'. 2017. Retrieved from www.yourunitedway.org/wp-content/uploads/2015/12/UWGRP-Guide-to-Outcomes-and-Logic-Models-6-8-15.pdf

Stories from the Field: RSPCA Queensland

Introduction

Internationally, some of the most prevalent not for profit (NFP) organisations are animal welfare charities. According to the USA Humane Society's statistics there are approximately one million animals worldwide that are reported as abused or mistreated every year (2016); therefore, sadly, there is a significant necessity for animal welfare organisations.[1] Animal welfare organisations, through methods of community engagement and awareness, attempt to rescue domesticated animals, livestock or wildlife from abuse, neglect, psychological detriment or unavoidable harm.

The leading NFP animal welfare organisation in Australia, the *Royal Society for the Prevention of Cruelty to Animals Queensland* (RSPCA Queensland), cares for approximately 51,000 abandoned, sick, or poorly treated animals per year. Although this is an alarming number of animals, RSPCA's influx rate reflects how far community awareness and education has come since the RSPCA was first established. This accomplishment is due to successful contemporary leadership styles within the walls of RSPCA Queensland.

The RSPCA began permanent operation within Australia in 1883, but the NFP quickly established offices and shelters throughout the country, including at multiple sites throughout the state of Queensland. However, in the last 30 years there was an evident lack of appropriate leadership styles. Previous RSPCA Queensland leaderships battled government parties and legislative delegations, and attempted to tackle short-term goals with a lack of appropriate technology, databases, organisational systems, protocols and directional tactics. Although RSPCA Queensland maintained a universal goal of diminishing animal cruelty throughout these stages, the NFP did not begin taking effective, leading strides until 2000 when Mark Townend was appointed CEO of RSPCA Queensland, whose head facility is located at the recently established campus in Wacol, Brisbane (Queensland's capital city).

Since Mark's appointment as CEO, RSPCA Queensland have begun leading the organisation towards a mission statement of *helping animals, enlightening people and changing lives*. Additionally, through community education and engagement, fundraising and marketing schemes, staff and volunteer recognition systems, and strong, motivated leadership methods, RSPCA Queensland is now a leading organisational body in Australia. Since 2000, the NFP has implemented employee and staff databases, appropriate adoption programs, software development and creative business strategies; and as a consequence, now operates all 13 facilities throughout Queensland.

The proof of these beneficial shifts in leadership are evident through the myriad of successful fundraising events, including the Million Paws Walk, innovative software initiatives, including Finding Rover, the highest adoption and rehoming rates of any Australian animal welfare charity (87% live release rate) and a successful relationship with local and state governments that eventuated in a valuable Act change in 2001. These accomplishments are evidence of Mark Townend's innovative and successful approach to leadership.

Originally RSPCA Queensland was governed with a generic managerial technique; however, with Mark's appointment as CEO a re-design of innovative leadership techniques has been adopted. This approach to a contemporary style of leadership has been adopted by a multitude of for profit (FP) and NFP organisations internationally, and has become widely known as *transformational leadership*. Transformational leadership can be defined as a pattern of collective behaviours that inspire worker productivity, enhance followers' ethical aspirations and motivate parties to strive toward mutual organisational purposes.[2] The organisation has always been united by their values and beliefs for a world where animal cruelty is absent; however, Mark's four pillars to transformational leadership—vision, innovation, perspective, collaboration—are what guided RSPCA forward to achieve shared values and the manifest accomplishments.

Vision

"Always be guided by your mission," Mark Townend

Successful transformational leadership relies on a unified organisational focus that is based on long-term vision, as opposed to specific daily goals. Although this may appear obvious, before Mark Townend's appointment as CEO RSPCA Queensland governed the organisation's advancement through the completion of diminutive, daily goals. This leadership mindset is problematic for a NFP organisation attempting to gain successful fundraising, as well as stretch funds, and eradicate animal cruelty universally. Although the organisation's mission statement of *helping animals, enlightening people and changing lives* has guided RSPCA to a transformed model of leadership, a key element to the NFP organisation's recent success is due to the CEO's personal vision for the future—*to make RSPCA, as a whole, redundant.*

Thus, if animal welfare organisations are needed within society, his ultimate goal of eliminating animal cruelty hasn't been achieved.

All aspects of Mark's transformational leadership traits are influenced by his concept of RSPCA's 'big picture' vision. However, in order to establish and maintain a successful organisational vision, two key elements are required—passion and strategy.

Without a passion for the overarching vision, there is no motivation to accomplish a task swiftly and accurately. Although RSPCA's employees, volunteers and interns are ignited and connected by their intrinsic passion for animals and animal welfare, passion needs to run deeper in order for there to be a consequential movement. In order to successfully advance the RSPCA and manage personnel performance, there needs to be a passion for, and within, the people and the organisation. Defining specific organisational values is a method to establishing and moulding a concrete vision, thereby shaping the behaviour within an organisation (James & Lahti 2011, p. 108).[3] Mark's attempt at establishing organisational passion is designed to instil drive within RSPCA's staff and volunteers, therefore keeping them enthused and motivated at work. According to workplace culture research, employees who are passionate about the job role's identity (i.e. the organisation's overarching vision) are also motivated to produce effective work styles and exceed managerial expectations—of course, this applies to volunteer work also.

Following these motivation techniques, to ignite an alternative sense of passion within the RSPCA team the organisation developed a reward and recognition software program in 2013, christened as *Make Your Mark*. The system is designed to honour and commend workers' accomplishments, as well as to keep employees in competition with themselves through an incentive system. Employees and volunteers receive complimentary badges, which are either gold, silver or bronze depending on individual achievements, and small prizes (e.g. $30 iTunes gift card) for each achieved level, as well as an annual awards night to honour successes.

However, volunteers and employees are also motivated with *Make Your Mark* travel incentives. Travel incentives offer motivated employees international trips to learn about cultural diversities within animal welfare programs. For example, one of the most recent travel grant winners went to China to learn about pandas and their wellbeing within animal care facilities. Therefore, this incentive scheme increases people's passion for the RSPCA as a workplace, but also increases workers' productivity and ultimately benefitting the organisation. Additionally, due to word of mouth promotion by staff and volunteers, the *Make Your Mark* program entices more community members to join the team. The software program was additionally recognised for its innovative development by winning the Peter Williams award for HR Technology at the Australian Human Resources Institute (AHRI) Awards in 2014.

Additionally, Mark believes there is a stigmatisation surrounding NFP organisations' employee wages. Firstly, there is a notion that because RSPCA rely significantly on donations and bequest dollars for organisational income, they cannot afford to appropriately pay employees. However, RSPCA Queensland has fought to meet fair market wages, contributing to employee incentive and performance management. Although income is not the sole incentive for RSPCA's employees, fair wages help to maintain motivation and also entice new employees to potentially join the organisation. Secondly, Mark believes, especially for newer employees, that there is a common idea that working for RSPCA or a NFP organisation means you can 'slack off' within your job tasks. In order to combat this mistaken notion, Mark provides training that he believes goes beyond FP organisations' employee training measures. With staff employed specifically to train new employee or volunteer groups, Mark believes this style of in-depth teaching provides a solid framework for new team members to base their service on. RSPCA's employees are also encouraged within training programs and throughout their duties to work just as hard as they would if they were working for a for-profit (FP) company.

Although RSPCA is a charity, Mark sees no vast difference between NFP and FP organisations' business styles, and therefore develops strategies to constantly advance RSPCA's reputation and success. Prior to Mark's leadership, RSPCA Queensland had 14 different databases with no relationship between them. When he was appointed CEO his first leadership act was to quickly develop a business strategy. He explains, "We had to seriously do something with our databases. As it was [previously], we could prosecute someone for animal cruelty, and then, unless we recognised them at the counter, adopt another animal to them." There was no consistency and no strategy in place to run the organisation as a regular business, which is how Mark sees the NFP organisation.

A key report that the organisational software now produces is emailed to key staff automatically at 6.00am each morning. It helps staff to identify logjams or delays in animals moving through the system. The report, which works as a metric or Key Performance Indicator system, provides details on every animal's status and location across the state and is a key management tool in improving efficiency of care for the animals in stock. The management efficiency of the inventory plays a huge role in the psychological and medical condition of shelter animals and impacts the length of stay reduction, and therefore financial gains. This metric system is now known as the 'In Care Inventory', and is a prominent managerial tool within RSPCA Queensland.

Each daily report details the following:

- The current location of the animal (throughout Queensland)
- When the animal was brought in

Animal ID Location	Type (Count)	Days At Current Status	Status	Animal Name	Primary Breed	Age Yrs	Age Mos	Age Wks	Source	Incoming Date	Days In Care
Wacol Animal Care Campus		(Avg)									
Type: Puppy Available For Adoption											
944715 Wacol Animal Care Campus	Puppy	6.1	Available For Adoption	Darla	English Staffordshire Bull Terrier	0	3	3	Owner Surrender	7-Jul-16	56.5
949210 Wacol Animal Care Campus	Puppy	1.3	Available For Adoption	James	English Staffordshire Bull Terrier	0	0	10	Humane Officer Surrendered	3-Aug-16	29.4
949211 Wacol Animal Care Campus	Puppy	1.3	Available For Adoption	Thomas	English Staffordshire Bull Terrier	0	0	10	Humane Officer Surrendered	3-Aug-16	29.4
949349 Wacol Animal Care Campus	Puppy	0.3	Available For Adoption	Harlequin	English Staffordshire Bull Terrier	0	3	2	Ambulance	4-Aug-16	28.4
951537 Wacol Animal Care Campus	Puppy	2.4	Available For Adoption	Tipsey	Labrador Retriever	0	0	10	Owner Surrender	27-Aug-16	5.6
952512 Wacol Animal Care Campus	Puppy	5.6	Available For Adoption	Riley	Bull Arab	0	3	0	Owner Surrender	23-Aug-16	9.5
952513 Wacol Animal Care Campus	Puppy	5.6	Available For Adoption	Monty	Bull Arab	0	3	0	Owner Surrender	23-Aug-16	9.5

| 952514 | Wacol Animal Care Campus | Puppy | 5.6 Available For Adoption | Mambo | Bull Arab | 0 | 3 | 0 Owner Surrender | 23-Aug-16 | 9.5 |
| 952516 | Wacol Animal Care Campus | Puppy | 5.6 Available For Adoption | Freya | Bull Arab | 0 | 3 | 0 Owner Surrender | 23-Aug-16 | 9.5 |

Available For Adoption—No Web Presence

953965	Wacol Animal Care Campus	Puppy	-0.1 Available For Adoption - No Web Presence		DogueDe Bordeaux	0	0	6 Transfer In	31-Aug-16	1.4
953966	Wacol Animal Care Campus	Puppy	-0.1 Available For Adoption - No Web Presence		Dogue De Bordeaux	0	0	6 Transfer In	31-Aug-16	1.4
953967	Wacol Animal Care Campus	Puppy	-0.1 Available For Adoption - No Web Presence		Dogue De Bordeaux	0	0	6 Transfer In	31-Aug-16	1.4

- Why the animal was brought in (abuse, neglect, stray etc.)
- If/if not the animal requires behavioural or psychological treatment
- If/if not the animal has received veterinary attention
- If/if not the animal requires medical treatment (surgery, de-sexing etc.)
- If/if not the animal requires euthanasia (in cases of untreatable illness or pain)
- If the animal has/has not received an adoption profile
- If that profile has/has not been promoted in public locations
- If that profile is/is not online (RSPCA website, social media etc.)
- If that profile is/is not in the designated locations on/off campus
- Overall adoption status

Statewide	Count	Avg Days At Status
All Dogs		
Awaiting Surgerv—Not Spav/Neuter	5	1.3
Awaiting Transfer	1	2.5
Awaiting Vet Approval—In Foster	2	5.5
Awaiting Vet Exam/Health Check	23	1.9
Court Hold	13	20.6
Disposition Under Final Review	9	2.9
Emergency Boarding	4	20.0
Hold	11	3.3
Hold For Possible Match	2	11.8
Hold In Foster	5	17.0
Hold In Vet Care	7	5.0
Hold Quarantine	5	5.8
ID Trace	17	2.8
In Foster	107	27.6
Owner Relinquishment	1	2.3
Police Hold	1	0.4
Protective Custody—Awaiting Foster	4	50.0
Protective Custody In Foster	10	43.1
Protective Custodv/Hold	6	42.1
Sanctuarv/Life Resident	4	188.0

Stray Hold	36	3.1
Stray Hold—In Vet Care	1	3.3
Under Behavior Modification	12	11.2
Under Vet Care	47	7.0
Total Dogs	782	15.5
Statewide Grand Total	1,698	17.1

The short-term goal of the system is to have the animal adopted within 14 days, as this is optimal for animals' physical, behavioural and psychological wellbeing. The metric system helps the RSPCA team to work to constantly reduce the average length of stay for shelter animals to increase their live release rate and to decrease expenditure. Additionally, the In Care metric system is designed to continuously lead the different sectors of the organisation toward the ultimate goal. For example, if a stray cat came into the shelter during the night, and has not yet received veterinary treatment, the report would clearly identify animals in hold or awaiting veterinary team intervention. Mark says he can now base his entire day from each morning's metric system reading. This software development not only took a major leap towards RSPCA's consequential vision, but also established steps to achieve throughout the day—developing both short-term and long-term strategies, as well as moving toward the consequential vision.

Without developing a successful strategy through means of technology, in this instance, the RSPCA would not have come as far as it has in the advancement of animal welfare procedures. Developing strategies that suit the mission statement and vision of the NFP organisation have helped to implement plans, maintain performance and enhance productivity while continuously striving toward RSPCA's consequential goal. However, these organisational aspects would not have been achieved without Mark's innovations.

Innovation

> "We have a 'nothing's off the table' mentality"—Mark Townend

Innovation has become a norm of successful leadership within contemporary businesses and organisations. Implementing innovative concepts and maintaining creative business strategies is a goal of both FP and NFP organisations in terms of constructing a renowned reputation; however, the term 'innovation' has a different representational meaning for each organisational structure. Although the modern term 'innovation' is often related to software development and technology, since Mark Townend's leadership commencement, RSPCA have taken on a broad range of innovative business techniques in order to renovate its image and reputation.

To achieve this, RSPCA Queensland have adopted a *nothing's off the table* mentality—no idea is too small, too extreme, or too unalike. Mark manages RSPCA with the ideology of "the more outside the box, the better." This style of creativity and innovation within a business setting sparks unique brand heuristics to the community, as well as a strong and recognisable reputation. In the passing decades, RSPCA Queensland has transformed from an organisation that once had no clear system for previously convicted animal cruelty offenders, to an organisation that has been domestically and internationally recognised for revolutionary animal shelter software and volunteer reward programs.

As previously discussed, prior to the introduction of this transformational leadership approach, RSPCA Queensland had approximately 14 different databases filled with confusing clusters of diverse information with no correlation between them. Therefore, arguably the most innovative concept RSPCA Queensland has initiated is the *ShelterBuddy* software. After being confronted by a lack of software, Mark decided there needed to be an internet database that connected all the animal shelters' useful information together—it should be noted that in 2000 the World Wide Web had only just become recognised by the public, with a large number of people predicting its fall in a matter of years. However, with Mark's trust in the internet's success, a database was developed that later became known as ShelterBuddy, or alternatively as ShelterMate in Australia.

This software manages the core functions and records of animal shelters. The software was originally developed by Microsoft and IT professionals in conjunction with Mark Townend, with the first BETA version being released in 2002—just two years after Mark was appointed CEO. The software is now sold and used internationally, with the most dominant buyers being from the USA and Canada, and saves almost 400,000 animal lives annually. Needless to say that despite public concerns about internet portals, the database was a huge success for the organisation.

Therefore, after witnessing the success of ShelterBuddy's software, RSPCA Queensland began developing a range of databases that assisted the core functions of a business, as well as moved towards the mission statement of helping animals and increasing live release rates. In 2005, the development of *adoptapet.com.au* quickly followed ShelterBuddy's innovative commencement by being the first online adoption centre in Australia. AdoptAPet was an additional method that was designed to get shelter animals into the public eye in order to be adopted, therefore further advancing the live release rate of animals across the country. The website allows users to select the specific type of animal wanted, or to follow a process to find an animal that suits specific lifestyles. The concept was to unite a chain of animal welfare organisations into one online entity for the public to view and adopt animals across particular areas.

However, RSPCA Queensland's most recent technological innovation is the integration of Finding Rover facial recognition software. ShelterBuddy was originally developing facial recognition software with the expertise of specialist programmers in Germany. At the same time, US practitioners from Finding Rover were working with the University of Utah in facial recognition. Mark saw that the repetition of programming across two locations was inefficient, and began collaborating closely with Finding Rover associates to form a partnership that would provide access to shelter animals seamlessly in return for ShelterBuddy software utilisation. This not only displays Mark's methods of sustainability and innovation, but also highlights the significance of his fourth pillar, collaboration, which will be discussed later in this case study.

The Finding Rover software is designed to reunite lost dogs with their rightful owners through a facial recognition system. The app and website have the ability to send push notifications to users when other users within a ten-mile radius report missing or found dogs. If facial recognition technology identifies the animal within the Finding Rover system, the rightful owner will be able to be contacted. Additionally, Finding Rover has social aspects by allowing app or webpage users to connect with each other based on common interests. The program is now used in conjunction with a range of US animal care facilities including SPCA Los Angeles and many of the USA's Humane Society entities. Since the launch of these software systems RSPCA Queensland has raised over $1 million worth of profit, with a majority being put toward the development and progression of these systems.

As well, although RSPCA Queensland's funding sources are spread across methods of fee for service, government funding, and donations, the NFP organisation also relies heavily on bequest revenue; however, bequest income reliance is also a potential risk especially if it is heavily relied upon. A sudden downturn could jeopardise the mission of the organisation. When Mark commenced his role as CEO, bequest income was $4 million, with the average total revenue being $6 million. In order to create optimal sustainability, Mark's goal was to reduce the bequest revenue to less than 20% of the RSPCA's general income.

Through methods of community engagement, sustainability plans and transformational leadership, within a little over 15 years, RSPCA's bequest income is now $14.5 million within a total revenue of $47.6 million—and so the bequest income is 14.5% of the total. This achievement was significant in terms of business sustainability, and is also not only extremely beneficial for the organisation as a whole, but highlights the pioneering initiative from the new transformational leadership style. Traditionally, NFP organisations are criticised for income gain, contributing to the fearful illusion that NFPs should not gain profit. However, Mark opposes this idea in stating, "We are a profit for purpose, not a 'not for profit'. We shouldn't be ashamed of making profit . . . the key is what happens to that profit and how it goes towards our mission."

However, Mark's leadership has also displayed models of innovation that steer away from finance and technology. An alternative innovation technique that was used to manipulate the perspective of community members was the re-design of brand and marketing aspects. Rather than having multiple diversified images and portals to appeal to the community, Mark decided to develop one unified system to control all online and offline portals. Currently, the majority of the online promotion techniques are facilitated by the marketing team through the utilisation of social media and web portals. The multitude of web-based platforms are now linked in order to create a unified appearance to the community. Furthermore, other types of advertising aimed at older demographics, including posters etc., are now branded in similar styles with a recognisable *RSPCA Queensland* logo appearing across all. By branding all the software and tangible promotion tools with one specific style the NFP organisation's reputation is enhanced through recognisability.

To move toward the ultimate mission, and to improve public engagement, innovative methods of community awareness have also been adopted in order to reduce the length of stay characteristics for animals. As previously stated, when animals are brought into Brisbane's Wacol campus, some have behavioural or psychological problems that need to be treated before adoption can take place. Therefore, Mark proposed that certain animals be fostered to local correctional facilities to not only rehabilitate the animal, but also provide volunteer work for inmates. The inmates are trained and assessed before being given an animal, and are also in a secure environment to maintain the animals' and inmates' welfare. Engaging members of the community that have been prominently underutilised to assist in animal rehabilitation is truly a transformational leadership facet.

It is because of these methods that RSPCA Queensland have become a notorious recognisable body across Australia and internationally. Through these creative concepts, RSPCA has not only taken an innovative step towards their mission goal, but has also raised awareness for animal care throughout the community.

Perspective

> "If we change the minds of the people . . . then we will improve the lives of the animals"—Mark Townend

Other key aspects that have rendered RSPCA the respected NFP organisational body that it is today are the perspectives of the vast diversity of affiliates and staff. Individuals contribute varied concepts and ideas to the overall team, therefore providing a unique and innovative final product to the organisation and its audiences. However, in order to produce optimal task efficiency and therefore meet the vision accordingly, there needs to be similar perspectives across the organisational hierarchy. Intellectual and modern leadership styles also have the role of instilling the same vision within everyone, but also beneficially manipulate perspectives. This tactic not only creates unity in vision, but also a unique sense of motivated autonomy within different sectors of the organisation. By contrast, sectors that are too diversified in perspective are problematic as there is no common ground—this was the case when Mark began his leadership in 2000.

Within RSPCA Queensland's current organisational system, there is a myriad of diversified job roles, including humane officers, inspectors, fundraising, marketing, events management, customer service, veterinary and animal husbandry, as well as a range of volunteers contributing to multiple different creative or animal care roles. Although these roles are now established, at Mark's commencement to leadership there was a need to change workers' views from an individualistic approach to become collective and motivated.

Initially, Mark established this by instigating a job role change among staff members. According to organisational psychology, when there is evidence of highly diversified job roles, and therefore a lack of worker productivity within organisations, job and task change can potentially be the optimal solution.[4] By reassessing the knowledge and capabilities of employees as well as personality and engagement levels, people were able to be arranged into appropriate roles. By having employees within a job role that appeals to them personally, worker's productivity, effectiveness, and workplace culture follow. Additionally, this tactic avoids resignation and redundancy rates, and in the circumstance of RSPCA Queensland keeps the knowledgeable and experienced employees within ideal job roles.

However, the most recent perspective transformation initiated by Mark was the relaunch of RSPCA Queensland's image. Recently, a new collection of offices and shelters were constructed for RSPCA Queensland's central campus at Wacol, Brisbane. In order to celebrate the re-launch of the new campus, the whole RSPCA team, including staff and volunteers within Queensland were provided with new uniforms, which gave a fresh and modern appearance to the organisation.

To accompany the new uniforms, a staff campaign video was launched to ignite a sense of unity across the state's volunteers and employees. Mark had each facility across the state participate in the video that featured the *Party Rock Anthem* song by popular contemporary band *LMFAO*, for which permission was achieved. This video was then uploaded to YouTube, the social media platform, and launched with the new uniforms to create the sense of comradery among employees. The video clip is now also played to new trainees and volunteers to welcome them to the RSPCA team as well as to display that RSPCA Queensland is a unique, united organisation to be a part of.

In addition to instilling the appropriate perspective in employees and volunteers, this video also establishes a relationship and new perspective with the wider community of RSPCA. From the public's perception, the NFP organisation was originally viewed as dull and overly professional under previous leadership; however, the *'Party Rock'* launch and uniform transition changed the image of RSPCA's brand and reputation. By being visibly perceived as a fun and friendly cohort, this intuitively creates the sense that the RSPCA Queensland team are approachable and ultimately want a relationship with the community. Consequently, this increases community awareness and engagement, as well as increases the likelihood of community members seeking information about fundraising events or animal cruelty reports, which ultimately moves RSPCA forward.

However, another key aspect influencing the community's perspective and therefore engagement with the RSPCA is the utilisation of media portals. The styles of marketing used are designed to create awareness, and educate the community through means of perspective transformation. RSPCA Queensland has no specific demographic that engages with content or adopt from the shelters—the age groups and demographical features are significantly varied throughout Australian society. As previously discussed, social media and web-based platforms are a significant tactic to engage multiple demographics; however, due to the nature of online platforms, the key users are between approximately 18 and 30-years-old. Therefore, in order to target demographics that fall outside of this bracket, face-to-face primary school and later life education have been introduced.

It is important for later life adults to have knowledge about the RSPCA's programs, campaigns and shelter animal information in order to evolve a relationship with them, and increase community awareness. RSPCA Queensland's Senior Media Adviser, Michael Beatty regularly attends local senior citizen clubs, including Returned & Services League (RSL) and Rotary clubs, to entertain and inform later life members of the community. Michael often uses entertaining visual presentations to reflect statistical measures of the NFP, and also highlights the organisational obstacles and successes—he also conducts similar presentations at universities throughout the state.

However, among elderly homes, Michael additionally explains RSPCA's *Pet Legacy* program. The Pet Legacy program is designed to leave later life adults the option to specify in their will that they would like RSPCA to claim ownership of their animal in the case of their passing. The elderly individuals also have the option to leave a small bequest amount to RSPCA in their will in this circumstance. However, at the other end of the spectrum, RSPCA additionally offers similar interactions with primary schools through their *Educational Mobile Unit (EMU)*. The EMU is a 'classroom on wheels' that regularly appears at primary schools, and small community events, along Australia's east coast. A team of humane education members present concise educational information to students or community members about pet ownership, farm animal care, and important facts about Australian wildlife conservation. The objective of EMU is to educate the community's entirety in order to decrease animal cruelty or accidental animal neglect. Each year the EMU educates more than 60,000 people, therefore showing the widespread community education as well as RSPCA's innovative steps toward their mission statement.

To increase further community awareness, another key marketing tool is print and televised media portals. One key media portal that proved a great success in terms of gaining community awareness was a television program, called *Animal Rescue*. The program aired for about five years in peak time and was featured on a popular Australian television network.

Animal Rescue was similar to a reality TV show as audiences followed the daily routine of RSPCA inspectors attending animal cruelty complaints, or vets and other staff rescuing animals which had been mistreated or injured. Additionally, the program featured success stories of rescued animals, but also promoted animals for adoption. The show was incredibly popular during its airtime and reached approximately 1.6 million viewers each week. In order to grasp the admiration of the show within Australia's walls, another popular Australian television show that aired around the same time, *Sea Patrol*, previously gained 900,000 viewers per episode, and cost producers approximately $800,000 each episode. Not only did RSPCA's *Animal Rescue* have almost double the viewers, but also its expenses were a fraction of the cost at $150,000 for each episode.

This was not only another revenue source for RSPCA Queensland, but was also a significantly innovative resource to gain societal awareness. Not only did the television show reap increased fundraising profit, but also enticed the community to attend the Adoption Centre, which increased live release rates, increased public knowledge about where to go when a pet is lost, and also specified who to call in the event of a mistreated animal.

Although the show ceased airing in 2012, multiple other social media and web portals have replaced the community engagement tool. A site that has been launched recently, *The Biscuit*, features funny and inspiring videos about RSPCA animals—ultimately providing similar benefits to RSPCA as *Animal Rescue*. The Biscuit is also linked to the myriad of marketing platforms in order to unite the portals, and therefore all demographics. The platforms' success of reaching multiple demographics as well as engaging the overall community is reflected through the number of calls RSPCA Queensland received between 2012/13 (approx. 209,889 calls) and 2015/16 (approx. 323,000 calls).

The key within an NFP organisation that relies heavily on bequest dollars and alternative forms of income for its advancement is to remember who is in charge. The organisation needs to stride towards the mission statement by focussing on community and audience perspective. Although RSPCA is methodised to help and stand for animals and their rights (as the name implies), the organisation is more being-orientated, rather than animal-orientated. By focussing on the human lives that are involved with the organisation, that is where true change for animals happens.

Collaboration

'The power of one' — Mark Townend

The final focal pillar of transformational leadership within RSPCA Queensland, which follows the ideology of being-orientated rather than animal-orientated, is the concept of collaboration—or something Mark Townend refers to as *'the power of one'*. By focussing on the people within an organisation, who are both internal and external bodies, shelter animals yield the benefits.

Prior to Mark's contemporary transformational leadership style, RSPCA Queensland organisers were running a campaign entitled *Kill the Bill*—a petition organised and promoted by RSPCA Queensland in a bidding attempt to cut links with the local and state governments. The motivation behind the campaign was to run the NFP organisation as a lone entity in an adversarial type system. This clearly worked against Mark's ideology of collaboration, highlighted in his statement, "There's no use being against something that is realistically above you in the hierarchy of power."

With Mark's transition in his leadership role, this campaign was quickly concluded and a relationship with all parties was encouraged. As predicted by RSPCA's transformational leader, the collaborative relationship with the government resulted in success. Not only did this relationship increase RSPCA's harmonious reputation with the public, as discussed previously, but it also resulted in a change to the *Animal Care and Protection Act 2001*—an Act which had not been amended since 1925. This amendment established RSPCA Queensland as the charity with the highest prosecution penalties for animal cruelty offenders in Australia—a huge success among animal welfare organisations. Although having a legislative stakeholder affiliated with the NFP organisation brings obvious strength to organisational progression, as a leader there can often be delegation issues. Knowing when, and when not, to intervene is essential to maintaining a positive relationship as well as moving the organisation towards the ultimate mission.

Intervention with governmental parties relates to RSPCA's compass of morality—the organisation will mediate discussions with the governmental bodies when there is something that is proposed that disagrees with RSPCA's mottos or values. If there is something the two entities cannot console or negotiate throughout private policy deliberations, that is when RSPCA will seek public attention (protests, media coverage etc.). For example, over the recent years a major animal welfare movement within Australia has been the fight to end greyhound dog racing.

Recently, after a tiring battle, an Australian state, New South Wales (NSW) had finalised legal delegations to ban greyhound racing, although this has since been revoked due to considerable political pressure. In that context, the country is now looking to RSPCA Queensland, as the leading body in animal welfare, to take the lead in this national animal welfare fight to ban such racing across the country. However, due to current legal issues with the Queensland government, RSPCA is unable to completely ban the racing currently. Therefore, they have delegated with the government to achieve the 'next best thing', which is an increased strictness on rules for greyhound owners and trainers. Although Mark believes you must fight for your business' moral and organisational stance, there also has to be a balance in power for any professional relationship to work. Instead of fighting the governmental affiliate, RSPCA Queensland has negotiated to maintain a positive relationship.

Mark uses this system of shared control within all of his professional collaborations. Since his appointment to leadership RSPCA Queensland has also introduced a list of corporate sponsorships and partnerships. The long list of corporate sponsorships includes major national partners including, Bendigo Bank, major Queensland partners including, GreenCross Vets, and a range of National ambassadors including Australian sleepwear designer Peter Alexander, Australian health and fitness professional Michelle Bridges, and Australian Olympic swimming champion Mitchell Larkin.

Having this range of national and state supporters in conjunction with RSPCA not only strengthens promotional tactics but also constructs an endorsed community reputation of relationships. While renowned Australian figures and businesses can sometimes be sought by RSPCA, current ambassadors and partners declare they often seek RSPCA out for collaboration due to personal alignment with the organisation's vision and their desire to promote the RSPCA message to gain increased bequest income. This not only proves the approachability and value recognition of the organisation, which Mark has established, but also the rapid growth in community awareness and reputation during the last decade of his leadership.

Maintaining the concept of relationship balance, Mark says he does everything he can to ensure that collaborators know RSPCA's appreciation of their involvement. By establishing and maintaining these positive relationships with external parties, RSPCA Queensland is not only increasing its promotional tactics and strengthening their community awareness and reputation, but is also building professionally beneficial relationships that progressively work toward the ultimate mission statement. In an interconnected world, as categorised by Archer & Cameron, organisations "need the ability to work together with [other] organisations from different backgrounds and cultures for ultimate success."[5]

Although RSPCA Queensland is defined as a charity, the transformational leadership style of Mark Townend has proved that there need be no difference in approach between a not-for-profit and a for profit organisation. As previously mentioned, not for profits should not have any shame about gaining profit as the income is progressing the organisation's mission statement. In Mark's words, "rather than spending the business's incomes on the

CEOs and superior staff as in a private company, NFP's spend their incomes on the mission statement . . . We are not a 'not for profit', we are a 'profit for purpose'."

Without the income the organisation receives through marketing activities, community engagement and relationship construction, RSPCA Queensland would not be as successful as it is today. The RSPCA Queensland has utilised methods of innovation, transformed perspective and collaboration in order to take the leading strides towards its shared vision. Mark's four transformational pillars to leadership—vision, innovation, perspective and collaboration—are what led RSPCA Queensland from an organisation that once had a lack of appropriate personnel, software databases, unified vision and healthy governmental relationships, to a NFP that is now described as *'one of the most successful animal welfare organisations in the southern hemisphere'*.

Chloe Wheeler

Background

- RSPCA's Animal Rescue television show aired between 2006 and 2012, and followed the daily routines of saving and helping animals within Queensland. You can view past episodes of the show here: www. lifestyle.com.au/tv/rspca-animal-rescue/episodes.aspx?series=2
- AdoptAPet was developed in 2005 in order to increase public awareness of shelter animal adoption via an online platform—the webpage was the first online adoption centre in Australia. You can view RSPCA Queensland's animals for adoption here: www. adoptapet.com.au/
- RSPCA Queensland's *Educational Mobile Unit*, or *EMU* was developed in order to increase community education regarding animal welfare and care. The 'classroom on wheels' appears at primary schools and local events within Queensland. You can read more here: www.rspcaqld.org.au/what-we-do/education-for-children/school-community-visits
- To accompany new uniforms for RSPCA Queensland, a *Party Rock* YouTube video was also uploaded in order to increase unison within the organisation, and to refresh the community's image of the NFP. You can view the video here: www.youtube.com/watch?v=kSOcuoWt_c8
- ShelterBuddy (known as ShelterMate in Australia) was the first database designed by Mark Townend at the commencement of his leadership in order to connect animal shelters' important information into one software entity. You can read more about Shelter-Buddy here: www.shelterbuddy.com.au/

- Finding Rover is a facial recognition system that was designed to reunite pet owners with their lost dogs. You can read more about Finding Rover here: www.shelterbuddy.com.au/rover.htm

Notes

1. The Humane Society. "Animal Cruelty Facts and Stats," 2016, www.humane society.org/issues/abuse_neglect/facts/animal_cruelty_facts_statistics.html?refer rer=www.google.com.au/
2. Jose Caballero and Didier Cossin. "Transformational Leadership: A Background Literature Review," *International Institute of Management Development*, 2013, www.imd.org/uupload/IMD.WebSite/BoardCenter/Web/213/Literature%20 Review_Transformational%20Leadership.pdf
3. Keith James and Ken Lahti. "Organizational Vision and System Influences on Employee Inspiration and Operformance," *Creativity and Innovation Management* 20, no. 2 (2011): 108.
4. Australian Psychological Society. "Organisational Psychology," 2016, www. psychology.org.au/public/organisational/
5. David Archer and Alex Cameron. *Collaborative Leadership: Building Relationships, Handling Conflict, Sharing Control* (London: Routledge, 2013).

Bibliography

Archer, David, and Alex Cameron. *Collaborative Leadership: Building Relationships, Handling Conflict, Sharing Control*. London: Routledge, 2013.
Australian Psychological Society. Organisational Psychology. 2016. Retrieved from www.psychology.org.au/public/organisational/
Caballero, Jose and Didier Cossin. Transformational Leadership: A Background Literature Review. International Institute of Management Development, 2013. Retrieved from www.imd.org/uupload/IMD.WebSite/BoardCenter/Web/213/ Literature%20Review_Transformational%20Leadership.pdf
James, Keith, and Ken Lahti. "Organizational Vision and System Influences on Employee Inspiration and Organizational Performance." *Creativity and Innovation Management* 20, no. 2 (2011): 108–20.
The Humane Society. 2016. Animal Cruelty Facts and Stats. Retrieved from www. humanesociety.org/issues/abuse_neglect/facts/animal_cruelty_facts_statistics. html?referrer=www.google.com.au/

About the Contributors

The Editors

Emeritus Professor Kenneth Wiltshire AO has enjoyed a long association with the Not for Profit Sector. As J. D. Story Professor of Public Administration and Leader of the Not for Profit Unit at The University of Queensland Business School he has conducted courses on Leadership for Not for Profits and Social Enterprises, research and consultancies for the sector, and is currently a Board Member of Not for Profits in the fields of Education, Indigenous Health, and Intellectual Disability.

Professor Wiltshire is also the author of 15 books and over 70 scholarly articles in areas of leadership, public policy, public sector management, intergovernmental relations, and government-business relations. He has served as consultant to parliaments, Royal Commissions, Prime Ministers, Premiers, government departments and enterprises, international organisations, and the private sector. He has chaired many government bodies and was Co-Chair of the Review of the Australian national school curriculum. Professor Wiltshire served for six years as Australia's Representative on the Executive Board of UNESCO. He is a National Fellow of the Institute for Public Administration Australia, a Member of the Australian Institute of Company Directors, and an Honorary Trustee of CEDA. In 1998 he was awarded the Order of Australia for services to public administration, development of public policy, and UNESCO.

Dr Aastha Mallhotra works as a Lecturer within the School of Health and Wellbeing at the University of Southern Queensland. Prior to this role, Aastha was Vice Chancellor's Research Fellow at the same University. Her current research projects are focused on building gender and culturally-sensitive capacity within and scaling up of women-led businesses in Australia and in an emerging country context.

Aastha holds a Masters in Human Services (specialisation management and leadership) and a PhD in Management from UQ Business School where she was awarded a full industry scholarship. During this time she also lectured and tutored for academic and corporate education courses. These included Small and social enterprises, Entrepreneurship and new ventures, Principles of strategic management, Introduction to management and Nonprofit leadership.

Aastha has experience working with fast growing nonprofits, public sector organisations and social enterprises in India, Canada and Australia. She has conducted workshops and assisted on numerous projects in the areas of enterprise development, strategic planning and business development for industry clients.

She continues to be actively involved in the nonprofit industry through management seminars, consulting projects and serving on panels and advisory committees and spends her free time on refining a design-led organisational diagnostic tool that builds on her PhD to aid nonprofit decision-making.

Dr Micheal Axelsen holds the position of Lecturer (Business Information Systems) in the UQ Business School, University of Queensland (UQ).

Micheal is an experienced IS professional and accountant with fifteen years' experience in the area of IS consulting. This experience and career includes the evaluation of IS projects, IS audit and IT management and governance. Micheal's published research is in the areas of the use of intelligent decision aids, Information Systems (IS) audit, and Information Technology (IT) governance. Prior to receiving his PhD, Micheal chaired the IT & Management Centre of Excellence for CPA Australia. Professionally, Micheal is a Fellow of CPA Australia, and was awarded the President's Award for contributions to the management of information systems in 2004.

Micheal has more than 15 years industry experience as a Director in an IS consulting practice with public, private, and community sector organisations as clients. He has significant experience in facilitating development programs, and currently teaches into the UQ MBA program and the Master of Commerce program at UQ.

Contributors

Karina Collins is the National Lead for BDO's consultancy division. Her role includes working with clients to develop strategies and solutions for complex business challenges. She has a background in innovation, technology, and transformation. More recently Karina has worked in areas of ICT Procurement and Transformation, Digital Transformation, Data Analytics,& Insights. Karina also sits on multiple Boards in the Professional Services, Health, Not for Profit and Social Sectors. She regularly presents sessions on Not for Profit leadership in UQ Business School's Executive Development programmes. Her widespread consultancies span the Government and Public Sector, Education, and Not for Profit sectors.

Dr. Susan Dann is Professor and Foundation Head of the Peter Faber Business School, Australian Catholic University. She has held prior academic appointments at QUT, Griffith University and University of Queensland. A former State President and National Deputy President of the Australian Marketing Institute, Professor Dann's expertise and research is in the strategic implication of marketing to non-commercial organisations with a specific interest in social marketing. Using this expertise she has spanned boundaries of academia and industry through consultancies and external appointments. She has served as a Director on a variety of governance boards including St. Vincent's and Holy Spirit health, St. Rita's College, and Ozcare, as well as being a member of two government tribunals. Susan has over 60 academic publications including eight books, two of which have been shortlisted for education awards.

Mark Dodgson is Professor of Innovation Studies at The University of Queensland Business School, and Visiting Professor at Imperial College London. He has written or edited 14 books and over 100 academic articles and book chapters on innovation. Mark has advised numerous companies and governments around the world and has researched and taught innovation in over 60 countries. He has served on the Board or Advisory Board of two multi-billion dollar companies and three start-ups. Professor Dodgson is a Fellow of the Royal Society of Arts and is widely recognised as an international authority on innovation.

Belinda Drew is the inaugural CEO of the Community Services Alliance CSIA, the new peak body for organisations engaged in Community Services. Prior to this she had 20 years of industry experience in various social sectors. Over the last decade Belinda successfully led Forresters Community Finance through a period of considerable change and cultural evolution focusing on Australia's social investment market in her role as CEO. Belinda's career has seen her developing her strong skillset in organisational management and strategic leadership harnessing and further honing her knowledge across social enterprise, social entrepreneurship, microfinance, community finance and social investment.

Robert Fitzgerald AM was appointed by the Australian Government as the inaugural Chair of the Australian Charities and Not for Profits Commission Advisory Board for three years in 2012. For more than 30 years he has also been involved in a voluntary capacity in numerous community services including as President of the Australian Council of Social Service and served on numerous non-profit boards and governing bodies. Robert has a diverse background and extensive experience in commerce, law, public policy, and community services. He was appointed a full time Commissioner with the Productivity Commission in 2004, and previously was the Community and Disability Services Commissioner and Deputy Ombudsman in New South Wales. He has been a commissioner or member of over 15 national inquiries including as Presiding Commissioner on the Productivity Commission's study into the Contribution of the Not for Profit Sector in Australia. A solicitor by profession he has degrees in commerce and law from University of NSW and an Honorary Doctorate from the Australian Catholic University. He was made a Member of the Order of Australia in 1994 for services to the community.

Dr. Stephen Jones is a lecturer in the Business School at The University of Queensland. He specialises in public policy research and has expertise in local government and intergovernmental relations. He also examines the role of governments in managing the development of cities and urban environments to encourage innovation and creativity to reduce the impact of climate change. Stephen has published extensively on these topics in high quality international and Australian scholarly journals. His book, Cities Responding to Climate Change: Copenhagen, Stockholm, and Tokyo will be published in 2017. Stephen had an extensive career in management and strategic policy positions in both state and local governments, and has extensive experience in establishing partnership arrangements between governments agencies and not for profit groups. He has worked closely with community groups in attracting support from government to achieve their objectives.

David Knowles heads Koda Capital's Philanthropic and Social Capital team. His primary responsibility is providing strategic advice to charitable, non-profit, and philanthropic investors. In a 27 year private wealth management career David worked for Coutts and Merrill Lynch in the UK and held senior leadership positions at Perpetual and JB Were where he was Managing Director and Head of Philanthropic Services. David is a member of the Centre for Social Impact's advisory council, Impact Investing Australia's market building working group, Raise Foundation's advisory council and a director of the charity BoardConnect. He also sits on the editorial advisory board of Generosity magazine. In 2012 David established a Public Ancillary Fund account to encourage philanthropy within his own family. In 2013 David completed the Governing for Non-profit excellence executive education course at Harvard Business School, and more recently completed the AICD's Governance Foundations for Non-Profit Directors course.

Christian Koch is a strategy and systemic organisational development consultant. He facilitates change projects in public administration, companies, and civil society organisations. Key for his work is the ability to switch perspectives, a competence he further developed working for more than 50 different projects of German International Cooperation (GIZ) in 30 countries worldwide over the last ten years. He is a Board member of More Than Shelters, a Hamburg based social enterprise which offers innovative architecture and social design solutions for the humanitarian context. This is one reason why he has become increasingly interested in adequate forms of organisational design for these 'zebras' that balance value orientation and profitability, goal orientation and participation.

Dr. Anna Krzeminska is a Lecturer in Strategy and UN PRME Director at The University of Queensland Business School and a Research Fellow at the Leuphana University Research Centre for Entrepreneurship Evidence Germany. After completing her PhD in Germany Anna held lecturer positions at Leuphana University and University of Technology Sydney as well as adjunct professor at HULT Business School in London UK. Her research publications include books, book chapters and articles in top-tier journals such as the Strategic Management Journal, R&D Management and the Nonprofit and Voluntary Sector Quarterly. Anna is an expert in strategic management of social impact organisations including the design of socially and commercially successful business models, growth and scaling strategies, competitive advantage, leadership and governance practices. Her teaching expertise centres around learning and development approaches that assist entrepreneurs and business students to understand their role and responsibility within society and business.

Paul Paxton-Hall established his legal practice in Brisbane in February 2007 after retiring from a national firm. He has worked in the commercial finance and tax areas of the law throughout his career. His focus remains in the company and commercial arenas with a passionate commitment to the not for profit sector. Paul acts for a variety of charities and not for profits organisations that include organisations in all charities' sectors, licensed and unlicensed clubs and sporting associations. His work in those areas includes structuring, corporate advisory, mergers and acquisitions. Amongst a range of board commitments Paul is the Deputy Chair of the Queensland Education Leadership Institute and a member of the Queensland Law Society's Not for Profit Committee and the Tax Institutes' Not for Profit Committee. He has also served in advisory roles to the Australian Charities and Not for Profits Commission.

Dr. Amanda Roan is an Honorary Research Fellow at the UQ Business School, University of Queensland. Throughout her academic career her research focused on work and employment across for-profit, government, and not for profit organisations. Her extensive lecturing experience includes examining the workplace relations systems and their impact on employees. Amanda's recent projects have examined issues of gender equity in architecture and in science, engineering and technology professions. Her research has been published in numerous book chapters and in Australian and International Human Resource Management and Employment Relations journals. Her postgraduate supervision has included projects on managing volunteers in the not for profit sector.

Rosie Simpson joined The Smith Family in 2009 and became Head of Fundraising in what is Australia's largest educational Not for profit organisation. Prior to this she served with Telstra as an Executive Director of Consumer Marketing, managing the communications, pricing, retail and product developing strategies for a large segment of Telstra's consumer market. She also has had previous appointments with The National Farmers Federation, the International Wool Secretariat in London, and the Australian Bureau of Agricultural and Resource Economics in Canberra. At The Smith Family she led the organisation's fundraising activity across all key market segments including individuals, corporates, major donors and

Trusts and Foundations. Also reporting to her were national community events and the supporter care and data entry teams. Rosie has recently been appointed CEO of the Children's Hospital Foundation in Brisbane.

David Swain is Chief Operating Officer of Churches of Christ in Queensland and a well respected leader of care and community services. He has been instrumental in harnessing the industry's voice in the state and nationally as well as promoting sustainable initiatives that result in positive social impact. He has been a strong advocate for cross sector collaboration. He is an alumni of Monash University, QUT, and University of Pennsylvania's Wharton School. He has a background as a health practitioner, army officer, quality auditor, educator, HR professional and company director. David is an active contributor to government and industry forums and has collaborated with University of Queensland over a number of years to promote understanding of, and interest in, the not for profit sector.

Kate Tully joined YWCA Queensland as CEO in 2011 with a lifelong focus on issues affecting women and children and has had extensive business experience in the private and not for profit sectors. She has a passion for social justice issues and originally trained as a journalist and editor. In addition to her role with YWCA Kate has extensive experience serving on Boards and other governing bodies. She is currently Chair of the Queensland Council of Social Service and a member of the board of governors of the national body ACOSS. She was appointed by the Premier to the Queensland Ambassadors Council and is also a member of the Queensland Government's Gender Equity and Violence Against Women Reference Group. In 2016 Kate was awarded the Alumna of the Year Award by QUT's Centre for Philanthropy and Nonprofit studies, for her contribution to the not for profit sector.

Greg Vickery AO is a corporate lawyer and special counsel at Norton Rose Fulbright Lawyers, and has been a Red Cross Volunteer for over 40 years. He is currently a member of the prestigious international Standing Committee of Red Cross and Red Crescent and is the immediate past president of Australia Red Cross Society (2003–2011). Upon the completion of his term the ARC Board established the Greg Vickery Scholarship, a valuable award for a joint research project involving a staff member and a volunteer. Greg is also a former member of the international governing Board of Red Cross and Red Crescent Societies. Greg is a former President of the Queensland Law Society and was the Honorary Consul in Queensland for Indonesia. He was made an Officer of the Order of Australia in 2013 for his contribution to the governance and leadership of international aid organisations.

Dr. Jay Weerawardena is Associate Professor of Strategic Marketing, and Marketing Discipline Leader at UQ Business School, University of Queensland. His core research area is entrepreneurship, dynamic capabilities and innovation-based firm competitive advantage. Over the years he has expanded into related areas; social entrepreneurship, social innovation, and social value creation, non-profit brand vulnerability, entrepreneurial marketing and high tech marketing. His pioneering work in social entrepreneurship (SE) with Professor Gillian Mort has made a notable impact to advance the SE field. He has conducted a number of case studies on Not for Profits including Surf Lifesaving Australia. He is currently interested in understanding business model innovation in Not for Profits.

Chloe Wheeler is a Creative Industries student, majoring in creative writing at the Queensland University of Technology. Throughout her studies she has also established and maintained a position in the Golden Key International Society for high academic achievement. In between her studies she also maintains an editorial position at Copeland Publishing (Brisbane CHILD) magazine and she has also undertaken multiple creative writing internships throughout her degree. One internship at RSPCA gave her an opportunity to extend her writing capabilities and share a passion for animal welfare with their committed staff.

Bruce Wilson AM had a highly successful career in both Commonwealth and Queensland governments starting as a civil engineer and including twenty-two years as a Chief Executive of a number of Queensland Government Departments, serving governments of both sides of politics twice each, and having responsibilities covering transport, public works, land management, trade and public sector reform. He built a reputation for delivering strong results, building effective team work with the private sector, and developing positive cultures. After retiring from government Bruce became part time Director and consultant to public, private, and not for profit sectors. He is the chair of a syndicate of the CEO Institute.

Chris Wilson is a key member of the Koda Philanthropy and Social Capital team. His responsibilities include bringing philanthropic opportunities and solutions to clients. He also provides strategic advice to charitable and non-profit organisations in relation to their governance, endowment practices, capacity building, sustainability, and donor relations activity. Chris has a decade of experience in financial services, working predominantly with high-net-worth individuals, corporations, and charitable institutions. Prior to joining Koda Capital, Chris was Director of JB Were's Philanthropic Services team. He is Chairman of the Reach Foundation and is a Founding Committee member of Impact100 Melbourne. Further to this Chris also chairs the Reach Foundation's Fundraising Sub-Committee and also sits on their Impact and Audit-Risk Sub-Committees. Chris holds a Masters of Commercial Law, Bachelor of Business (Economics and Finance) and a Diploma in Financial Planning. More recently he completed the AICD's Governance Foundations for Non-Profit Directors course.

Index

For Product Safety Concerns and Information please contact our EU
representative GPSR@taylorandfrancis.com
Taylor & Francis Verlag GmbH, Kaufingerstraße 24, 80331 München, Germany

www.ingramcontent.com/pod-product-compliance
Ingram Content Group UK Ltd.
Pitfield, Milton Keynes, MK11 3LW, UK
UKHW020937180425
457613UK00019B/435